THE NEW MUTANTS

Postmillennial Pop

GENERAL EDITORS
Karen Tongson and Henry Jenkins

THE NEW MUTANTS

Superheroes and the Radical Imagination of American Comics

RAMZI FAWAZ

New York University Press
NEW YORK AND LONDON

NEW YORK UNIVERSITY PRESS
New York and London
www.nyupress.org

LIBRARY OF CONGRESS CATALOGING-IN-PUBLICATION DATA

Fawaz, Ramzi.
The new mutants : superheroes and the radical imagination of American comics / Ramzi Fawaz.
pages cm
Includes bibliographical references and index.
ISBN 978-1-4798-1433-6 (cl : alk. paper)
ISBN 978-1-4798-2308-6 (pb : alk. paper)
1. Comic books, strips, etc—United States—History and criticism.
2. Superheroes in literature. I. Title.
PN6725.F37 2015
741.5'973—dc23

2015021427

THE AMERICAN LITERATURES INITIATIVE

A book in the American Literatures Initiative (ALI), a collaborative publishing project of NYU Press, Fordham University Press, Rutgers University Press, Temple University Press, and the University of Virginia Press. The Initiative is supported by The Andrew W. Mellon Foundation. For more information, please visit www.americanliteratures.org.

For
Roula, Kathy, Melani, and Robert,
my Fantastic Four.

The myth . . . of Science Fiction . . . is quite simply the myth of the end of man, of the transcendence or transformation of the human—a vision . . . of radical transformation (under the impact of advanced technology and the transfer of traditional human functions to machines) of homo sapiens into something else: the emergence—to use the language of Science Fiction itself—of "mutants" among us.

—LESLIE FIEDLER, "The New Mutants" (1965)

Mr. Fantastic: *There was another Human Torch . . . a much older one . . . more than 20 years ago! . . . He was amazing! There seemed to be nothing he couldn't do with that flaming body of his. But, there were rumors that he wasn't fully human!*

The Thing: *Nowadays, who is??*

—FANTASTIC FOUR ANNUAL #4 (November 1966)

Contents

Color plates follow page 124.

Acknowledgments

I read my first comic book when I was thirteen, during the summer between seventh and eighth grade. It was the Thirty-fifth Anniversary issue of *The Uncanny X-Men*, America's most popular superhero comic, which, for over three decades, had narrated the lives, loves, and losses of a band of mutant outcasts gifted with extraordinary abilities because of a difference in their genetic makeup. Even back then I was spectacularly gay and exceptionally bookish, not to mention loud about both. I was a mutant in suburban Orange County, California. These qualities had made middle school a nightmare and life lonely. But that summer day, returning home exhilarated by the sights of the local comic book store, I sat by the family pool, slipped my *X-Men* issue from its bag, and carefully opened the dazzling holographic cover; what I discovered there has kept me dreaming and made life far, far less lonely ever since. This book is one outcome of that encounter, but it is even more a product of the crossings, friendships, and bonds that my thirteen-year-old self could only wish for and my adult self has been lucky enough to live.

This book is dedicated to four people without whom it would not exist. My mama, Roula Fawaz, is everything to me. She survived a war zone, emigrated with her family to a new country, dared to pursue the lifestyle that sustained her, and built a thriving business from the ground up, all so that her children could live their dreams. She did all this with unconditional love. Your spirit is all over this book, Mama, just my version of it. I met Kathleen Moran as a sophomore at UC Berkeley on the first day of her course on the 1980s. Ten minutes into a lecture on *Back to the Future* and Reaganism, I knew she was going to change my life. Kathy introduced me to the study of popular culture, convinced me I could take comics seriously as scholarly objects, and believed in me enough to let me teach in Berkeley's American studies program as a very green twenty-one-year-old. Because of her, American studies became my life's work. Kathy was first my mentor and is now family. After leaving Berkeley I couldn't have dreamed that I'd find mentors as extraordinary and inspiring. In Melani McAlister and Robert McRuer, I did. From the moment I met her, Melani has challenged me to be the most rigorous and exacting scholar I can imagine, provided me with love, support, and insight to last a lifetime, and has modeled a form of intellectual generosity I aspire to every day. In case you were wondering, she's my favorite superhero. Robert McRuer is my other favorite. He has always modeled for me what it means to live one's intellectual values as an ethics, to be bold, experimental, and epic with my ideas, and to remember to pursue intellectual life with as much playfulness as rigor (which he might say are the same thing). Each in their own voice, these four have always told me "Go ahead."

This book began as an undergraduate dream research project at UC Berkeley. My mentors Mark Brilliant, Carol Clover, Kevis Goodman, Richard Hutson, Greil Marcus, Christine Palmer, Carolyn Porter, and Hertha D. Sweet Wong shared with me more of their brilliance, generosity, guidance, and support than any undergraduate could ever hope for. What I learned from them could fill another book, or two. I'm honored now to count them as my friends and colleagues. The intellectual and social community of George Washington University's American Studies Department is unparalleled. It was my absolute fortune to spend the six years of my doctoral study there. At GW, I want to especially thank Tom Guglielmo, the late Jim Miller, and Jennifer Nash for their friendship and their tireless support of my scholarship and my career. Elisabeth Anker and Kip Kosek were the most incisive and generous committee members one could hope for. Julie Passanante Elman was the first graduate student I met at GW, when she was starting to write her dissertation proposal. (It's now a book.) She has been mababaay! ever since—an extraordinary intellect, true friend, and all-around Amazon warrior. Sandra Heard was a constant source of inspiration, laughter, and strength (she still is), and Stephanie Schulte was my role model of the scholar I wanted to become (she still is). Laura Cook Kenna, David Kieran, Laurel Clark Shire, and Kevin Strait always led the way.

Damon Young has been my longest running interlocutor for this project. We met just as I started writing, read drafts of each other's work for years, and developed a friendship I cherish every day—he is the truest of companions and one of the most infuriatingly exacting thinkers I've ever known. This book came into its final form during my first two years as a member of the English Department at the University of Wisconsin, Madison. The friendships and intellectual community I've developed here in a short time have left an indelible mark on me and this project. Stephanie Elsky and Aida and Alyssa Levy-Hussen have helped make the last years of finishing this book an experience filled with laughter, good conversation, and mutual support. This book would not be what it is now without Nirvana Tanoukhi. Since I arrived at Madison, she has been an extraordinary friend and confidant, a fiercely devoted interlocutor, and my combination cheerleader and drill sergeant for getting this book out in the world. I am eternally grateful for the love and camaraderie she's brought into my life.

During the years that I worked on *The New Mutants*, I received support from a number of institutional sources. A Yale Summer Undergraduate Research Fellowship in 2005 led me to write the undergraduate thesis that inaugurated this project. My Yale faculty mentor, Jonathan Katz, believed in my ideas from the start and was the first person to encourage me to use the critical tools of queer theory in my research. A generous Visual Studies fellowship from the Social Science Research Council allowed me to conduct preliminary research as a first-year graduate student that fundamentally shaped the trajectory of the project. The incisive research advice of my SSRC mentors, Vanessa Schwartz and Anne Higgonet, strengthened the project's historical archive immeasurably. Participating in the Cornell School of Criticism and Theory in 2008 had a decisive impact on my methodology; the conversations I had as part of Elizabeth Povinelli's seminar on the politics of liberalism were practically revolutionary for defining the political stakes of my project. A writing workshop sponsored by the New York University Institute for Public Knowledge, led by Linda Gordon and Crystal Parikh, offered a generative environment for sharing ideas with students in a variety of fields when I was preparing to articulate the most crucial interventions of my work. Finally, shortly after this project found a home at NYU Press, my manuscript was awarded the 2012 Center for Lesbian and Gay Studies Fellowship for best first book project in LGBT studies, a humbling honor.

I am also indebted to a number of archives whose staff were welcoming and informative during stays that lasted anywhere from one day to a month. These include Michigan State University's Russell B. Nye special collection in popular culture, the Columbia University Rare Books and Manuscript Library, UC Berkeley's Bancroft Library, and the University of Oregon's Knight Library. At Michigan State, Randy Scott, the collection's lead archivist, taught me everything I could ever hope to know about the collection and provided me with the resources I needed to make the most of my visit. I'm inspired by his enthusiasm and support for comics research. The first true archive for this project was my local comic book store in Tustin, California, Comics Toons & Toys. It all started there. This magical place was a safe haven and treasure trove of stories that ignited my imagination and made me feel at home. The owner, Matt Powers, showed me generosity and kindness that I will not soon forget.

Portions of this book originally appeared as the essay "'Where No X-Man Has Gone Before!' Mutant Superheroes and the Cultural Politics of Popular Fantasy in Postwar America," published in *American Literature* 83.2 (Copyright 2011): 355–88. This material appears in substantially revised form in my introduction and chapter 4 by permission of the publisher, Duke University Press. I'm grateful for the editors of the June 2011 special issue of *American Literature* on speculative fictions, Priscilla Wald and Gerry Canavan, who championed my work and included it among an exceptional group of essays. Working with the journal's chief copyeditor, Emily Dings, was an extraordinary experience. Her exacting attention to detail, incisive questions, and genuine enthusiasm for my work embodied all that is great in scholarly life.

My editor at NYU Press, Eric Zinner, believed in this project before it was even completed. His unwavering support, sometimes brutal honesty, and acute insights about the book have made it a product I am proud to bring into the world. I am also thankful for the guidance of my series editors, Henry Jenkins III and Karen Tongson, who shepherded this project with incredible enthusiasm and guided me through the complex process of revision, and to Alicia Nadkarni, without whose leading hand through the publication process this book would still be a stack of paper on my desk. I have boundless gratitude for the remarkably generous and precise commentary of my two anonymous reviewers, which helped me bring the project to a new level of insight and acuity.

My family has shaped this project in more ways than they might imagine. My father is the most authentic intellect I've ever met. He instilled in me his passion for worldly ideas and endless learning. He is the most generous and loving man I know, and I continue to aspire to his example. My brother's boldness and creativity and his unflinching pursuit of his professional goals have provided a blueprint for my own life path. When

I was seven, Jean Mylen showed me the boundless possibilities of fantasy when she placed an epic fantasy novel in my hands and told me to start reading. I've been hooked ever since.

This book is a testament to the power of queer world-making, but it is also a product of queer world-making itself. The queer families, kinships, and communities I have inhabited these past ten years have sustained me in my writing, in my vision, and in life. No amount of words can capture the love and gratitude I feel for those companions who've built worlds with me, memory by memory, conversation by conversation. Let's just say I really, really love these people. My thanks, and a full heart, go to Steve Abate, Bridget Brew, Meghan Drury, Travis Eby, Mark Farrier, Olivia Friedman, Erin Hawkins, Scott Larson, Michael Horka, Michelle May, Uri McMillan, Shannon Davies Mancus, Nedda Mehdizadeh, Margo Padilla, Crystal Parikh, Gary Patterson, Aaron Potenza, Dan Rudmann, Anne Showalter, Paul Schwochow, Shanté Paradigm Smalls, Matthew Tinkcom, Matt Veltkamp, Bob Venable, and Sam Yates. Olivia Friedman is my rock. Through every twist of fate, every success and disappointment, every mental block, and every revelation that unfolded during the writing of this book, she has been there providing unconditional love. The feeling is utterly mutual. Michael Horka was a surprise that entered my life five years ago. He has never ceased to amaze me. The depth of our conversations, the sincerity of our laughter and our vulnerability, the true friendship we have built have been constants through every storm. Finally, the fifth secret behind this book is Nedda Mehdizadeh. We met on the first day of graduate school, and she has been my soul mate ever since. My greatest interlocutor, the most loyal, loving, and brave friend, the sister I never had, and a companion any superhero epic would be proud to depict. She is mababe for life. This book is what it is because of our friendship.

Since the day I finished reading my first superhero comic book, my greatest fantasy was to become a member of the X-Men, a band of mutants who find a home in the world among rebels, outcasts, and visionaries. Among this group of friends, I got my wish.

THE NEW MUTANTS

Introduction: Superhumans in America

*We might try to claim that we must first know the fundamentals of the
human in order to preserve and promote human life as we know it. But
what if the very categories of the human have excluded those who should
be described and sheltered within its terms? What if those who ought to
belong to the human do not operate within the modes of reasoning and
justifying validity claims that have been proffered by western forms of
rationalism? Have we ever yet known the human? And what might it take
to approach that knowing?*
      —JUDITH BUTLER, *Undoing Gender* (2004)

We've changed! All of us! We're more than just human!
      —THE FANTASTIC *four* #1 (November 1961)

In November 1992 Superman died. The Man of Steel would fall at the
hands of the alien villain Doomsday, a thorny-skinned colossus who
single-mindedly destroys life throughout the cosmos. Arriving on Earth
seeking his next conquest, Doomsday meets his match in the planet's
longtime guardian, known to few in his civilian garb as the meek journalist Clark Kent but beloved by all as the caped hero Superman. After
an agonizing battle in the streets of Metropolis, Superman's urban home,
Superman and Doomsday each land a final fatal blow, their last moments
of life caught on camera and broadcast to devastated viewers around the
world.[1] The fictional media firestorm surrounding Superman's death
mirrored real-world responses to DC Comics' announcement of their
decision to end the life of America's first superhero earlier that year.
Months before the story was even scripted, national print and television
media hailed Superman's death as an event of extraordinary cultural
significance, propelling what initially appeared as an isolated creative
decision into the realm of public debate.

Public opinion ranged widely, from those who interpreted Superman's downfall as a righteous critique of America's moral bankruptcy to
those who recognized it as a marketing stunt to boost comic book sales.
In an editorial for the *Comics Buyer's Guide* years later, leading comic
book retailer Chuck Rozanski claimed that upon hearing about the decision, he had called DC Comics editor Paul Levitz, pleading with him that
"since Superman was such a recognized icon within America's overall
popular culture . . . DC had no more right to 'kill' him than Disney had

the right to 'kill' Mickey Mouse." According to Rozanski, by choosing to kill Superman for sensational purposes, DC would be breaking an implicit promise to the American people to preserve the hero's legacy as a "trustee of a sacred national image."[2]

Compounding such hyperbolic claims to Superman's national iconicity, *Superman* #75, the famed death issue, was visually presented to readers as an object of national mourning. The issue was wrapped in a sealed plastic slipcover containing a series of memorial keepsakes: a fold-out obituary from the *Daily Planet* (Metropolis's official newspaper), a trading card in the form of a tombstone declaring the Man of Steel's last resting place, and a black armband embroidered with the red Superman logo for readers to wear as a public symbol of shared grief.[3] As potentially valuable collectibles, these keepsakes targeted hardcore fans who coveted memorabilia linked to beloved characters and narratives. As performative objects associated with and intended to elicit public displays of mourning and commemoration, they captured the attention of a wider national audience. Through these items virtually anyone could articulate affective attachments to a popular culture icon that embodied a dense network of feelings, ideals, and fantasies about the nation itself; indeed in news media, the comic book press, and print culture, everyone from fans to cultural critics and to ordinary Americas did just that.

The public debates over the meaning of the death of an American icon would be redoubled in the fictional narrative following Superman's passing. In subsequent comic book issues, Superman's seemingly stable identity as an emblem of American values—in fact *the* paragon of public service to the nation and a broader global community—would fracture beneath the weight of competing claims to his mantle. In his absence four mysterious figures appeared in Metropolis vying for his title as the city's heroic representative. These potential "supermen" included the teenage clone Superboy, the African American engineer turned construction worker John Henry Irons, a cyborg known as "the Man of Tomorrow," and a humanoid alien calling himself "the Last Son of Krypton." At a moment when Americans were embroiled in conflicts over multiculturalism, the ethics of genetic science and new medical technologies, immigration reform, and the proper education of the nation's youth, it was fitting that Superman's identity crisis would be embodied in four primary figures of the American culture wars: minorities, cyborgs, aliens, and teenagers.

For nearly twenty issues each of these figures took center stage in one of the four *Superman* comic book titles. Each series, respectively, explored what Superman would be like if he was an African American vigilante fighting crime in Metropolis's black ghetto, a rebellious and ego-centric teenager using his powers for media publicity, an alien wanderer encountering life on Earth for the first time, or a cyborg war machine programmed to maintain law and order by any means necessary.[4] By depicting the literal proliferation of Superman's body in these four alter egos, comic book creators presented the superhero as a dynamic and contested figure through which readers and creators alike could make claims about who might legitimately represent the American people, and the wider human race, as their heroic ambassador. Ultimately it was revealed that Superman never really died, his body hibernating to allow him to heal before making his miraculous return. For those who followed the story to its conclusion, however, it was clear that despite the Man of Steel's triumphant return, the "reign of the supermen" would forever shatter the national myth of a one true Superman.

The death of Superman begs a central question of this book: How could a figure commonly associated with seemingly trivial childhood fantasies become a site for debating questions of political significance and collective public concern? In *The New Mutants*, I argue that Superman's death and the subsequent fracturing of his identity bookended nearly three decades of creative innovation in American comics that transformed the superhero from a nationalist champion to a figure of radical difference mapping the limits of American liberalism and its promise of universal inclusion in the post–World War II period. On the one hand, the depiction of Superman's four alter egos cynically played on popular debates about multiculturalism and diversity in the early 1990s in order to sell comic books; on the other, the very fact that such minority figures could vie for Superman's vaunted place as an American icon—two of these characters even garnering their own comic book series—suggested that the superhero had undergone a symbolic reinvention that enabled previously ignored or marginalized identities, including African Americans and "alien" immigrants, to inhabit the space of superheroic power. *The New Mutants* narrates the history of this creative transformation by showing how the American superhero, once an embodiment of nationalism and patriotic duty, became a popular fantasy of internationalism and the concept of universal citizenship in the second half of the twentieth century.

With its inception in the late 1930s, the superhero quickly became a popular national icon that wedded a fantasy of seemingly unlimited physical power to an ethical impulse to deploy one's abilities in the service of maintaining public law and order. The great superheroes of the 1930s and 1940s—among them Superman, Batman, Captain America, and Wonder Woman—were legendary crime fighters who protected civilians from the machinations of organized crime, saved innocent victims from natural disasters, and, in the case of Captain America, battled foreign threats to American democracy like the Nazi menace. Despite their disparate and often nonhuman origins, these inaugural characters were perceived as exceptional Americans whose heroism could provide an aspirational model of ideal citizenship for the nation's impressionable young readers.

Starting in the late 1950s, this model of the American superhero as a local do-gooder and loyal patriot was radically transformed by a generation of comic book creators who reinvented the figure to speak to the interests and worldviews of postwar youth. Unlike their fictional forebears, whose powers were natural extensions of their body, postwar superheroes gained their abilities from radioactive exposure, technological enhancement, and genetic manipulation. Where once superheroes were symbols of national strength and paragons of U.S. citizenship, now they were framed as cultural outsiders and biological freaks capable of upsetting the social order in much the same way that racial, gendered, and sexual minorities were seen to destabilize the image of the ideal U.S. citizen. Rather than condemn these figures, superhero comics visually celebrated bodies whose physical instability deviated from social and political norms. Consequently they produced a visual lexicon of alliances between a variety of "inhuman" yet valorized subjects as a cultural corollary to the cosmopolitan worldviews of movements for international human rights, civil rights, and women's and gay liberation.

The traditional view of the superhero as a nationalist icon has blinded scholars of cold war cultural history to the dynamic role the figure has played in offering alternative and often radical reinterpretations of the central political terms of liberal democracy in the post–World War II period. I complicate this view by exploring how superhero comics articulated the tropes of literary and cultural fantasy to a variety of left-wing projects for political freedom. In the chapters that follow I show how postwar superhero comics made fantasy a political resource for recognizing and taking pleasure in social identities and collective ways of life commonly denigrated as deviant or subversive within the political logics of cold war anticommunism and an emergent neoconservatism. In case studies of *The Justice League of America* (1960) and *The Fantastic Four* (1960), I show how these comic book series recast the vigilante superhero as a member of a democratic collective through the invention of the "superhero team." The egalitarian image of the superhero team as an intergalactic peacekeeping force provided readers with a popular fantasy for imagining alternative social and political responses to the cold war, including international cooperation and cross-cultural alliance, rather than unilateral military power. In later chapters I investigate the emergence of mutant, cyborg, and alien superheroes in comic books like *The Silver Surfer* (1968), *The X-Men* (1974), and *The New Mutants* (1981) as visual allegories for racial, gendered, and sexual minorities. Though socially outcast by a bigoted humankind for their monstrous biology and alien lineages, benevolent mutant superheroes like the X-Men and alien warriors like the Silver Surfer were celebrated in comic books as figures who sought alliances on the basis of shared ethical goals rather than national or ethnoracial identity. Tracking these and a variety of other fictive innovations in superhero storytelling, I argue that postwar comic books used fantasy to describe and validate previously unrecognizable forms of political community by popularizing figures of monstrous difference whose myriad representations constituted a repository of cultural tools for a renovated liberal imaginary. *The New Mutants* tells the story of these monsters and the world of possibilities they offered to readers who sought the pleasures of fantasy not to escape from the realities of cold war America but to imagine the nation and its future otherwise.

From American Marvels to the Mutant Generation: Reinventing the Superhero

The superhero was introduced to American culture in 1938, when Superman made his first appearance in *Action Comics* #1, a variety adventure serial produced by publisher Detective Comics (later known as DC Comics). The superhero's debut launched the comic book medium to national notoriety while providing Americans with a fantasy of unlimited physical power and agency in an era when the promise of individualism and self-determination appeared all but impossible in light of an unremitting economic depression. Comic books emerged as a distinct cultural form in the early 1930s, originally sold as pamphlets containing reprinted newspaper comic strip materials; cheap, portable, visually sensational, and accessible for repeat readings, comic books embodied the populist ideals of folk culture but packaged in mass cultural form. As the medium gained public attention and sales figures expanded, publishers began developing original content in a variety of genres, including crime and suspense, romance, and war stories. It was the invention of the superhero, however, that would cement comics as one of the most influential forms of twentieth century American popular culture, by linking the populist character of the comic book medium to a fantasy figure that embodied American ideals of democratic equality, justice, and the rule of law. DC Comics initially refused to publish Joe Shuster and Jerry Siegel's *Superman* comic in 1936, fearing that the character was too "unbelievable," but they soon discovered that if someone could draw the Man of Steel, readers would believe in him.

First introduced as the opening feature of *Action Comics* #1, Superman immediately became a national sensation, soon starring in his own series and spawning countless imitations that would compose a growing pantheon of American superheroes. Between the late 1930s and the end of World War II, superhero comic books like *Superman* (1938), *Batman* (1939), and *Captain America* (1941) reached monthly circulation figures of nearly 900,000 issues, making superheroic fantasy a common fixture in American households and an anticipated monthly escape for GIs on the front lines of war.[5]

Gifted with abilities beyond the ken of normal humans, superheroes possessed an unprecedented capacity to extend their bodies into space and manipulate the material world with physical powers—among them extraordinary strength, speed, agility, and energy projection—that mimicked the capacities of modern industrial technologies. Both scholarly and fan literature often locate the American superhero at the tail end of a long tradition of mythic folk heroes, namely the frontier adventurers and cowboy vigilantes of nineteenth-century westerns. Though the superheroes of the late 1930s limned these figures through recourse to heroic masculinity and the embrace of vigilante justice, the superhero is historically distinguished from these previous icons by its mutually constitutive relationship to twentieth-century science and technology. Unlike the frontier hero escaping the constraints of civilization, the modern superhero is an embodiment of the *synthesis* between the seemingly "natural" biological self and the technologies of industrial society.

What distinguished the superhero from the merely superhuman, however, was its articulation of an extraordinary body to an ethical responsibility to use one's powers in service to a wider community. When attached to the prefix *super*, the word *hero* irrevocably transforms the concept of a body gifted with fantastic abilities by framing the bearer of such power as an agent of universal good. At once capable of refashioning the world in his image yet ethically committed to the well-being of a broader community beyond his own self-interest, the superhero has historically functioned as a visual meditation on the political contradiction between the values of individual liberty and collective good.

I conceive of the superhero's dual relationship to individual agency and public life as embodying the central tension of American liberal democracy, which articulates a belief in the unfettered autonomy of the individual with a form of governance dedicated to protecting political freedom for all citizens through collective political representation. Liberalism can be defined broadly as a worldview that values individual agency as the ultimate goal of organized politics and recognizes the rights of individuals on the basis of their universal humanity;[6] alternately, democracy is a collective solidarity between disparate individuals equally vested with political power, who seek to achieve a common good for a community above the pursuit of individual license. In the United States the uneasy alliance between liberalism and democracy has consistently been threatened by the historical exclusion of those deemed outside the boundaries of legitimate humanity, including the disabled, the stateless, and those believed to lack the capacity for reason on the basis of their race, gender, or class.[7] In its commitment to protecting the political interests of these alienated social groups the superhero had the potential to redefine the meaning of political freedom in America by recognizing the rights of those excluded from the national community. The lack of definition surrounding the superhero's ethical purview—whether her commitments ended at the borders of the nation or the broader sphere of humanity or included all life in the cosmos—and to whom the superhero was ultimately accountable in the use of her powers made the figure a generative site for imagining democracy in its most radical form, as a universally expansive ethical responsibility for the well-being of the world rather than an institutional structure upholding national citizenship.

During World War II this creative potential was mitigated by the superhero's affirmative relationship to the state. The comic books of this period depicted the superhero as an American patriot with definite national loyalties; often deploying his abilities in service to national security, the superhero's robust masculinity served as a metaphor for the strength of the American body politic against the twin evils of organized crime at home and fascism abroad. As Bradford Wright argues, the superheroes of this period embodied an idealized form of liberal citizenship as champions of individual freedom who supported outside intervention (whether in the form of the superheroic vigilante himself or the strong state) to protect and expand the political rights of individuals and maintain law and order.[8] This form of liberal citizenship embraced the use of science and technology in forwarding the goals of American democracy by imagining that mechanical or biological enhancement of the body would grant Americans an unprecedented ability to perform acts of civic duty beyond the physical capacity of ordinary humans.

The most famous cultural product of comics' articulation of science and liberal citizenship during World War II was Marvel Comics' Captain America (1941). Once a sickly army reject, Steve Rogers is transformed into the supersoldier Captain America, the nation's premier Nazi fighter, when the government backs the invention of a "super-serum" that alters his physiognomy, granting him unparalleled strength, speed, agility, and invulnerability.[9] With his exceptional physical powers and rigorous military training, Rogers is able to take on the Nazis with few physical or moral limits. Captain America manifested the belief that science was a vehicle for political freedom and that scientific and technological enhancement of the human body could produce more capable citizens. As Rogers's transformation from scrawny stripling to muscular powerhouse suggested, this particular image of ideal citizenship through scientific intervention was consistently coded as masculine and virile (not to mention white and heterosexual); with rare exceptions the defining characteristic of World War II superheroes was an invulnerable male body whose physical strength functioned as a literal bulwark against threats to the nation's borders and ideological values. No surprise, then, that this period of superhero storytelling is traditionally dubbed "the Golden Age" of comics, implying a nostalgic reverence for an era defined by the superhero's triumphant embodiment of American ideals.

Alternatively, postwar superheroes emerged as the monstrous progeny of the age of atomic and genetic science, no longer legitimate citizens of the state or identifiable members of the human race. Their mutated bodies and bizarre abilities—variously obtained from radiation exposure, genetic mutation, and alien science—suggested that the innovations of molecular engineering might destabilize the biological integrity of the human, producing political subjects whose abnormal physiologies rendered them unfit to engage in national civic life. What comic book historians call "the Silver Age" of comics was defined by an interest in exploring how various experiences of superhuman transformation might change what it means to be human and, consequently, what kind of community the superhero might affiliate with when the traditional markers of belonging—namely, proper humanity and national citizenship—no longer held true.

A variety of historical circumstances made this creative project viable for the comic book industry beginning in the late 1950s, including demographic shifts in reading audiences; changing social attitudes toward race, gender, and sexuality; new technologies of media production and circulation; and national interest in atomic and genetic science. A central motivating force, however, was the transformation of the relationship between the comic book industry and the U.S. government from one of mutual affirmation during World War II to one of clashing political and cultural interests in the postwar period. Following the war, crime and horror comics supplanted superhero stories as the highest selling genres among teenage readers. Narrating the violent exploits of criminals and social deviants, these comics joined other contemporary cultural genres such as film noir and dystopian science fiction that uncovered the seamy underside of postwar prosperity.[10] Responding to public criticism of the violent content of crime and horror comics by Catholic decency groups, psychologists, and school officials, in 1954 the House Un-American Activities Committee convened a special Senate session on juvenile delinquency, which threatened comic book publishers with regulatory action if they refused to develop content standards for their publications.[11] In the wake of government chastisement, mainstream comic book producers returned to the superhero as a fantasy figure traditionally understood to embody patriotic American values. Ironically this creative shift allowed writers and artists to explore bodies whose monstrous abnormality offered a rich site for critiquing the regulatory powers of the state and its inconsistently applied guarantee of national citizenship based on liberal ideals. Galvanized by such possibilities, the two most productive publishers of superhero comics, DC Comics (creator of Superman, Batman, and Wonder Woman) and Marvel (creator of Captain America), reinvented the superhero as a biological misfit and social outcast whose refusal or failure to conform to the norms of social legibility provided the ground for a new kind of political community.

This new generation of heroes challenged dominant assumptions in three key arenas of postwar cultural and political life. First, postwar superheroes upended the assumed relationship between scientific enhancement of the body and liberal citizenship. Simultaneously made superhuman by scientific interventions on the body, yet physically and symbolically shattered by such experiences, postwar superheroes were as damaged and vulnerable as they were powerful. By making vulnerability the ground upon which unexpected forms of solidarity might flourish, superhero comics reorganized the dominant narrative of liberal progress that associated science with man's mastery over nature and the body; according to these new stories, it was the *failure* to manage the consequences of scientific and technological innovation that laid bare the instability and unpredictability of the human. Second, these vulnerable figures overturned traditional hierarchies of gender and questioned presumptions about the physical superiority of the virile white male body. In the 1960s and 1970s male superheroes were repeatedly depicted as physically and psychologically unstable beings, their bodies seeming to switch genders through an array of anatomical metamorphoses or appearing incapable of performing the proper sexual functions of heterosexual masculinity. Unlike earlier depictions of the rigid male body struggling to secure its boundaries from perceived hostile forces, a new generation of superhero comics presented the unpredictable transformations of the male physique as a far more pleasurable and liberating form of embodiment than traditional models of sex and gender could ever conceive. These texts also showcased the development of empowered female superheroes, using the ecstatic visual cultures of women's and gay liberation to depict the exercise of superhuman powers as an expression of liberated female sexuality, pleasure, and agency.

Both the qualities of bodily vulnerability and gender instability constituted the postwar superhero as a figure in continual *flux*, visualized on the comic book page as constantly moving among different identities, embodiments, social allegiances, and psychic states.[12] At first glance the extraordinary physical malleability (and sometimes *literal* flexibility) exhibited by postwar superheroes—such as Mr. Fantastic's seemingly limitless physical pliability—might appear an expression of what some cultural critics have called neoliberal flexibility. Neoliberalism describes a shift in the ideological and political structure of capitalism in the late twentieth century—the same period as the superhero's reinvention—that involves the increasing imposition of market demands on all aspects of American culture, politics, and social life. Under neoliberalism formerly vilified or outcast social identities—for instance being gay or lesbian—have been revalued on the basis of their profitability, both as new target markets for consumer products and as sites of cultural expertise that aspiring entrepreneurs can claim "insider" knowledge about on the basis of their own racial, gendered, or sexual identity. This accelerated diffusion of market demands into private life has encouraged the development of the "flexible subject," a social type who exhibits the capacity to flexibly adapt every aspect of her identity to accommodate the demands of neoliberal capital and its periodic crises, including recessions, market fluctuations, and increased economic risk.[13]

Rather than performing flexibility, I argue, the monstrous powers and bodies of postwar superheroes exhibited a form of *fluxability*, a state of material and psychic *becoming* characterized by constant transition or change that consequently orients one toward cultivating skills for *negotiating* (rather than exploiting) multiple, contradictory identities and affiliations. Fluxability identifies one mode of being, fictionally depicted in the superheroes' many mutated or transitional forms, that exists in tension with neoliberalism's co-optation of oppositional identities. The visibly unruly and in flux bodies of superheroes like the Hulk, the Fantastic Four, and the mutant X-Men not only identified them as social deviants but also made them notoriously bad laborers, neither capable of holding down steady jobs nor interested in conceiving of their ethical service to the world in economic terms. The postwar superhero's fluxability attenuated the figure's potential as an effective laborer and also came to describe a form of material existence in which one's relationship to the world and its countless others was constantly subjected to questioning, transformation, and reorganization. This fact defines the third intervention of the postwar superhero: its generative engagement with the production of alternative alliances across difference at local, global, and cosmic scales.

Specifically, postwar superhero comics depicted the social communities and solidarities produced by a new "mutant generation" of heroes as the ground upon which progressive social transformation could take place. If cold war political rhetoric touted the hyperindividual, heterosexual, and presumably middle-class citizen as the antithesis of the communist subversive, superhero comics presented such individuals as narcissistic, alienated, and potentially destructive of social community. Against this self-centered figure of liberal politics, superhero comics celebrated the production of implicitly queer and nonnormative affiliations that exceeded the bounds of traditional social arrangements such as the nuclear family and the national community. Whether willfully choosing alternative solidarities or unwittingly thrown into relation with a host of mutated or monstrous others, postwar superheroes produced complex and internally heterogeneous communities of fellow travelers—often brought together under the rubric of the superhero "team" or chosen "family"—who sought to use their powers for shaping a more egalitarian and democratic world. Like the bodies and identities of the superheroes, aliens, mutants, and outsiders that composed their ranks, these alternative solidarities were depicted as being in constant flux, expanding, retracting, and transforming their stated values on the basis of unexpected encounters with a wider world.

Few superheroes exemplified these transformations more than Marvel Comics' Incredible Hulk (1962). Bombarded by radiation rays during the testing of a "gamma bomb," the shy, gentle scientist Bruce Banner is unwittingly transformed into a giant green monster with mammoth strength and invulnerability. As the Incredible Hulk, Banner is a physical powerhouse of unparalleled magnitude, yet in mutated form, he recurrently loses control of his emotions, destroying everything in sight during bouts of uncontrollable rage. The Hulk was a material expression of Banner's repressed psyche, manifesting at moments of extreme emotional distress. The competing halves of Banner's identity would have public ramifications as well: as a respected scientist for the military-industrial complex, Banner is an asset to national security. Yet as the Incredible Hulk, he is a violent threat to the American people, making his alter ego a target for the U.S. military. In the Incredible Hulk comic book creators linked scientific interventions on the body to biological and psychic instability, depicting the superhero's body as a vulnerable, porous surface always on the verge of radical transformation and consequently threatening the very definition of citizenship as the mutual recognition between individual subjects and a governing state.

At the same time, just as Steve Rogers's transformation into Captain America was gendered masculine, his enhanced body expressing virility and strength, Banner's mutation was troubled by an excessive and unstable performance of gender. On the one hand, the Hulk's physical appearance as a muscled green giant and his outbursts of violent rage identified him as hypermasculine; on the other, Banner's vulnerability to science and his subsequent emotional struggles to control his unpredictable abilities indicated a newfound association between the superhero and those traits commonly associated with femininity, including fragility and emotionality. In figures like the Hulk, comic books presented what appeared to be physically masculine bodies failing to live up to the norms of proper gender and sexuality or else threatening the boundaries between male and female, invulnerability and vulnerability, human and inhuman. At every level these were figures in flux.

As the superhero evolved from a rigid representation of law and order to a dynamic figure of flux negotiating multiple identities and affiliations in the postwar period, it straddled overlapping, and often competing, commitments to liberal and radical political ideals. On the one hand, superhero comics continued to espouse a liberal belief in individual free-dom and political choice, remained committed to science and reason as avenues for human progress, and endorsed human rights discourse, which confers political recognition on the basis of a universally shared humanity among all people. In its increasingly radicalized form, how-ever, the superhero comic book expanded who counted as legitimately "human" within liberal thought by valuing those bodies that were com-monly excluded from liberal citizenship, including gender and sexual outlaws, racial minorities, and the disabled. It highlighted human (and nonhuman) difference as the defining feature of all social creatures rather than their universal sameness, while also suggesting the need for a polit-ical common ground that would bind people across multiple identities and loyalties. I identify this project as radical because it actively under-mined the philosophical basis of liberal thought—namely the concept of a universally shared humanity underpinning each individual's claim to political rights—while also promoting collective freedom above the securing of individual rights and privileges. The tension between these various political impulses—to endorse human rights while undermin-ing the basis of the human, to value scientific discovery as the basis of progress while questioning the very idea of objectivity, to embrace cross-cultural solidarity while taking pleasure in difference—would form the conceptual ground upon which postwar superhero comic books would develop their greatest adventure stories.

In shifting the creative weight of superheroic fantasy from a focus on individual power and agency to bodily transformation and the question of collective belonging, postwar superhero comics contested and imag-ined alternatives to the cold war political logics of containment and integration. Recent scholarship in cold war cultural history has shown how containment—the political policy of halting the global spread of communism through economic and military coercion—existed alongside competing ideological formations. In *Cold War Orientalism*, Christina Klein has argued for a more complex reading of containment as a political policy and cultural ideology that worked in tandem with a policy of global *integration*, which saw Americans' active engagement with foreign cultures as an avenue for promoting U.S. interests abroad. Like containment, the policy of integration worked through cultural formations such as Hollywood musicals, popular travel memoirs, and foreign aid campaigns to encourage Americans to see themselves as civilian ambassadors to the U.S. government and supporters of anti-communist ideals abroad.[14]

Alternatively scholars like Julia Mickenberg and Cynthia Young have shown how, for a variety of left-wing activists and intellectuals, culture became an avenue for performing radicalism during a period of intense political repression.[15] In her cultural history of children's literature during the cold war, Mickenberg uncovers a diverse network of left-wing artists, intellectuals, and activists of the 1930s Popular Front era who rerouted their political energies toward the field of children's publishing after World War II. These Old Left writers, artists, editors, and librarians produced and circulated stories with egalitarian political messages for a new generation of American youth who would become the political activists of the New Left in the 1960s. Similarly Young narrates how an emergent Third World Left deployed a variety of cultural and intellectual forms—including film, literature, and scholarly research—to forge links between racial and class minorities in the United States and colonized peoples across the globe by identifying their shared experiences of poverty, social inequality, and political violence.

The New Mutants contributes to this body of work while focusing greater attention on the fantasy content of cold war popular culture. I seek to uncover the radical political possibilities contained in a fantasy form that was not produced by self-proclaimed left-wing activists or artists but rather emerged as the product of an ongoing negotiation between competing liberal and radical visions among creators and readers of comic book texts. To capture the cultural and political work of postwar superhero comics, I forward a model of world making that treats comic books "as a form of politics, as a means of reshaping individual and collective practice for specified interests."[16] World making describes instances when cultural products facilitate a space of public debate where dissenting voices can reshape the production and circulation of culture and, in turn, publicize counternarratives to dominant ideologies.[17] I am drawn to the concept of world making because of its dual reference to the aesthetic production of imaginative worlds and political practices that join creative production with social transformation. Michael Warner and Lauren Berlant identify world making as a practice engaged by sexual minorities and other social outcasts to create forms of culture, as well as public spaces, that offer recognition to nonnormative social relations and hail audiences commonly ignored by mainstream mass-media forms. Warner and Berlant posit that the term "world . . . differs from community or group because it necessarily includes more people than can be identified, more spaces than can be mapped beyond a few reference points, modes of feeling that can be learned rather than experienced as birthright." They continue, "The queer world is a space of entrances, exits, unsystematized lines of acquaintance, projected horizons . . . alternate routes, blockages, incommensurate geographies."[18] José Esteban Muñoz adds to this description social practices and performances that "have the ability to establish alternate views of the world" that function as "critiques of oppressive regimes of 'truth' that subjugate minoritarian people."[19] These definitions of world making underscore the importance of both social *and* creative practices in the construction of alternative ways of life for a variety of marginalized groups and point to the kinds of open-ended political projects that take flight in directions that are clearly incommensurate with, or actively resistant to, dominant social formations.

Berlant and Warner's description of the "queer world" as a "space of entrances, exits, unsystematized lines of acquaintance [and] projected horizons" beautifully captures both the aesthetic and symbolic thrust of post–World War II superhero comic books, whose visual elaboration of new heroic identities and alliances, lush fictional worlds, and enchanting phenomena would break the traditional aesthetic borders of the comic strip form, while offering readers "alternate routes" for imagining left-wing politics during the cold war and after. World making in postwar superhero comics involved a conceptual, narrative, and visual scaling upward of the superheroes' orientation from the local frames of city life and national affiliation, toward an expansive idea of "the world" as the object *at stake* in a variety of superheroic endeavors. As political theorist Ella Myers elaborates, "To say . . . that the world is 'at stake' in politics means that although the specific motivations and sentiments that inspire collective democratic action vary widely and produce outcomes that are uncertain, an underlying impulse, the 'wish to change the world,' is shared by even the most divergent democratic actors."[20] With the birth of a mutant generation of superheroes in the early 1960s, the formerly touted values of the superhero comic book, including law and order, nationalism, and virile masculinity, were increasingly sidelined in favor of producing imaginative fictional universes infused with a democratic political orientation toward the world. I call this ethos a "comic book cosmopolitics."

Comic Book Cosmopolitics

I use the term *comic book cosmopolitics* to describe the world-making practices of postwar superhero comic books. Unlike the liberal spirit of

World War II comics, which championed individual freedom and the defense of a national community against outside threats, the cosmopolitan ethic of postwar superhero comic books valued the uncertainty of cross-cultural encounter and the possibilities afforded by abandoning claims of individualism in exchange for diverse group affiliations. This ethic was both an aesthetic and a social achievement. It was formed in the mutual transformation of the creative content of superhero comic books *and* the changing values of an emergent participatory reading public that actively conversed with comic book creators about the formal and political content of the fantasy worlds they produced.

By attaching the label of *cosmopolitanism* to the American comic book, a medium commonly associated with "nonrealist" juvenile entertainment, I aim to relocate a seemingly apolitical form of mass culture within a genealogy of American political and intellectual thought. Following David Hollinger, I understand cosmopolitanism as an ethos that "promotes broadly based, internally complex, multiple solidarities equipped to confront the large-scale dilemmas of a 'globalizing' epoch while attending to the endemic human need for intimate belonging." Expanding on the ethical implications of Hollinger's description, Amanda Anderson elaborates that cosmopolitanism "aims to articulate not simply intellectual programs but ethical ideals . . . for negotiating the experience of otherness. . . . Although cosmopolitanism has strongly individualist elements (in its advocacy of detachment from shared identities and its emphasis on affiliation as voluntary), it nonetheless often aims to foster reciprocal and transformative encounters between strangers variously construed."[21] Postwar superhero comics facilitated such "transformative encounters between strangers variously construed" on multiple levels. They depicted expanding casts of superhuman characters "negotiating the experience of otherness" within a vast cosmos, while fostering "ethical ideals" of democratic debate between creators and readers about the aesthetic and political content of superhero stories. These varied scales of engagement produced countless opportunities for developing multiple, "internally complex" solidarities—between and among comic book characters, readers, creators, and various political visions—that embodied a cosmopolitan willingness to be transformed by encounters with new worlds, bodies, ideas, and values.

Comic book cosmopolitics was cultivated in three ways. First, as the superhero came to embody a model of universal citizenship, the visual locus of superhero comic books dramatically expanded. Where once superhero comics focused on the happenings of local city life, depicting the crime-fighting exploits of urban vigilantes, now they presented the superhero as a freewheeling adventurer within a vast web of relations between human and nonhuman actors across the cosmos. This expansion of the visual field of superhero comics took advantage of the comic book medium's vast representational capacities, captured in the conceit that *whatever can be drawn can be believed*. As a low-tech visual form requiring only pencil and paper, comics allow for the visual depiction of extraordinary scales of existence and embodiment without the need for costly technical special effects. With the advent of global satellite imaging technology, technical innovations in film and television media, and the emergence of new discourses of globalism in the 1950s and after (including postwar internationalism, cold war geopolitics, and environmentalism), comic book creators began to exploit the capacity of their medium to represent grand totalities in such figures as the world, the universe, and the cosmos.

Corollary to the expansion of comics' visual scale, editors at DC and Marvel Comics reconceptualized their individual publishing houses as overseers of distinct fictional "universes" inhabited by particular cadres of superhuman characters. They encouraged readers to see each of the company's superheroes as inhabiting the same unified social world rather than characters isolated in their own discreet stories. This diverged from the comic book publishing model of the 1930s and 1940s, in which complete, bounded stories were narrated in the space of a single issue so that on-again, off-again readers could follow the plot of a given serial regardless of which issue they purchased. By the late 1950s comic book publishers found themselves catering to a regular reading audience who wished to follow multi-issue story lines and see character development over time. The trademarking of distinct DC and Marvel universes boosted sales by luring readers with the promise of various character crossover stories. Yet it also expanded the "worldliness" of comic book content by encouraging creators to depict individual superheroes' unfolding interactions with countless other figures who populated their daily lives, interactions that now took place across vast geographical terrains on Earth and beyond.

As these fictional worlds took shape, superhero comics became less about common crime fighting and more about the unpredictable encounters between an expanding cohort of superhumans, aliens, cosmic beings, and an array of fantastical objects and technologies. As a result, cross-cultural *encounter* rather than assimilation became the primary site of political world-making in the superhero comic book, offering an alternative to the one-sided model of cultural tolerance promoted by the cold war logic of integration. If the goal of cold war integration was a stable postcommunist world dominated by American cultural and economic values, the open-ended serialized narratives of postwar comics, as well as the increasingly complex fictional worlds they produced, promised indefinite instability. Each new issue of a series offered creators an opportunity to critique, reimagine, or wholly transform the narrative and visual trajectory of previous stories so that narrative outcomes were always unpredictable and provisional. This fact was redoubled in the sequential character of comic book art, which became a formal tool for underscoring the transformative and unpredictable nature of the superhero's body.

In the post–World War II period, comic book creators began to underscore the serial visuality of comics—its use of sequential images unfolding across space to depict change over time—as a formal corollary to the superhero's unstable anatomy. They experimented with the visual layout of sequential images to depict bodily flux as a visual effect of transition between panels on a page. What would appear as an ordinary human body in one panel might appear in the next as a body in flight, as invisible, aflame, shape-shifting, encased in metal, or altogether *not there*. The visual instability of the superhero's body across time and space negated the figure's previous iconic status as a seemingly invulnerable masculine body by proliferating countless permutations of the superhero that refused to cohere into a unified image or physiology.[22] Such bodily fluxing and its articulation to the cosmopolitan ideal of unpredictable, worldly encounter became both a central "problem" of superhero stories—requiring superheroes to negotiate their bodily transformations and encounters with similarly mutant, nonhuman, or hybrid beings—as well as a site of cultural and political investment for a new generation of comic book readers.

The emergence of a participatory reading public as a fixture of postwar comic book culture would form the second foundation of comic book cosmopolitics. In the late 1950s DC Comics editor Mort Weisinger began including a letters page at the end of the company's best-selling title, *Adventure Comics*. There Weisinger published short letters from readers across a wide demographic spectrum that commented on the company's creative productions, including praise and criticism of various story lines, the aesthetic details of specific issues, and suggestions for new characters. The popular response to these letters pages was so powerful that both DC and Marvel instituted regular letters pages in all their best-selling comic book titles. By offering readers the possibility of greater interaction between characters and increasingly elaborate fictional worlds, creators put themselves in the position of having to respond to a growing audience demand for *more* innovations in comic book storytelling.

By the mid-1960s these print forums had produced an affective counterpublic (which included the institution of fan clubs and comic book conventions) where readers could voice their relationship to the characters and worlds they followed monthly while democratically debating the comics' content. Just as fictional superheroes were encountering a cosmos filled with alien life in a spirit of cosmopolitan engagement, so too the heterogeneous members of a growing postwar readership were using a popular media form to engage one another across race, class, gender, generation, and geographical space. As I show in chapter 3, while a majority of letters across titles focused on aesthetic concerns, some of the most acclaimed comic book series of the period, particularly *The Fantastic Four,* became famous for printing letters that directly addressed the relationship of superheroes to contemporary political concerns, including civil rights and race relations, the women's movement, and the Vietnam War. Consequently superhero comics became an evolving creative site for exploring questions of cultural difference, social inequality, and democratic action that would form the basis of a comic book cosmopolitics.

The alignment of a new reading generation's emergent political investments with the superhero's increasingly cosmopolitan outlook on the world was underwritten by a third, and final, transformation in comic book culture: the medium's resurgent investment in the liberal values of antiracism and antifascism alongside its absorption of the more radical politics of New Left social movements. Though few comic book creators voiced commitments to radical political ideals—many even politically conservative—the generation of writers, artists, and editors who helped forge the industry in the late 1930s was deeply invested in liberal egalitarian values. These primarily Jewish creative producers were shaped by the dual experiences of being second-generation immigrants as well as witnesses to, and sometimes active military participants in, the battle against Nazism. These experiences led them to espouse the ideals of religious and ethnoracial tolerance, as well a broader commitment to universal political freedom and equality. Writing in his monthly editorial, "Stan's Soapbox," in December 1968, Marvel Comics editor Stan Lee proclaimed:

Let's lay it right on the line. Bigotry and racism are among the deadliest social ills plaguing the world today. But, unlike a team of costumed supervillains, they can't be halted with a punch. . . . The only way to destroy them is to expose them—to reveal them for the insidious evils they really are. . . . Although anyone has the right to dislike another individual, it's totally irrational, patently insane to condemn an entire race—to despise an entire nation—to vilify an entire religion. . . . Sooner or later, if man is ever to be worthy of his destiny, we must fill our hearts with tolerance.[23]

By the late-1960s this commitment to liberal tolerance had become a defining value of superhero comics. In its most progressive iterations, this antiracist and antifascist worldview intersected with and helped theorize an emergent radical sensibility among postwar youth that combined liberal ideals of political freedom with a powerful critique of the interlocking oppressions of race, class, and gender and the government institutions that underwrote the violent conflicts of a global cold war.

The young readers who galvanized this increased radicalism in comic book content were growing up in a world where the rhetoric of civil rights and anticolonialism was in ascendancy, offering a utopian political alternative to the cold war's rigidly antagonistic view of the world divided between a capitalist United States and a communist Russia. An increasingly international readership hailing from every major demographic welcomed the superhero comic book's expanded visual scope and its attendant ideal of universal human (and "inhuman") equality. Frustrated with the normalizing social expectations of 1950s America, these readers also valued the superhero's physiological nonconformity with proper humanity. Consequently they facilitated the invention of an array of new figurations of the superhero, including aliens, cyborgs, and mutants, while encouraging the demographic diversification of comic book characters.

From the production side, the diversification of superhero comics through the introduction of racial minorities and women to previously white, male-centered superhero stories was ostensibly a *liberal* response to the traditional homogeneity of comic book content. It was also a transformation conditioned by economic demands to appeal to a more diverse readership. From the perspective of readers, however, the demand for greater representational diversity was less about the mere visibility of minorities in comics and more an appeal to creators to develop stories and worlds that explored the cultural politics of identity. As a generation attuned to the emerging cosmopolitan visions of the New Left, and later black power, Third World movements, and women's and gay liberation, many readers and cultural critics of comics understood that *differences* (whether of race, class, sex, or gender, geographical location, ability, or religious orientation) were not only sites of political oppression but potent cultural resources for articulating new forms of social and political affiliation, questioning the limits of democratic inclusion, and developing new knowledge about the world from the position of the outcast and the marginalized. An increasingly politically minded readership took seriously the idea (presented by superhero comics themselves) that the internal heterogeneity of the fictional universes of Marvel and DC Comics could facilitate interactions between differently situated characters that might foment debates about the political possibilities, pleasures, and limits of cultural differences. The very fact that superhero comics were conceptually obsessed with phenotypic and physiological difference, expending vast narrative and visual space depicting new species, bodies, abilities, and identities, meant that the introduction of previously unrepresented differences (whether real-world ones like race or fictional categories like mutation) demanded a substantive recalibration of the social relations between characters, the visual depiction of new distinctions, and a language with which to discuss such differences.

This approach to difference dovetailed with the values of women of color feminism and other radical critiques of race in this period, which "were fundamentally organized around *difference*, the difference between and within racialized, gendered, sexualized collectivities."[24] As Roderick Ferguson and Grace Hong elaborate, "The definition of difference for women of color feminism . . . [was] not a multiculturalist celebration [or] an excuse for presuming a commonality among all racialized peoples, but a cleareyed appraisal of the dividing line between valued and devalued, which can cut within, as well as across, racial groupings."[25] Comic book readers were surprisingly adept at articulating these ideals in their own words. They demanded that creators value commonly devalued identities and bodies in comics (including women, people of color, and the working class) and that the fictional narratives of these characters honestly dramatize the uneven social value attributed to different kinds of superhumans within their distinct fantasy worlds based on the magnitude of their abilities, specific form of mutation, or level of social standing. Readers understood, for instance, that the introduction of an African female superhero, Ororo Monroe (Storm), in the pages of the popular *X-Men* (1974) series might force writers to address the distinctions between African and African American experiences of race, *as well as* the gendered dynamics of a black woman superhero capable of controlling the elements working alongside predominantly white, male teammates whose powers were largely extensions of physical strength; similarly, when creators introduced the first African American super-hero, Luke Cage, in his own series, *Luke Cage: Hero for Hire* (1972), as an economically struggling private detective, readers lauded the series for taking seriously the race and class implications of hero work (including the expense of costumes, travel, and headquarters space) especially for inner-city minorities. Readers' willingness to embrace the liberal project of representational inclusiveness in comics, then, was conditioned by a more radical investment in comic books as sites of political world-mak-ing where the presence of diverse actors in expansive fictional universes of encounter, conflict, and negotiation could provide substantive creative responses to social difference.[26]

One of the most radical outcomes of this attentiveness to differ-ence within a cosmopolitan frame was to facilitate the reinvention of the superhero as a distinctly "queer" figure. I invoke the term *queer* to describe how postwar superheroes' mutated bodies and alternative kin-ships thwarted the direction of heterosexual desire and life outcomes and cultivated an affective orientation toward otherness and difference that made so-called deviant forms of bodily expression, erotic attachment, and affiliation both desirable and ethical. The postwar superhero comic's embrace of indefinitely unfolding narratives with no predetermined outcome, its unraveling of the traditionally gendered physiology of the white, male superhero, and its centralizing of cross-cultural encounter and mutually transformative engagement popularized a mode of story-telling that was largely uninterested in traditional heterosexual repro-duction, family forms, or gender norms. Even when comics told stories of superheroes getting married or having children, these narratives were shot through with contradictions about the supposed social normalcy of such practices. The weddings of superheroes were attended by motley crews of alien, mutant, and cyborg guests dressed not in formal wear but in flamboyant superhero costumes, and when superheroes looked forward to child rearing, they fretted over the queer potential of prog-eny born from nonhuman parents.[27] Instead of solidifying a "straight" future organized by the nuclear family and the promise of heterosexual reproduction, postwar superhero comics framed the proliferation of dif-ference, its ceaseless alteration of the social world, and the pursuit of ever more complex forms of affiliation and collective action *across* all manner of cultural and geographic divides as the goal of a comic book cosmopolitics.

Taken together, the expanding visual horizon of the superhero comic book, the emergence of a participatory reading public, and the alignment of comic book content with the egalitarian ideals of left-wing political projects constructed the parameters of comic book cosmopolitics. I locate the political productivity of comics—understood as their capacity to imaginatively innovate and make public aesthetic and social responses to the limits of contemporary political imaginaries—in the generative relationship between comic book producers, an emergent countercultural readership, and the expanding visual and narrative content of comic book texts. Yet I place my greatest analytical emphasis on the actual visual and narrative content of superhero comic book texts themselves. This content, and the broader cosmopolitan aspirations it articulated, was the common object of concern that brought creators and readers into dialogue in the first place; it was also the material outcome of their various engagements with each other and the wider cultural and political contexts within which they articulated their distinct positions. Taking a dual-pronged approached, I conceive of comics as historically constituted objects emerging from distinct social and material conditions—including shifting economic demands, the biographies of different creators, demographic transformations in readership, and new printing technologies—while also seeing their rich narrative and visual content as producing imaginative logics that offer ways of reconceiving, assessing, and responding to the world that are *not* reducible to any single historical factor. In other words, I never assume that the "meaning" of a given comic book text, story, character, or fictional event can be deduced from a single biographical element of a creator's life, or by laying bare the economic conditions that encouraged a specific creative decision, or by making an abstract reference to a historical event that took place shortly before a story was scripted. Rather, following Foucault, I see the interpretive possibilities of texts (not their ultimate meaning, but what people *do* with them) as emerging within a field of dynamic interactions and antagonisms between competing actors who exercise power in different ways that ultimately shape and proliferate *multiple* meanings and interpretive possibilities around a text.[28] Consequently my method for analyzing comics involves a form of close reading that centralizes questions of literary scale to bridge the distances between the historical and the imaginative valences of comic book content.

In her essay "The Scale of World Literature," Nirvana Tanoukhi conceptualizes scale as "the social condition of a landscape's utility." By "landscape" Tanoukhi means the field of social and aesthetic relations that surrounds the production of and composes the creative content internal to a given literary text. Tanoukhi theorizes scale not merely as geographical or historical distance but as the *conceptual distance* that must be traversed by a reader in order for a particular element of a text (including characters, themes, tropes, or literary and visual techniques) to have meaning or use to them in varied contexts.[29] This understanding of scale allows us to consider, for instance, what conditions enabled readers to take up the visual depiction of the mutant (or genetically outcast) superhero as a figure for Third World politics or internationalism or any number of cosmopolitan political projects attuned to the relationship between marginalized identities and broader scales of affiliation beyond the nation. From this perspective the categories of world making (as a creative practice) and comic book cosmopolitics (as an ethos) can be understood as tools or *metrics of scale*. Each offers a framework for analyzing how a local, material, worldly object like the superhero comic book aspired to broad scales of conceptual and political experience, what I am labeling a cosmopolitics, through both shifting conditions of production and innovative aesthetic practices. To analyze superhero comic books this way is, in a sense, to aspire to the world-making possibilities of comics themselves, but with critical attention to how those possibilities were historically produced and articulated, taken up by various actors, and revised over time. The basic fact that so many readers and cultural critics were able to make political meaning out of the fantasy content of superhero comic books suggests the capacity of these texts to elicit imaginative acts of scale-making from its audiences, ones specifically oriented toward a cosmopolitan ethos, *despite* the numerous economic, social, and political constraints on the production of comics themselves.

A variety of business histories of both Marvel and DC Comics have shown how, since the 1960s, economic demands to maintain operating budgets, pay salaries, make profits, and increase market share have placed incredible pressure on creators and editorial management to produce salable comic book content.[30] While taking into account the economic pressures that mediated the relationship between creators and readers, I narrate a different story that explores how the social conditions of comic book production and circulation from the 1960s onward helped produce figures and stories that often exceeded, contested, or altogether repudiated the mandates of profitability at both Marvel and DC Comics. The postwar superhero's fluxability was one such figure, an imaginative tool for thinking outside the framework of economic profitability that also encouraged the sale of comics. The fluxible superhero was not innocent of economic interests, but neither were his meanings reducible to them.

Because comic book production in the 1960s was less constrained by corporate demands and underpinned by the basic need of creators to make a living wage, I approach this period as one of relatively unrestrained creative innovation when the economic interests of creators dovetailed with the political radicalization of a growing countercultural audience. By the mid-1970s and early 1980s, Marvel and DC would become fully corporate ventures (owned by Cadence Industries and Warner Communications, respectively) with increasing investments in making comic books profitable to publishers, CEOs, and shareholders. This transformation attenuated open-ended dialogue and creative experimentation between readers and creators but also heightened tensions between a new generation of creative talents and their corporate employers. Rather than reducing all comic book content to corporate pandering, then, these constraints added another dynamic variable to superhero comics' production that encouraged innovative creative responses to corporate economic pressures. Because of this, in later chapters I analyze how the political and visual content of superhero comics since the mid-1970s became an index of the shifting scales of negotiation among creators, fans, and a newly appointed corporate management within an increasingly profit-driven industry. As I discuss in chapter 5, this included a bold critique of corporate capital lobbied by writers and artists in the pages of mainstream comics as a response to the economic devaluation of their artistic labor in the 1970s. Simultaneously the aesthetic innovations that creators used to articulate their economic frustrations—including recasting the superhero as an icon of working-class virility—provided readers with a new set of conceptual tools for scaling downward from the cosmic worldviews they had become accustomed to and addressing the daily living conditions of racial minorities, the working class, and the homeless. Both a product of dynamic dialogue and contestation *and* a figure mediated by the vicissitudes of the mass entertainment market, the comic book superhero would come to articulate a variety of potential solutions to the impasses of contemporary social politics within the constraints of industry realignments.

If bridging the conceptual distances between the fictional world of superhero comics and the political world was the central project of a comic book cosmopolitics, then the vehicle for this work was undoubtedly fantasy. The capacity to invent and depict a near-limitless range of fantasy figures, scenarios, and worlds was an imaginative skill that creators and readers both exercised but that comic book texts visually manifested and circulated to mass audiences. It was fantasy that made the scale-making aspirations of superhero comics both possible *and* pleasurable, displaying the worlds that might unfold from a cosmopolitan view of life, while imbuing those worlds with endless desire.

The Cultural Politics of Popular Fantasy

Fantasy is distinguished from other modes of communication by its use of figures, tropes, and scenarios that are impossible or inexplicable by scientific means. It is a particular kind of fiction making, which invents or describes things that do not actually exist with the hope of expanding what is imaginable at a given historical moment.[31] A variety of intellectual traditions have theorized fantasy and its cultural operations by defining it as a psychic mechanism, a narrative genre, or a utopian political longing. Psychoanalytic theory views fantasy (or "phantasy") as a psychic wellspring of desires expressed in imagined narratives or scenarios that would potentially fulfill unconsummated wishes, while genre studies examines fantasy as a mode of storytelling that destabilizes traditional conceptions of reality by making that which is assumed impossible appear possible or imminent. A third approach, Marxist theory, has explained fantasy through the concept of "utopia," or the idea that fantasy allows one to produce maps of alternate worlds that resist the limits of the present, especially those imposed by class hierarchy; the ability to imagine or invent a world without money or class distinctions, for instance, is the central idea of Thomas More's *Utopia* (1560), which set the standard for utopian fantasy as an alternative mode of rethinking the present relations of production.[32] This open-ended quality of fantasy, however, is usually set against the more classical Marxist understanding of fantasy as false consciousness, or an ideology that actively mystifies the real conditions of social and economic hierarchy. Marxism, then, traditionally locates fantasy in a dialectic of ideology and utopia, with its radical potential related to whether or not it can function as a legitimate critique of capitalism. All three approaches imply a subversive potential in fantasy that can work as an imaginative resource for resisting and potentially altering a given set of norms that constrain one's world—whether those be gender and sexual norms, class expectations, or the demands of "good" citizenship. Despite their distinctive locating of fantasy in various sites (unconscious desires, narrative, or ideology), all see fantasy as a definable structure whose outcomes can be clearly predicted and described.

In *The New Mutants*, I treat fantasy as a dynamic aesthetic and social phenomenon, a mode of communication deployed as a tool of world making rather than a psychic mechanism, genre, or dialectic whose meanings are determined in advance. I posit a new analytical category I call "popular fantasy" as an alternative to traditional genre analysis and ideology critique. Popular fantasy describes the variety of ways that the tropes and figures of literary fantasy (magic, superhuman ability, time travel, alternate universes, among others) come to organize real-world social and political relations. On the one hand, I take fantasy on its own terms as a mode of communicating that invokes impossible, magical, or enchanted phenomena; on the other, I consider the social and public dimensions of fantasy, including how it is taken up in the production of collective narratives of political possibility and desire. Comic book cosmopolitics was an exemplary twentieth-century popular fantasy, a set of aesthetic and social practices oriented toward the invention of a cosmopolitan ethos through the unfolding of elaborate fantasy worlds.

In *The Anatomy of National Fantasy*, Berlant develops the concept of "national fantasy" as a mechanism by which local, atomized individuals come to see themselves as citizens of a national community. In this view, fantasy is neither a discreet psychic structure nor a literary genre but a social and cognitive practice of scale-making that involves projecting oneself into broader registers of existence.[33] National fantasy circulates discourses of national belonging (including the promise of democratic inclusion or the shared status of citizenship) in fiction, political rhetoric, and folklore to provide people with conceptual tools to enact a cognitive leap, or *fantasy*, of imagining themselves as an organic part of a collectively shared national identity. Berlant's approach retains the imaginative qualities of fantasy, its capacity to encourage cognitive creativity, while assessing how those qualities can be understood as a *social* process that produces political realities, including shared affective attachments to the nation. Despite her attention to the heterogeneity of national fantasy, however, Berlant describes it as a consolidating project that produces a relatively unified and durable national subject. She claims that the fantasy of "national identity provides . . . a translation of the historical subject into an 'Imaginary' realm of ideality and wholeness . . . by being reconstituted as a collective subject, or citizen." Because this experience of "wholeness" is predicated on individuals having to strategically "forget" the local realities of national citizenship—including racism and sexism, the institution of slavery, and class hierarchy—national fantasy appears as an ideological project that produces citizens through a willful covering over of real historical conditions.[34]

My conception of popular fantasy builds on Berlant's understanding of fantasy as a collective social practice of scale-making, while exploring its unique ability to destabilize, alter, or altogether unravel existing frameworks in order to present new ways of perceiving the world. Specifically I use the term *popular fantasy* to identify expressions of fantasy that suture together current social and political realities with impossible happenings to produce figures that describe and legitimate nascent cultural desires and modes of social belonging that appear impossible or simply out of reach within the terms of dominant political imaginaries. The fantastical or seemingly impossible character of popular fantasies signals the continued "otherness" of the potential social relations they seek to describe, while making that otherness desirable as an alternative to normative social aspirations. The entertainment value of popular fantasy—its ability to induce pleasure in witnessing impossible phenomena or experiencing lifeworlds that have no everyday corollary, or else unevenly map onto reality—signals its embeddedness in commodity culture but also highlights its capacity to inaugurate or invent new political desires, new worlds, through modes of enchantment and wonder. This experience of wonderment is galvanized by the production of impossible figures that surprise and exhilarate because of their seemingly miraculous or fantastical qualities.

Superhumans, mutants, aliens, cyborgs, and "companion species" of all kinds enchant us. These figures capture the imagination, spark pleasure and wonder, and offer new ways of seeing the interrelations between bodies, objects, and worlds. This fact is so obvious as to go unspoken, but without it we misunderstand the diverse pleasures and political possibilities that audiences have derived from superheroic fantasy in the twentieth century. If, as I have been arguing, fantasy describes a form of communication that encompasses a set of tropes, figures, and narratives of the impossible and imagined, then enchantment describes the *affective experience* of witnessing or encountering fantasy in its varied forms.[35] Enchantment captures a constellation of emotions that might include wonder, exuberance, excitement, pleasure, and a host of ambivalent feelings that necessarily come with a "surprising encounter" with the unknown, including fear, uneasiness, and confusion. Yet, as Jane Bennett argues, "the overall effect of enchantment is a mood of fullness, plenitude, or liveliness, a sense of having had one's nerves or circulation or concentration power tuned up or recharged." For Bennett the enchanted quality of fantasy figures—including any number of hybrid, monstrous, and magical creatures from art and literature—derives from their seemingly unlimited capacity for transformation. Mobile, mutating, and morphing, these figures "enact the very possibility of change; their presence carries with it the trace of dangerous but also exciting and exhilarating migrations."[36]

The complex and knotted set of affective states that make up enchantment might also just be called *fun*, which is the experience most people have with fantasy. That sense of fun or exuberance or desire for the impossible is often disregarded as a minor entertainment effect of mass culture, or worse, an ideological ruse that blinds audiences to the underlying politics of the fantasies they consume. Yet, as a number of theorists of enchantment have shown, the affective pull of enchantment is not only capable of underpinning progressive politics but might be a necessary prerequisite for ethics. According to Bennett, to be enchanted can also involve a feeling of attachment or care for the miraculous phenomena before you and, by extension, an attachment to the world that houses and proliferates such wonders.[37]

A progressive ethical orientation to the world is not a necessary outcome of enchantment, but enchantment can be a potent tool for cultivating it. This fact is most obvious when one seeks out enchantment in places where we usually do not expect to find it, namely the realm of politics and social activism, which is commonly associated with hardheaded realism and grounded strategies and tactics. Describing the political affects that drive and sustain social movements, the sociologist Deborah Gould writes, "I would venture that social movements sustain themselves at the level of desire. A movement milieu . . . expresses desire for different forms of social relations, different ways of being, a different world. In doing so, a movement allows participants to feel their own perhaps squelched desires or to develop new ones that through articulation can become contagious, flooding others' imaginations and drawing them into the movement. In articulating and enacting what previously might have been unimaginable, a movement offers a scene and future possibilities that surprise, entice, exhilarate, and electrify."[38]

One can substitute the term *popular fantasies* for *social movements* in each of Gould's sentences and the statement still rings true. Cultural fantasies like comic book cosmopolitics can operate in ways similar to modes of political action, using creative figures to "offer a scene of future possibilities that surprise, entice, exhilarate, and electrify" or, as the cultural historian Robin Kelley claims, "to take us to another place, envision a different way of seeing, perhaps a different way of feeling."[39] Disparate thinkers like Bennett, Gould, and Kelley remind us that no form of ethics or political action can be motivated without an attendant vision of the world one wishes to forge through such ethical and political commitments. Just as a social movement's desires for a different world can "flood others' imaginations," so too popular fantasy enchants its potential audience by presenting a vision of a different world and offering encounters with figures of radical otherness that provide tools to subvert dominant systems of power and reorient one's ethical investments toward bodies, objects, and worldviews formerly dismissed as alien to the self.

The radical transformation of identity in the service of producing new standards for ethical action is a central project of popular fantasy, and the postwar superhero in particular. From the late 1950s onward, a new generation of comic book mutants, aliens, and cyborgs encouraged audiences to form deep attachments to figures of deviancy, monstrosity, and marginalization. These fantasy figures spoke "to people at the level of desire" by identifying bodies, worldviews, and behaviors commonly denigrated by American public culture as both pleasurable and desirable.[40] Such attachments, when woven into the fabric of contemporary political concerns, forged a new ethics based on the dream of a world where difference and nonconformity might be valued as necessary components of social justice and collective well-being. This articulation of enchantment to political ethics was brilliantly modeled for readers in the 1961 origin story of the Marvel Comics superhero team the Fantastic Four, whose intergalactic exploits would become the best-selling comic book stories of the decade.

After being bombarded by cosmic rays from outer space, four anticommunist space adventurers—Reed Richards, Ben Grimm, and Sue and Johnny Storm—experience monstrous bodily mutations. Each initially reacts with terror and confusion at their "freakish" transformations, none more so than Johnny, whose body spontaneously bursts into flame (figure I.1). When Johnny realizes that he can survive the flame, however, even using his body's radiant energy to fly, his horror turns into exuberance as he gleefully takes to the skies. Witnessing Johnny's extraordinary flight, his three companions are jolted from their initial panic, now enchanted by his superhuman skill. In response to the transformations they have witnessed in each another, the four think in unison: "We've changed! All of us! We're *more* than just human!" Clasping hands in a gesture of solidarity, they vow to deploy their newfound powers to "help mankind."[41] In the transformations of these figures, Marvel

FIGURE I.1. The birth of the Fantastic Four. Stan Lee (writer) and Jack Kirby (penciller), "The Fantastic Four!," *Fantastic Four* #1, November 1961, Marvel Comics, reprinted in *Fantastic Four Omnibus Vol. 1* (New York: Marvel Comics, 2005), 21.

Comics visually modeled how enchantment might reorient ethical commitments and political attachments. Following their physical evolution, the four are compelled to redirect their previous anticommunism toward a more egalitarian interest in protecting mankind from violence and injustice; this ethics is materialized by the physical contact of visibly mutated bodies whose touch invokes new bonds between unlikely partners as they struggle to come to terms with their fantastic, yet monstrous, superhuman abilities.

Such abilities and the novel solidarities they facilitated figured the Fantastic Four as part of a new, *queer* generation of American superheroes, bound together by attachments that exceeded the dictates of heterosexuality, traditional family life, and national loyalties. To theorize the superhero as a distinctly queer figure of twentieth-century popular culture, I approach popular fantasy and its political affects from the perspective of queer theory. Queer theory is a body of knowledge that concerns itself with the ways queer or nonnormative figures generate alternative desires, bring into view unexpected objects of passionate attachment, and facilitate the production of novel forms of kinship and affiliation. It is a sustained attempt to theorize the social relations of desire, linking the heterogeneity of local, intimate, erotic attachments to the broader scales of political desire, aspiration, and affiliation in public life.

Within this framework a number of theorists have used *queerness* to describe a utopian horizon or way of being in the world that imbues social relationships with the hope and possibility of nonnormative social and sexual relations. For Eve Sedgwick queerness "can refer to: the open mesh of possibilities, gaps, overlaps, dissonances and resonances, lapses and excesses of meaning when the constituent elements of anyone's gender, of anyone's sexuality aren't made (or can't be made) to signify monolithically. The . . . adventures attaching to the very many of us who may at times be moved to describe ourselves as (among many other possibilities) pushy femmes, radical faeries, fantasists, drags, clones, leather folk, ladies in tuxedoes, feminist women or feminist men, masturbators, bulldaggers, divas, Snap! Queens, butch bottoms . . . transsexuals . . . or people able to relish, learn from, or identify with such."[42] Sedgwick's understanding of queerness is expansive and elastic, an orientation from which to articulate numerous identities and desires that do not fit into the schema of heterosexual normativity, yet it is also committed to endless specificity and distinction within a broad frame of reference, attending to the fact "that people are different from each other."[43] This aspiration for queerness to be broadly inclusive *and* attentive to difference, while creating an alternative world for an endless variety of people to inhabit, is similarly captured in Muñoz's conception of queerness as "a structuring and educated mode of desiring that allows us to see and feel beyond the quagmire of the present."[44]

Superhero comic books provide a remarkable example of a queerly inflected, "educated mode of desiring" in late twentieth-century American culture. The developing imaginative worlds of superhero narratives visually and affectively oriented readers toward an expanding array of queer figures, worldviews, and social relationships while engaging innovative experiments in the organization of the comic book page to articulate the "gaps, overlaps, dissonances and resonances" of social identity to the *formal* gaps, overlaps, dissonances, and resonances of comic book visuality. Sedgwick's freewheeling, open-ended list of queer identifications uncannily echoes any similar inventory of the fantasy figures who came to populate the Marvel Comics universe: mutants, Asgardians, Eternals, Atlantians, Inhumans, Avengers, allies, Morlocks, alpha and omega levels, Celestials, Agents of S.H.I.E.L.D., Hellions, Shi'ar Guardsmen, time travelers, Black Queens, teammates, or just simply "all in the family." Readers came to "relish, learn from, or identify with" this expansive collection of queer beings, and they developed sophisticated ways of aligning their own feelings of dislocation and alienation from the dominant ideologies of cold war America with the creative practice of imagining, depicting, and critically assessing the efficacy of a variety of alternative modes of queer belonging. One way readers did this was to engage with progressive and radical politics as activists, allies, or simply sympathetic observers; another was to read, respond to, and collaborate in the production of superhero comic books. Both were forms of political world-making, though in different registers. Consequently in each of the following chapters I narrate the emergence of a new kind of figure, trope, or narrative mode in superhero storytelling as a form of political theorizing that sought to overcome the impasses of various left-wing political projects at moments when the ideals of a cosmopolitan left appeared to fracture from internal conflict or external backlash.

In chapter 1 I explore how the creative reinvention of the "superhero team" as an intergalactic peacekeeping force in DC Comics' *Justice League of America* (1960) recast the superhero as a global citizen whose ethical purview was not limited by national affiliation. Chapters 2 and 3 extend my analysis of the superhero team in a two-part case study of Marvel Comics' *The Fantastic Four* (1961). Chapter 2 analyzes how the series framed its four heroes' newfound powers as expressions of deviant gender and sexuality, thereby recasting the superhero's mutating body as a site for enacting an array of queer modes of identity against the rigid sexual politics of cold war America. Chapter 3 elaborates on how the deviant bodies of the Fantastic Four oriented them toward numerous encounters with other similarly nonhuman or "inhuman" figures; these encounters and their narrative consequences were directly shaped by the ongoing dialogues between creators and readers about the cosmopolitan values of the series in the age of civil rights and anticolonial movements. This chapter analyzes written correspondence between fans and creators alongside specific *Fantastic Four* storylines to show how the former galvanized an extended visual meditation on questions of racial and species belonging in the late 1960s. Chapters 4 and 5 narrate the evolution of the superhero in two genres that came to dominate comic book storytelling in the 1970s: the science fiction space opera and the urban folktale. Chapter 4 conducts a pair of case studies of Marvel Comics' *The Silver Surfer* (1968) and *The X-Men* (1974) that track the evolution of the space opera from a melodramatic narrative of lament for the moral degradation of mankind in the late 1960s to a cosmopolitan story of interspecies encounter in the mid-1970s. I identify *The X-Men* as a paragon of the cosmopolitan space opera and argue that the series provided the most nuanced conception of superhuman difference in modern comics by imbuing its narrative with the visual and cultural politics of women's and gay liberation. Chapter 5 explores the concurrent return of space-faring superheroes to poverty-stricken and racially segregated inner cities in DC Comics' *Green Lantern/Green Arrow* (1970) and Marvel's *Captain America and the Falcon* (1974). Through a comparative case study of these series, I argue that the urban folktale positioned itself against cosmopolitan projects like those depicted in *The X-Men* by identifying the remasculanization of iconic male heroes, including their "hard-nosed" return to the gritty conditions of America's inner cities, as the solution to racial conflict and economic inequality in the post–civil rights era. Chapter 6 documents the emergence of the trope of demonic possession in the superhero comics of the 1980s, which depicted formerly benevolent superheroes overtaken by malevolent otherworldly forces that would unleash their most violent psychosexual fantasies. I focus on *The X-Men*'s "Dark Phoenix Saga" (1980) and *Spider-Man*'s "Venom Saga" (1984–89) as paradigmatic examples of demonic possession, showing how both texts linked the superhero's loss of self-possession and rapacious desire for power with an equivalent loss of control over one's sexual and gender identity. I suggest that these texts exhibited an increasing ambivalence among comics creators about the efficacy of 1960s and 1970s liberation movements in the context of neoliberal capitalism, where the oppositional identities of the previous decades were now commoditized and exploited for profit in the global marketplace. Chapter 7 develops a sustained analysis of Marvel Comics' *The New Mutants* (1982), an offshoot of the *X-Men* series. Against the utopian identity politics of *The X-Men* a decade before, *The New Mutants* presented a cadre of teenage mutants who no longer perceive themselves as bound by a shared mutant identity or ethical imperative to save the world; in the absence of a predetermined heroic identity, *The New Mutants* offered a novel conception of the superhero not as crime fighter or icon of identity politics but as a vehicle for forging political alliances across multiple axes of difference and diverse spiritual and ethical worldviews. Taken together, these case studies coalesce an archive of "new mutants," a powerful collection of figures, tropes, and genres of deviant and queer fantasy that proliferated in the pages of American comic books.

In June 1965 the noted literary critic and public intellectual Leslie Fiedler delivered a talk at Rutgers University titled "The New Mutants." In it he argued that the countercultural youth of the late 1950s and 1960s—most visible in the Beatniks and hippies but also apparent in political groups like the student movement and civil rights activists—represented a "new mutant" generation defined by a rebellious disengagement from the traditions of liberal humanism.[45] This included turning away from the values of human reason and progress and embracing "anti-rational" aesthetics, or forms of art and literature that parody the supposedly foundational institutions and narratives of American social life, including the family, romantic love, and upward mobility. Fiedler associated this new sensibility with the willful relinquishing of attachments to traditional masculinity and an increasing identification among American youth with the outcast elements of American society: racial minorities, the homeless, and women. He claimed, "To become new men, these children of the future seem to feel, they must not only become more Black than White but more female than male. . . . Literary critics have talked a good deal during the past couple of decades about the conversion of the literary hero into the non-hero or the anti-hero; but they have in general failed to notice his simultaneous conversion into the non- or anti-male."[46] Amassing a wide array of literary and cultural examples—from Beat poets to suburban literature, from experimental fiction to postmodern cinema—alongside his own ambivalent homophobia and illiberalism,

Fiedler attempted to prove that this shift in values and desires signaled the collapse of genuine ethical commitments to progressive social transformation while undermining the importance of art and literature in transmitting meaningful cultural ideals. Fortunately for us, there were also superhero comic books.

1 / The Family of Superman: The Superhero Team and the Promise of Universal Citizenship

All men are brothers. Being endowed with reason and conscience, they are members of one family. They are free, and possess equal dignity and rights.
—DRAFT OF "The Universal Declaration of Human Rights" (June 1947)

Maybe that's what our world needs—simple understanding among men, no matter what their race, color or creed!
—WONDER WOMAN, *The Justice League of America* #15 (November 1962)

Dear Editor: The Justice League of America is more than just a comic book. . . . It is every police force, every detective, and every citizen that upholds law and order. A spark of hope, a dash of faith and a lot of trust in human nature are all the Justice League members. They are constantly proving that the world can be a much better place to live in.
—DANNY ANDERSON, letter to the editor, *The Justice League of America* #15 (November 1962)

In the spring of 1991, with an Iranian fatwa weighing on his shoulders, Salman Rushdie issued a statement defending the novel.[1] Against conservative claims of the "ungodly" character of contemporary literature, the same kinds of charges that had made the Booker Prize–winning author a target for assassination, he celebrated the novel as an exceptionally democratic literary form. According to Rushdie, the open-ended storytelling conventions of the novel—including its capacity for sustained character development and narration across historical time and space—allowed for a cacophony of worldviews to exist side by side in a single text, providing readers with multiple perspectives on reality. Near his conclusion he invoked a beloved literature of his youth, American superhero comic books, as an example of narrative fiction's ability to reorient one's outlook on the world:

Among the childhood books I devoured and kissed were large numbers of cheap comics. . . . The heroes of these comics books were . . . almost always mutants or hybrids or freaks: as well as the Batman and the Spiderman there was Aquaman, who was half-fish, and of course Superman, who could easily be mistaken for a bird or a plane. In those days, the middle 1950s, the super-heroes were all . . . hawkish law and order conservatives, leaping to work in response to the Police Commissioner's Bat-Signal, banding together to form the Justice League of America, defending what Superman called "truth, justice and the American way." . . . In spite of this extreme emphasis on crime-busting, the lesson they taught children . . . was the perhaps unintentionally radical truth that exceptionality was the greatest and most heroic of values; that those who were unlike the crowd were to be treasured . . . that this exceptionality was a treasure so great and so easily misunderstood that it had to be concealed, in ordinary life, beneath what the comic books called a "secret identity."

Rushdie then compared the novelist to the "freakish, hybrid, mutant, exceptional beings" that were superheroes. He suggested that in a world where writers were persecuted for exercising literature's capacity to depict a different way of life or present political alternatives to the present, a novel might function as an author's heroic "secret identity," a material expression of the writer's superhuman ability to recast the world anew for readers from all backgrounds.[2]

How did it come to be that a cultural form so deeply associated with American nationalism and white masculinity—the superhero comic book—could be marshaled by an Indian British writer in defense of transnational literature in the early 1990s? Rushdie's unlikely reference to the culture of superhero comics at midcentury points to a largely untold story about the historical and creative circumstances that made the superhero available as an icon of exceptionality and difference in post–World War II America. During the same years that Rushdie's childhood imagination was swept up by tales of superheroic adventure, a creative renaissance in superhero storytelling was transforming a figure of juvenile fantasy into an embodiment of the values of postwar internationalism and human rights. Throughout the late 1950s what Rushdie referred to as comic books' "extreme emphasis on crime-busting" increasingly gave way to stories about the development of international, and intergalactic, solidarities between previously independent heroic vigilantes to combat a variety of threats to global peace and security. Where previously these heroes were exceptional due to their superhuman abilities, now their exceptionality stemmed from being "citizens of the world."[3]

No comic book helped reinvent the superhero as a global citizen more than *The Justice League of America* (1960). The *Justice League* narrated the adventures of a cadre of superpowered crime fighters who join forces as Earth's guardians—among them DC Comics' iconic heroes Superman,

Batman, and Wonder Woman. It was one of the first postwar comics to revitalize the concept of an ongoing alliance between individual super-heroes, and it helped the superhero team to become the most popular figuration of the genre in the second half of the twentieth century.

In this chapter, I develop a case study of *The Justice League of America* between 1960 and 1965 that shows how the comic book transformed the superhero from an icon of American nationalism to a champion of inter-nationalism and universal citizenship. Even as they operated under the assumed banner of "America," the Justice League members articulated their ethical commitment to the world in universal terms, refusing to limit their heroic service to anyone based on national origin, geographi-cal location, or ethnoracial identity. This was impressed upon readers in the opening scene of the series' first issue. In this sequence the Justice League member Flash encounters two extraterrestrial refugees, Saranna and Jasonar, fleeing a maniacal despot who has overtaken their alien home world. The Flash is initially introduced to readers in his civilian identity as policeman Barry Allen; just before he meets the alien exiles, he transforms into his heroic alter ego, a red-clad superhuman speed-ster. After hearing Saranna and Jasonar's plight, the Flash reassures his companions, "Don't give up hope! The Justice League of America has been fighting for liberty and justice on Earth—why not for a dimensional world? Perhaps we can help."[4] Where minutes before, the Flash had been an ordinary protector of law and order in a small American town, now, as a member of the Justice League of America, an intergalactic peace-keeping force, he speaks for anyone in need of aid across the galaxy.

A decade earlier comic book superheroes would not have brandished such grandiose claims to protecting the universe from tyrannical threats. The Golden Age heroes of the World War II era were resolutely nationalist in their vision of justice, fighting homegrown criminal mas-terminds and limited international threats to national security.[5] Now *The Justice League of America* dramatized the conflicting relationship between national and postnational forms of citizenship by framing the team members as putative Americans, while linking the League's com-mitment to political freedom with the interests of all life forms in the universe. It did so by visualizing the teammates' civilian and superhe-roic identities as metaphors for their dual loyalties to national and global forms of citizenship. As civilians, the Justice League members were U.S. citizens; as superheroes, they were citizens of the world.

Central to *The Justice League*'s vision of intergalactic justice was a conception of science and technology as vehicles for cross-cultural understanding and humanitarian action. Despite their extraordinary powers, the members of the Justice League repeatedly defeat their foes using scientific know-how and ingenuity, displaying the universal application of science as both an instrument of justice and a transferable body of knowledge that can be shared between superheroes and ordinary people alike. The valorization of science as a form of knowledge that can be applied universally worked hand in hand with the series' vision of postnational affiliation by locating scientific knowledge as a bridge between the Justice League and the wider world it served. By articulating the relationship between science and citizenship as a prerequisite to global service, *The Justice League* was the first comic series to make the superhero available as a popular fantasy for critiquing cold war nationalism and the state's use of science as a tool of American military supremacy.

Late 1950s "team books" like *The Justice League* and DC's *Legion of Super-Heroes* (1958) capitalized on readers' eagerness to buy comics showcasing greater visual action among multiple heroes in a single story. Yet the resurgent popularity of superhero comic books in the early 1960s following more than a decade of declining readership cannot be explained merely by the presence of additional characters or the pandering of comic book creators to reader preference. After all, *The Justice League* was a remake of an earlier 1940s series, *The Justice Society of America*, which depicted a team of vigilante heroes who join forces to combat local criminal menaces none are capable of defeating alone. Despite its popularity in the immediate postwar period, *The Justice Society* went the way of most superhero comics in the 1950s that were indefinitely suspended due to reader disinterest. Why, then, did the return of the team book inspire resurgent interest in superhero comics in the early 1960s? While it paid homage to its creative predecessor, *The Justice League* presented the superhero team as a self-governing political body that engaged the world outside the urban stomping grounds of each member, and well beyond the borders of the nation. Consequently *The Justice League* offered a sustained exploration of the conflict between loyalty to national citizenship and a broader commitment to global justice. This conflict defined postwar American liberalism, an ideology that simultaneously aimed to bring about universal political freedom while stamping the future of self-determining peoples with the seal of Americanism.[6] It was this contradiction between the political impulses of worldly egalitarianism and national economic and political interest that a new generation of readers responded to in their return to a mode of storytelling that had long been dismissed as childish escapism.

Against a traditional understanding of national citizenship as a legal relationship to the state, *The Justice League* posited "ethical citizenship" as a form of belonging based on an individual's performance of good deeds that promote global peace and solidarity while "making the world a better place to live." By presenting the Justice League members as paragons of ethical citizenship, the series offered a vision of postnational political affiliation that worked against the narrow frame of cold war antagonisms. The series opposed the cold war politics of containment by activating a competing strain of liberal thought grounded in postwar internationalist initiatives, such as the Atlantic Charter, the United Nations, and the Universal Declaration of Human Rights. In the wake of the atrocities of total war and the Nazi final solution, these treatises and institutions framed the rights of all human beings to peace, prosperity, and economic opportunity as superseding the interests of national citizenship.[7]

The Justice League embodied these values in the teammates' dual identities as literal or figurative immigrants to the United States who maintain multiple loyalties to the human race and their own home worlds. The original Justice League roster included the iconic heroes Wonder Woman, a mythical, warrior princess of the Amazons gifted with superhuman strength, speed, agility, and invulnerability; Martian Manhunter, a shape-shifting Martian possessing the ability to fly, enhanced senses, and extraordinary strength; Flash, a superhuman speedster able to move faster than the speed of sound; Green Lantern, an ordinary man chosen by the alien Guardians of Oa to wear a power ring that materializes anything its wearer imagines; Aquaman, the super strong sea king, able to communicate with all marine life and control the Earth's oceans; and Green Arrow, an archer and gymnast of unparalleled accuracy and physical agility who gained his "powers" through exceptional training. The classic heroes Batman and Superman served as auxiliary members, with other DC heroes, including the size-shifting Atom and the winged aviator Hawkman, joining the team in later adventures.

Questioning the assumed "American" character of this diverse group of heroes, one reader wrote to the editors, "I believe the name Justice League of America isn't right. It should be Interplanetary League of Justice. Let's consider J'onn J'onnz—is he really an American? Hardly! We all know he was born on Mars! Superman is a native of the planet Krypton. You'd have to stretch a long point to consider Aquaman an American. And of course Wonder Woman's birthplace is the Amazon Paradise Island." Despite the heroes' un-American origins, the editors stressed, "It's not the birthplace of our super-heroes that counts—it's their allegiance to their 'adopted' country."[8] Here the editors highlighted a contradiction at the heart of the Justice League's vision of ethical citizenship: even as that they sought to reaffirm the League members' American affiliations, they stressed the voluntaristic quality of national citizenship, recalling the language of Article 15 of the Universal Declaration of Human Rights, which states that "everyone has the right to a nationality," and "no one shall be arbitrarily deprived of his nationality nor denied the right to change his nationality."[9]

On one hand, then, the League members were framed as ideal immigrants, "adopting" the American way of life and offering loyalty to a national government; on the other, their performance of global civic acts suggested that assimilating to any nation or community was a willful choice individuals could make, or unmake, at their discretion. The series' ambivalent attachment to a distinctly American form of political freedom even as it appeared to espouse postnational humanitarian values reflected its continued commitment to liberal thought—particularly the values of self-determination, freedom from institutional coercion, and scientific rationalism—alongside an egalitarian vision of human action taken in the name of a collective good. In this sense the Justice League's reinvention of the superhero sought to recuperate an increasingly insular and self-interested American liberalism by articulating it to the concept of universal human rights.

"To Fight All Foes of Humanity!"
The Justice League's Universalism

The Justice League of America was introduced to readers in the March 1960 issue of The Brave and the Bold, a variety adventure serial. In their first story the newly formed Justice League face off against an alien menace, Starro the Conqueror, a giant, space-faring starfish in search of material resources to feed its boundless hunger for energy. "Starro the Conqueror" was arguably the first superhero comic book narrative to present a villain capable of obliterating life on Earth, expanding the scope of superhero storytelling to include the entire planet as well as life throughout the cosmos. The depiction of a colossal starfish as a menace to mankind might have seemed ridiculous were it not for the real threat of nuclear holocaust in this period, which many assumed would wipe out life on Earth and mutate plant and animal life into monstrously enlarged forms. In this context Starro was a genuinely fearful allegory for the potential destructive outcomes of atomic warfare. The global scope of Starro's plan to eliminate humankind and ravage the planet's resources is counterbalanced by the distinctly American locus of its malevolent activities: as the narrative unfolds, Starro seeks to access America's nuclear arsenal to foment a global atomic war that will release extraordinary amounts of radiation it can absorb as a source of energy. At the same time as it fights for the survival of mankind, the Justice League must protect America's military resources and secure its borders against an alien threat.

This contradiction between global guardianship and national security would form the conceptual core of the series and is vividly displayed in the comic book's opening splash panel (plate 1). At the center of the page appears Starro's five-tentacled body, its long arms extending to the edges of the spread. Seven circles frame its limbs, featuring silhouettes of each of the Justice League's members. Their worried faces stare at the center of Starro's body, which appears as a red, white, and blue bull's-eye. These elements appear against a background of alternating red and white vertical bars with a blue banner at the top that reads "Justice League of America." A square banner at the bottom displays the League's mission: "Foes of evil! Enemies of injustice! To the mighty heroes of the Justice League of America all wrong-doing is a menace to be stamped out—whether it comes from outer space—from the watery depths of the seven-seas—or springs full-blown from the minds of men! Banded together to fight all foes of humanity, the mightiest heroes of our time battle the menace of . . . Starro the Conqueror!"[10]

This bold image locates the Justice League within a series of competing national and global frames. Its multilayered visual organization simultaneously references the nation—through the use of an American flag as its backdrop—and a monstrous threat supposedly "alien" to the nation but whose central consciousness is visually linked to national culture. (Starro's red, white, and blue center complements its purple epidermis.) This division is redoubled in the arrangement of Justice League silhouettes, which are associated with the United States through visual reference to the flag yet whose ethical commitments are identified as oriented toward all of humanity. As they stare into Starro's red, white, and blue heart, the teammates appear to fret over the intended target of their heroic actions, an alien menace or America itself.

By invoking the language of universalism through the claim to combat "*all* wrong-doing" and "*all* foes of humanity" regardless of their geographical origin, the Justice League's charter echoes the language of midcentury humanitarian declarations like the Atlantic Charter and the Universal Declaration of Human Rights. These treatises spoke in the name of a "human family" for the purpose of creating shared ethical standards for global justice.[11] The Atlantic Charter, the statement of shared values issued by Franklin Roosevelt and Winston Churchill in 1941, rhetorically appealed to a universal human good by proclaiming the right of "*all* people to choose the form of government under which they live" and a shared investment in "establishing a peace . . . which will afford assurance that *all* the men in *all* the lands may live out their lives in freedom from fear and want" (my italics). The Justice League charter is similarly founded on the premise of a universal ethical responsibility to humanity that necessarily begins with guardianship over the cosmos, indicated by the reference to "outer space," then scales down to the geography of planet Earth ("the watery depth of the seven-seas"), and finally moves to the hearts and minds of men. The team's first villain manages to encompass all of these valances, a menace from outer space who manipulates Earth's ocean life to materialize mankind's destructive fantasies of nuclear war. With such villains *The Justice League* blurred the lines demarcating distinctly national from global concerns. The team's charter suggested that the forms of injustice that plagued the world in the postwar period exceeded the boundaries of national life and demanded novel forms of postnational solidarity.

Following this opening display, we learn that Starro's first order of business after arriving on Earth is to locate three organisms with similar genetic structures (ordinary starfish) that it transforms into telepathically controlled doubles to serve as its henchmen. Starro's scouting mission over the Atlantic is detected by an observant puffer fish that promptly informs the sea king and Justice League member, Aquaman, of the alien intruder's plan. Aquaman alerts his teammates of the threat to Earth, and the League promptly delegates the task of hunting down Starro's three emissaries.

Green Lantern discovers the first mutated starfish scouting Yosemite National Park, where it hijacks a military jet with an atomic warhead. Wonder Woman and Martian Manhunter discover the second starfish attempting to telepathically absorb the combined knowledge of the nation's greatest scientists who are assembled at an annual conference at "the Hall of Science." The Flash finds Starro's third emissary brainwashing the residents of the suburban coastal town Happy Harbor. Starro's plan to conquer Earth thus begins with an attempt to gain control over three key sites of American cold war political and cultural life: the atomic weapons associated with national security, the scientific brainpower fueling the government's defense technology, and the suburban nuclear family upholding the ideals of national citizenship. Starro's interest in atomic weaponry, its ability to duplicate itself through similitude to Earth creatures, and its capacity to mentally manipulate human beings coalesce a number of the cultural anxieties that circulated around the concept of the communist menace, namely the belief that communism is an ideology that promulgates itself through aggressive forms of psychological control or brainwashing to encourage political submission.[12]

Yet the simple allegorization of Starro to communism is undercut by a crucial fact: in the story's logic the same sites intended to protect domestic life from communism—scientific progress and the family unit—are revealed as distinctly susceptible to psychic manipulation *because* of their affiliation with a form of citizenship that demands blind conformity to the nation. When Wonder Woman sees Starro's second deputy carrying the Hall of Science in its clutches, she proclaims, "The greatest scientific brains of the United States are gathered in that Hall of Science!" To which the starfish responds, "My mission is to rob the brainpower of the scientists inside this building. The scientists have been put into a state of suspended animation so they'll remain alive until their mind knowledge is taken from them!" The comic depicts scientists as a single unified mass, faceless and identifiable only as bearers of knowledge frozen in "suspended animation" in a public building whose generic name similarly suggests the homogenization of scientific culture within the frame of national citizenship. (The only identifiable marker separating these scientists from anyone else is that they are Americans.) Here Starro becomes not simply an outside threat but an embodiment of the U.S. state itself, which funds such gatherings of great thinkers in the hopes of relaying their knowledge to its own project of global political and military supremacy. Similarly, when Starro's third emissary brainwashes the people of Happy Harbor, the first image we see is that of a family standing outside their suburban home in a zombie-like trance as they obediently listen to Starro's mental commands. When Snapper Carr, a young hipster tending to his family's lawn, sees them possessed by Starro, he yells, "Hey! What's with the family circle?" Both the Hall of Science and Happy Harbor are generic spaces that stand in for the specificities of national research facilities and suburban American towns, their populations similarly collapsed into empty types ("the scientist" and "the family circle," respectively) defined by mass mental manipulation. The only instances in which locations like these stand out is when extraordinary individuals such as the Flash in Central City or Snapper Carr in Happy Harbor become associated with them, indicating the characters' non-conformity through acts of ethical citizenship.

The smooth-talking hipster Snapper Carr is bizarrely unaffected by the alien's telepathy. When Starro's third deputy tries to destroy the teenager with an "atomic power lance," Snapper is saved by the Flash, who speedily battles and defeats the clone. Intrigued by Snapper's invulnerability, the Flash asks Green Lantern to use his power ring "as a spectroscope" to reveal if any unusual chemicals appear on Snapper's body. Projecting a rainbow-hued spectrum against Snapper's body, Green Lantern's ring reveals that the teen is covered with "calcium oxide . . . lime," the same chemical he used as turf builder for the family lawn. Aquaman promptly explains, "Oyster men use quicklime to fight starfish who prey on oysters in the sea!" "That's the answer!" Flash adds. "The lime protects Snapper from Starro! And lime will help us defeat Starro!" Locating barrels of lime on a nearby farm, Green Lantern carries them aloft with his power ring, dousing Starro with a chemical avalanche that imprisons the creature in "an un-breakable shell—a living statue of lime!" (figure 1.1).[13] Having previously battled Starro to no avail with the combined might of their superhuman powers, it is the team's scientific know-how and shared knowledge with ordinary, open-minded American youth that allow them to develop a strategy for defeating the alien monster.

In its short twenty-six pages, "Starro the Conquer" set the stage for a dramatic transformation in the American superhero that would lead to the figure's reinvention as a model of postnational affiliation in the second half of the twentieth century. In its depiction of team members democratically delegating individual responsibilities for a common goal, in its blurring of the boundaries between threats to domestic security and threats to humanity's flourishing, and in its critique of the military-science complex in favor of scientific egalitarianism, *The Justice League of America* rearticulated the American superhero's former function as an icon of national power to the image of a global Samaritan placing the needs of humankind above the local interests of sovereign states. The induction of Snapper Carr into the Justice League as an honorary member displayed for readers the possibility of a teenager much like themselves whose family ties could be supplemented, if not wholly supplanted, by a new kind of alternative solidarity based on ethical commitments to the world. When one fan denounced Snapper as a foolish, immature addition to the series, a defender responded, "I guess—to you— the name *Justice League of American* [sic] means 'super-powers.' Well, to me, it means loyalty and honor, two qualifications, which fit *Snapper Carr* very well."[14] Even in his minor role as a recurring supporting character, Snapper

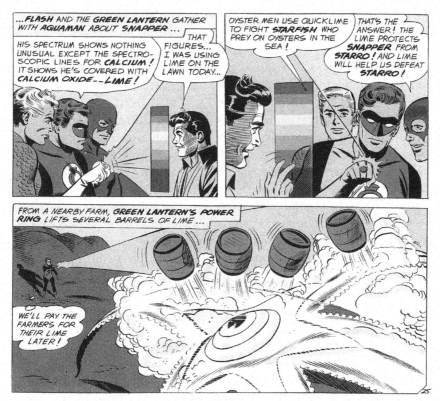

FIGURE 1.1. The Justice League of America defeat Starro with scientific ingenuity. Gardner Fox (writer) and Mike Sekowsky (penciller), "Starro the Conqueror," *The Brave and the Bold* #28, March–April 1960, DC Comics, reprinted in *Justice League of America Archives Vol. 1* (New York: DC Comics, 1997), 38.

represented the possibility of inhabiting an egalitarian political vision for a new generation of cold war youth, one that the Justice League sought to reignite as the wellspring of superheroic action in the postwar period.

"DC Comics Print the Truth When It Comes to Science!"
Scientific Internationalism and the Contradictions of Global Citizenship

In its commitment to the idea of global security through collective acts of ethical citizenship and its celebration of teamwork above individual action in the maintenance of law and order, *The Justice League of*

America can be understood as a cultural corollary to postwar interna-tionalism. Between 1945 and the late 1950s the United States backed a variety of political projects that linked national political and economic interests with a broader vision of global uplift, including the self-deter-mination of colonized peoples, the development of international laws against unprovoked warfare and "crimes against humanity," and the creation of multilateral global peacekeeping institutions.[15]

This last project was consistently displayed in the Justice League's democratic decision-making process, which was presented as a fic-tional parallel to the United Nations. Throughout the series the team often appeared deliberating on their future peacekeeping missions at a round table in their secret headquarters that visually referenced the UN's Security Council chambers. Formed in 1946, the UN was conceived as an international political body that would empower member nations to enforce universal standards of action for maintaining global peace and security. The birth of the UN signaled the beginning of a distinct era of international cooperation whose ideological currency was powerful enough to withstand the nationalist fervor of the early cold war.

Culture served a crucial role in selling the image of global integration. The U.S. government, as well as numerous local community groups, circulated American cultural products, technological innovations, and "national treasures" around the globe. In turn, through Hollywood films, travelogues, letter-writing campaigns, and museum exhibits, Americans were introduced to global customs, languages, religions, and political systems utterly foreign to "the American way of life."[16] Argu-ably the most successful cultural project of the politics of integration was Edward Steichen's *The Family of Man* exhibit in 1955, which premiered at the New York Museum of Modern Art. The largest photographic dis-play of its time, *The Family of Man* presented images of global peoples for the purpose of evoking the idea of a universal human kinship above the petty conflicts of ethnic and national divisions. Consisting of 503 photographs spanning the entire half-century's photographic produc-tion, the exhibit was organized around central themes in the human life cycle: birth, childhood, family, work, leisure, creative pursuits, aging, and death. Despite its intended universalism, the exhibit concluded with a distinctly political message. Its final image, the only color photo in the show, captured the mushroom cloud of a hydrogen bomb. With this vision Steichen sought to compel a visceral response from viewers to the threat of human annihilation posed by global conflict.[17] Consequently "the family of man" became a common trope with which a variety of cultural and political projects framed their ideological message, often masking distinctly American interests beneath the language of universal human uplift or conflating the American way of life with the political and social trajectory of the world.

In its varied political and cultural forms, postwar internationalism put into question a series of previously held assumptions about the national interest: in politics it troubled the primacy of national citizenship by demanding an ethical orientation of all peoples toward their fellow man; in science it questioned the morality of the alliance between scientific research and national military interest, suggesting that scientific knowledge should be shared freely in the service of improving the quality of life for all peoples; and in culture it contributed to a species-wide discourse that spoke to the common bond between members of the human race rather than narrating their differences in the deleterious language of racism, xenophobia, and classism.[18]

The Justice League's visual and narrative logic actively pressed each of the vexing contradictions of postwar internationalism, most pointedly in its reevaluation of science as a tool for promoting cross-cultural exchange and global peace. Despite the egalitarian thrust of projects like Atoms for Peace (1953) and the People to People program (1956)—government campaigns to distribute nuclear technology internationally and provide opportunities for cross-cultural exchange between Americans and the international community—these initiatives ultimately served the purpose of global American scientific and cultural supremacy. Alternatively *The Justice League* promoted the idea that science should be free of all ideological manipulation and was the linchpin to producing ethical citizens committed to a postnational vision of political freedom.

The series presented this worldview through three visual and narrative techniques. First, the comic book served a dual role as a vehicle for superheroic adventure and scientific pedagogy. Rather than distinguishing between entertainment and education, the series wove scientific knowledge into the heroic exploits of its characters, repeatedly linking such knowledge with the ability to overcome threats to global security. Second, through its depiction of numerous villainous scientists bent on world domination alongside the League's egalitarian use of science and technology, the series distinguished between narcissistic forms of scientific practice that deploy knowledge for personal gain and democratic knowledge production committed to the collective search for universal "truths" rather than individual self-interest. Third, the series articulated knowledge of science with the exercise of free will, suggesting that greater understanding of the material properties of life on Earth translated into the ability to move through the world with greater purpose and agency. These latter capacities were seen as the sine qua non of the Justice League members, who were visually displayed performing heroic feats in every physical environment—including outer space—equipped with their knowledge of the material properties that organize life in the universe.

From the series' first panel, *The Justice League* presented a nearly obsessive interest in scientific facts. Each issue presented readers with countless pieces of information regarding the chemical composition of glass and lead, the material properties of light, and the physics behind meteorological events like tornadoes and tides. Factoids culled from a variety of natural sciences, including astronomy, geology, zoology, chemistry, and physics, were presented as educational information for readers and critical pieces of knowledge that help the Justice League triumph over enemies. In "The Weapon's Master of Space," the Martian Manhunter uses his super breath to spin sand, potash, soda, and aluminum at a speed that superheats them into a mirror, allowing him to deflect the fatal beams of a "de-evolutionizing ray." In a later story, when Superman spies an isotope of Kryptonite, the one material that negates his powers, an omniscient narrators explains, "Isotopes are elements . . . possessing the same atomic numbers and chemical properties but having different atomic weights!" In one of the team's earliest adventures, they are baffled by the disappearance of zoological specimens from scientific laboratories around the world. Among the stolen property are a European catfish and an ordinary cicada. Using recently obtained scientific knowledge, Snapper chimes in, "I'm batting out a term paper on the life span of animals! According to my research the European catfish lives longer than any other fish . . . about 60 years! The cicada . . . with a life span of 17 years . . . is the Methuselah of the insect kingdom." With this information, the Flash deduces that the thief is developing an "immortality elixir" that will allow him infinite time to fulfill his plans for world domination; in response the team concocts a plan to visit the location of each of the oldest members of the animal kingdom before the culprit can obtain their precious biological samples. In these and countless other scenarios scientific knowledge offers clues for uncovering the machinations of the team's villains and allows the League to take action against threats to world security with civic purpose—in this case compelling the Leaguers to fan out across the globe. As the teammates race to their various animal targets, readers see an image of Snapper standing before a world map, with each of the superheroes' destinations marked with their names (figure 1.2).[19] Snapper's lay scientific knowledge

FIGURE 1.2. Snapper maps the Justice League of America's global exploits. Gardner Fox (writer) and Mike Sekowsky (penciller), "Case of the Stolen Super Powers!," *The Brave and the Bold* #30, July–August 1960, DC Comics, reprinted in *Justice League of America Archives Vol. 1* (New York: DC Comics, 1997), 74.

paves the way for global acts of ethical citizenship, while the comic book itself functions as a form of postnational pedagogy.[20]

Early issues of the series included "feature-pages" that presented scientific trivia and puzzles for readers to solve in between scenes of heroic adventure, including games that asked readers to identify and debunk scientific myths. By presenting scientific facts as public knowledge freely circulated among readers, the series championed the value of transparency in scientific research and discovery during an era of heightened secrecy around American military technology. In turn fans used the series' informative adventure stories as evidence of the positive social character of comics, validating their enjoyment of a supposedly "juvenile" form by indicating its contribution to creating educated readers. Reader Gary Freidrich wrote in a local high school newspaper a defense of reading superhero comics on the basis of their scholastic content, which was subsequently reprinted in the letters page of *Justice League of America* #5; according to Freidrich, if those who denounced comics would read even one superhero comic, they would see that "three or four pages . . . contained nothing but scientific information. Take, for instance, the first issue of a comic called *Justice League of America*. . . . The League battled a foe who was, to put it bluntly, a huge starfish. Therefore, the publishers added a page to the book which contained several interesting facts about the starfish. . . . The information on this page conformed perfectly to information found in this high school's textbooks, thus disproving the statement that comics are worthless."[21]

Other readers lauded the comic book for depicting the Justice League traveling internationally and into the cosmos, linking the series' interest in the physical properties of planet Earth to its global imaginary. One letter writer expressed delight over an adventure that took the Justice League to Victoria Falls, Lake Como, Greenland, and the Indian Ocean in a single issue, while another thanked the editors for printing a letter of hers that led to her gaining pen pals in India and the United Kingdom. Yet another writer voiced pleasure in reading *The Justice League* as a world traveler interested in science: "Since my father is in the service, I have had the chance to travel throughout this fine country of ours, and be an American Ambassador of good will overseas. Traveling by boat, plane, or train, with no television. I find nothing more interesting than a comic book. . . . I especially enjoy DC Comics, since I specialize in science at my school, and know that your comics print the truth when it comes to science." Like many of her fellow readers, this writer located the practice of reading comics within a larger context of global travel and expanding scientific knowledge about the material world.[22]

The series' investment in scientific knowledge focused less on laboratory work and more on the global connections that the search for empirical knowledge produces. The scientific feature-pages that dot the visual landscape of the comic were paired with public service announcements on the global outreach work of institutions like the UN and UNICEF. Like the stories presented in the narrative proper, these features depict global peoples struggling with famine and lack of water, clothing and shelter while presenting institutions like the UN combating such atrocities and requiring readers' support for the maintenance of a free world. One feature, titled "People Are People!," displays a series of images of mankind progressing from a homogeneous tribal culture to distinct ethnoracial groups (figure 1.3). The narrative reads, "Scientific surveys have proven that no one race is superior to another. . . . All races are capable of performing the same work, of reaching the same level of education. . . . All can and must work together for peace and the advancement of mankind—as they are doing right now in the United Nations!" This public service announcement invokes science to provide empirical proof supporting the ethical value of universalism while grounding the ideals displayed in the fantasy narrative of *The Justice League of America* in the real-world political work of internationalist organizations.[23] All people are equalized in their humanity and in their shared capacity to contribute to ethical citizenship: this, the comic book suggested, was what made anyone a potential superhero.

The Justice League offered a vision of science not merely as a technical practice of gathering empirical knowledge but as a fully formed way of

FIGURE 1.3. "People Are People!" Artist unknown. Printed in Gardner Fox (writer) and Mike Sekowsky (penciller), "For Sale—The Justice League!," *Justice League of America* #8, December 1961–January 1962, DC Comics.

life defined by the open-minded seeking out of truth grounded in "the values of tolerance and honesty, publicity and testifiability,' and 'universalism' and 'disinterestedness.'"[24] Consequently *The Justice League* culturally materialized a midcentury intellectual tradition described by David Hollinger as scientific cosmopolitanism, an ethos espoused by left-wing social scientists and philosophers in the 1930s and 1940s, which identified science as a worldview based on rational, unbiased deliberation and knowledge production that sought to combat the irrationalism and xenophobia of contemporary totalitarian politics. Scholars in this tradition invoked "those images of science . . . serving to connect the adjective scientific with public rather than private knowledge . . . with universal rather than local standards of warrant, with democratic rather than aristocratic models of authority. . . . These men and women saw a world filled with 'prejudice' and . . . efforts to 'impose certain opinions by force.' Against these evils one must affirm 'free inquiry' and 'open-mindedness' in order that our society might be organized realistically on the basis of the conditions life actually presents."[25] This philosophy permeated the pages of *The Justice League of America* and shaped its conflicted depiction of the "evil scientist," the series' most recurrent villainous figuration.

Mad for Power: The Evil Scientist and the Value of Empirical Truth

Following World War II, American scientists struggled to reconcile their professional allegiances with their responsibilities to the U.S. government. When the U.S. Defense Department sought to maintain secrecy over nuclear science research, many former Manhattan Project scientists who had worked on the creation of the atom bomb during the war organized nationwide information networks for disseminating public knowledge about the possibilities and potential hazards of atomic science. In these instances scientists linked their role as researchers to their civic duty to facilitate the free exchange of ideas.[26] Government-funded scientists, however, often had to inhabit dual roles as global ambassadors and state informants, traveling to international scientific conferences to amass data on the laboratory work and political intentions of perceived scientific competitors.[27] Playing off this ideological and professional conflict *The Justice League* presented both its greatest villains and its central heroes as scientists with competing commitments to scientific self-interest and scientific cosmopolitanism.

Though many of the villains presented in the series are scientists, it is the ethical misuse of their knowledge that is condemned by the comic, not science itself. The comic book affirmed this by presenting many of the Justice League members as scientists in their civilian identities. Unlike the Justice League members, whose individual scientific pursuits are consistently linked to their collective peacekeeping projects, the villainous scientists depicted in the series are nearly always misanthropic loners or outcasts who have spent their lives perfecting knowledge of a single scientific specialty in isolation from larger communities of scientists and the public that might benefit from their discoveries. In "The Last Case of the Justice League," the physicist Dr. Light admits to having spent his entire career in isolation perfecting the manipulation of light rays, while in "The Wheel of Misfortune," the endocrinologist Professor Amos claims to have been obsessed with discovering a biological basis for personal luck to capitalize on his gambling habit. Such revelations revealed *The Justice League* villains as having a deeply narcissistic relationship to science, based not on unbiased observation or the universal applicability of their discoveries for a common good but on unfettered self-interest.[28]

While *The Justice League* indicted the moral failings of human scientists, it also critiqued the cold war geopolitics that underwrite the malevolent use of science and technology. In a number of stories the Justice League aids the inhabitants of alien worlds suffering from the apocalyptic aftereffects of their own military technologies. In "Journey into the Micro-World," the League members are transported to a microscopic planet, Starzl, where they encounter an alien civilization on the brink of extinction due to radiation emitted by their atomic weaponry. In "The Slave Ship of Space," the League members are abducted by an alien tyrant, Kanjar Ro, who hopes to use the heroes as weapons of war against three adversaries, all alien despots engaged in an ceaseless battle for domination over a distant galaxy. Unwilling to concede or find a way to live in peace, the dictators remain in permanent stalemate, spending their days developing ever more advanced weapons, hoping to outgun their adversaries.[29] Like the major combatants in cold war conflict, the alien civilizations in these stories associate scientific progress with the development of more efficient technologies of mass destruction. Questioning this logic, the series sought to uncover a central ideological illusion upheld by military scientists in the postwar period: that a technologically advanced society was also necessarily more democratic or politically free as a result of its scientific progress.

The villainous scientists depicted in *The Justice League of America* were not the only masters of illusion, however, for the majority of the League members themselves maintained double lives as heroes and scientists. Moreover, as civilians nearly all of the Justice League's heroes work for the state in some capacity: Diana Prince (Wonder Woman) works for the Department of Defense; Barry Allen (the Flash) and John Jones (the Martian Manhunter) are detectives, the former also a forensic scientist; Ray Palmer (the Atom) is a government physicist; and Hal Jordan (Green Lantern) is an air force test pilot. This alliance with state interests potentially undermined the team's claim to fight on behalf of a global constituency. Moreover it begged the question of whether or not the heroes would be commanded to serve in a military capacity should their superhuman alter egos ever be revealed. As the team's brief enslavement by Kanjar Ro attested, in the right circumstances the heroes' own bodies could be deployed as weapons of war. In the series' narrative logic, what distinguishes the members of the League from their greatest adversaries is the fact that they maintain a "scientific" worldview across their dual identities as civilians and superheroes, espousing the spirit of objectivity, free exchange of knowledge, and the use of that knowledge for the good of mankind. This ethical orientation toward science is framed as an expression of their extraordinary will power, a strength of character that enables each team member to make deliberate choices to use their knowledge, skill, and abilities to benefit others. The recourse to will power worked to reconcile liberal and egalitarian (or democratic) ideals by celebrating self-determination without espousing a careless individualism.

The series presented the free circulation of scientific knowledge as a prerequisite to willful agency. So key is this force to the League's success that a number of villains focus their energies on nullifying the team's will power and thus their ability to apply their knowledge about the world in the service of global peacekeeping.[30] Consequently the ability to encourage willful determination in others is often the key to the League's success against its most formidable adversaries. In "The Riddle of the Robot League," the League faces off against robotic doppelgangers programmed to exceed the abilities of each member. By coincidence Aquaman has no adversary since the aliens who produce these automatons live on a waterless planet and cannot create a cyborg to combat the sea king's abilities. Seeing his companions outmatched by their combatants yet depowered himself by the absence of nearby ocean life, Aquaman gives each teammate words of encouragement. He exclaims to Green Lantern, "A man who won't be beaten can't be beaten!" Energized by Aquaman's support, Green Lantern thinks, "Aquaman's got something there! This is a battle of will powers, which makes the ring work! As long as I'm determined to win I will!" Rejoining the battle with full force, Green Lantern surmises, "Aquaman's boost gave me that little 'extra energy' I needed! Just as an athlete responds to the cheers of a crowd—so I responded to Aquaman's voice!" Here the dual meaning of *will*, as a psychic force and a physical expression of agency, becomes one and the same as Aquaman's pep talk incites Green Lantern to action.[31]

The Justice League's vision of ethical citizenship grounded in a willful exercise of individual agency was materialized both narratively and visually. In spectacular visual displays of superhuman bodily feats, the series repeatedly sutured the values of liberalism to mobile and agentic bodies whose extraordinary abilities functioned as vehicles for acts of global citizenship. By virtue of their superhuman bodies, the Justice League members can traverse the globe in seconds, reform the physical contours of the planet, and access rare material resources to be deployed against combatants or repurposed for everyday human use. Accordingly the visual landscape of the series is dominated by images of superhuman bodies rapidly moving through space: carried aloft by air currents, agilely dodging physical obstacles, or barreling through metal, rock, and ice. The League members manage their superhuman bodies with razor-sharp skill, combining enhanced bodily speed, strength, and flexibility with rigorous physical discipline. In his drawings Mike Sekowsky presents the team members not as muscular gods but as lean, lithe gymnasts and swimmers. Acrobatic images of gliding, bending, swooping, and dodging with finesse abound, as do visually bombastic moments depicting the complete loss of control that can result when such skill is derailed by both natural and man-made phenomena. When the League travels to the microworld of Starzl, the narrative depicts the teammates cascading through a kaleidoscopic landscape of atoms and electrons before landing on the tiniest civilization in the universe. There they discover entire solar systems, planets, and societies with their own unique political realities and conflicts. As the heroes explore the reaches of outer space, they discover life existing throughout the cosmos and in multiple alternate universes.

To imagine bodies capable of traversing space at such infinitesimal and gargantuan scales was an imaginatively daring reinsertion of the human body into the realms commonly demarcated for observation by scientific professionals like physicists and astronomers. This enabled readers to envision the geographically expansive scale of the material world as being related to the conceptually expansive scale of cosmopolitan political commitments, which demanded the cognitive capacity to account for multiple valences of local and global lived experience to make ethical decisions across these frames of reference. What linked all the fictional worlds encountered by the Justice League, and invariably brought the team within the orbit of such disparate civilizations, was their shared experience of interspecies conflict, political oppression, and social inequality. When the peace-loving energy beings of Ersilane travel across the cosmos to enlist the Justice League's help in stopping the genocidal alien Skarn, they inform the teammates that their heroic deeds have become legendary across the universe. In the Ersilanes' claim the series suggested that despite the manifold differences among life forms in the cosmos, ethical citizenship could function as a universally recognized force of goodwill that could scale the distance between planets and species rather than a project to manage or claim supremacy over global political relations.

By training its readers to identify scientific knowledge with cosmopolitan social aspirations, *The Justice League of America* renarrated one of the prevailing ideologies of postwar American science: the equation of medical, scientific, and technological progress with global U.S. military power and the ideal of man's mastery over nature. While this fantasy of global scientific power was attenuated by mass anxieties about the negative effects of new technologies of warfare and potential atomic fallout, it was also promulgated by the nation's most established institutions, including the American Medical Association, the Department of Defense, and the FBI.[32] *The Justice League* aligned itself instead with the cosmopolitan intellectuals who rallied against these institutions and celebrated science as an ideal of objectivity, open-minded inquiry, and rationalism. In so doing the series elevated science to a heroic vocation, enacted through the fantastical bodies of superhuman Samaritans. This necessarily put the League at odds with official national ideology as well as the legal structures of international peacekeeping organizations like the UN, whose distinct political investments and economic interests did not always align with the expansive egalitarian mission of the team.

While the League outwardly supported state power both in its national and transnational forms, its interactions with these institutions consistently encouraged readers to see the Justice League members as victims of government self-interest, bureaucratic ineptitude, and the false authority of government scientists. In nearly every instance of conflict between the Justice League of America and legal institutions, governments and peacekeeping bodies mistake the duplicitous machinations of the team's villains as misdeeds of the League members themselves, turning against the heroes for supposed crimes against humanity. In "The Super-Exiles of Earth," the League is forced to curtail its heroic endeavors by government decree after civilians witness the heroes engaging in acts of theft, assault, and vandalism. We soon learn that an evil scientist, Dr. Destiny, has invented a technology capable of materializing dream doubles of League members, criminal versions of the superheroes invented by his twisted imagination.[33] When the League members go to court to defend themselves against false charges, the narrative boldly states, "For the first time in their long and honorable career, [the Justice League members] are opposed by the law forces which they have sworn to uphold! What can be the outcome of this strange conflict?" Unable to convince the court of their innocence (as their doubles are identical copies of themselves), the team engages in a self-imposed exile from Earth to prove that they are not the culprits. Their loyalty to national law through willful exile belies the fact that the state is patently wrong; as readers, we are constantly reminded that the government not only fails to uncover the larger mystery behind Dr. Destiny's handiwork (it is government mismanagement of the prison system that frees Destiny before the end of his sentence) but that it similarly cannot subdue the duplicate Justice League members brought to life by science run amok.

Ultimately the teammates hatch a plan to return to Earth and fight their doubles without breaking the law. They collectively decide to exchange their superhero costumes for their civilian garb in order to lay claim to their U.S. citizenship, returning to the scene of their arrest and uncovering Dr. Destiny's plot and subsequently exonerating their superheroic alter egos. Much like the cold war scientists who had to navigate competing affiliations to the U.S. government and an egalitarian ethos of global scientific exchange, the Justice League's conflicts with governments and international peacekeeping institutions highlighted the possibility of playing competing forms of belonging against one another through the teammates' strategic movement between superhuman and civilian personas. For *The Justice League of America* it was this capacity to deftly move between varied scales of belonging and affiliation that defined a new form of ethical citizenship necessary for progressive social change in a postwar world defined by the increasing centrality of international political engagement and competition between the so-called Great Powers.

Extra-ordinary Bodies

Working at the nexus of postwar internationalism, popular science, and expanding state power, *The Justice League of America* offered a visually exuberant expression of the contradictions of cold war political culture in the early 1960s. The ascendancy of the security state and McCarthyism's curtailment of civil liberties, the public display of postwar scientific discoveries alongside increasing military secrecy, and the promise of a postwar international order, an imagined "family of man," coupled with virulent nationalism were all contradictions that circulated in the pages of *The Justice League of America*. Far from espousing a singular vision of the appropriate relationship between these three sites of the American body politic, *The Justice League* was often ambivalent in its positions. Yet the series' broader embrace of a collective, egalitarian model of ethical citizenship performed through a visually expansive depiction of the body's movement across national, global, and intergalactic borders meant it was not simply a reflection of cold war geopolitics; rather it was an alternative global imaginary that sought to revitalize the democratic promise of American liberalism within the discourses of internationalism and scientific cosmopolitanism.

If the comic book took any position, it was to claim, if obliquely, that while the juridical category of citizenship and the political institutions that claimed to protect it could be highly ineffective, the values that accrued to both were worth preserving. *The Justice League* worked to visualize what a successful manifestation of such values might look like in a world increasingly driven by monumental scientific and technological innovations and the shifting conceptions of citizenship that accompanied them. Such conceptions included the idea of "global citizenship" espoused by organizations like the United Nations—which encouraged consideration of one's belonging to a global community above that of national citizenship—and the scientific cosmopolitanism of American left-wing intellectuals, both notions of belonging that emerged in response to wartime technologies of mass murder like the Nazi concentration camps and the atomic bomb. It was ultimately the extraordinary bodies of the League's heroes that mediated between the scales of technological innovation and citizenship, for according to the series' logic, the superhuman body links scientific knowledge with acts of ethical citizenship as a vehicle for materializing collective good in the everyday world. Yet what *The Justice League of America* fails to address are the countless ways in which the relationship between science and citizenship remakes the body, unsettling the category of "universal humanity" at the same time that it claims to solidify it.

The Justice League's emphasis on the virtues of ethical citizenship bypasses any serious discussion of the physical experience of being superhuman. Like the liberal subject itself, which comes to stand in for all people as a figure of universal human will and agency, so too in

The Justice League of America "the superhuman" becomes a metaphor for the self-determining character of all people, subsuming bodily differences and alternative expressions of agency beneath the ideal of an exceptionally able-bodied superhero. Because of this, the *Justice League* cannot conceive of a subject position *not* allied to a liberal egalitarianism founded on exceptional, embodied performances of civic engagement. In the mid-1960s such a position ultimately made its entrance in the form of the disabled body. This figure would prove the limit to the series' egalitarian ethos by revealing how a purportedly universal category of ethical citizenship was implicitly underwritten by the assumption of a normative able-bodied subject inhabiting the identity of the global Samaritan.

In the June 1965 story "The Case of the Disabled Justice League," five members of the League visit a local hospital where they regularly drop in to "cheer up the patients."[34] On this day the doctor who coordinates these visits claims to have "special patients for [the superheroes] to see." Directing them to an unfamiliar room, he continues, "In here are my handicapped ones, boys who have lost the will to fight their afflictions! Nothing we say or do can reach them! I only hope a special visit from the Justice League will do what we cannot!" Accompanying this statement is a picture of five disabled teenage boys: one missing both arms, another missing a leg, a blind boy, a severe asthmatic, and a boy on crutches with a stutter that restricts his control over his body. The doctors hope that the visual presence of the League's superhumanly robust bodies, "special" in a very different way from the patients', will have the effect of producing will power in the disabled boys to overcome their "handicaps." And that is exactly what happens: when the Leaguers make their entrance, the boys immediately perk up, star-struck by their visitors. "Amazing!" the doctor exclaims. "All of a sudden they're filled with new life! I was right! The Justice League is the best medicine I could prescribe!" The narrator adds, "That vital force called 'will to live' surges strongly into youthful chests."

With their newfound "will to live," the boys express their desire to see the Leaguers perform heroic feats of skill. Prepared for the request, the superheroes return to their headquarters, where Batman, transformed by Green Lantern's ring into a reptilian monster, lies waiting to play-act a dramatic battle scene with his teammates. As soon as they attempt to subdue this illusory menace, however, the heroes are suddenly waylaid by disabilities of their own, each taking on the affliction of one of the young boys at the hospital. The Flash finds his legs glued together; Hawkman experiences the blistering pain of asthma, unable to maintain the strain of flight; Superman is blinded; Green Lantern gets a terrible stutter, preventing him from calling forth the power of his ring; and Green Arrow finds himself without arms to handle his bow and arrow. Initially baffled by their circumstance, the teammates soon learn that their former villain Brainstorm, a master of illusion, has escaped a local penitentiary. Believing Brainstorm may be the cause of their disabilities, the team travels to the spot of his last sighting, though without their usual ease of movement. Finding it difficult to run with one leg, the Flash suggests to Hawkman, "We'd make better progress by joining forces!," to which his teammate replies, "No—we can't team up, Flash! We must overcome our individual handicaps by ourselves!" Green Lantern chimes in, "W-we h-have to inspire these b-boys! They'll see we have physical difficulties—and b-by overcoming them we'll s-set a good example." Green Arrow adds, "By watching us, they'll learn to depend on themselves, not on others!"[35] Of all the menaces to plague the League in its illustrious history, disability is the first to cleave the team's commitment to collective action; where menaces to international security traditionally require the team to act in concert, this story suggests that threats to their bodily integrity must be managed by heroic individualism.

In the following scene the Leaguers take on Brainstorm and his marvelous illusions–living rock formations with murderous intent—each hero ingeniously adapting his disabilities to work alongside his superpowers. The visual field becomes a celebration of individual initiative as the arrangement of panels literally fragments the team by segmenting each hero's successful overcoming of his disability into self-contained action shots (plate 2). Unable to see, Superman relies on his sense of touch to destroy a massive rock hand that springs from the earth to crush him; the Flash furiously tunnels into the ground using his single powerful leg to help destroy Brainstorm's earthen creations; Green Arrow falls to his back, holding an arrow and the string of his bow with his teeth while employing his feet as leverage to let fly an explosive-tipped arrow that destroys a rock hammer threatening to flatten him.

Having successfully overcome their handicaps and triumphed over Brainstorm, the teammates make a final visit to the hospital. There the boys proclaim, "You sure taught us a lesson! Handicapped people can adjust! . . . We're going to use our handicaps as you used yours—as an incentive to make us even better than we would have been without them!" The final page depicts a disability pledge that rhetorically mimes the U.S. Constitution:

We, the people of a united nation, aware that all human beings are created equal, and realizing that some of us are more fortunate than others, are resolved: 1. That we shall meet those among us who are physically handicapped, as fully our equals. . . . 2. That we shall control our feeling of pity as they would want it controlled and treat them as they want to be treated: not as people apart, but as people normal and intelligent, and desirous of making their own way in life as a result of their own efforts. May we have understanding and wisdom and the power to carry out our pledge, the pledge of a free people. The Justice League of America is united with us in making this pledge.[36]

Beneath this message of tolerance appear images of Franklin Delano Roosevelt, Helen Keller, John Milton, and Beethoven alongside the caption "Here are just a few of the great people who made their mark in spite of their handicaps." Joining these historical greats are the five disabled boys, their faces encircled to the left of the page along with the smiling visages of the League members, arrayed at the bottom.

According to the charter, overcoming disability is a prerequisite to making worthwhile social and cultural contributions to the world and, implicitly, to becoming a citizen of humanity. Yet the collective vision of the charter is offset by its celebration of individual human genius, which reads history as a series of singular achievements distinct from collective forms of action. Unlike the classic splash panel of Starro the Conqueror that presented the League's mission statement alongside a threatening alien menace, here the nation's monstrous other is not figured as an intergalactic threat but as disability itself. Disability haunts the image both in the form of those with actual physical infirmities (the historical figures and the young boys who suffered and overcame their "handicaps") and as the Justice League members themselves, who might be read as something other than human due to their superpowers. Refusing to address the disabled body's uneasy relationship to *The Justice League of America*'s liberal project—or the superhero's own "inhuman" body—the comic book disavows this threat by espousing a discourse of tolerance that values will power as opposed to physical nonconformity: both the will to overcome one's handicaps and the will to treat those "less fortunate" as equals. Ironically, by the time the boys voice their own commitment to using their disabilities as the League members did—to become "better than [they] would have without them"—every character in the narrative has mouthed the line of "overcoming" disability so that the story's central values of individualism and free will become expressions of mass conformity. Unable to imagine a monstrous "we" made up of those who *don't* fit the idealized frame of able-bodied citizenship, *The*

Justice League makes recourse to a national banality, the presumed "we" of a "free people," apparently free only to the extent that one is willing to acknowledge the universal superiority of the extraordinary or superhuman body.

With its ethos of universal humanism, *The Justice League of America* brought the figure of the American superhero into a wider set of debates about what a true "family of man" might look like in an new international era. This same ethos, however, made it difficult to map the failures of the liberal project and address the specificities of human experience potentially effaced by a taken-for-granted universal citizenship. Where in this model did such concepts as disability, monstrosity, and mutation reside? Despite its ability to metaphorically stand in for a host of affiliative modes in the postwar period, *The Justice League of America*'s commitment to "the family of man" left it unable to deal with these deviant categories, ones that, in the cold war politics of containment, belonged squarely in the intimate sphere of the nuclear family. The conservative political and cultural rhetoric that lauded the nuclear family as a bulwark against communism and a bastion of normative gender and sexuality also paradoxically located sexual deviancy and social nonconformity within this same social structure.

In the early 1960s Marvel Comics' *The Fantastic Four* would overtake the popularity of *The Justice League of America*, rapidly becoming the favored comic magazine of a generation of readers. *The Fantastic Four* was understood by readers and creators to be a radical departure from the classic superheroes represented by the DC Comics label. It would be the first comic book series to focus on the personal lives of superheroes, to present its characters as inhabitants of a real-world metropolis (New York City), and to directly address the everyday financial and emotional cost of hero work. These innovations were negligible, however, compared to the series' conceptual breakthroughs in superhero storytelling. First, where *The Justice League* offered a vision of liberal universalism in an intergalactic police force maintaining the rule of law across the cosmos, *The Fantastic Four* depicted the chaotic energies of a dysfunctional family unit as they struggled to maintain their solidarity in a world divided by competing political interests and proliferating forms of difference. Second, *The Fantastic Four* highlighted the capacity of science to transform the body with monstrous results, offering an extended exploration of the place of the body in mediating the relationship between science and citizenship in postwar America. The four heroes' bizarre powers are a result of their encounter with cosmic rays that permanently alter their bodily morphology, undermining their claim to a proper "humanity" that is a prerequisite to national, racial, and species belonging. Finally, by locating the intimate sphere of the family as the social site where popular science and state power attach to citizenship, *The Fantastic Four* opened up the figure of the superhero to the categories of gender and sexuality, the material textures of everyday life, and the dynamics of generational conflict at the dawn of the turbulent 1960s. Where *The Justice League* presented its central characters as unmarked by sexuality, class, or race, *The Fantastic Four*'s success would lie in its reinterpretation of the body as a highly contested site for the production of identity in an age where one's bodily integrity was constantly undone by the flexible object world that surrounded it. If *The Justice League* flatly assumed the humanity of all, *The Fantastic Four* put the very notion of the human into question.

2 / "Flame On!": Nuclear Families, Unstable Molecules, and the Queer History of *The Fantastic Four*

Few tales of teenage angst could compete with the experience of young Johnny Storm as his body bursts into flame before his very eyes. Watching horrified as his three closest friends, among them his sister, miraculously transform into a human plastic, an invisible trace, and a rock-like behemoth, Johnny can only imagine they have become nothing short of monsters. As a terrifying heat overtakes his body, Johnny's horror at his own violent transformation quickly evaporates into a newfound sense of freedom: he can survive the flame. He can fly. Released to popular acclaim in 1961, the inaugural issue of Marvel Comics' *The Fantastic Four* tells the story of four companions who attempt an unauthorized rocket flight into space, hoping to outrace the communist menace. Their fateful trip ends with their bodies bombarded by "cosmic rays" that would alter their molecular structure, their skin absorbing substances once thought alien to the touch. Ben Grimm's rocky epidermis, Johnny Storm's flaming body, Sue Storm's invisible silhouette, and Reed Richards's physical pliability were marvelous gifts and social burdens that collapsed objects and bodies in decidedly abnormal ways. Now the four had been made as deviant as the threat they had sought to contain.[1]

More than any previous figuration of the superhero, *The Fantastic Four* dramatized a fantasy of bodily vulnerability to the forces of science and to the social norms of national citizenship in the era of anticommunism. The transformation of the team's biology into "unstable molecules" that mimicked the malleable plastics and synthetics of postwar material science revealed that the interaction between the physical self and the material world could produce nonnormative or "queer" effects. I use the term *nonnormative* to describe those behaviors that mark the failure to conform to the proper performance of gender and sexuality; this wider designation folds within it distinctly queer modes of intimacy and affiliation, or ways of being in the world that thwart the assumed direction of heterosexual relations. In the logic of cold war containment, those who stepped outside the bounds of sexual and gender norms—including homosexuals, people practicing premarital sex and nonmonogamy, and gender outlaws—were understood as abnormal or queer, and hence lacking the qualities associated with good citizenship.[2] As David Serlin and Robert McRuer have shown, this mark of sexual or gender perversion implying failed citizenship commonly extended to the disabled, people whose apparent distance from the "normal" human body was interpreted as a material expression of their inability to perform the proper functions of able-bodied heterosexuality.[3]

The Fantastic Four's powers played on this logic as a physical mark upon the flesh that indicated their failure to live up to the sexual and gender norms of cold war culture and, more broadly, their abjection from proper humanity. Consequently the narrative's central conceptual conflict was not the split between a civilian and a superheroic identity, as it had been in *The Justice League of America* (unlike most heroes, the four claimed no secret identities) but between what the members of the team felt or *believed* themselves to be and what their mutated bodies suggested they *actually* were: something "more than just human." By rewriting the superhero as a figure that highlighted the impossibility of suturing an unpredictable body (and identity) to the narrowly construed social norms of cold war America, the series presaged and oriented itself toward the radical political reappraisals of self-making that would take place in the coming decade.

In *The Fantastic Four* between 1961 and 1967, the series' first sixty issues, writer Stan Lee and artist Jack Kirby developed the foundational attributes of the fantastic foursome and introduced more than a hundred supporting characters, a cadre of fellow superheroes, villains, cosmic beings, and human allies who collectively made up a growing "Marvel Universe." I frame *The Fantastic Four* as a popular fantasy that bridged the gap between the ideological conservatism of 1950s anticommunism and the emergent radical political sensibilities of the 1960s. It accomplished this by visually critiquing the relationship between sexual and gender identity and cold war politics, namely McCarthyism's powerful political framing of the heterosexual nuclear family as a bulwark against communism.[4] Against this worldview *The Fantastic Four* imaginatively crafted a new kind of citizen capable of engaging cosmopolitan political projects without an attachment to narratives of heterosexual normalization and bodily regimentation. In so doing *The Fantastic Four* became a visual repository of an array of nonnormative identities, affiliations, and kinships that were gaining public visibility due to the politics of civil rights, the New Left, and an emergent counterculture, movements that resisted the political constraints placed on private life by the imperatives of the cold war security state.

During the cold war the state increasingly sought to regulate private life—particularly individuals' sexual orientation, gender identity, and intimate social relations—with the rationale that private conduct was symptomatic of political loyalties. Government officials argued that deviant forms of gender and sexual identity indicated a tendency toward communist sympathies.[5] This attitude was bolstered by the popularization of psychoanalysis, and the rise of a postwar therapeutic culture, as a medical practice that purported to identify nonnormative sexual proclivities as expressions of underlying neurosis and expunge them through sustained investigation of the "interior self" or individual psychology. Psychoanalysis promised to cure neurotic psychosomatic symptoms by helping the mind conform to the prevailing sexual and gender norms of the time; in so doing it echoed the ideological thrust of a variety of cutting-edge medical treatments—including plastic surgery, hormone replacement therapy, and prosthetics—which sold people on the idea that they might remold their physical body to comport with their mental self-image.[6]

The most publicized expression of this will to align the psyche with an ideal body was the case of Christine Jorgenson, a former U.S. naval officer who, in 1952, was the first American to undergo sex-reassignment surgery. Jorgenson's public declaration of having transformed her formerly male body to comport with her female self-image was celebrated as an act of unprecedented individual empowerment.[7] In Jorgenson the public saw proof of people's capacity to use the tools of modern medicine to remake themselves into the image of the ideally normal American. The alignment of popular discourses of normalcy with institutions of political and medical coercion that Jorgenson's case exemplified produced a cold war regime of normalization that enforced a prevailing set of ideals about what a healthy and adjusted life (and body) should look like. That well-adjusted life was overwhelmingly heterosexual, able-bodied, family-oriented, upwardly mobile, and traditionally gendered.[8] Jorgenson was celebrated because medical technology had helped transform her into a blond bombshell who embodied the ideals of postwar femininity and because that femininity was "purchased" through a willful act of self-making; however, when Americans realized that Jorgenson's procedure had not given her a female reproduction system, many were disgusted by what they now perceived as an inauthentic performance of femaleness. Jorgenson found herself trapped between a valorized practice of empowered self-fashioning and the drive to conform to real or imagined sexual and gender norms.

The Fantastic Four visually celebrated the transitional body and depicted perceived "neurotic" or pathological social types who failed to live up to unrealistic sexual and gender ideals as paragons of heroic nonconformity. In so doing it linked existing critiques of the culture of conformity lobbied by liberal intellectuals throughout the postwar period to the production of new kinds of citizenship grounded in difference and abnormality that were gaining traction in the early to mid-1960s. It did so in three ways. First, the comic book visually dislocated individual psychology from the physical body by depicting the bodies of its heroes as explicitly contradicting their self-image. By magnifying and widening the gap between the body's radical (and often monstrous) capacity for transformation and the psychic desire to live up to the impossible social norms demanded of that body, The Fantastic Four dramatized McRuer's contention that "able-bodied identity and heterosexual identity are linked in their mutual impossibility and their mutual incomprehensibility—they are incomprehensible in that each is an identity that is simultaneously the ground on which all identities supposedly rest and an impressive achievement that is always deferred and thus never really guaranteed."[9] The Fantastic Four's superpowers were presented as a series of chaotic material surfaces whose unpredictable effects destabilized each of the characters' sense of self or else encouraged them to reorient their psychic lives toward new ways of being and acting in the world; this included taking pleasure in the ways their powers unraveled their previous gender and sexual expressions as well as their claims to a properly "human" body. In this sense, while the characters did not explicitly embody Jorgenson's sought-after transition from male to female, they played upon the emergent transsexual or transgender conceit of the mismatch between social performance and embodied realities to identify the putatively white, middle-class, straight American body as riven by sexual and gender conflict and, as a result, in a continual state of political transition or flux.[10]

Each of the four characters initially appeared as ideal social "types" whose physical comportment reflected the common categories of identification associated with the 1950s nuclear family in the decade's popular culture: Reed Richards, the emotionless scientist and proud father figure; Sue Storm, his doting fiancée and surrogate mother to her sibling; Johnny, the hip teenage rebel with a soft spot for pretty girls; and Ben Grimm, the former fighter pilot with a temper to match his hypermasculine demeanor. Though initially depicted as monolithic types, the physical transformations the four undergo ultimately reveal the tenuousness of these roles and the social anxieties attending their performance. As each character's superheroic identity took shape, they grew to embody a host of 1960s countercultural figures—the left-wing intellectual, the liberal feminist, the youth activist, and the maladjusted queer—all nonconformist figures that flatly contradicted the teammates' original self-presentation as patriotic, traditionally gendered, family-oriented anticommunists.

Second, the series explicitly identified those objects most associated with cold war normalcy—consumer goods and the material innovations of postwar science—as the wellspring of *nonnormative* and implicitly queer desires. By recasting the question of both sexual and social identity as one of orientation toward particular bodies and objects, the series conducted what Sara Ahmed has called a "queer phenomenology" of postwar material culture. Ahmed claims, "If orientation is a matter of how we reside in space, then sexual orientation might also be a matter . . . of how we inhabit spaces, and who or what we inhabit spaces with."[11] The Fantastic Four's physical proximity to the rockets, synthetics, and technology of the atomic age—not to mention a host of alien, mutant, and cyborg others—meant that they literally and figuratively "inhabited space with" bodies, objects, and worlds that existed far outside the acceptable boundaries of cold war heterosexual family life. The series envisioned what might happen when subjectivity and the material world that helped shape its psychic contours were collapsed onto a physical body, much as they had been in anticommunist logic. The result was both a reorientation of the putatively "normal body" toward sites of radical queer encounter, as well as an expansion of comic book forms' visual capacity to depict such encounters as the wellspring of alternative desires.

Even as it creatively engaged with the social norms and personality types common to 1950s culture, as a distinctly 1960s cultural phenomenon *The Fantastic Four* deployed the developing cold war space race and the Kennedy administration's New Frontier ideology as fertile ground for linking the social norms of the 1950s to the political life of a revolutionary decade. Though it still retained the policy of containment, Kennedy's New Frontier sought to reorient the cold war from a normalizing project to a dynamic national mission to propel mankind into a technologically advanced and democratic, space-age future. As Lynn Spigel explains, "The Kennedy administration . . . adapted its own political agenda to the new space-age metaphors that were based on the tenets of progress, democracy, and national freedom. The forthright do-gooder citizen to whom Kennedy appealed was given the promise of a new beginning in abstract terms. . . . The ride into space proved to be the most vivid concretization of such abstractions, promising a new-found national allegiance through which we would not only diffuse the Soviet threat but also shake ourselves out of the doldrums that 1950s life had come to symbolize."[12] *The Fantastic Four* framed its reinvention of the rigid social types of the 1950s within the utopian technological imaginary of the New Frontier, depicting its seemingly domestic and ordinary heroes as champions of American space exploration. Yet far from making the four heroes paragons of cold war citizenship, their first rocket flight into space would irrevocably transform them into biological "freaks" and security threats to the government they had risked life and limb to serve.[13] Moreover it produced in them a desire to reorient their commitments to all those who similarly stood outside the bounds of humanity.

At the dawn of the 1960s, advances in rocket science and utopian hopes for a space-age future made the potential for encounters with extraterrestrial life appear genuinely possible; in 1961 *Time* magazine described projects by the nation's leading astrophysicists to transmit radio waves into space in hopes of contacting intelligent life beyond our solar system.[14] If contact was a potential outcome of such endeavors, *The Fantastic Four* suggested that the rigid social types of the 1950s would merely extend the conservative worldview of the cold war into an uncharted cosmos, negating possibilities for cosmopolitan cultural exchange beyond planet Earth. Through the dramatic transformations of its four central characters, the series sought to develop the affective and intellectual faculties required to approach a world of fantastic and unexpected encounters with life in the universe.

Third, the comic book contradicted the cold war ideal of the conflict-free nuclear family as a bulwark against communism by depicting the family as a site of democratic debate that equipped individual members to engage with a heterogeneous world. The team took the shape of the nuclear family—simulating the mother-father pair of Reed and Sue and their two surrogate children, Johnny and Ben—while altering its form through the production of a chosen kinship based not on the conception of a universally shared humanity but on the mutual experience of difference *from* it, an "inhuman" cosmopolitics. Just as the team's bodies were transformed into billions of unstable molecules, their kinship was similarly depicted as an unstable molecular unit capable of accommodating a variety of social relations. I argue that the series' recurrent depiction of the family as a site of generative conflict and willed affiliation aligned its values with left-wing political movements that similarly sought to recast social relations as chosen bonds anchored by shared values rather than social conformity or biological kinship. As they came to embody the oppositional spirit of an emergent counterculture in the 1960s, the Fantastic Four inaugurated a renaissance in superhero storytelling while becoming iconic figures in the remaking of American liberalism.

Soft Touch: The Queer Textures of Cold War Masculinity

In the narrative of *The Fantastic Four*, Reed Richards, Ben Grimm, and Johnny Storm took literal and figurative shape against three figures of nonnormative masculinity in the cold war: the liberal, the neurotic, and the queer. In visually referencing these figures, the comic book self-consciously performed and critiqued the bodily and textural rhetoric of anticommunism. During the early cold war, the terms *hard* and *soft* were used to describe conservative and liberal orientations, respectively, toward anticommunist politics. In the political logic of McCarthyism, *softness* took on a double meaning, referring to a psychological susceptibility to communist ideology that was also understood as an expression of effeminized or "weak" masculinity associated with homosexual tendencies. The liberal, the neurotic, and the queer were understood as interrelated psychic and material manifestations of "soft" masculinity whose desires for particular ideologies and love objects were seen as two sides of the same coin.[15]

The negative social meanings that came to attach to these figures were articulated to textural language: alongside the "hard" and "soft" rhetoric of anticommunist ideology, postwar psychology described the perceived fragility of the male psyche in terms of "inner-directed" and "other-directed" personalities, the latter suggesting weakness of character and a will to conformity. The popularization of phrases like the "man in the gray flannel suit" and "the doughface liberal" to describe the postwar subject's submissive pliancy extended the textures of anticommunism to embodied figurations linking somatic experience with ideological loyalties.[16] In the bodies of the Fantastic Four's three male characters, these social types and their related textural economies would reappear in extraordinarily mutated ways, transforming the meanings of masculinity, heterosexuality, and ideological conformity in postwar America.

Reed is initially presented to readers as a paragon of patriotic masculinity, a loyal anticommunist using his scientific genius to help the United States win the cold war space race and a committed family man. His subsequent transformation into the superhumanly elastic Mr. Fantastic, however, placed the physical pliability of his body in opposition to both the social "type" his previous performance of gender embodied—the hard-minded scientist—and his responsibility to the state as a producer of objective knowledge whose ideas supported anticommunist goals. As the heroic Mr. Fantastic, Reed can stretch any portion of his body to incredible lengths, flatten or balloon his physique at will, and take the shape of a variety of objects. Mr. Fantastic gave visual expression to somatically inflected terms like *softness* and *plasticity*, which described the material qualities of postwar consumer goods as well as psychic qualities associated with the effete and "soft-minded" liberal.

Reed's newfound abilities would have a direct effect on his psychological orientation toward state-sponsored anticommunism. Following the team's failed rocket flight into space, Reed is the first member of the team to voice the need to use their powers for the good of mankind, a liberal egalitarian impulse that leaves him in a precarious relationship with the government's national security interests. His ambivalence toward these competing commitments is showcased in *The Fantastic Four* #13. In this issue the team attempts to thwart the diabolical plans of an evil Russian cosmonaut, Dr. Kragoff, to transform himself and three apes into superpowered beings like the Fantastic Four. Just as the four are poised to confront Kragoff on the dark side of the moon, Reed exclaims, "This is wrong! Why should we battle Kragoff? Why can't we leave our differences behind us! This is the first step to the stars—and we should all make that trip together—as fellow earthmen!"[17] In the prevailing conservative rhetoric of his time, had Reed uttered such a statement anywhere besides the dark side of the moon, he would have undoubtedly been accused of being "soft on communism." Though Reed is ultimately convinced of Kragoff's villainous intentions, his belief in the right of all humans to share the fruits of technological advance echoes throughout the team's many adventures. As the series progressed, Reed found intellectual camaraderie with scientists and thinkers from an array of advanced alien and "inhuman" civilizations that would provide the impetus for reconsidering his unwavering loyalty to the nation.

Reed's contradictory loyalties are best illustrated in a Mr. Fantastic feature page at the conclusion of *The Fantastic Four* #16 (plate 3). Feature pages were stand-alone splash panels in the back matter of comic book issues that gave readers in-depth looks at characters and their unique superpowers. In this feature page Reed stands tall and stoic in his Fantastic Four costume to the left side of the scene. To the right, he appears in four miniature action sequences dynamically taking on a variety of shapes and forms as Mr. Fantastic. As he performs these feats, he explains to the reader, "The shapes into which I can mold my pliable body are virtually limitless . . . from a spare auto tire . . . to a delicate, life-saving parachute! These shapes can be assumed with the speed of thought, but only because I have spent long hours practicing and developing my agility! . . . Due to the extreme flexibility and elasticity of my molecular structure, I can absorb the impact of any type of shell (except an atomic missile)."[18]

On the one hand, Reed presents his power as an egalitarian, even promiscuous pliability whose boundlessness holds untapped potentialities; on the other, the visual presentation of his skill ties his feats of bodily transformation to the accouterments of the military-industrial complex: mass-produced rubber, synthetic fibers, and atomic weaponry. As he points out, the limit of his flexibility is marked by the highest achievement of military technology: the atom bomb. Similarly the transparency of his display, his willingness to publicly present visual evidence of his bodily elasticity and the possibilities inherent in the technologies he emulates—a particularly bold move in an era of intense government secrecy about American military science and technology—is offset by his reference to rigorous physical discipline as a prerequisite for his amazing feats. The chaotic energies of Reed's power become acceptable only within a discourse of physical discipline and control—captured in his initial rigid stance—that was the hallmark of the hard-bodied anticommunist type. Yet, as Reed explains, the farther he stretches his body, "the weaker [his] muscles become." His power enhances his body but has the potential to effeminize and weaken him.

The precariousness of Reed's masculinity was impressed upon readers in his physical interactions with other bodies and objects. The series recurrently displayed Mr. Fantastic wrapping himself around the bodies of other men, usually villains, using his pliable frame to contain and neutralize a combatant's powers. In these instances of physical homosocial bonding, Reed's masculinity is placed in crisis, his body distended to the point where his gender is no longer clearly identifiable. These moments of homosocial bonding recalled the cultures of male-dominated professional spaces in the 1950s and early 1960s. The American scientist, for instance, was often depicted in popular culture as a bland "egghead" whose lack of personality made him interchangeable with a seemingly endless procession of fellow lab-coated male researchers. Even as he was celebrated as a national hero, the American scientist was also perceived as antisocial and effete, more suited to interact with molecules and microscopes than human beings.[19] By the early 1960s, however, this image had been superseded by a refashioning of the liberal intellectual as an icon of "style, virility, and glamour." As K. A. Cuordileone argues, this transformation was enabled by the Kennedy administration's celebration of public intellectuals as part of the "boy's club" of national politics and high society, while periodicals like *Life* and *Time* touted scientists as brave and adventurous "explorers of the unknown."[20] Reed straddled the dual personalities of the virile scientific adventurer and the antisocial, and potentially queer, lab geek, while pointing to a third possibility: the rerouting of the liberal intellectual's mind and body toward cosmopolitan social relations *not* predicated on masculinity and heterosexuality.

Mr. Fantastic's implicitly queer encounters with the bodies of other men referenced both his detailed knowledge of and work with "unstable molecules" and the instability of his own heterosexual desires, which were often derailed by his devotion to the inanimate object world of the laboratory. On one pinup page Reed is depicted playfully straddling a gigantic alien laser gun in his lab. At the top of the page appears a note to readers written in flowing cursive letters: "Just between us, I don't know what this silly contraption is, either! Keep smiling—Reed." Despite his brilliance and masculine bravado, Reed appears more like a clueless Boy Scout or amateur scientist fooling around in his garage; the image suggests that scientists might just be "silly little boys" obsessed with playing with their "joy-sticks." Cheekier still, that joystick appears like a giant mechanical phallus Reed gleefully fauns over, while the cursive flourishes of his note offers yet another campy expression of his over-the-top feminine masculinity. Despite his physical flexibility, Reed's attachment to the rigid, sterile tools of cold war science and technology damages his emotional connection to Sue, who is repulsed by her fiancé's obsessive focus on experiments and technogadgets. In this way Reed materialized the ever-proliferating contradictions of cold war masculinity, which demanded physically hard bodies yet intellectually flexible minds, sexually virile husbands yet docile government workers, creative applications of science yet uniform and useful results. Despite his extraordinary powers and unparalleled intellect, Reed still laments in issue #14, "I've always thought of myself as being able to accomplish . . . anything! With my scientific talent, and my super-flexible body, it seemed that nothing could ever defeat me! . . . Though the world knows me as the invincible Mister Fantastic, I am unable to win my most cherished goal! I am unable to . . . conquer the heart of the girl I love!"[21]

Visualized as a dramatic foil to Reed's pliable body, Ben Grimm's power encases his body in rigid orange rock, an invulnerable stony edifice combined with extraordinary strength. As the teammate with no control over the presentation of his powers and the figure whose affiliation to the group is nonfamilial, the Thing's struggles to come to terms with his monstrous form became a central trope of *The Fantastic Four*, positioning him as the neurotic subject of failed masculinity.

Throughout the series the Thing's personality took shape in relation to a form of popular Freudianism that saw the drive to conform to particular gendered and sexual norms as the source of insecurity and neuroses. In the early twentieth century, Freud's discovery of the unconscious— a component of the human mind that he claimed housed fundamental instinctual drives and unfettered desires that had to be repressed beneath our everyday conscious life for the purpose of normal socialization—led many radical thinkers to believe that cultivating mechanisms for unleashing the energies of the repressed psyche might liberate individuals from the shackles of social conformity.[22] During World War II psychoanalytic therapy gained professional standing as it was incorporated into wartime medical practice to treat neurotic behavior. In this period the neurotic came to be understood as a social type defined by a lack of emotional and sexual control or else psychologically incapable of dealing with the stresses of everyday life. The stresses of modern warfare led countless soldiers to experience mental breakdowns and neurotic psychosomatic symptoms, while the male-dominated environment of the military became a hotbed for homosexual activity. The U.S. government treated these two concerns as part of the same psychopathology, dispatching psychoanalysts to the front lines of war to conduct mental evaluations on overstressed soldiers.[23] Psychoanalysis came out of the war with a new image as a mental cure-all that could dissipate neurotic symptoms and perceived deviant behaviors therapeutically.[24] The great

paradox of postwar psychoanalysis was that it simultaneously identified the overwhelming demands of gender and sexual conformity as the
source of psychopathology but sought to reorient individual behavior
toward the fulfillment of those norms. By the mid-1950s and early 1960s
this contradiction would become the site of sustained critique by left-
wing intellectuals who sought to recapture the earlier radical thrust of
psychoanalysis by highlighting its capacity to unleash the charismatic
and nonconformist aspects of human potential, including sexuality, creativity, and individuality.[25] This critique would be anticipated and taken
up by superhero comics, beginning with *The Fantastic Four*.

In Benjamin Grimm, the monstrous yet lovable Thing, *The Fantastic
Four* celebrated the neurotic personality as a desirable state of being that
described a productively maladjusted stance toward contemporary gender and sexual norms. First presented as a loud-mouthed, aggressively
masculine fighter pilot, Ben is soon revealed to be a deeply insecure
man unable to express affection without devolving into violence or self-
deprecating humor. Heckled by his former inner-city posse, the Yancy
Street Gang, and reminded of his physical ugliness by his teammate
Johnny Storm, Ben humorously employs the language of psychoanalysis
to deflect the thrust of these taunts. When Johnny tries to humiliate his
teammate by publicly announcing that Ben is a fan of *The Mickey Mouse
Club*, Ben yells, "Okay, okay! You tryin' to give me an inferiority complex?" In one telling encounter with the Yancy Street Gang, Ben walks to
his old neighborhood looking to settle a score over a derogatory drawing
of him they have sent to the team's Manhattan headquarters, the Baxter Building (figure 2.1). As Ben takes his stand on the corner of Yancy
Street, we see the image held tightly in his fist, a drawing of the Thing
in a tutu with a rose in his mouth. Across the top of the page is scrawled
"The Thing is a sissy!"[26]

By manifesting the normative personality of the "hardened," masculine male subject of postwar culture as a second skin, Ben is paradoxically
unable to perform the assumed functions of hard masculinity—obtain-
ing a job, getting married, having sex—which makes him a "sissy."
Rather than a cautionary tale, however, it was the Thing's neuroses
that audiences identified with, similarly encouraged by the logic of the
comic book to refuse identification with normative masculinity. In fact
the Thing's seemingly flexible gender identity was invoked as a progressive sign of the times. In a humorous scene, the Yancy Street Gang send
the Thing a gag gift in the form of a Beatles wig, presumably intend-
ing to compare the former football star to the androgynous and lilting

FIGURE 2.1. "The Thing is a sissy!" Stan Lee (writer) and Jack Kirby (penciller), "The Mad Thinker and His Awesome Android!," *Fantastic Four* #15, June 1963, reprinted in *Fantastic Four Omnibus Vol. 1* (New York: Marvel Comics, 2007), 375.

rockers. Attached to the package is a note: "A perfect gift for a man who has nothing!" Rather than rage at their insult, the Thing gladly dons the bowl-cut wig, claiming he's "always wanted to try one." Standing next to his girlfriend, Alicia Masters, the Thing is indistinguishable as man, woman, or living rock with a fake hairdo. Turning earlier cold war fears about gender inversion and the emasculation of American men on their head, the Thing joins the Beatles and other 1960s pop icons in celebrating androgyny and gender bending.[27]

Marvel Comics found in Ben Grimm an icon for a new generation of superheroes whose powers rendered them sexual deviants and species

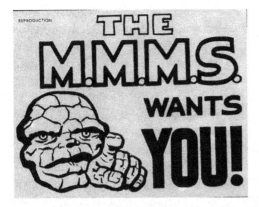 

FIGURE 2.2. Promotional materials for the Merry Marvel Marching Society. Peter Sanderson, *The Marvel Vault: A Museum-in-a-Book with Rare Collectibles from the World of Marvel* (New York: Running Press, 2007), 99.

outcasts. Ben's psychological struggles to square his monstrous exterior form with his internal sense of self catapulted him to stardom as readers' most beloved and sympathetic character in the growing Marvel Comics pantheon. When Marvel inaugurated its official company fan club, the Merry Marvel Marching Society, in 1964, it would take the neurotic Thing as its mascot. Creators emblazoned his mug shot on membership cards as a latter-day Uncle Sam, pointing his rocky finger at potential fans with the injunction, "THE M.M.M.S.WANTS YOU!" (figure 2.2).[28] These potential "Marvelites" were hailed as self-made outsiders and maladjusts to the norms of social acceptability through a rhetoric of alternative belonging; as Marvel editor and writer Stan Lee explained to readers, "You can't describe the normal Marvel fan—nobody can! The minute someone gets hooked on Marvel, he stops being normal!"[29] If Uncle Sam hailed citizens as a masculine father figure protecting the universal values of the nation, the Thing's androgynous visage spoke to an audience of peers as fellow deviants bound by their symbolic (if not actual) refusal of the gendered logic of cold war politics.

In the narrative proper, Ben struggled between impulses to resist or embrace his abnormality. This psychic conflict was externally dramatized in a variety of scenes in which his rock-like body briefly morphs back into his "normal" human form. In early issues of the series, Reed works tirelessly to develop a serum to transform the Thing back into Ben, occasionally succeeding at providing Ben with short-term returns to his human form. Though Ben is initially ecstatic about regaining his human form in these brief instances of reconversion, he almost always regrets the loss of his power when he realizes he is unable to join his friends in combat or protect them from harm in his traditional body. Ironically his transitions back to human form would reconsolidate his gender, confirming his status as a full-fledged man—in the first of these instances, Ben exclaims, "I'm human again!! I'm Ben Grimm at last! . . . A man!! I'm a man!"—but would rob him of his extraordinary abilities, which hinged on his gender indeterminacy. Thus Ben's literal transitions from human to rock form were also coded as transitions in gender identity, while his feeling of being "trapped" in his mutated body echoed emergent discourses of transsexual (and later transgender) identity, which increasingly used the leitmotif of being trapped in the wrong body as a powerful description of the lived experience of transsexuality. As Jay Prosser claims, "If the goal of transsexual transition is to align the feeling of gendered embodiment with the material body, [then] body image . . . clearly already has a material force for transsexuals. The image of being trapped in the wrong body conveys this force."[30] In Ben comic book creators imagined what it would mean to "transition" *into* a state of indeterminacy or flux, hence their repeated visualization of his transitions from human to rock form and between man and androgyne, while exhibiting his powers. For Ben the concept of being trapped in the wrong body did not convey the consolidating force of body image in underwriting his material form, as it did for those who identified as transsexual. Rather it conveyed the productive failure of any body, especially the normatively heterosexual male body, to capture an authentic sense of self. In this way the comic book suggested that a variety of discourses of bodily nonnormativity deployed to *consolidate* alternative sexual and gender identities in the face of homophobia and transphobia (such as the transsexual language of being "trapped in the wrong body") could also be used to *destabilize* normalizing structures like heterosexual masculinity.

It is here, in the body's failure to present a specifically fixed gender identification, both at the level of physical appearance and the direction of its psychic desire, that the question of sexuality is made manifest on the bodies of the Fantastic Four. Though at times the direction of the characters' desires seems obviously normative (all four characters romantically pursue members of the opposite sex), such desires are shot through with "queer" feelings that attend the team's more obviously abnormal bodies: Ben's desire for his own monstrous second skin; Reed's split affections for Sue and his scientific research; Sue's equally split feelings for Reed and for Prince Namor, the team's on-again, off-again villain and king of Atlantis—all pointed to the fact of heterosexual desire gone awry. I use the term *direction* here to indicate the ways that the Fantastic Four articulated questions of sexuality and desire in the visual rhetoric of orientation or physical proximities between bodies and objects. Ahmed posits, "To become straight means not only that we have to turn toward the objects given to us by heterosexual culture but also that we must turn away from objects that take us off this line. The queer subject within straight culture deviates and is made socially present as a deviant."[31] The members of the Fantastic Four become visually present on the comic book page, and hence "socially present" to readers, as figures whose bodies and desires "turn away" from the objects "given to us by heterosexual culture" in every attempt to embrace them; this outcome identified the four as deviants (and ecstatically so) and recast the structures of postwar heterosexuality as amenable to deviation.

No character of *The Fantastic Four* exemplified deviation from sexual norms more than Johnny Storm, the Human Torch. A youthful playboy and lover of fast cars, Johnny seems at first glance to represent the heterosexual spirit of male teenage youth associated with the popular rebel figure of the 1950s. At the same time, his bodily condition is consistently presented as literally and figuratively overheating his sexual desires. In this way Johnny's blazing body functioned as both a visual expression of excessive heterosexuality—the hypersexualized teenage rebel—as well as its seeming opposite, the "flaming" homosexual of popular political rhetoric. From the very first issue of *The Fantastic Four*, the flame that the Torch loves derails his heterosexual attachments.

In his first appearance as the Human Torch, Johnny is in the front seat of a hot rod he is remodeling with a friend (plate 4). "There's only one thing in the world that interests me more than cars!" he declares. In the ensuing space between panels, the direction of his statement seems destined to lead to "girls," the obvious object of affection for all teenage boys. In the next panel, however, his thought is interrupted by the sight of a fiery number 4 etched in the sky, Reed's signal for the team to assemble. Immediately Johnny begins to steam and blaze, exclaiming, "Remember me saying there was only one thing that interests me more than cars?! Well this is it!!" With this last statement, Johnny flies out of the car's roof at full burn, melting the vehicle in a puddle of metal and rubber.[32] Here the physical manifestation of Johnny's flame symbolically enacts a queer narcissism that reroutes his assumed heterosexual desire for women toward a queer desire for an unruly, flaming body. In the space between Johnny's first appearance as an ordinary body and the last, as a human torch, the visual trajectory of the images on the page disorients our expectations of a heterosexual outcome to his initial statement. Instead both Johnny's body and the flow of the comic book narrative are made to "extend differently into space," providing Johnny and the reader with the possibility of an alternative, or queer, orientation toward the self and the material world in the figure of his flaming body.[33]

In issue #2 Johnny's transformations into the Human Torch became paired with his now famous exclamation, "Flame On!," a performative utterance that brings into being the condition it describes. Couched in the language of consumer durables—recalling increasingly ubiquitous terms such as *nylon* and *rayon*—the force of its pronouncement both references and refuses identification with these plastic textures and their social realities, linked to domestic order, self-control, and the sublimation of desire in material goods.[34] Johnny's powers point to the ordered material world of consumer durables (including hot rods) only to ignite them in chaotic flame, unhinging their structural integrity with a physical heat that functions as an orgasmic display of his equally charged sexuality.[35]

As the team's resident youth, Johnny circulates within another network of meaning that positions him as the team's link between 1950s heterosexual youth culture and the politically antagonistic and sexually polymorphous 1960s counterculture. It would be impossible to visualize bodies aflame in the postwar period without invoking the fiery death worlds of the Nazi final solution and the incinerated bodies of Hiroshima and Nagasaki. Moreover Johnny was directly tied to World War II history by dint of being the second incarnation of the Human Torch, Marvel Comics' first wartime superhero invented in 1939, a human android who deployed his extraordinary pyrotechnics to fight the Nazis.[36] Johnny's teenage form brought the flame of his forebear into the orbit of contemporary struggles of American youth against the devastating moral storms of racism and the cultural and environmental inferno that was the Vietnam War. On the one hand, Johnny's ecstatic joy in zooming through the stratosphere materialized images of rocket flight and the pleasures of a technologically liberating future central to the utopian vision of Kennedy's New Frontier. Yet this image of unbridled human flight into the cosmos was haunted by the specter of modern bodies aflame in the global conflicts that attended cold war politics. Alongside spectacular photographs of NASA's rocket launches into space, perhaps no contemporary image attended Johnny's flaming body more immediately than that of the Buddhist monk whose act of self-immolation in 1963 shocked the world, one of the first public acts of protest that would mark the decade into which *The Fantastic Four* was unfolding with its readers. In the coming years the bodies of 1960s youth would be literally and figuratively aflame, radically queered by the sexual revolution, massacred by military violence, and incited to answer affirmatively with Johnny's claim "There's only one thing in the world that interests me more than cars!": "the search for truly democratic alternatives to the present."[37]

Object Lessons

We regard men as infinitely precious and possessed of unfulfilled capacities for reason, freedom, and love. In affirming these principles we are aware of countering perhaps the dominant conceptions of man in the twentieth century: that he is a thing to be manipulated. . . . We oppose the depersonalization that reduces human beings to the status of things.—STUDENTS FOR A DEMOCRATIC SOCIETY, *The Port Huron Statement* (1962)

I ain't Ben anymore—I'm what Susan called me—the Thing!—BEN GRIMM, *The Fantastic Four* #1 (November 1961)

Throughout the postwar period critics of the cold war culture of conformity repeatedly identified consumerism and the valorization of material wealth with a decline in democratic public life.[38] *The Fantastic Four*, however, argued that a willingness to be psychically and physically transformed by commodities in nonnormative ways could be an avenue for shaping a critical relationship between citizens and the products they commonly took for granted. By relating the disorienting psychic life of its characters to an equally unwieldy material object world presumed to produce "normal" citizens, *The Fantastic Four* located consumer durables and their everyday somatic textures as legitimate sites for theorizing an alternative or queer orientation toward self and society. Specifically *The Fantastic Four* redirected the homophobic and sexist logic of anticommunist political rhetoric by reframing the world of commodities as a playground of queer pleasures that could provide tools for enacting nonnormative performances of gender. As Ahmed argues, "If the sexual involves the contingency of bodies coming into contact with other bodies . . . then sexual disorientation slides quickly into social disorientation, as a disorientation in how things are arranged."[39] Across the span of the series, the visual attention given to the tactility of Reed's, Ben's, and Johnny's physical forms encouraged readers to take pleasure in the display of bodies and objects whose encounters disoriented the arrangement of normative heterosexuality, becoming a locus for unpredictable, queer desires.

The Fantastic Four #14 offers an exemplary instance of such queer encounters. In this issue Reed, Ben, and Johnny travel to the depths of the Atlantic Ocean to confront Prince Namor after he kidnaps Sue. The ensuing battle is visually staged as a series of encounters between the chaotic bodies of the three superheroes and an array of tactile ocean creatures that Namor deploys as weapons against his adversaries (plate 5).[40] First, Namor takes on the Human Torch with a "flame eater," a pole capped with two giant sea anemones whose tentacles sap the heat from Johnny's flaming body. Next, Namor confronts the Thing, initially stalling him with a "dagger-needle coral," its sharp spines piercing the hero's rocky skin, then entrapping him in a fast-growing ocean fungus that hardens into bone. Finally, Mr. Fantastic transforms his body into a living net, extending his arms into a vast latticework that ensnares Namor before he summons another weapon.

In this visually exuberant and entertaining scene, the battle between the Fantastic Four and Namor is presented as a struggle between competing material textures that carry the imprint of both natural and man-made objects. The flame-eater resembles a household mop, the dagger-needle coral a pincushion, and the fungus dishwashing foam. Namor explicitly links his creatures to such products when he describes the flame-eater as "absorbing the heat" from Johnny's body like "a sponge absorbs water." The visual pleasure of the scene lies less in physical violence than in the bizarre encounters between the fantastic bodies of the teammates and the unusual physical properties of Namor's ocean creatures. The scene elicits wonder in unexpected physical transformations that result from the vulnerability of the putatively straight male superhero's body to outside forces. Not only do Namor's various sea creatures appear as feminine domestic products; they also temporarily emasculate the Human Torch and the Thing, the former brought to his knees by the flame-eater's enervating touch. Similarly, by using his own body to subdue Namor, Reed simultaneously exercises his masculinity even as the visual display of his soft and distended limbs implies his body's loss of specific gender. The gendered politics of the team, then, were implicated in the proximities of bodies to particular kinds of objects and their somatic experiences, both of which were situated in the historical specificities of postwar domestic material life.

Concurrent with the sensory political discourse of anticommunism and the normalizing project of psychoanalysis, postwar American culture was flooded with an array of consumer durables born in the age of plastics, the synthetic revolution facilitated by wartime manufacturing and extraordinary advances in the study of molecular engineering. These innovations brought engineered substances like nylon, rayon, and a variety of moldable hard plastics into daily proximity with the bodies of ordinary citizens. By 1960 "baby boomers played with Wham-O hula hoops [and] Barbie dolls... and their families experienced Tupperware... laundry baskets... Saran Wrap" as part of everyday life.[41] The malleability of these inventions alongside an unprecedented material durability figuratively captured the wider cultural contradictions between the boundless possibilities of postwar economic and social progress and desires to contain such possibilities within rigidly gendered heterosexual spaces.

As we have seen in the three male figures of *The Fantastic Four*, the series' conceptual project was to offer the contradictions inherent in the postwar discourses of anticommunism and psychological "normality" as the very condition by which the body's materiality took shape, by dissolving the distinction between a private biological self and a public world of consumer objects. This project took on its most radical expression in the series' lead female character, Sue Storm, the Invisible Girl. In her revolutionary 1963 polemic, *The Feminine Mystique*, Betty Friedan identified the domestic housewife as a paragon of women's social invisibility, a figure whose professional ambitions and political influence were rerouted toward the maintenance of normative family life. It would be in performing that same role that Sue Storm would become a *literal* invisible woman, capable of vanishing from sight at will. Unlike her teammates, who *fail* to identify with normative masculinity, Sue is better understood as *disidentifying* with proper femininity. According to Muñoz, disidentification describes an attempt to transform the limits of one's subject position by performing it in unexpected or unpredictable ways. To disidentify is neither to "buckle under the pressures of dominant ideology" nor "to break free of its inescapable sphere" but rather to rearticulate a set of norms to new meanings through spectacular and critical performances of those norms.[42] Just as contemporary feminist thinkers sought to make visible the taken-for-granted structure of patriarchy in the 1960s, Sue's power similarly made the concept of women's social invisibility an object of visual critique by making invisible bodies and objects conspicuous on the comic book page. When using her powers, Sue commonly appears as a ghost-like outline clearly visible to the reader, marking the very performance of invisibility as worthy of symbolic recognition. It is *through* invisibility, rather than an attempt to escape the social stigma of being invisible and unrecognized, that Sue would alter the meanings that attached to postwar women's supposedly docile, domestic bodies.

One strategy the series took to highlight Sue's disidentification with normative femininity was to show her powers evolving, granting her two new abilities in issue #22: an invisible force shield and the ability to extend her invisibility to other objects and bodies. These transformations were the result of readers' insistence that Sue model empowered woman-hood in the 1960s. To induct her newfound abilities into the visual logic of the comic book, a series of tests are presented by way of encounters between the physical form of Sue's shield and the textural surface of her teammates' bodies (plate 6). At first Sue's shield recalls the structure of weak plastic, softening under the pressure of Reed's elastic arm. But with concentration she soon wields a shield powerful enough to repel the Thing, proving herself literally impenetrable to "hard" masculinity. In this jocular scene Sue's invisibility becomes not merely a social meta-phor she struggles against but a tactile force that extends her disidenti-fication with normative femininity into the world at large.[43] As Judith Butler writes, "It may be precisely through practices which underscore disidentification with those regulatory norms by which sexual difference is materialized that both feminist and queer politics are mobilized. Such collective disidentification can facilitate a reconceptualization of which bodies matter and which bodies are yet to emerge as critical matters of concern."[44] By physically manifesting invisibility as a material skin, Sue was forced to inhabit it—and the gendered norms it attached to—as a condition of her claiming a self. The outcome was to make her body *mat-ter to* audiences but also to *matter forth* on the page through the exten-sion of her powerful body into space.

The transparent surfaces of Sue's power carried a host of gendered meanings. Her invisible force shield resembled the flexible hardness of Tupperware and the translucent sheen of cellophane, two postwar inven-tions that became household staples of suburbia's invisible woman, yet its spherical shape and impenetrable surface also referenced tools of wom-en's liberation, such as the diaphragm and the birth control pill.[45] These dual meanings would compete in Sue's deployment of her powers both as a powerful containment device and a flexible material extension of her self-determination. Throughout the series Sue is called upon to employ her shield as a powerful vacuum that helps contain air and water, its edges capable of being raised and replaced like the famous Tupperware seal. At other times it becomes a tool of self-expression and libidinal pleasure. In one instance, when Sue becomes the central focus of a *Life* magazine editorial on the Fantastic Four, she poses flirtatiously for the cameraman, alternately making herself invisible from the waist down and the waist up, making different parts of her body available for visual consumption.[46] Even as she is forced to work within the visual conventions of the male gaze, she exploits her invisibility as a site of visual pleasure that highlights both her ability to control what the camera looks at and the desirability of her body.

Sue's exercise of her evolving powers and the subsequent transformations in personality that made her a more "visible" actor in the Fantastic Four's unfolding dramas were not merely willful acts of agency or a simple refusal of the norms of womanhood, but were taken up in and through the very act of performing "femaleness" that had once seemed to make her invisible both socially and materially. This was made clear in a 1963 Invisible Girl Pin-up Page that presented Sue in her Fantastic Four costume waving to fans from the cockpit of the team's "Fantasticar" high above the Manhattan skyline (figure 2.3).[47] Sue's pose is a direct visual reference to Marilyn Monroe's sultry wave in her famous cover photo for the inaugural 1953 issue of *Playboy*. Sue's bobbed hair and regal manner, however, link her to the elegant femininity of Jacqueline Kennedy. Sue performs these competing types of hyperfemininity within the traditionally male role of a superheroic adventurer. Ironically, rather than call attention to her femininity, the narrator's note above her head reads, "In answer to many requests, note the details in the control panel of Sue's section of the fabulous Fantasti-car!" These details can be see through the translucent portion of Sue's legs, implying that readers' fandom of Sue is as much linked to her femininity as to their interest in the technologies of the space age, technologies that *The Fantastic Four* articulated to an array of unwieldy, playful, and erotically charged bodies across gendered types.

Certainly Sue's powers did not liberate her from the meanings attached to invisibility, and such displays as the *Life* magazine photo shoot and the Fantasti-car pinup displayed the extent of objectification that could result from the public performance of her powers. Yet these instances of feminine performance also presented a playful working against the normative underpinnings of the visibility of female bodies by displaying Sue's shifting skein of invisibility as a polymorphous surface of pleasure that echoed new conceptions of women's sexuality emerging in the mid-1960s from the writings of radical feminists and popular sexologists. If

FIGURE 2.3. "Sue Storm, the Glamorous Invisible Girl." Stan Lee (writer) and Jack Kirby (penciller), "The Return of Doctor Doom," *Fantastic Four* #10, January 1963, reprinted in *Fantastic Four Omnibus Vol. 1* (New York: Marvel Comics, 2007), 266.

traditional conceptions of sexuality in the 1950s limited the locus of a woman's pleasure to the opposite sex, a new understanding of women as capable of gaining autonomous bodily pleasure through interaction with their own body (masturbatory or otherwise) became increasingly popular in the wake of the Kinsey reports (1948, 1953) and the Masters and Johnson study (1966) on human sexuality.[48] In scenes like the *Life* magazine photo shoot and the Fantasti-car pinup page, Sue's body visually develops just such an autonomous female subject capable of commanding her own sexuality as well as the pleasures of those around her, simultaneously laying bear and disidentifying with the visual conventions of heterosexual desire. In Sue Storm *The Fantastic Four* attempted to wed femininity with a queerly inflected feminism through a symbolic restructuring of the relations between women's bodies and the material object world of postwar domesticity.

Unstable Molecules

In the early 1960s *The Fantastic Four* recast the superhero as a figure of nonnormativity that functioned as a visual palimpsest for a host of postwar discourses of normalization that would be radically undone by the unstable physiology of the superhuman body. In each character the series took on a primary narrative of postwar normalization—anticommunism, psychoanalysis, consumer society, domesticity—and used the mutated biology of the superhero to alter or wholly upend the meanings that attach to these regulatory regimes. This transformation in the symbolic structures of normalization was effected by an equivalent reworking of the gender and sexual identity of each character. Reed's and Ben's physical softening and hardening rendered them unable to embody ideal masculinity, Johnny's flaming body destabilized his performance of proper teenage male heterosexuality, and Sue's shifting surface of invisibility simultaneously identified her as a figure of hyperbolic femininity and radical feminism. In this way *The Fantastic Four* worked within the very ideological structures of cold war America to produce an array of nonnormative or queer bodies that would be oriented toward a more politically radical and sexually polymorphous future.

Yet, like any political project or ideology, these transformations required an image to organize and direct the social relations that might unfold from them. If Kennedy's New Frontier took as its emblem the sleek, phallic figure of the rocket flight into space, *The Fantastic Four* found its greatest icon in the molecule, a miniature elastic world small enough to reside in human DNA but vast enough to form complex chains that made up the synthetic materials of an external object world. The link between the molecular structure of material objects and the most intimate aspects of human biology was dramatized in the Fantastic Four's costumes, blue and white jumpsuits made of a synthetic variant of the same unstable molecules that constituted the four heroes' mutated bodies. This allowed the suits to adapt to the teammates' powers—stretching with Reed's body or turning invisible at Sue's command—because of their shared molecular properties. Just as the teammates' bodies were physical manifestations of molecular structures gone haywire, they were also enveloped by and in turn helped shape the contours of experimental material substances.

As a physically bonded structure relying on varying degrees of solidarity between individual atoms to produce increasingly complex molecular chains, the molecule became a rich metaphor for dynamic human interactions and affiliations. In *The Fantastic Four* the unstable molecule came to stand in for both the instability of the distinction between human and inhuman and the dysfunctional or volatile character of familial relations. As *The Fantastic Four* developed in its first years of publication, the family and the team became synonymous as a chosen kinship whose connections were never assured but required reaffirmation through acts of willed solidarity. Rather than being the foundational unit of national community, as it was understood by the rhetoric of cold war containment, the Fantastic Four's familial bond functioned as one site among many through which cosmopolitan forms of affiliation could be developed. When the characters attempt to rely on idealized notions of family—including heterosexual intimacy and gendered power relations—their sense of security is undone as they realize that their "family" ties involve alternative forms of relationality based on shared *differences* rather than the assumption of traditional heterosexual familial roles.

The most visible heterosexual union of the foursome was that of Reed and Sue, who were initially presented as fiancés. The team's inaugural trip to space derails their plans for marriage, while Sue's expanding repertoire of powers gives her a newfound sense of confidence to stand up to Reed's patronizing ways. The team's many crossings with an expanding world of superhumans further complicates their romance. When the Fantastic Four first battle the Ocean King, Prince Namor, in a struggle to save New York from his vengeful plans to flood the city, Namor is taken aback by Sue's beauty and compassion for someone whose life experiences seem so different from her own.[49] Though he often expressed his affections in violent displays of machismo, Namor came to represent a compelling alternative to Reed's rigid, scientific worldview, as a dreamy, exotic, half-naked ocean god. The incipient romance between Namor and Sue would produce an interspecies love triangle that unfolded for nearly thirty issues before Sue finally expressed her unwavering love for Reed. Even so, marriage would not provide the Fantastic Four with a "normal" outcome to the queer bonds they had forged. The marriage between Sue and Reed in the 1965 *Fantastic Four Annual* was a hyperbolic expression of domestic bliss, undercut by its own theatricality and by the disruption of the ceremony by countless villains attempting to destroy the foursome on the special occasion.[50] Moreover naïve gestures toward traditional matrimony surely rang hollow to a teenage readership growing up in the midst of a burgeoning sexual revolution. As though anticipating this fact, the creators gave their audience the marriage they had been expecting, while depicting Reed and Sue's married life as highly dysfunctional in ensuing issues.

Simultaneously the team members' wish to see one another achieve "normal," happy lives in wedded bliss often conflicted with a shared attachment to their alternative kinship. In the opening scene to issue #32, Reed unveils a new device that he claims might permanently transform the Thing back into his human form. Hearing the news, Johnny thinks out loud, "Then he can marry Alicia...and settle down! It's what he wants....He's my big buddy...and I want him to be normal to marry the gal he loves...but why can't he be the Thing also??! He's one of us...he belongs! Nuts! If the experiment fails, I'll be sorry for him...but if it works I'll be sorry for me! I don't know what to hope for!" Johnny's ambivalence over Ben's potentially permanent transformation into human form—his desire to both retain the "queer" elements of Ben's mutated body that makes him an integral part of the team while acknowledging the normal heterosexual life he could lead without them—speaks to a desire for a family that, like an unstable molecule, could hold all of these possibilities within it. These family dysfunctions and internal conflicts signaled a desire for queer bodies within the space of the family form, a willful embrace of nonnormative expressions of gender and sexuality that become the ground of alternative modes of intimacy and affiliation.

* * *

Across the 1960s *The Fantastic Four*'s queer solidarity modeled on the figure of the unstable molecule came to resonate with a countercultural worldview that celebrated nonnormative kinship structures and alternative political alliances. This same worldview sought to create a new relationship between U.S. citizens and the products of postwar science that was not based on exploitation, alienation, and violence. As I discuss in the next chapter, the overwhelmingly positive reader response to the series' radical reinvention of the superhero helped articulate *The Fantastic Four*'s narrative and visual content to larger political realities unfolding across the 1960s, including early feminist politics and cold war geopolitics. In its early years *The Fantastic Four* was driven by the question "What difference does it make what or who we are oriented toward in the very direction of our desire?"[51] By the mid-1960s its answer would be *worlds of difference.* This world-centered mode of thinking was made possible by *The Fantastic Four*'s recasting of the superhero as a paragon of nonnormative gender and sexual identity, a figure whose deviant bodily morphology could open up the superhero to a universe of equally deviant relations. A final image can help illuminate how *The Fantastic Four*'s queering of the superhuman became a common trope extending into the 1970s.

The attendees of the 1974 Comic Art Convention, an annual meeting of the greatest creative talents and fans of the mainstream comic book industry, were in for a humorous surprise when they opened their program books that year. Amid black-and-white advertisements, interviews, and convention venue logistics, Marvel Comics proudly displayed a double-page spread of the Thing posing nude in the mode of a *Playboy* pinup (plate 7). Against a bright red background, the Thing reclines on a leopard-print rug, the knee of his leg covering his presumably unrepresentable nether regions. In his left hand he carries a cigar, while a rose sticks out from behind his ear, his head coquettishly resting on his right arm as he winks at his fans. "You were expectin' maybe Burt Reynolds?" he intones, referencing the provocative 1972 *Cosmopolitan* magazine spread of the sultry movie star on which the image is based. Only months prior to the convention, Marvel had printed a special issue of its company fan magazine *Foom* (Friends of Ol' Marvel), dedicated to Benjamin Grimm. In contrast to the eroticized Comic Art Convention pinup, the opening page of the main article presented the Thing dressed in full cowboy regalia with two revolvers pointed at the reader, stand-ins for the appendage so conspicuously occluded in the later display (plate 8).[52]

Rather than solidify the hard-bodied stereotype of the superhero, this hyperbolic performance of dual gender roles speaks to the ways the Thing's rock-like skin made his body open to erotic pleasure and semiotic play, allowing his character to accommodate the varied gender identities demanded by visual genres as diverse as the pinup and the western. In these moments, so often enacted in the comic book itself, connotations of masculine "hardness" and impenetrability commonly attached to Ben's body were made to articulate with softness, femininity, and eroticism. More important, the sexualization of the Thing in such displays, particularly in the scopophilic interest in the textures of his stony skin, suggests the ways the narrative of the Fantastic Four opened up the body of the superhero to the politics of sexuality and the relationship between postwar sexual discourses and material culture.[53] By 1974 sex and gender had indeed dramatically changed in the modern United States: that Burt Reynolds could pose nude in a mainstream fashion periodical as an object of erotic visual pleasure attested to the degree to which the regulatory regimes that had guarded men's bodies from visual display in American culture had been deeply shaken by the sexual revolution, women's liberation, and the counterculture. That the Thing could stand in for this transformation was evidence of *The Fantastic Four*'s long-term investment in recasting the rigidly defended body of the cold war citizen as an unpredictable and adaptable surface of pleasure and transformation.

Such bodily fluidity and its material effects was not lost on the Fantastic Four themselves, who were made fully aware of the deviant potential of their genetic difference when the question of heterosexual reproduction took center stage. In 1968, on the eve of *The Fantastic Four*'s eightieth issue, Sue would announce that she and Reed were going to have a baby.[54] Amid much celebration a lone soul grew increasingly anxious about the biological consequences of bearing a child from genetically mutated parents. This was one possibility Reed found he could not control, scientifically or otherwise. In a stunning display of rigid biologism that foreshadowed debates about the existence of a "gay gene" and prenatal disability testing, Reed wondered to himself if the baby he and Sue had conceived would be born a "freak." Perhaps he had seen *Life* magazine's famous 1965 sequence of photographs charting the development of a healthy human fetus; perhaps that same image of pristine humanity was punctured by memories of his own fateful exclamation about the team's rocket ship years before, "She's behaving like a baby! Everything is perfect," just before a hail of cosmic rays changed the Fantastic Four's lives forever. Though in the narrative proper Marvel's first family prepared for the birth of a potentially superpowered freak, no narrative act of contrition could erase a basic fact: it was in the pages of *The Fantastic Four* that the queer generation of superheroes was born.

3 / Comic Book Cosmopolitics: *The Fantastic Four*'s Counterpublic as a World-Making Project

The main thing that made my heart sing is the latest in your concerted effort to bring comic literature to a more adult level by portraying members of races other than the white. I have a feeling that the Black Panther will turn out to be the first great Negro hero-villain in comic book history! . . . An African king at that! Most of all, I am gratified at the introduction of Wyatt Wingfoot to your pantheon of characters. Being partially of American Indian ancestry myself, I am always happy to see a modern Indian shown as being something besides a poor relic of the past. Wingfoot's pride, his skill, and his dignity are in keeping with the real tradition of the past.
—KEN GREENE, letter published in *The Fantastic Four* #55 (October 1966)

In September 1964 a note from Bruce Hall of Winchester, Indiana, was published in the letters column of *The Fantastic Four* #30: "Dear Stan and Jack: I simply must send my thanks and congratulations for so many super stories. You guys make me feel like I know you personally when I read the fan pages. . . . I don't know exactly how to say this but I feel like all the comic characters are my personal friends."[1] In his heartfelt praise for *The Fantastic Four*, Hall voiced a common sentiment among both hardcore and mainstream fans of the series. Like Hall, these readers used the language of intimacy and emotional identification to describe a developing relationship between creators and fans of *The Fantastic Four*. The reasons for this relationship were numerous. Fans alternately pointed to the comics' "realism" and social relevance, the emotional dynamic between characters, the pleasures of artist Jack Kirby's bombastic visual style, and the sincerity of the rapport that Kirby and writer Stan Lee developed with their readership, as sources for the powerful emotional bond forged between readers, creators, and an expanding world of non-human and "inhuman" characters. Moreover these sentiments were expressed in numerous printed letters by a larger and diverse body of readers—including women, minorities, and college-age and elderly readers—who were not previously comic book devotees.

While a number of *The Fantastic Four*'s most avid followers read DC Comics—their missives also featured in DC letters columns—countless other mainstream fans claimed it was Marvel's unique narrative and visual style that led them to read the comics they had derided as juvenile entertainment only a few years before. Unlike *The Justice League of America*, which played on the well-worn narrative structures of pre–World War II superhero comics (if in a decidedly internationalist vein), *The Fantastic Four* used narrative irony, a hyperbolically "campy" visual style, and a playful reworking of gender and sexual norms to garner a politically literate readership attuned to the comic's urbane sensibilities. In the series' first letters column, Lee and Kirby noted that, "unlike many other collections of letters in different mags, our fans all seem to write well, and intelligently. We assume this denotes that our readers are a cut above average, and that's the way we like 'em!"[2] The sense that Lee and Kirby genuinely trusted the opinions of their readers seems to have galvanized fans and critics to write more elaborate letters addressing a variety of aesthetic, political, and technical concerns regarding the series' developing story lines. In response to growing fan correspondence, *The Fantastic Four* letters column was expanded to two full pages in issue #10. In this enlarged format, Lee and Kirby responded more frequently to the letters they published, cracking jokes and poking fun at their readers as much as they responded seriously to their ideas, and solicited opinions on controversial topics regarding the series' visual and narrative content.

From the outset Lee and Kirby self-consciously framed *The Fantastic Four* letters column as a forum for discussing the transformations taking place in Marvel Comics, and U.S. culture more broadly, in the 1960s. It soon became a social laboratory for the production of a new counterpublic, the Marvel Comics readership. Here, in keeping with Michael Warner's concept of a "counterpublic," readers were welcome to express politically unfashionable or radical ideals through the discursive apparatus of a culturally denigrated medium. As Warner explains, "A counterpublic maintains at some level, conscious or not, an awareness of its subordinate status. The cultural horizon against which it marks itself off is not just a general or wider public but a dominant one. And the conflict extends not just to ideas or policy questions but to . . . the hierarchy among media. The discourse that constitutes it is not merely a different or alternative idiom but one that in other contexts would be regarded with hostility or . . . indecorousness."[3] In all of their creative productions, Lee and Kirby acknowledged the subordinate status of the medium in which they narrated their greatest stories, while encouraging readers to identify themselves with the pleasures and possibilities of comic book fandom. They also openly celebrated the seemingly contradictory juxtaposition of serious aesthetic and political debate in a form commonly derided as trash. By taking the superhero comic book seriously as a site for developing an alternative reader sociality, one that was often (though not always) organized by distinctly left-of-center political ideals, Marvel writers and artists encouraged readers to see comic book aesthetics as a vehicle for producing alternative social and political imaginaries. Readers responded by developing sophisticated interpretive practices through which they linked the fantasy content of Marvel Comics to larger questions of political concern, consequently demanding new forms of conceptual innovation and political accountability from the creators of their favorite stories.

In calling the Marvel readership a counterpublic, I do not intend to suggest that it was an easily identifiable or delimited group of specific individuals motivated by clearly defined or universally shared goals. After all Lee and Kirby's expansive "familial" vision of the Marvel community as a growing kinship modeled on the supposed camaraderie of the company's "Bullpen" (the collective of editors, writers, artists, and office personnel who composed Marvel's staff) accommodated multiple and often competing forms of fandom within the growing Marvel Comics readership. This included so-called Marvel Zombies, the moniker given to hardcore fans who obsessively collected every comic book issue Marvel creators produced, as well as a wide-reaching mainstream readership drawn to particular Marvel comics like *The Fantastic Four* because of their socially aware content, visual exuberance, and participatory reading community.[4] Rather I understand the counterpublic status of Marvel's readership to be a product of the complex discursive production of *The Fantastic Four* letters column; this production took shape through an ongoing negotiation between critical fan responses to Marvel Comics' content, editorial curatorship of fans' extraordinary written output, and writers' and artists' creative responses to fan commentary within the actual fantasy narratives of the comics themselves.

According to numerous personal and journalistic accounts of Marvel Comics in the mid- to late 1960s, their offices in Manhattan received hundreds, sometimes thousands of letters a month in response to their various comic book productions, with *The Fantastic Four* garnering the most enthusiastic response rate of Marvel's lineup. Because of the difficulties involved in cataloguing and storing this expansive archive, the vast majority of fan letter output is lost to the historical record, usually destroyed by companies to preserve space for storing artwork. Printed correspondence in comic book letters columns could be considered extremely limited as a representative sample of actual readers compared to the massive outpouring of letters received by Marvel. Letters columns appeared as one- or two-page inserts following the conclusion of an issue's main story, generally showcasing between six and twelve letters, depending on length; editors often pared down or abridged longer letters, exercising a powerful editorial hand over which letters (and what parts of those letters) were displayed and which remained inaccessible to the public. A true sense of the heterogeneity of Marvel's readership is further occluded by the overrepresentation of so-called hardcore fans in both the American comics archive and comic scholarship. These fans' intense commitment to comic book readership and collecting led them to produce fanzines, keep extensive comic book collections, and maintain records of their correspondence with other fans and creators, all of which have provided a rich but narrowly focused set of sources that scholars have often used to narrate the history of comics fandom.[5]

Despite all this, letters columns, and *The Fantastic Four*'s in particular, stand out as an important source of cultural knowledge because of their extraordinary range of demographic representation, aesthetic and political points of view, and forms of fan response to both the content of superhero comics and the opinions of other fans. Unlike the local reach of fanzines and interpersonal correspondence between members of fan clubs, printed letters in the monthly letter columns of *The Fantastic Four* circulated to hundreds of thousands of readers, thereby projecting a small sampling of audience responses to a wider mass public whose effects, including the solicitation of ever greater volumes of fan correspondence, far exceeded their limited number.[6] The heavy curatorship of editors in shaping the letters column self-consciously produced it as a space of debate, dialogue, and transformative disagreement; undoubtedly this was an editorial strategy to distinguish Marvel as a "hip" company catering to youth and the counterculture, yet regardless of editorial motives, it ultimately produced the conditions under which Marvel fans and letter writers became active participants in shaping the visual landscape and ideological worldview of *The Fantastic Four*. Reading the series over time, fans could observe how the content of printed letters (and the aggregate opinions of unpublished letters they stood in for) had a tangible effect on the visual and narrative content of *The Fantastic Four* issue by issue. In this way, even as they could not possibly represent the entire mass of actual fan letters to Marvel Comics, printed letters came to embody the spirit of a critical counterpublic, appearing as an alternative textual voice within the actual content of a given issue that influenced the future trajectory of the series.

In this chapter I analyze the development of *The Fantastic Four*'s counterpublic as an extension of the series' critique of normative gender and sexuality and its attempt to develop a new ethical stance toward the concept of "the human." I conceive of this counterpublic as a worldmaking project rather than merely a series of discreet exchanges because it fostered the development of a new social world between previously disconnected comic book fans *through* the literal invention of an expanding imaginative world, the Marvel Universe. Over the course of the series' first six years of publication, readers encouraged creators to expand the geographical and political limits of *The Fantastic Four*'s imaginary world far beyond the borders of the nation, introduce more racially diverse characters, and offer alternative images of cross-racial and cross-species solidarity that were not sanctioned by state power. It would be at the nexus of an emergent reader sociality and the production of an ever expanding fantasy world of alien and nonhuman "others" that a new cosmopolitan orientation to American social and political life would be forged within *The Fantastic Four*'s counterpublic.

As this counterpublic took shape, Lee and Kirby developed new forms of address to better connect readers to one another. In 1964 they introduced their growing fan base to Marvel's company fan club, the Merry Marvel Marching Society. Within the rhetoric of this new institution, to be a Marvel reader was simultaneously to be part of the "Marvel family," a kinship of strangers and intimates that mirrored the ever expanding familial bonds of the characters in Marvel's pantheon (and the real-world associations among Marvel staffers). This Marvel family took shape against a loosely defined social outside made up of so-called normal people who failed to understand the appeal of the comics Marvel readers held in such high regard. These included people who saw comics as worthless or labeled those who read them as weird or nerdy; people who supported antidemocratic, racist, or sexist worldviews; and people who were simply "square" or unwilling to experiment with new forms of popular culture.

The sensibility of this counterpublic linked a shared pleasure in superheroic fantasy with a value for the status of the outsider or socially maladjusted, a figure that the superhero, and its fans, had clearly both become. This valuation of the social outcast had a distinctly ethical dimension; in the published record of letter columns, one finds that while readers disagreed, often vehemently, on specific political or aesthetic issues, they collectively expressed a commitment to democratic dialogue and mutual respect for divergent ideas while working to cultivate skills in negotiating multiple experiences of difference and outsider status. To belong to the MMMS, it was implied, was to be both open-minded toward popular fantasy and liberal-minded toward social change. This fact was affirmed in *The Fantastic Four* letter columns, where readers repeatedly articulated the pleasures of superheroic fantasy to progressive political desires or investments. In a letter published in issue #32 Isabelle Kamishlian and J. Geoffrey Magnus of Bard College claimed, "Though to many others [comic books] seem to consist of light matter, we have become attuned to . . . their role in promoting cultural unity and integration."[7] As the epigraph to this chapter attests, readers like Ken Greene saw *The Fantastic Four* as a creative space where ethnoracial minorities subject to bigotry and violence in the real world could be represented as courageous allies or even heroes in their own right, who were valued by the misfits and social outcasts of the fictional Marvel Universe. By asking creators to expand the diversity of the Fantastic Four's social relations, offer more innovative and progressive expressions of the teammates' individual identities, and bring new and unexpected characters into the fold of their kinship, readers helped make the Fantastic Four itself into a fictional counterpublic that mirrored the ideals and values of an emergent Marvel comics family. Simultaneously, by curating letters in such a way as to highlight substantive differences of opinion on both aesthetic and political concerns, Lee and Kirby helped bring into being and performatively modeled the cosmopolitan spirit of engagement they imbued their characters with.

As I argued in chapter 2, *The Fantastic Four's* visual transformation of cold war gender and sexual norms helped make the nuclear family a site for exploring a variety of progressive political aspirations. As the series evolved, these aspirations came to include the struggle for domestic racial and class equality and Third World decolonization. This transformation was the result of the shifting political ideals of the series' readership but also an organic evolution of *The Fantastic Four's* own creative premise: if the Fantastic Four were "more than just human," the series asked, did that make them another *species*? Alternatively, did their biological difference from humanity make them a different *race* despite their putative whiteness? If so, what forms of affiliation and solidarity might address the uneven experience of human difference while binding diverse peoples together in the struggle for political freedom? These were not only imaginative questions that unfolded in the pages of the comic but also the political inquiries that drove the radical social projects of the New Left in the 1960s.

Through a series of mutually transformative dialogues between readers and creators in the mid-1960s, *The Fantastic Four*'s initial focus on gender and sexual nonnormativity evolved into a focus on questions of ethnoracial and species identity. Consequently the comic book's visual content became aligned with an emergent form of radical internationalism modeled by groups like Students for a Democratic Society, the Third World Left, and the Black Panther Party. This was not the liberal internationalism of *The Justice League of America* but rather a radical critique of cold war geopolitics that identified and condemned the unequal distribution of economic, cultural, and political resources to Third World nations, refugees, and ethnoracial minorities at home and abroad. Like the radical movements it spoke to and borrowed from, *The Fantastic Four*'s comic book cosmopolitics emerged from a genuine investment in valuing the lives of those deemed "inhuman" or disposable by the standards of Western imperialism.

Politics in Unlikely Places: The Letters Column as a Counterpublic

The letters column was first introduced to readers in the September 1958 issue of DC Comics' *Superman*. It provided readers of postwar superhero comics a space to publicly voice their affective, aesthetic, and political orientations toward the visual content of their favorite popular fantasies. Early DC Comics letters pages were organized by a clear hierarchy of power between editors and readers. In the letters section of *The Justice League of America*, editors consistently defused potential political clashes between readers, commonly responded to readers' critiques of narrative inaccuracies with condescending rebuttals, and made only minor adjustments to the series' content based on reader feedback. Creators saw themselves as pedagogues offering readers limited opportunities to voice their opinions while reserving the last word on conversations fomented within the space of the column.

Under the creative oversight of Stan Lee and Jack Kirby in the early 1960s, Marvel Comics transformed the affective dimensions of letters columns by recasting the relationship between creators and fans as a form of creative camaraderie. This was impressed upon readers when, in *The Fantastic Four* #10, the creative duo abandoned the salutation "Dear Editor" in printed letters in favor of the informal greeting "Dear Stan and Jack." They informed their readers, "Enough of that 'Dear Editor' jazz from now on! Jack Kirby and Stan Lee (that's us!) read every letter personally, and we like to feel that we know you and that you know us! So we changed the salutations in the following letters to show you how much friendlier they sound our way."[8] Lee and Kirby actively courted controversy and generated dialogue among readers by putting a variety of issues—from Invisible Girl's hairdo to the representation of communists—up for a vote while encouraging fans to voice their opinions about these matters across the political spectrum.

Unlike DC Comics, which tried to recapture the attention of its now significantly older pre–World War II readership, Marvel Comics sold its worldview to anyone willing to give their comics a passing glance, while seeking out a college-age youth market that was often amenable to countercultural ideals, if not avowedly leftist. Certainly not all or even the majority of Marvel's readership believed that comics should espouse liberal ideals or express any political orientation, yet Lee and Kirby spotlighted letters that interpreted the content of Marvel Comics as a form of progressive social commentary, empowered fans from the entire political spectrum to join dynamic debates about anticommunism, the representation of women and minorities in comics, and the ethics of the space race. If there was any pedagogical thrust to Lee and Kirby's editorial responses it was toward convincing skeptical readers of the values of liberal tolerance (in the form of antiracism and antifascism), social responsibility, and awareness of personal privilege. Such values were not only espoused by Lee and Kirby, as well as their characters, but were also performed by fan writers themselves, often in radical ways that far exceeded the limits of Lee and Kirby's liberal imaginary.

Fan letters are an extraordinary archive for documenting the development of a political imagination among comic book readers, but they are notoriously unwieldy documents. Unlike the visual content of comics, which is explicitly fictional, fan letters are presented as putatively real responses *to* fictional texts. Yet they also produce their own social worlds, modes of address, and internal regulations. Letters also have the potential to be falsified or doctored by editors. Finally, as I have already suggested, the winnowing down of presumably hundreds (even thousands) of letters to a select few to be published in each month's column was necessarily informed by editorial determinations and market interests. One way to approach published letters, then, is with skepticism about the potentially questionable veracity of some letters (even though many can be reasonably identified with actual fan writers) as well as the creative control that editors exerted over these forums. While such a view can be seen as legitimate, it has the disadvantage of highlighting the structural constraints of fan-creator correspondence at the expense of the actual discursive content and modes of creative interaction that such correspondence enabled; thus it severely limits what we can learn about the kind of sensibility and worldview these letters may have transmitted for readers and creators. Keeping in mind the historical limitations that frame letters columns, I strategically bracket concerns about the veracity and representative quality of individual letters, treating them instead as genuine expressions of fan communication to spotlight the conversations they fomented and the cosmopolitan ethos they cultivated in their form and content.

The aesthetic and political dialogues in *The Fantastic Four*'s letters column followed no single or clearly defined trajectory; conversations overlapped, contradicted, were taken up or dropped in rapid succession. Yet from these competing lines of flight emerged trends and recurrent dialogues that would have lasting effects on the visual and narrative content of the Marvel Comics universe and the social character of its evolving counterpublic. The overarching trajectory of these conversations was a movement from questions of visual representation—the depiction of certain kinds of superhuman and gendered bodies—toward questions of world making that addressed the series' broader political commitments and the formal tools through which it made claims about the "real" world. These conversations captured a general shift in the scale of dialogue (from individual bodies to social worlds) that reflected the expanding imaginative locus of the Marvel Universe. I analyze these conversations by attending to the ways that fan letters' content, structure, and mode of address articulated varying scales of intimacy—from local attachments between readers and their most cherished fictional characters to "global" affiliations between comic book texts and grand philosophical ideals—for the purpose of attaching wider political meaning to the interactions among characters, readers, and creators.

* * *

Among the handful of fan letters published in *The Fantastic Four* #6 was a brief missive by one Martin Ross: "Dear Editor: [*The Fantastic Four* is] the greatest! But I think Susan Storm ought to be thrown out. She never does anything."[9] Despite their seeming innocence, Ross's three short sentences would spark a furious debate in *The Fantastic Four* letters column about the role of the Invisible Girl in the team's unfolding adventures. This debate was facilitated by the spirited response to Ross's letter offered by Lee and Kirby in the same issue: "Well, this is the first anti–Invisible Girl letter we've received! What do the REST of you fans think?"[10] The sense that Invisible Girl's contributions to the team were limited was not merely subjective but an actual fictional dilemma in the narrative proper. Sue's powers often appeared weak and ineffectual next to her teammates', and she remained peripheral to their most exciting battles. Prior to Ross's bold assertion, more tempered fans like Scotty Smith had voiced similar complaints. "The FF is fantastic, wonderful, and amazing!" he claimed in issue #5, "But how about more action with Invisible Girl?"[11] That this problem should warrant Sue's removal from the team, however, was greeted with an emphatically negative response from fans.

"Angry Artie Starr" of Miami was the first to offer a rejoinder to Ross's letter. In issue #8 he declared, "Dear Editor: Who does Martin Ross think he is? In your #6 issue he wrote a letter saying that Susan Storm ought to be thrown out because she never does anything! If you ever throw that doll out, I want to know where you throw her, because I'm making a bee-line for that place! Take it from me . . . don't change anything bout your mag, and especially your characters."[12] Artie's vehement rebuttal was followed two issues later with the printed results of the poll Lee and Kirby had solicited in issue #6. According to the editors, "eight letters favored dropping Sue Storm, BUT 639 demanded that she remain one of the team!"[13] Starr's letter indicated readers' willingness to address one another directly, speak confidently about their interpretations of the text, and discuss the characters in affective or personal terms.

That Sue Storm, a figure invented and animated within the discourses of postwar patriarchy, would become the site for some of Marvel Comics' greatest fan controversies about making women more central (and hence more visible) to the narrative of the superhero comic book seems highly unexpected considering that these debates were fomented by young men whose investments were assumed to be in displays of masculine prowess and male-dominated adventure. These unlikely dialogues, however, were emblematic of a narrative that encouraged affiliations deemed socially taboo or underplayed in other modes of popular culture.

Having "proven" Sue's popularity among fans with their poll, Lee and Kirby unwittingly opened themselves to critiques of their failure to adequately represent her importance to the team. Here was an instance in which their careful curating of fan debate made possible an opening for counterpublic engagement, where fans sought to hold the creators accountable for their supposedly progressive social values. In the following months a variety of letters would voice frustration at Lee and Kirby's lack of creativity in maximizing Sue's heroism. One fan wrote: "Under the head of complaints, I have only one. It concerns the Invisible Girl. Now let me make it plain that I don't want her eliminated. She has too much potential for that. My complaint is that her potential is seldom utilized. I object chiefly to the fact that in eight stories, she has been captured by four of the villains. I think she would make a better action character than a hostage."[14] These criticisms led directly to the evolution of Sue's powers in issue #22 of the series, encouraging Lee and Kirby to recast her invisibility as an offensive force that she could extend into the world at large rather than merely a defensive posture.

These dialogues were powerful enough to transform not only the visual content of the narrative proper but also the hearts and minds of readers. In issue #13 Martin Ross would write to *The Fantastic Four* to amend his previous claims:

> Well, it looks about time for me to eat crow! . . . After having read *A Day with the Fantastic Four* in FF #11, and seeing the part where Sue goes to pieces, I realize what a mistake I made. I guess my mind slipped back to the days of the old time serials, and the damsels in distress. You know, it's the same way in life as it is in comics. You tend to think little of someone because you don't understand them or what they stand for. In closing, I say that Lee and Kirby convey my deepest apologies to Sue . . . and tell her that from now on, she's a friend of mine.[15]

In his hyperbolic mea culpa, Ross revealed a telling paradox in the logic that framed his change of heart: at the same time that he claimed it took real-life experience with people different from oneself to develop understanding and goodwill toward others, he implicitly equated such experiences with reading *The Fantastic Four*, a fictional text that, arguably, required little if any physical interaction with the outside world to entertain its audience. In this way Ross suggested that certain popular texts had the capacity to reproduce the *feel* of real-life interaction. In the case of *The Fantastic Four* such interaction was an inherent element of the reading experience itself. The presence of the letters column encouraged any single reader to take into account the reading community that shaped the narrative they were enjoying in isolation; simultaneously the serial temporality of monthly publishing allowed fans to follow and comment on each other's responses to the comics' content across time, collaboratively producing a shared reading history. In the story Ross cites, "A Visit with the Fantastic Four," Lee and Kirby directly referenced their readers' fan mail by depicting Sue distraught by a series of letters the team receives from local fans who believe she doesn't contribute enough to the team.[16] The scene acknowledged the influence of readers' correspondence on *The Fantastic Four*'s content, while asking them to consider the affective consequences of their communication—the capacity of a letter to hurt someone's feelings, for instance—with distant readers they still considered friends or fellow travelers. What Ross obliquely made reference to in his letter was what countless other readers consistently identified as *The Fantastic Four*'s "realism," a term that offered a shorthand way of conveying Ross's bold claim that "it's the same way in life as it is in comics."

From its inception *The Fantastic Four* self-consciously positioned itself as a "realist" take on the superhero. Like all Marvel series, *The Fantastic Four* was set in a world that was socially and politically identical to America in the early 1960s. By the third issue, every location the team traveled to was identifiable by name—including downtown Manhattan, their base of operations—or by more general geographical markers. References to globally scattered atomic power plants, the existence of the DNA molecule, advanced synthetics, and space-age rocketry indexed contemporaneous real-world scientific discoveries. Most important, the comic concerned itself with the same sociopolitical issues that were most salient to Americans in this period, including the threat of atomic fallout, the outcome of a cold war space race, anticommunism, changing gender and sexual norms, the dual evils of racism and fascism, and the problem of displaced populations and refugees.

Despite these real-world referents, there was much in the narrative that could *not* be considered properly realist. Whether one took Reed's miraculous discovery of "the negative zone," a dimensional portal to multiple universes, or the Human Torch's ability to produce the heat of a supernova, not all or even a great deal of the comic reflected the actual limits of the possible.[17] That these very fantastical elements were understood as legible and relevant to a diverse readership is, I would argue, what made *The Fantastic Four* an artifact of midcentury American "realism." As Ross's letter suggests, it was identification with characters, scenarios, and encounters depicted in the text *regardless* of their ability to reflect lived realities that made the comic book "real" to its audience. These identifications were encouraged by the text but cemented through interactions among members of *The Fantastic Four*'s counterpublic, a space in which representations of fantastical phenomena could be interpreted as politically salient, and hence *real*, to the series' readers.

In issue #9 the team faces financial ruin when Reed loses their money in the stock market, which they had acquired from patents for his scientific inventions. Many hailed the story as an exemplary instance of *The Fantastic Four*'s realist depiction of superheroes as "ordinary people." Others, however, suggested that the story ruined the fantasy of superhuman power. Fred Bronson complained, "[*Fantastic Four*] #9 was kind of silly. The idea of heroes going bankrupt is ridiculous! Fans read comics because the heroes in them *act* like comic book heroes, and not like real-life people. For Heaven's sake, don't ruin *The Fantastic Four!*"[18] While most other readers disagreed, lauding the story's authenticity, Martha Beck took a different tack. She eschewed a discussion of realism as the mere reflection of everyday life by articulating the concept through reader identification:

> [Fred Bronson says] that fans read comics because the heroes don't act like real-life people. . . . First of all, in order to enjoy almost any creative work (including comics), it is necessary to identify with some person. . . . And now comes Fred Bronson, wanting to remove any shred of believability from your marvelous characters—an act which would make identification impossible. . . . It is no accident that your best stories . . . are those in which the personalities of the FF . . . play a main role in determining the outcome. I don't presume to know why most fans read most comics, but this fan reads this comic because its characters act like real-life people and not like comic book heroes.[19]

Where Bronson saw the "realistic" situations of *The Fantastic Four* as puncturing the pleasure of superheroic fantasy, Beck's logic implied that the characters' complex affective responses to such circumstances made the fantasy of their mutated bodies legible to readers in the first place. For Beck it was not important that the Fantastic Four went bankrupt "like real-life people" do, but that their responses to this circumstance made sense or were "believable" in relation to their fictional personalities. In this sense *The Fantastic Four*'s realism paradoxically underwrote its central fantasy of bodily transformation: what was enchanting about these figures was that one could still identify with them despite, or perhaps even *because* of, their radical difference from ordinary humanity. As we have seen, the series' primary way of encouraging reader identification was by making the "queerness" of the characters themselves—their failure or refusal to inhabit postwar gender and sexual norms—a desirable orientation to the world.

In his second published letter, discussed earlier, Ross identified the story "A Visit with the Fantastic Four" as inspiring his renewed identification with the Invisible Girl. Presented as a special introductory feature to *The Fantastic Four* #11, "A Visit with the Fantastic Four" offered readers an "insider's" look at a typical afternoon in the lives of Marvel's first family.[20] The story quickly became one of fans' most beloved tales. It showcases *The Fantastic Four*'s ability to develop reader identification with the superheroic body and its queer orientation to family and kinship. The feature opens with the Fantastic Four taking a walk past a local newspaper stand, where a crowd of eager fans stand in line to purchase the latest issue of *The Fantastic Four*. Reed, Sue, Johnny, and Ben stand nearby in the background, wearing civilian garb, frustrated at having arrived too late to purchase a copy of their own monthly adventures. Not only do they appear cognizant of their status as fictional characters, but the scene features readers as visible actors in the production of the Fantastic Four mythos. Standing in the foreground, a teenage fan holds up a copy of his issue of *The Fantastic Four* folded over to display the letter column (plate 9). Motioning to his friend, the boy excitedly proclaims, "Hey, Charlie, look! I just got the latest copy! And my letter's on the fan page!"[21] Here the series' letters column is incorporated into the narrative itself, allowing readers to see their own participation in *The Fantastic Four*'s counterpublic reflected back at them; a banner at the top of the page boldly states, "Special bonus to our readers! The type of story most requested by your letters and post cards," suggesting readers' direct involvement in initiating the production of comic book narrative.

As the story unfolds, Lee and Kirby present a variety of interactions between the Fantastic Four and their fans that reveal how each team member's identity is constituted through the very social norms that their bodies appear to contradict. Following the opening scene, the team encounters a group of children—three boys and a girl—pantomiming the Fantastic Four's powers using everyday props. One boy carries long wooden boards with white gloves at the end to make his arms look elongated like Mr. Fantastic; another carries lighted sparklers, mimicking the Human Torch's flame; the third boy wears an orange papier-mâché mask and a cotton-filled suit to look like the Thing; finally, the young girl hides behind a lamppost, disappearing from sight like the Invisible Girl. Introducing themselves to the star-struck children, Reed, Sue, and Johnny offer their youthful counterparts unsolicited advice. Stretching his arm toward a bouquet of flowers in a nearby planter, Reed tells his young fan, "Look, son, if you want to play Mr. Fantastic, here are some flowers you can give to the Invisible Girl!" Sue showcases her powers to the girl, explaining, "*This* is how I turn invisible, dear! I just have to will myself to do it!" Finally, Johnny presents his look-alike with a miniature fireball display while admonishing, "Throwing fireballs is easy for *me*, fella, but don't *you* ever play with fire! It's too dangerous for little kids!"[22] In each interaction the three heroes perform their powers while framing their use in the language of normative behavior: heterosexual courtship, willful self-determination, and exuberant play within limits.

Ben's response is different; though the three companions seem satisfied with what they've taught the children, he exposes the falsity of their performances when he boldly asserts, "Sure—they'll tell how they met four *freaks* in the street!" The Thing's dark statement reminds the other three heroes and the reader that no amount of *performing* normalcy will actually make them a traditional family. The lessons imparted by Reed, Sue, and Johnny ring hollow when compared to their own experiences. Despite Reed's gentlemanly gestures of affection, a gift of flowers cannot resolve Sue's ambivalence about her love for him, as is made clear when she expresses indecision about Namor's marriage proposal three pages later. Similarly Sue's seeming self-confidence in controlling her powers doesn't make her any more capable of controlling her insecurities over public perceptions of her as a shrinking violet. And Johnny's fire-prevention tips seem like so much big talk coming from a young "hot head" unable to ignite a romantic flame beyond a teenage crush. Unsurprisingly, then, it is the team's resident queer "monster," The Thing, who reminds his companions that working to live by certain norms isn't the same as achieving them.

At least one reader understood that even Lee and Kirby's most earnest attempts to present their characters outside of the narrow stricture of gendered stereotypes were problematic and still took place within the language of those types:

> Ordinarily I enjoy your scripts and find them remarkably fresh and original . . . however, you need to do quite a bit more character development than was done in "A Visit with the Fantastic Four." . . . It is altogether unbelievable that characters of the complexity of the 1962 fantastic group should have emerged from the stereotypes you portrayed. Granted, you were being quite brief, but even so, couldn't Ben Grimm have possessed more than muscles and bravura? And Reed Richards would be more plausible if he were not intelligence personified. Can't they be more human beings, and less mere foils to each other?[23]

In her criticism of Lee and Kirby's most daring experiment in "realism," this reader highlighted a key element of the Fantastic Four's ability to elicit wide identification from its readership: the recurrent visual depiction of material and psychic contradiction that was the hallmark of the team's experience of their bodies was itself an expression of the political contradictions of the world their readers inhabited: that of America in 1962.

No contradiction generated more discussion about the ultimate political values of the series than the Fantastic Four's simultaneous desire for an expansive cosmopolitan worldview and their initial commitment to anticommunism for the purpose of national security. Between 1962 and 1964 Lee and Kirby frequently presented communists as archvillains of the Fantastic Four, a creative decision that sparked a prolonged and heated debate among readers regarding the creators' heavy-handed approach to cold war politics.

Veterans of World War II and staunch liberals, Lee and Kirby tacitly supported anticommunism as part of their investment in global democracy. Members of their fan base increasingly pointed out the ideological paradox of their position, espousing democratic ideals while appearing to denigrate opposing political values. For many readers, the debates fomented by this critique were not merely about personal political convictions but about the underlying values of the Marvel family itself. This was a question of political imagination and the capacity of superhero comics to figure the world in terms not limited by cold war rhetoric. In issue #25, following a series of stories featuring scheming communist scientists and superhumans, Lee and Kirby published a letter by Jimmy Edelstein admonishing the duo's anticommunist rhetoric: "Enclosed you will find pages from several of your comic books. Each one has something about the hero fighting Communists (or as you call them, Reds or Commies). Are you trying to encourage World War III? . . . Don't you have enough imagination to think up new enemies. . . . I believe in the American way of life and do not believe in Communism, however, why can't we have our beliefs and let them have theirs, and still exist in friendship?"[24] Despite their willingness to consider a variety of opinions and allow readers to do the same, Lee and Kirby saw no problem with their creative approach to communism since they were merely reflecting a popular consensus regarding this much maligned political form.

Though we have only their word to go on, Lee and Kirby suggested that the opinions they solicited from readers regarding their position on the use of communists as villains was "heavily in favor of calling a spade a spade, or a red a red."[25] Two responses summed up arguments on this side of the debate:

> I feel that you should definitely continue to pit your heroes against the forces of Communism, which is a much bigger threat to our nation than crime is [and] under whose domination lives one out of every three persons in the world. There is no way that . . . "We can have our beliefs and let them have theirs" because one of their principal doctrines is complete world domination.[26]

> After reading your letters page in the August issue of *FF* I decided to write you and let you know that your fans at this college are definitely in favor of your having Communists as the villains in your stories. Communism is like a cancer infecting the body and mind of the West and it must be fought in all ways possible.[27]

Regardless of what position readers took, writers on both sides of the debate consistently made recourse to liberal democratic ideals like freedom of speech and political self-determination to explain why denouncement of communism was warranted. One reader critiqued those who claimed Marvel was ideologically biased by reminding them that a majority of readers had voted in favor of anticommunist themes in the comic even after willingly hearing out the opposing side.[28] Similarly one young woman pointed out that if others (presumably the Soviets) were free to deride our government, free speech permitted an equally forceful rejoinder.[29] Despite their vehement reasons for denigrating communism, these criticisms often missed a larger conceptual argument about whether or not anticommunism accorded with the imaginative ideals of *The Fantastic Four*. The most powerful voices of dissent against the chorus of anticommunist supporters, including Edelstein, were those readers who identified such a position as antithetical to the egalitarian values espoused in stories of *The Fantastic Four* and embodied by Marvel's company philosophy. It was no accident, for instance, that Edelstein's own moving wish for a world in which Russian communists and Americans could forge different ways of life but "still exist in friendship" directly echoed Reed Richards's own sentiments about the team's conflict with the Russian cosmonaut Dr. Kragoff in Fantastic Four #13 when he implored, "Why can't we leave our differences behind us! This is the first step to the stars—and we should all make that trip together—as fellow earthmen!"[30] These dissenting readers argued that the series contradicted its own ideals when it made recourse to conservative forms of anticommunism. One letter writer encouraged the creators to take a tack more true to the series' worldview, namely pointing their social critique at the horrors of global racism: "If, as you say, 'someone's gotta be the villain,' why not make it something even worse than the Communists, such as the Ku Klux Klan or the politicians of South Africa?"[31]

One of the boldest condemnations of Lee and Kirby's anticommunist rhetoric came from letter writer Dan Clark. As part of his criticism, Clark defended the comments of a previous letter writer whose avowed affiliation with a left-wing political organization was unfairly lambasted by Lee and Kirby:

> As the Fantastic Four leave the domain of the Skrulls in issue #37, they say, "It's a different galaxy . . . with a different race of living beings . . . and yet . . . it seems that ambition, and hate, and love, are the same everywhere in the universe! Perhaps we're really not so different from others . . . either on earth . . . or in the void of space! . . . And, the day all mankind realizes that lesson . . . we shall come a step closer to brotherhood . . . and universal peace!" A fine sentiment! But you aren't as humane to Earth people. In *Suspense* #64, a devilish dictator, called "comrade leader" forces Black Widow to carry out his "evil purposes." Fighting against the Russian ghouls is one of the "richest, handsomest, most glamorous munitions makers of all time." Iron Man says the Russian gunmen talk "like true Commie tintypes." Man, the John Birch Society must love Marvel when you come up with something like that! Let's face it, there's no purpose behind that kind of anti-Communist tintype except prompting hate, and [Reed's] *FF* speech is in direct contradiction to that. George Carter, the guy from England whose letter appeared in *FF* #37, said, "Your magazines are intended to be used for entertainment, not political indoctrination." Yes! And your answer seemed to scorn his membership in a left-wing organization and said that your "democratic British fans would set him straight." Well, Prime Minister Wilson is a member of a left-wing organization, the Labor Party, and I don't think that he is considered undemocratic by many responsible people. . . . Marvel's too good to be involved in rightist name calling.[32]

Clark's criticism of Lee and Kirby's political views deploys the imaginative content of their own stories to point out the creative team's hypocrisy. Essentially Clark treats the statements made by a fictional superhero team as constituting the foundation of an alternative political imaginary that Marvel Comics readers are presumably called upon to help nurture in the service of egalitarian political goals; for Clark, Lee and Kirby's disavowal of that imaginary dishonors the values of their creative world making while also encouraging antidemocratic discourse among readers. Clark attempts to recapture these values both in his impassioned dissent against what he perceives to be an undemocratic practice and also by performing democratic dialogue in his letter, actively quoting other readers and participating in a wider discussion rather than shutting down communication across differences of opinion or worldview.

Published in 1965—less than a year after the defeat of Barry Goldwater, whose extreme conservative politics dovetailed with that of the John Birch Society—Clark's letter spoke to a rising sentiment among 1960s youth that the rabid anticommunism of the postwar period was a detriment to democracy. As in earlier debates, the discursive struggle over anticommunism in *The Fantastic Four* had an enduring effect on the creative trajectory of the series. In 1978, nearly a decade after the publication of *The Fantastic Four*'s first sixty issues, a student interviewer at James Madison University asked Lee to comment on Marvel Comics' contribution to anticommunist sentiment in their 1960s publications. Lee candidly responded, "It was really a more naïve time, in those years, and I'm a product of the times . . . [and] had been conditioned. During WWII, we were told that we were the good guys, and the Nazis were the bad guys . . . and I still believe it. . . . A few years later, when the word came down from D.C. that the Commies are the bad guys, I just acted like one of Pavlov's dogs. Then came Viet Nam, then came student protesters, then came a whole change in the country. I think you'll find that at that point we got off the kick."[33]

As Lee said, following *The Fantastic Four*'s issue #24 in 1964, anticommunism never appeared in the comic again. It would be supplanted by an expansive cosmopolitan vision of worldly encounters among diverse others. If debates over questions of appropriate character development and *The Fantastic Four*'s aesthetic realism initially seemed like minor quibbles over readers' personal preferences, the conflicts over Lee and Kirby's depiction of anticommunism went to the heart of the series' political values. Moreover it revealed these previous debates as necessarily political by virtue of the fact that they were part of a larger conversation about the ideological construction of a fictional world whose various elements readers believed should reflect utopian or progressive ideals. In this light, whether or not Lee and Kirby represented Sue Storm in more empowered ways or developed characters that effectively spoke to their readers' multiple identifications said something about the capacity of popular fantasy to recast current social and political realities in radically new ways.

The Fantastic Four's evolution from a narrative of sexual and gender nonnormativity to a story of cosmopolitan cross-species encounters was facilitated by a reframing of the series' central contradiction—the disjuncture between a gendered self and an unwieldy physical body—as a question of racial and species membership. Now it was the disjuncture between the characters' sense of humanity and their visibly nonhuman bodies that took center stage in their unfolding adventures. It was no coincidence that this transformation became most apparent following Reed and Sue's marriage in 1965. This issue marked a prolonged period in which the series presented the family more conservatively, depicting Sue as a doting housewife even as she became a more powerful and active team member, and Reed as an overbearing patriarch even as his clan repeatedly rebelled against his leadership. Yet the radical expansion of the four's social world and affective bonds—through a series of pan-ethnic and cross-species affiliations—would function in ways similar to its earlier gender and sexual radicalism, identifying the family as an unstable molecular unit continually reshaped by unexpected encounters with a heterogeneous cosmos. As the family appeared to contract its intimacies in these later issues, the lineaments of its worldly attachments grew so that its boundaries expanded into uncharted territories where the narrow imperatives of cold war geopolitics paled in comparison to the epic struggles of diverse species to find a place in the world.

Cosmopolitanism and The Fantastic Four's "Inhuman Anthropology"

I simply want to convey the core of cosmopolitanism, considered as an extended family of responses to the problem of solidarity, and to point to one supremely important insight about our contemporary world. . . . If you do not take on as much of the world as you can, the world will come to you, and on terms over which you will have even less control than you did previously.—DAVID HOLLINGER, *Cosmopolitanism and Solidarity* (2006)

David Hollinger's description of cosmopolitanism as an "extended family of responses to the problem of solidarity" succinctly captures the logic that underpinned the fictional lives of the Fantastic Four. Quite literally presented to readers as a family of material responses to the problem of solidarity in postwar America, the Fantastic Four negotiated a chaotic social bond in a wider world shaped by increasingly complex forms of social, cultural, and biological difference. From the woefully exploited Mole People to the shape-shifting aliens of the Skrull Empire; from Prince Namor's long-lost Atlantian tribe to the majestic Silver Surfer, exile of a distant planet; from the Black Panther, African King of Wakanda, to the mutant outcasts the X-Men—the ever-expanding Marvel Universe the Fantastic Four called home was defined by a proliferating cast of others whose existence made any notion of a stable human identity a distant and disagreeable fantasy. The sheer heterogeneity of different kinds of peoples, objects, and imaginary locales that appeared in the pages of *The Fantastic Four* identified diversity as a central value of Marvel Comics. Yet in the logic of the series, diversity was not an achievement in itself but a worldly fact that had material consequences and required substantive collective responses. Consequently it was the ongoing depiction of complex and uneven yet *mutually transformative* encounters among diverse actors that gave *The Fantastic Four*'s comic book cosmopolitics its distinctly radical dimension.

In Reed Richards's personal files the team maintained records of their numerous encounters documenting the cultural norms, habits, and abilities of the human, alien, and mutant creatures that composed their fictional universe. These files were presented to readers in colorful pinup galleries in *The Fantastic Four Annuals*. In this way *The Fantastic Four* produced an "inhuman anthropology," a visual lexicon of bodies and objects that marked the limits of the human. As the second part of Hollinger's statement suggests, cosmopolitanism can function as an expansive vision of mutual interaction but also a defensive attempt to diffuse potential threats to one's cultural integrity. Within the fictional narrative the team's anthropological interest in the others they encountered was presented as both a product of their genuine inquisitiveness about the world's diverse inhabitants and a potentially imperialist impulse to exploit critical knowledge to anticipate those who wished to do them harm.

How could one lay claim to a "family of man," *The Fantastic Four* asked, when one was not *man* at all? More important, how might one rethink the limits of family and solidarity without recourse to a fixed humanity? Unlike the universalist ethos espoused by *The Justice League*, which exceptionalized the human while ignoring alternative experiences of bodily disability or nonhuman physical morphology, the Fantastic Four acknowledged difference not only as a necessary and difficult reality of human experience but as the very ground upon which the human took form. While the series consistently attended to questions of gender and sexuality, it had a significantly more uneven, though no less productive relationship to race. *The Fantastic Four* narrated race in species terms by defining it as a form of biological difference from humanity. On the one hand, the conflation of the categories of race and species had the effect of flattening out the specificities of ethnoracial experience; though the series often made bombastic gestures toward condemning racist ideology (including a particularly over-the-top story in which the team combats a villainous bigot, "the Hate Monger," who is later revealed as a Hitler cyborg dressed in Ku Klux Klan garb), the creators rarely directly addressed the vicissitudes of U.S. racial conflict in the 1970s.[34] On the other hand, the series' expansive definition of race as a form of species belonging allowed the Fantastic Four, who were putatively white well-to-do urbanites, to explore broad hierarchies of social and political power that were organized around the uneven distribution of the category of the human. In the figure of Prince Namor and his Atlantian tribe, for instance, the comic book presented a highly advanced "species" of underwater dwellers who were clearly foils for the Japanese, a real-world ethnoracial group. Namor is coded Japanese in his visual presentation—with his upraised eyes, lithe frame, and sleek black hair—while Atlantis is depicted as having barely survived the consequences of ocean atomic testing, echoing the real-world suffering of the Japanese following the dropping of the atomic bombs on Hiroshima and Nagasaki during World War II. Rather than function as mere stereotype, however, the depiction of Namor and his people as *potentially* Japanese, while more broadly understood as an entirely different species, allowed a conceptual expansion of the distinct plight of one ethnoracial group to a larger network of global relationships affected by the negligent actions of U.S. imperialism. Through its depiction of a variety of alien and superhuman beings exiled from their home worlds or else forced into hiding by a bigoted humanity, the series addressed how the rights and privileges of a supposedly free democratic society were withheld from those perceived as less than or perhaps "more than just human." Often themselves scorned by the public they claimed to serve because of their mutant physiologies, the Fantastic Four were also figuratively racialized by the stigma of biological difference.

The Fantastic Four's creative world making and its rearticulation of ethnoracial categories to broader questions of human inclusion and equality came to make sense in relation to the emergence of a radical left-wing internationalism in the mid- to late 1960s. This form of *radical* internationalism—embodied by groups like Students for a Democratic Society, the Third World Left, and the Black Panther Party—linked the political interests of global anticolonial movements with domestic minorities. In his historiography of 1960s black radicalism, Richard O. Self explains, "Black internationalism challenged the notion that racism and its attendant forms of subordination were merely flaws within the liberal American political order, flaws whose disappearance over time was assured. By linking the color line in the United States with an international color line . . . in the context of anticolonial struggle and the emerging Cold War, black internationalists interpreted racial domination in the United States as part of the history of Western imperialism."[35] According to Nikhil Singh, this radical strand of left-wing political activism "[redefined] integration and equality not as a moment of entry into the American mainstream, but as a commitment of solidarity with all those who defined America's margins and all the victims of Americanism at home and around the world."[36] Unlike the liberal ideal of universal inclusion embodied in institutions like the United Nations, which sought to ameliorate the atrocities of racial apartheid and colonial violence through political reforms to national policies, radical internationalism offered a powerful critique of liberalism by proclaiming the necessity for a new political imaginary that could account for the uneven distribution of economic and racial power in the postwar geopolitical order. Though *The Fantastic Four* did not identify U.S. imperialism as the primary reason for global economic and racial inequality, it did recast notions of integration and equality in terms of proliferating "commitments of solidarity with all those who defined" the margins of the human internationally.

Few documents more clearly display the relationship between *The Fantastic Four* and the ethos of a radical internationalism than *The Port Huron Statement* (1962). This New Left radical manifesto circulated contemporaneously during the series' first two years of publication to a college-age audience that was a primary demographic of its readership. *The Port Huron Statement* offered a sophisticated reassessment of the undemocratic political and social realities of 1960s America, while outlining the ideological worldview of a New Left youth movement that would underpin support for civil rights, antiwar, and decolonization movements for over a decade. In their introductory statement of values the Students for a Democratic Society (SDS) declared, "Our own social values involve conceptions of human beings, human relationships, and social systems. . . . Human interdependence is contemporary fact;

human brotherhood must be willed however, as a condition of future survival and as the most appropriate form of social relations. Personal links between man and man are needed, especially to go beyond the partial and fragmentary bonds of function that bind men only as worker to worker, employer to employee, teacher to student, American to Russian."[37] The values of human relationships grounded in respect for individual agency were decidedly liberal but with a cosmopolitan bent. For the SDS, as for a variety of New Left groups, the encounter between radically different peoples and the collective transformations that emerge from them were at the heart of producing a nonviolent world that allowed for the flourishing of political freedom for all beyond mere securing of individual rights. As Reed Richards would declare, following the team's second encounter with the alien Skrulls, "It's a different galaxy—with a different race of living beings—and yet . . . it seems ambition, and hate, and love, are the same everywhere in the universe! Perhaps we're not really so different from others—either on Earth—or in the endless void of space! And the day all of mankind realizes that lesson—we shall come a step closer to brotherhood and universal peace!"[38] Reed's liberal claim of a shared universal humanity throughout the cosmos was complemented by a tacit acknowledgment that humankind had much to learn from encounters with other civilizations, whether alien, "inhuman," or mutant. Like the members of SDS, Reed did not "deify the human" but rather expressed "faith in [man's] potential" for social and political consciousness of his interconnectedness with life in the universe.[39]

This was highlighted in the Fantastic Four's unprecedented encounter with the Black Panther, the first African superhero, introduced to readers in July 1966. In issue #52 the Black Panther invites the Fantastic Four to visit his African kingdom, Wakanda, as guests of honor. Accompanied by Johnny Storm's college roommate and friend Wyatt Wingfoot, the team travels by sonic jet to the African continent. Upon arrival they are shocked to discover an African nation whose tribal society exists alongside a highly advanced technological infrastructure. As their ship hovers above Wakanda's jungle landscape, Sue admits, "It's so hard to believe that a ship such as this one could have come from a land with no sign of . . . industrial development!" When the group lands in a forest clearing, they soon realize that a wide swath of the jungle is composed of man-made technology. Their guide explains, "The entire topography and flora are electronically-controlled mechanical apparatus."[40] In the fictional nation of Wakanda, the series joined modern technology with the so-called natural or premodern world of African tribal culture. Faced with Wakanda's extraordinary scientific and technical achievements, the Fantastic Four are forced to reevaluate their assumptions about Western technological supremacy.

This unexpected juxtaposition of modern and premodern lifestyles is spectacularly displayed in the introductory splash panel to *The Fantastic Four* #53 (plate 10).[41] In this image the Wakandan people honor the Fantastic Four and their Native American companion, Wyatt Wingfoot, with a traditional tribal "Dance of Friendship." The scene depicts the Black Panther perched on his tribal throne atop a raised dais with his five guests seated before him. Six tribesmen dressed in traditional Wakandan garb—long white headdresses and flowing skirts—dance ecstatically before this audience. Arrayed around this scene are the tribe's musicians with drums and rain sticks to the right, and guardsmen carrying both traditional tribal spears and modern machine guns in the foreground. Witnessing the display, Ben jokes, "Sheesh! A bunch'a Fred Astaires they ain't!," to which Johnny replies, "Relax Ben! It's better'n being shot at by them!" Reed whispers to Sue, "Though the Wakandan tribe lives in the traditions of their forefathers, they possess modern super-scientific wonders we can only marvel at!" Wyatt observes, "They are not the ordinary native tribe they seem to be!"

At first glance the scene appears to rehearse the worst forms of racist visual anthropology, depicting a series of exoticized black bodies in a hyperbolic display of tribal dancing before an audience of white foreigners. Yet the scene undermines the logic of this stereotype through a series of visual reversals. First, the image inverts the assumed racial hierarchy of imperial encounters by visually positioning the Black Panther seated *above* his guests, while they must sit at his feet. This literal hierarchy of black bodies above white ones is also officially asserted by the Black Panther's status as royalty and the four as guests of his court. The scene complicates a traditional black-white binary, however, by including the Native American Wingfoot among the guests of honor. Wingfoot's statement that the Wakandans "are not the ordinary native tribe they seem to be" questions the imperialist portrait of atavistic tribal cultures by reminding us that the Wakandans' cultural heritage underlies a technologically sophisticated society. As a Native American, Wingfoot might be expected to recognize the Wakandans as akin to his own people; however, rather than conflate Wingfoot's native ancestry with that of the Wakandan tribe, as though all indigenous cultures are cultural copies of one another, the scene offers a moment of misrecognition wherein Wingfoot voices both confusion and genuine interest in encountering an unfamiliar culture in which technology and tribal custom are seamlessly woven together.

Second, this literal and figurative inversion of racial hierarchy is redoubled in Reed's admission that the Wakandans possess technology vastly superior to that of the West; the scene suggests that their advancement is not only by virtue of their technical genius but because of their ability to reconcile tribal traditions with modern technoculture. The Fantastic Four's visit to Wakanda was arguably the only image of a socially and economically independent Africa to appear in American mass culture outside of the black arts movement, the cultural arm of black radical politics in the 1960s. In so doing it alerted readers to the existence and specificities of the African experience while identifying Africa with the future of global political and technological freedom. As James Baldwin wrote in a 1962 op-ed for the *New York Times*, "The American Negro can no longer . . . be controlled by white America's image of him. This fact has everything to do with the rise of Africa in world affairs. . . . This could not but have an extraordinary effect on [African American youths'] own morale, for it meant that they were not merely the descendants of slaves in a white, Protestant, and Puritan country; they were also related to kings and princes in an ancestral homeland, far away. And this has proven to be a great antidote to the poison of self-hatred."[42] In its depiction of a youthful, modern-day, globally educated African king who values tribal customs equally with home-grown technological innovation and fights on behalf of the anticolonial project, *The Fantastic Four* further cemented the idea of an empowered black heritage for its minority readers, not only in kings and princes but in superheroes too.

Third, the image presciently captures the dual facets of cosmopolitanism, at once presenting a lively and exciting moment of cross-cultural exchange, while visually admitting the characters' deep ambivalence over the outcome of such interactions. Even as they express respect for the Wakandan people, the Fantastic Four fear the tribe's technological superiority and their own vulnerability as outsiders in unfamiliar territory. Johnny's remark that the Wakandan dance of friendship is "better'n being shot at by them" reminds us that all forms of cross-cultural encounter are fraught with the potential for violence. Visually ecstatic scenes of cross-cultural encounter like this one recalled the pleasures of witnessing the intermingling of bodies and objects in earlier displays, revealing that the enchantments of physical transformation and tactile encounters could be rerouted toward similar pleasure in cosmopolitan exchange.

In the story's concluding panels, the narrative depicts a contemplative Black Panther considering abandoning his mantle now that his people are safe from the machinations of the imperial hunter Klaw, whom the Fantastic Four had joined the Panther to defeat. Laying their hands on Black Panther's shoulder in a spirit of solidarity, the four encourage him (with more than a little humor) to set his sights on hero work as a broader vocation to fight injustice for all people (figure 3.1). The Panther replies, "I shall do it! I pledge my fortune, my powers—my very life—to the service of all mankind!" This scene visually echoes the original clasping of hands enacted by the Fantastic Four when they first discovered their extraordinary abilities and devoted themselves to using those powers for mankind's benefit, yet it also reverses, or at least complicates, the original thrust of their pact. Here the Fantastic Four's broader cosmopolitan commitments have been turned toward an African nation and its revolutionary leader, while the Black Panther's local commitments to tribe and country are turned outward, toward the world. In this double movement, the comic book depicted cosmopolitan encounter as mutually transformative in its capacity to scale upward and downward through varied valences of political and ethical commitment.

As the story of the Black Panther suggests, by far the most anthropologically intriguing scenes of encounter that Lee and Kirby developed in *The Fantastic Four* stories of the mid- to late 1960s were those in which the team engaged a host of other races, species, and civilizations. In these encounters the delimited category of race would be opened up to more expansive questions of species belonging that allowed characters who belonged to radically different ethnoracial communities to forge meaningful bonds.

The Fantastic Four's struggle to redefine the limits of species belonging was powerfully captured in their first meeting with the mysterious Inhumans in 1966, the same year as their visit with the Black Panther.[43] The Inhumans were a genetically engineered race of superpowered beings preexisting Homo sapiens by thousands of years. For generations they dwelled in the "Great Refuge," a soaring underground metropolis hidden in the High Andes, where a benevolent royal family, led by the king Black Bolt, ruled as their leaders and guardians. When the royal family proclaim their wish to reveal themselves to the human race in hopes of fomenting a cross-species solidarity, Black Bolt's megalomaniacal brother Maximus publicly accuses them of treason and demands their exile. Under the threat of death, the royal family—including Black Bolt's wife, Medusa; her sister, Crystal; their guards Triton, Gorgon,

FIGURE 3.1. The Fantastic Four in solidarity with the Black Panther. Stan Lee (writer) and Jack Kirby (penciller), "The Way It Began . . . !," *The Fantastic Four* #53, August 1966, reprinted in *Fantastic Four Omnibus Vol. 2* (New York: Marvel Comics, 2007), 616.

and Karnak; and their companion animal, Lockjaw, a superpowered pit bull—flee their home seeking safe haven, ultimately landing in the belly of the world's busiest metropolis, New York City. The Inhuman royal family offered a foil for the Fantastic Four, a kinship network similarly bound by shared values rather than blood ties, whose commitments to cosmopolitan engagement have made them refugees.

Johnny Storm first encounters the Inhumans when he stumbles upon Crystal, the youngest of the royal family, in an abandoned New York ghetto where they live in hiding. By framing the Inhumans as refugees in the slums of New York, the series cannily articulated the economic hardships of inner-city life—with its uneven distribution of resources and deteriorating infrastructure—with the experience of displaced peoples fleeing colonial rule and political violence.⁴⁴ The Inhumans were, in a sense, what the Third World Left called an "internal colony," a term deployed by black radicals to describe how nonwhite populations in the United States lived under forms of poverty and degradation akin to the experiences of colonized people. Upon learning that Johnny possesses superhuman powers like her own, Crystal eagerly leads him to meet her family, assuming he is also an Inhuman. Johnny is taken aback, however, when he sees that a member of their clan, Crystal's older sister, Medusa, is one of the Fantastic Four's most recent foes. He hastily concludes the Inhumans are supervillains intent on destroying humankind, while the Inhumans assume that Johnny represents an immanent threat to their survival. When the rest of the Fantastic Four arrive at the scene, an all-out brawl ensues.

In the heat of battle the royal family suddenly ceases the attack and teleports away from the scene. Reed surmises, "I realize now that they are a slightly different type of life which evolved without mankind knowing it—and they've combined all their inhuman powers for their mutual safety." Sue replies, "Then Medusa wasn't some sort of freak—but rather part of a strange unsuspected race!," to which Johnny vehemently counters, "Nobody can tell me that Crystal isn't as human as any of us!"⁴⁵ Johnny's exclamation captures the core problem of the Fantastic Four's encounter with the Inhumans: the struggle to define a proper humanity even as that category is undermined by the proliferation of differences that fracture the unity of a presumed "human family." Here the narrative plays on the dual meaning of the term *race*, as both a category of cultural difference and a form of species membership. Johnny's attempt to identify Crystal as distinctly human against accusations of inhumanity, or "freak" status, only further destabilizes any claim to that category: if Crystal is indeed as human as the Fantastic Four, then that implies that she is something far from human indeed, since the four themselves are biological aberrations within the human race. Indeed it was in the expression of Johnny's own "freakish" superpowers that Crystal recognized him as kin, or to use his words, "as *Inhuman* as any of us." The scene underscores the social construction of categories like race, species, and family. It dramatizes the strategic necessity of claiming these categories to make the lives of those most neglected or subject to violence because of their perceived difference from humanity "count" as subjects worthy of care and interest.

In the aftermath of their skirmish, the Fantastic Four are convinced of the need to learn more about the Inhumans, ultimately deciding to join them in solidarity against the injustices heaped upon them by Maximus. The Fantastic Four soon uncover the royal family's historical lineage as genetic mutants and learn of the threat they face from the Seeker, a hunter sent by Maximus to capture and return the renegade group to the Great Refuge. When the Seeker arrives in Manhattan searching for the royal family, the Fantastic Four stealthily follow him back to the Great Refuge, where Black Bolt and his clan have willingly returned to face their fate. There they combine forces with the royal family to reclaim the throne and save the Inhumans from Maximus's tyrannical rule. Though ultimately ousted from his corrupt reign, just before he surrenders Maximus activates an impenetrable shield that permanently traps the Inhumans within their mountain fortress. Barely managing an escape before the barrier seals them in forever, the Four lament the tragic circumstances of their newfound companions and commit to finding a way to release them from their self-inflicted exile. In their last moments together, however, Medusa rhetorically invokes a powerful bond between the Inhumans and the Fantastic Four when she proclaims, "Richards was right! We are not the natural enemies of the human race! We are not inhuman! We are the same as they. For years we have hidden . . . thinking the humans would destroy us because we are a different race! But we are human too! It is only our powers that are different."

Like Johnny's contention that Crystal is "as human as anyone," Medusa's invocation of a shared humanity acknowledges difference at the same time that it brings into being a willed solidarity based on the shared *experience* of difference from a proper humanity that has shaped the lives of both the Inhumans and the Fantastic Four. Yet it simultaneously reveals the "necessary error" of claiming a shared identity to build common bonds for the mutual survival of those made other by the same categories that define what kind of lives may or may not count as legibly human. If throughout their adventures the Fantastic Four disidentified with proper humanity, expanding the limits of what might count as human by performing their identities through chaotic and mutated bodies, so too Black Bolt's family disidentifies with their Inhumanity for the purpose of thinking and feeling beyond the limits of their kind.

More than any previous story in the Fantastic Four mythos, the saga of the Inhumans highlighted the cosmopolitan ethos at the core of the team's familial drama. By activating the categories of race and species alongside the more local affiliations of the family form, the narrative dramatized how such categories came into being in relation to one another, while simultaneously offering critical positions from which to voice differing social and political requirements for survival at varied scales of community. When Sue initially suggests that they should avoid getting involved in the troubles of the Inhumans, Reed reminds her, "Where injustice exists, it is our affair, Sue! Even our marriage can never change that!" In true cosmopolitan form, Reed's statement confirms that the most intimate and local bonds of family need not negate the development of more expansive affiliations.

In the saga of the Inhumans, "Marvel's First Family" lived up to its nickname as the first of many marvelous "families" whose manifold expressions across the second half of the twentieth century would rearticulate the superhero to questions of kin and kind, race, species, and population, and the biological narratives that both underpinned and undermined claims to such categories. In relating the history of the Inhumans as a scientifically advanced race that quickly outgrew early human civilization, Reed explains that the Inhumans shaped their society around the "science of controlling genes." The introduction of the genome as a figure of difference in the wider world of superhero comics was one of the most revolutionary moves of the Marvel Universe. If superheroes were now understood as genetic aberrations or, as was the case with the X-Men, mutants who represented the next step in human evolution, they could become a rich site for performing and contesting the ways that biological realities—including genetic lineage—were understood or constructed *as* realities. Far from becoming a fixed material fact, the concept of "mutation" or genetic diversity in the Marvel Universe worked as an elastic metaphor for a vast array of differences based on race, class, gender, sexuality, generation, and ability that would become the mainstay of late 1960s and early 1970s cultural politics.

PLATE 1. Introducing the Justice League of America. Gardner Fox (writer) and Mike Sekowsky (penciller), "Starro the Conqueror," *The Brave and the Bold* #28, March–April 1960, reprinted in *Justice League of America Archives Vol. 1* (New York: DC Comics, 1992), 14.

PLATE 2. The Justice League members overcome their disabilities. Gardner Fox (writer) and Mike Sekowsky (penciller), "The Case of the Disabled Justice League," *The Justice League of America* #36, June 1965, reprinted in *Justice League of America Archives Vol. 5* (New York: DC Comics, 1999), 147.

PLATE 3. "Spotlight on Reed Richards, Mr. Fantastic." Stan Lee (writer) and Jack Kirby (penciller) "The Micro-World of Doctor Doom!," *Fantastic Four* #16, July 1963, reprinted in *Fantastic Four Omnibus Vol. 1* (New York: Marvel Comics, 2007), 419.

PLATE 4. Johnny transforms into the Human Torch. Stan Lee (writer) and Jack Kirby (penciller), "The Fantastic Four!," *Fantastic Four* #1, November 1961, reprinted in *Fantastic Four Omnibus Vol. 1* (New York: Marvel Comics, 2007), 14.

PLATE 5. Johnny and Ben take on Prince Namor's ocean creatures. Stan Lee (writer) and Jack Kirby (penciller), "Prince Namor and the Merciless Puppet Master," *Fantastic Four* #14, May 1963, reprinted in *Fantastic Four Omnibus Vol. 1* (New York: Marvel Comics, 2007), 362–63.

PLATE 6. Testing Sue's shield. Stan Lee (writer) and Jack Kirby (penciller), "The Return of the Mole Man!," *Fantastic Four* #22, January 1964, reprinted in *Fantastic Four Omnibus Vol. 1* (New York: Marvel Comics, 2007), 609–10.

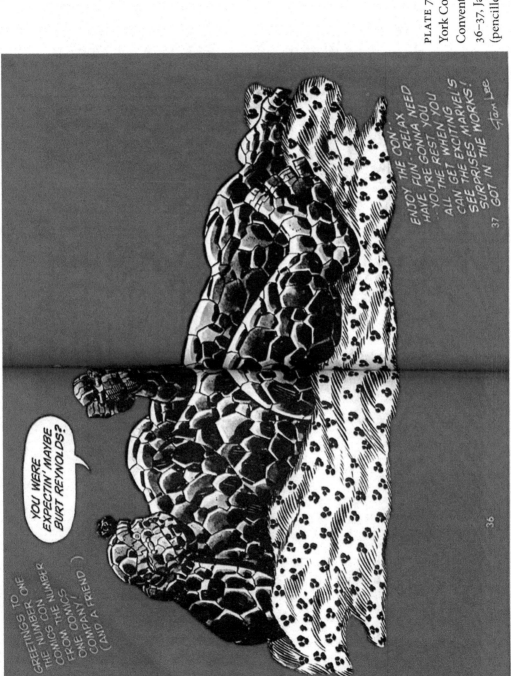

PLATE 7. 1974 New York Comic Art Convention program, 36–37, Jack Kirby (penciller).

PLATE 8. "Marvel's Greatest Hero: The Thing," *Foom* #5, Spring 1974, Marvel Comics. Jack Kirby (penciller).

PLATE 9. "A Visit with the Fantastic Four!" Stan Lee (writer) and Jack Kirby (penciller), *The Fantastic Four* #11, February 1963, reprinted in *Fantastic Four Omnibus Vol. 1* (New York: Marvel Comics, 2007), 271.

PLATE 10. The Wakandan "Dance of Friendship." Stan Lee (writer) and Jack Kirby (penciller), "The Way it Began . . !," *Fantastic Four* #53, August 1966, reprinted in *Fantastic Four Omnibus Vol. 2* (New York: Marvel Comics, 2007), 597.

PLATE 11. The Surfer's lament. Stan Lee (writer) and John Buscema (penciller), "The Origin of the Silver Surfer!," *Silver Surfer* #1, August 1968, reprinted in *Marvel Masterworks: The Silver Surfer Vol. 1* (New York: Marvel Comics, 2010), 6.

PLATE 12. Left: The Surfer's tortured visage. Stan Lee (writer) and John Buscema (penciller), "Worlds without End," *Silver Surfer* #6, June 1969. Right: The suffering hero. Stan Lee (writer) and John Buscema (penciller), "When Lands the Saucer!," Silver Surfer #2, October 1968, reprinted in *Marvel Masterworks: The Silver Surfer Vol. 1* (New York: Marvel Comics, 2010), 202, 40.

PLATE 13. Mephisto reigns over human suffering. Stan Lee (writer) and John Buscema (penciller), "The Power and the Prize," *Silver Surfer* #3, December 1968, reprinted in *Marvel Masterworks: The Silver Surfer Vol. 1* (New York: Marvel Comics, 2010), 106.

PLATE 14. "Deadly Genesis," Len Wein (writer) and Dave Cockrum (penciller), *Giant Size X-Men* #1, May 1975, reprinted in *Uncanny X-Men Omnibus Vol. 1*, (New York: Marvel Comics, 2006), n.p.

PLATE 15. "Enter: The Phoenix!" Chris Claremont (writer) and Dave Cockrum (penciller), "Like a Phoenix, from the Ashes!," *X-Men* #101, October 1976, reprinted in *Uncanny X-Men Omnibus Vol. 1* (New York: Marvel Comics, 2006), 176.

PLATE 16. The X-Men meet the Shi'ar Guard. Chris Claremont (writer) and Dave Cockrum (penciller), "Where No X-Man Has Gone Before!," *X-Men* #107, October 1977, reprinted in *Uncanny X-Men Omnibus Vol. 1* (New York: Marvel Comics, 2006), 294–95.

PLATE 17. Green Lantern flies through the skies of Central City. Denny
O'Neil (writer) and Neal Adams (penciller), "'No Evil Shall Escape My
Sight,'" *Green Lantern/Green Arrow* #76, April 1970, reprinted in *Green
Lantern/Green Arrow Collection Vol. 1* (New York: DC Comics, 2004), 10–12.

PLATE 18. "More deadly than an atom bomb." Denny O'Neil (writer) and
Neal Adams (penciller), "They Say It'll Kill Me but They Won't Say When,"
Green Lantern/Green Arrow #86, October–November 1971, reprinted in *Green
Lantern/Green Arrow Collection Vol. 2* (New York: DC Comics, 2006), 75.

PLATE 19. "What Can One Man Do?" Eliot S. Magin (writer) and Neal Adams (penciller), "What Can One Man Do?," *Green Lantern/Green Arrow* #87, December 1971–January 1972, reprinted in *Green Lantern/Green Arrow Collection Vol. 2* (New York: DC Comics, 2006), 116.

PLATE 20. Left to right: Jean as Lady Wyngarde, Black Queen, and Dark Phoenix. Respectively in Chris Claremont (writer) and John Byrne (penciller), "There's Something Awful on Muir Island!," *Uncanny X-Men* #125, September 1979; "Dazzler!," *Uncanny X-Men* #130, February 1980. Right: "Dark Phoenix!," *Uncanny X-Men* #135, July 1980.

PLATE 21. Cover to Chris Claremont (writer) and John Byrne (penciller), "Dark Phoenix!," *Uncanny X-Men* #135, July 1980, reprinted in *Marvel Legends: The Dark Phoenix Saga* (New York: Marvel Comics, 2006), 112.

PLATE 22. Jean consumes the energy of a star. Chris Claremont (writer) and John Byrne (penciller), "Dark Phoenix!," *Uncanny X-Men* #135, July 1980, reprinted in *Marvel Legends: The Dark Phoenix Saga* (New York: Marvel Comics, 2006), 124–25.

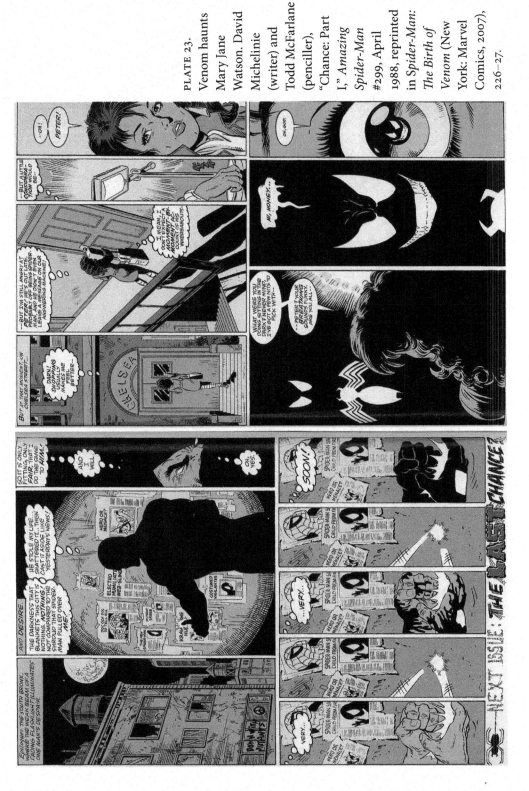

PLATE 23. Venom haunts Mary Jane Watson. David Michelinie (writer) and Todd McFarlane (penciller), "Chance: Part I," *Amazing Spider-Man* #299, April 1988, reprinted in *Spider-Man: The Birth of Venom* (New York: Marvel Comics, 2007), 226–27.

PLATE 24. Left to right: Illyana, Magik, and Darkchylde. Respectively in *New Mutants Classic Vol. 1*, back matter; Bret Blevins (penciller), "Illusion!," *New Mutants* #68, October 1988; Bret Blevins (penciller), "Limbo," *New Mutants* #71, January 1989.

PLATE 25. Dani confronts the Demon Bear. Chris Claremont (writer) and Bill Sienkiewicz (penciller), "Death-Hunt," *The New Mutants* #18, August 1984, reprinted in *The New Mutants Classic Vol. 3* (New York: Marvel Comics, 2008), 19.

PLATE 26. The Badlands. Chris Claremont (writer) and Bill Sienkiewicz (penciller), "Badlands," *The New Mutants* #20, October 1984, reprinted in *New Mutants Classic Vol. 3* (New York: Marvel Comics, 2008), 50–51.

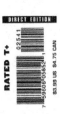

WHERE WERE YOU
WHEN CAPTAIN AMERICA DIED?

PLATE 27. Front and back covers to Ed Brubaker (writer), Steve Epting (penciller), and Mike Perkins (penciller), "The Death of the Dream Part One," *America*: 2007.

PLATE 28. Wrap-around cover to Marjorie Liu (writer) and Perkins (penciller), *Astonishing X-Men* #51, variant edition, August 2012.

4 /   "Where No X-Man Has Gone Before!":
Mutant Superheroes and the Cultural Politics
of the Comic Book Space Opera

In The Silver Surfer #7, a much-avoided issue was brought up in the letters page.... The topic was minorities. It was said it "really doesn't concern you as comic publishers." This is fatally incorrect. True, a comic is a fantasy media. But, once you finish a comic, are you to go on the outside, believing things such as racism don't exist?... Being ignorant of an evil is about the same as supporting it. The comic is a unique thing; both young and old read it. Is it bad if children are taught that people can hate others for ridiculous reasons? Is it bad if an adult is reminded, just once more, that we don't have a perfect world, that people do suffer, and that it can be helped?... Your stories are still fantasy, good fantasy. But, how can it be wrong... if you're trying to build a better world?
    —CHARLES SWIFT, letter published in *The Silver Surfer* #8
(September 1969)

Writing for the *New York Times* in 1971, Saul Braun claimed, "Today's superhero is about as much like his predecessors as today's child is like his parents." In an unprecedented article on the state of American comics, "Shazam! Here Comes Captain Relevant," Braun wove a story of an industry whose former glory producing jingoistic fantasies of superhuman power in the 1930s and 1940s had given way to a canny interest in revealing the power structures against which ordinary people and heroes alike struggled following World War II. Quoting a description of a course on comparative comics at Brown University, he wrote, "Now heroes are different—they ponder moral questions, have emotional differences, and are just as neurotic as real people. Captain America openly sympathizes with campus radicals ... Lois Lane apes John Howard Griffin and turns herself black to study racism, and everybody battles to save the environment." Five years earlier *Esquire* had presaged Braun's claims about comic books' generational appeal, dedicating a spread to the popularity of superhero comics among university students in their special "College Issue." As one student explained, "My favorite is the Hulk, I identify with him, he's the outcast against the institution." Only months after the *New York Times* article saw print, *Rolling Stone* published a six-page exposé on Marvel Comics, and *Ms.* emblazoned Wonder Woman on the cover of their premier issue—declaring "Wonder Woman for President!," no less—and devoted an article to the origins of the latter-day feminist superhero.[1]

Where little more than a decade earlier comics had signaled the moral and aesthetic degradation of American culture, by 1971 they had come of age as America's "native art": taught on Ivy League campuses, studied by European scholars, artists, and filmmakers, and translated and sold around the world, they were now taken up as a new generation's critique of American society. The concatenation of these sentiments among such diverse publications revealed that the growing popularity and public interest in comics (and comic book superheroes) spanned a wide demographic spectrum, appealing to middle-class urbanites, college-age men, members of the counterculture, and feminists alike. As the title of Braun's article suggests, in the early 1970s *relevance* became a popular buzzword denoting a shift in comic book content from oblique narrative metaphors for social problems toward direct representations of racism and sexism, political corruption, and urban blight. *Relevance* also came to describe the intertextual nature of modern superhero comic books, now discussed alongside epic poetry, Shakespearean drama, Hollywood film, and the American novel.

While news media and mainstream readers assumed comic books could be at once political and entertaining, creative producers, editors, and hardcore fans struggled over the appropriate balance between fantasy as pure entertainment and as a vehicle for social-consciousness raising. This tension over the dual role of comic books as forms of social critique and mass market entertainment rapidly intensified and came to dominate discussions of comic book culture at the same historical moment when many members of the youth market that formerly made up the ranks of teenage comic book readers in the 1960s had become politically active young adults who now embraced the radical values of the New Left, black power, and women's and gay liberation movements. The complementary struggles of creators and readers to develop a political consciousness that could move beyond the limits of 1960s liberalism would reshape the American superhero and the genres in which it had previously thrived, namely popular science fantasy and urban realism. In this period, superhero comics increasingly trained a self-reflective eye at the limits of the cosmopolitan vision that had animated series like *The Fantastic Four* throughout the previous decade, lobbing a scathing indictment of American political culture in the form of a moral complaint against the entire human race for its failure to embrace cultural difference and nonviolence. This sense of exhaustion and disappointment with "humanity" would fuel the flight toward ever greater heights of superheroic fantasy, imagining limitless worlds far distant from our own, as well as a variety of creative attempts to revitalize a liberal progressive worldview grounded in affective attachments to egalitarian principals rather than institutional political reform and social activism.

Two genres came to embody these competing projects: the space opera and the urban folktale. These genres reworked earlier science fiction and "realist" conventions of superhero comics to account for American political life after the fracturing of New Left political coalitions in 1968 and the rise of identity politics. In this and the following chapter, I analyze the visual and narrative logics of the space opera and the urban folktale as *the* paradigmatic generic formations through which the American superhero was articulated between 1967 and 1979.

Expanding on the space adventures of *The Fantastic Four*, the space opera depicted Earth as a tiny planet within a vast cosmos teeming with enigmatic and potentially dangerous alien and divine forces capable of destroying humankind with unparalleled space-born powers. By the early 1970s Marvel Comics had introduced its readers to a pantheon of secular gods in such figures as the planet-devouring Galactus; the immortal observer of human folly, the Watcher; the god-like guardian of interstellar life, the Stranger; and lord of the underworld, Mephisto. Space operas expanded the superhero's locus of action to a variety of spiritual, psychic, and otherworldly realms. Where the mutated bodies of the Fantastic Four oriented them toward a heterogeneous outside world of mutants, cyborgs, and aliens, the space opera explored how these species exiles and social minorities dealt with the existential experience of being adrift in a limitless cosmos.

Concurrently the urban folktale emerged as the space opera's geographic and conceptual foil, narrating the return of space-faring heroes to their local origins, the cities where they once labored to safeguard ordinary citizens from the hazards of metropolitan life. If the space opera's primary players were alien species and distant civilizations, the urban folktale was populated by the American underclass, including the homeless, orphaned children, and minorities of all stripes, struggling to survive the harsh realities of urban decline in post–civil rights America. These urban or "ghetto" narratives can be understood as folktales because they played upon American myths of local folk heroes who came to identify with and sought to protect working-class communities from exploitation. The first African American superheroes found popular expression in the urban folktale, most notably Luke Cage, a Harlem youth framed and sent to prison for a crime he did not commit, and the Falcon, a social worker turned superhero who became Captain America's street-smart sidekick in the early 1970s. I explore the urban folktale in chapter 5.

Where the politics of 1960s superheroes were articulated through the materiality of the body, either presented as willful subjects capable of extending superhuman bodies into space or mutated beings stretching the limits of the human, in the 1970s the superhero was reshaped and visually presented as a product of its physical location and the cultural geographies it inhabited. This shift in the locus of meaning making around the superhero from the materiality of the body to the cultural geographies of post-1960s space and place involved a concurrent shift in the visual pleasures of the superhero away from the tactile economies of the body (and encounters with the material object world) toward affectively charged moral identification cemented through images of the superhero's hyperbolic emotional suffering or psychic liberation. The space opera and the urban folktale both relied on the assumption of an intimate reading public that collectively engaged the political failures of American liberalism as a *felt* experience, a loss of morale and trust in institutional reform and the democratic process that could be assuaged only by a turn away from politics toward affective forms of affiliation. In these genres creators used the biologically and socially unstable body of the superhero to explore and potentially bring into being the states of bodily and psychic liberation that a variety of countercultural movements espoused: whether it was the "getting loose" philosophy of the hippie generation or the consciousness-raising projects of liberal feminism, the ecstatic physical states of disco culture or the spiritual communion with nature celebrated by popular ecology, the call for a countercultural politics grounded in felt experience manifested in the visual culture of mainstream superhero comics, which presented readers with superhuman figures whose powers literally materialized these ways of being as physical extensions of the self.

In this chapter I map the trajectory of the space opera from its origins in the late 1960s as a melodramatic narrative of lament for the moral degradation of mankind to its regeneration as a cosmopolitan story of interspecies encounters across the cosmos in the mid-1970s. I begin by describing the emergence of a distinct subgenre of the space opera I call "the messianic melodrama," which narrated the psychic torture of heroic alien visitors to Earth whose altruistic intentions are denied by the "unreasoning hatred" of bellicose humans. In a case study of the influential series *The Silver Surfer* (1968), I show how the messianic melodrama relied on visually hyperbolic expressions of affective frustration with human intolerance to galvanize responses against racism and xenophobia in its readership. In the second half of the chapter, I explore how the genre responded to the resurgence of utopian political visions promulgated by a radical counterculture. I argue that the genre evolved from a narrative of moral complaint to a vehicle for modeling new kinds of social, sexual, and political relations celebrated by the hippie counterculture and women's and gay liberation. To illustrate this I develop a close reading of Marvel Comics' *X-Men* series in the mid-1970s. The highest selling superhero comic of the late twentieth century, *The X-Men* tells the story of an international cadre of superpowered beings known as "mutants," genetically evolved humans outcast by a bigoted and fearful humanity. In a series of epic space adventures, the X-Men were depicted negotiating competing affiliations with nations, minorities, and war-ravaged alien civilizations, while their own chosen kinship reimagined the superhero team as a radical expression of the shift from a celebration of universal humanity in the 1960s to the birth of a "queer mutanity" in the 1970s.

Messianic Melodramas and the Hero's Complaint

While brainstorming a new villain for the Fantastic Four's latest adventure in 1966, Stan Lee and Jack Kirby decided to invent a character with cosmic powers rivaling any to appear in comics past. As Lee put it, "The FF's next super-foe would be more than just a man, more than just a group of men, more than a mere creature from another planet, or any group of planets."[2] Expanding outward through a great chain of being to the universe itself to find their next great villain, Lee and Kirby would present their readers with Galactus, Devourer of Worlds. Galactus is a cosmic entity taking the form of an armored titan who travels the cosmos sapping the physical nutrients from planets that support organic life in order to maintain the balance of living and dead matter in the universe. In the process he obliterates the worlds he visits. As the story goes, Lee and Kirby planned a three-part epic in which the Fantastic Four would battle Galactus for the fate of Earth. When Lee received Kirby's original proofs for the first installment, he was "surprised to find a brand-new character floating around the artwork—a silver skinned, smooth-domed, sky-riding surfer atop a speedy flying surfboard." "When I asked ol' Jackson who he was," Lee claims, "Jack replied something to the effect that a supremely powerful agent like Galactus, a godlike giant who roamed the galaxies, would surely require the services of a herald who could serve him as an advance guard."[3] Dubbed the Silver Surfer, this seemingly minor character would inaugurate an entire genre: the comic book space opera. The Surfer was a hyperrational, alien superpowered being sent in advance of Galactus to seek out worlds for him to consume. Though a harbinger of doom, the Surfer would unexpectedly become an ally to the Fantastic Four when his humanity is awakened by an encounter with Alicia Masters, Ben Grimm's wise and gentle paramour.

Initially unconvinced of humanity's value and steely-eyed in the face of his duties, the Surfer is transformed by Alicia's empathy for his experiences as a lone scout shorn of all worldly attachments and forced to witness the destruction of countless civilizations. Appealing to the Surfer's lost sense of compassion, Alicia implores him, "Perhaps we are not as powerful as your Galactus . . . but we have hearts . . . we have souls . . . we live . . . breathe . . . feel! Can't you see that??" Moved by her plea, the Surfer replies, "Never have I known this strange . . . new emotion. There is a word some races use . . . a word I have never understood until now! At last I know . . . beauty!" In the ensuing battle between the Fantastic Four and Galactus, the Surfer would take a stand on behalf of humanity, turning against his master as he develops feelings of compassion, pity, and pride, all emotional registers previously denied him as Galactus's herald. Ultimately Galactus retires from Earth unsated; though he leaves the human race in peace (at least temporarily), he exiles the Surfer to Earth, revoking the Surfer's immortality while leaving him with his space-born powers. In the years to come, the Silver Surfer would question his allegiance to humanity as he found himself unwillingly trapped on a world replete with countless forms of human cruelty that contradicted Alicia's sympathetic portrait of Earth's highest life form.

Between 1967 and 1978 alien and otherworldly beings like the Silver Surfer and Galactus took center stage in the comic book space opera. As a subgenre of science fiction narrative, the space opera was commonly defined by three characteristics: first, it visualized Earth within an infinitely vast universe whose contents were unknown and potentially threatening to the survival of mankind; second, it employed the limitless geography of outer space as a backdrop for epic struggles between competing forces—alien, human, or cosmic—and a metaphor for the psyche as both a void of loneliness and potential connection, contemplation, and insanity; and third, it used superhuman figures to mediate between space and Earth as bodies whose powers allow them to physically traverse these locales and survive their harsh conditions and also symbolically straddle the social worlds of humans and aliens and the shifting scales of earthly and cosmic conflicts. This expansive vision of the universe as a delicate web threatened by cosmic conflict spoke the language of 1970s environmentalism—with its ecological vision of life on Earth as a chain of interdependencies between humans and animals, organic and inorganic life—while reworking the cold war discourse of global crisis to show how the political policies of nuclear brinksmanship had produced the apocalyptic circumstances they claimed to defend against.

In its early incarnations the space opera commonly took the form of an emotional screed against the petty cruelties of human civilization set against the backdrop of a vast cosmos that evoked awe and humility before the magnitude of life in the universe. I call these early stories messianic melodramas because they inaugurated the space opera as a narrative about the psychic suffering of powerful salvation figures who ambivalently fight on behalf of a humanity they deem morally degraded yet capable of redemption. In August 1968 the Silver Surfer debuted in his own comic book series. Though the series lasted only eighteen issues, retired in 1970 due to creative conflicts over the future direction of the character, it laid the foundation for the narrative and visual tropes that would animate the messianic melodrama in the early 1970s. Following in the footsteps of the Silver Surfer, both the alien warrior Captain Marvel and the omnipotent android Warlock, Christ-like savior figures representing the forces of "good" against a host of human and otherworldly evils, similarly receive spotlight attention in their own series between 1968 and 1976. In these three figures the messianic melodrama developed a new subject-position for the American superhero, no longer a universal citizen nor a fantasy of limitless bodily transformation but a god-like observer and judge of the human race.

Distanced from humankind by their alien origins and their moral superiority, messianic heroes forced readers to realign their previous modes of identification, which traditionally rested on desires to inhabit the identities of their favorite characters. Rather than desiring to *be* the Silver Surfer, readers were encouraged to sympathize with his emotional longings and moral fortitude against human injustice. This alternative mode of identification was displayed in a fan letter published in *The Silver Surfer* #4. Referring to scenes from an earlier issue in which bigoted humans deny the Surfer shelter and companionship the writer states:

What made this issue stand out was the message it contained. In many of your other comics . . . you have portrayed man's unreasoning fear of the unknown, and his hatred of the different and alien. But never has this message been so real . . . as in *Silver Surfer* #2. In scene after scene I felt the anguish and grief of the noble glistening skylark as he was shunned by the very men he risked his life to save; and I felt shame that I, as are all members of the human race, am guilty of the aforementioned sin. This issue seemed pointed at all racists and bigots that roam the Earth, hating and fearing all that is different. If this message was not enough to stop this hatred and fear of the strange of anyone who reads it, nothing will![4]

As this writer suggests, the Silver Surfer reminded readers of their complicity in the moral shortcomings of humanity by inciting feelings of shame and guilt over humankind's intolerance. These tortured emotions were intended to activate a shared investment in making amends for heinous acts of inhumanity, partly through a personal identification with the righteous indignation of the lone alien hero.

Despite its melancholic tone, the messianic melodrama was a resolutely idealist subgenre. It depicted the personal suffering of its heroes not as underwritten by cynicism or lack of moral conviction but from a frustrated desire to transform mankind and nurture universal moral feelings such as goodness, compassion, and love. This ethos described the worldview of the liberal counterculture, particularly in the mainstreaming of hippie culture and environmentalism, which celebrated the freedom of human affective expression and an organic relationship to nature as alternatives to political activism; the genre's relationship to countercultural lifestyles, however, was ambivalent, taking up its egalitarian ethos but avoiding its themes of "loosening" the body through sexual and psychotropic experiences.[5] In this way the messianic melodrama was committed to free will and agency as abstract values but remained wary of the free or promiscuous use of the physical body, presenting its heroes as highly self-disciplined allegorical ciphers for universal humanist ideals.

Messianic heroes were commonly members of alien races or nonhuman cosmic beings whose travels unexpectedly led them to Earth. There they were simultaneously horrified by humanity's petty cruelties while enamored with its "innate goodness" and the individual's purportedly unlimited capacity for love and generosity. Responding to the discrepancy between humanity's moral potential and real-world injustice, the messianic melodrama was articulated in the register of what Lauren

Berlant has called "the female complaint," a rhetorical mode organized by an affective lament over the failure of democratic political life to adequately live up to its promise of universal inclusion and equality. This rhetorical mode, primarily associated with women's culture, foregrounds emotional or felt responses to political failures by encouraging sentimental identification between similarly alienated individuals who, despite their differences, are made to feel that their experience of disaffection from the political realm is equivalent and widely shared.[6]

This rhetoric of complaint is commonly gendered female because it was inaugurated by the emergence of a distinct women's culture in the early nineteenth century that was underwritten by the recognition of women's exclusion from American political life. Conceptually speaking, its association with both socially marginalized groups and hyperbolic emotionality also makes the complaint a uniquely "gender-marked" form of address. What is most distinctive about the female complaint is its combination of frustrated critique of systemic inequality alongside a fervent attachment to the very norms and values that underwrite the unequal social world it admonishes, identifying the female complaint as "a space of disappointment, but not disenchantment."[7] Berlant argues that the penultimate genre for this complaint is melodrama, which pits the martyrdom of a victimized hero against the evil machinations of institutional powers (the government, private industry, or a cruel or unjust world) but seeks to reward personal suffering and moral fortitude through the generic construct of the love plot. The cultural texts of the female complaint repeatedly suggest that where political justice and social transformation fail, the fulfillment of romantic desire in private life can ameliorate the inability to reform or revivify the institutions of liberal democracy.[8]

The messianic melodrama similarly reflected a broader disappointment with liberal politics while attempting to ameliorate political failures by interpolating a reading public putatively identified with the moral lament of a powerful but struggling salvation figure. This lament found its greatest expression in *The Silver Surfer*, a series that became famous for its lengthy diatribes against humanity's flawed character. Nearly every issue of the series begins with an extended soliloquy by the eponymous hero decrying his horrible fate, trapped on Earth and denied the company of his former beloved Shalla Bal, and the barbaric actions of the hate-mongering species with whom he must live out his days. In the series' inaugural issue, the Surfer reflects upon time spent with the human race since first meeting the Fantastic Four. Gliding across the landscape of the majestic Rocky Mountains, he pleads to the heavens, "In all the galaxies . . . in all the endless reaches of space . . . I have found no planet more blessed than this . . . no world more lavishly endowed with natural beauty . . . with every ingredient to create a virtual living paradise! Possessed of rainfall in great abundance . . . soil fertile enough to feed a galaxy! And a sun . . . ever-warm . . . ever constant . . . ever symbolizing new life, new hope! It is as though the human race has been divinely favored over all who live! And yet . . . in their uncontrollable insanity . . . they seek to destroy this shining jewel . . . this softly-spinning gem . . . which men call earth! While, trapped upon this world of madness . . . stand I!" (plate 11).[9] Were it not to be found in the pages of a superhero comic book, the Surfer's lament would fit in any environmentalist polemic of the late 1960s. Predating but presciently capturing the sentiments of environmentalism's soon-to-be-famous slogans "Give Earth a Chance!" and "I Have Seen the Enemy, and He Is Us," this paradigmatic example of the Surfer's numerous critiques of man's folly positions the human race as antagonists to the planet and its natural riches.[10] The Surfer's lament is foregrounded by the natural beauty of the Rocky Mountains, brightly colored in psychedelic hues of red and orange against a vivid blue sky, splashing through streams of fresh water, and finally reaching heavenward with an upturned hand as though directing his address to the cosmos itself. The visual structure of the sequence encapsulates the broader project of the messianic melodrama: to transcend the realm of the political—identified in the previous scene by U.S., Russian, and Chinese military leaders who dispatch missiles against the peaceful Surfer—through recourse to a universally shared experience of the natural world, the latter necessarily understood as a sentimental site for moral regeneration squandered by humans.

No social movement of the late 1960s and early 1970s harnessed the language of the female complaint more directly than environmentalism, which deployed an emotionally charged moral rhetoric lobbied against ecological destruction to galvanize human investment in planetary survival. By the early 1970s environmentalism's "whole earth" ideology, which imagined the planet as a complex web of human and nonhuman interdependencies requiring care and aid for their mutual flourishing, had infused a wide array of popular culture forms: dystopian science fiction films depicting bleak outcomes of environmental catastrophe, lifestyle periodicals like the *Whole Earth Catalog* that sold forms of sustainable living, and national public events like the first Earth Day celebration in April 1970 that sought to ignite social consciousness about the ecological health of the planet.[11] Popular expressions of environmentalism often eschewed direct appeals for environmental policy reforms, instead eliciting emotional or sentimental investment in ecological concerns through an impassioned plea to take personal responsibility for Earth's future.

The Surfer's cosmic perspective on the privileges afforded by Earth's rich biosphere encouraged a form of enlarged thinking as a corollary to environmentalism's demand that humans consider the needs of the planet in ecological rather than political or partisan terms. In his speech the Surfer juxtaposes the "insanity" of human folly with the natural order of the planet, akin to the perfect shape or organization of a "jewel" or a "gem." This rhetoric echoed whole earth environmentalism, which used the famous 1972 NASA images of Earth as a floating orb in space to project an image of a self-contained ecosystem whose natural majesty should be honored and protected.[12] The Surfer's repeated reference to Earth's fertility and abundance also recalls a conception of the planet as a distinctly gendered figure (codified in James Lovelock's "Gaia hypothesis" in 1979, which posited a universal feminine force connecting all elements of the natural world), a nurturing mother or lover, abused by her kin. Combining rich figurative description with hyperbolic visual majesty, the scene sutures the natural beauty of Earth to the Surfer's anguish, cutting from the expanse of the Rocky Mountains to the hero's suffering visage, an iconic mask of despair that functions as the moral anchor demanding an ethical relationship to the natural world.

The messianic melodrama linked worldly political traumas to otherworldly moral structures by visually juxtaposing the epic vistas of Earth's natural landscape and outer space with the intimate features of the human face, often contorted in pain in response to the suffering that took place amid such beauty (plate 12). *The Silver Surfer* exhibits a near-obsessive depiction of the Surfer's face twisted in horror, often an exact echo of Edvard Munch's *The Scream*, or outrage at the circumstances that bind him to Earth. Alongside facial close-ups, messianic melodramas fetishized images of the hero's tortured body, lying prostrate in emotional defeat, fists clenched in fury at some injustice, or else wracked with physical pain inflicted by demonic villains or humankind's advanced military weapons. Eliciting universal empathy for the outcast martyr, the tortured expressions of the suffering hero became the visual horizon that stood in for direct political critique.

Messianic superheroes were gifted with powers so vast—cosmic abilities that included nearly unlimited strength and speed, supersonic ght, telepathy, energy projection, and invulnerability—as to make any confrontation with ordinary corporeal foes meaningless. Just as messianic heroes embodied goodness, compassion, and love, so in the classic melodramatic formula, they faced all-powerful cosmic villains who allegorically embodied evil, greed, and hatred. The Surfer's archnemesis Mephisto, for instance, appeared as a latter-day devil (a cross between Lucifer and Dracula with crimson cape and fangs), one of the Marvel Universe's most powerful villains and lord of the underworld who desires nothing but the destruction of mankind.[13]

Echoing the Surfer's tortured soliloquies, Mephisto appears throughout the series proclaiming his love of all things base and mean in the human condition. In one arresting splash panel, his imposing figure looks down upon a montage of images depicting human greed in the form of a cigar-smoking hustler delighting in a wad of cash, homelessness, violent mobs in a race riot, and the burning landscape of a war-ravaged city as tanks roll over its muddy streets (plate 13). Over this kaleidoscopic vision of human catastrophe, Mephisto intones, "So long as I can appeal to man's basest instincts—to his greed—his envy—his hatreds and aggression—his fear and distrust of his fellow man—so long as man takes the law into his own hands—both in the streets—and on the fields of battles—and so long as crime covers the planet like a deadly creeping fungus—then, only Mephisto shall reap the final reward!"[14]

Mephisto's hell is grounded in the daily realities of human moral conflict. Significantly this vision collapses highly divergent phenomena under the banner of human moral bankruptcy: in scenes like these, everything from domestic political activism to global warfare are swept into a homogeneous maelstrom of evil. Moving between Judeo-Christian frames of moral decline in its references to the seven deadly sins, while simultaneously calling upon the language of environmental decline and evolutionary backsliding—comparing crime to a deadly fungus and denying human progress by highlighting man's "basest instincts"—Mephisto's celebration of human degradation reveals the messianic melodrama's problematic investment in identifying and critiquing both moral and political corruption as two sides of the same coin. The genre's emotional intensity is so powerful as to drown out significant differences between various forms of human conflict, refusing to distinguish between truly fascistic forms of power and progressive struggles for political freedom.

One contradiction consistently performed in these texts was the contention that their lead characters were embodiments of pure good but were potentially susceptible to evil by their very proximity to a flawed humanity. In *The Silver Surfer* and *Warlock* series especially, the fear that either hero might ultimately repudiate humanity and their commitment to fight for universal good was an underlying concern of a variety of plots. When the Surfer is ambushed and imprisoned by an angry mob after trying to save a young woman's life, he thinks to himself, "I dared not use my power against them, lest I destroy them all! But, how much longer . . . before I, too, am afflicted by the virus of human savagery?"[15] Like Mephisto's reference to the "fungus" of crime, humanity's barbarism is naturalized as a disease to which all, including those with seemingly limitless moral fortitude, are susceptible.

These texts also reflected ambivalence about the efficacy of both religious worldviews and scientific authority to make up for the failings of humanism and liberal democracy. As the Marvel Universe grew in scope with the introduction of new characters, plots, and genres, an intricate cosmology took shape that included a growing cadre of otherworldly forces who allegorically stood in for broader moral categories (such as Mephisto, who embodies pure "evil") as well as traditionally sacred icons across a variety of religious systems. The relationship between Galactus and the Silver Surfer, for instance, could easily be read as an allegory for the relationship between God and Christ, while also functioning as a metaphor for humanity's dual character as a resource-devouring leviathan and a potentially moral race whose innate goodness is reflected in the Surfer's decision to help save the planet from extinction. Likewise Warlock appears to his "master," the High Evolutionary, as a long-lost son who might rid the world he created of its inherent evil. Having engineered an alternate Earth in a direct echo of God's seven days of creation, the High Evolutionary appears as both scientist and deity, while his genetically engineered progeny takes on Christ's mantle as a religious savior.

Despite their apparent moral and intellectual superiority, god-like figures like Galactus and the High Evolutionary consistently undermine the concept of a benevolent higher power by appearing mired in humanity's moral corruption. In every appearance these minor deities are depicted as petty, cruel, and self-serving, while the heroes of the Marvel Universe reveal them to be false gods manipulating their worshipers and using their knowledge and power for destructive ends.[16] Just as these cosmic beings discredit notions of divine leadership, they similarly undermine the utopian hope that human evolution will ultimately solve the species' internecine conflicts. In the *Warlock* series the High Evolutionary uses an advanced technology to transform himself into what man "will be at the end of a million centuries of evolution." Far from granting him transcendence from worldly concerns, his metamorphosis fails to ward off loneliness, self-doubt, and an extraordinary narcissism that manifests as a god complex. It is precisely in his evolved state that the High Evolutionary unleashes the very evil he was intent on eradicating, by genetically engineering a race of advanced human-animal hybrids that seek to exterminate mankind.[17]

The messianic melodrama's distrust in traditional icons of spiritual moral authority was paired with a deep suspicion of utopian visions of technological progress. In the first issue of *The Silver Surfer* the alien wanderer recounts the journey that led him to become herald to Galactus. Originally named Norrin Radd, the Silver Surfer was a brilliant but tortured scientist on his home world, Zenn-La, a society so technologically advanced it had become a utopia where all needs and desires were attended to without personal effort. Unsatisfied with an empty existence of unearned pleasure, Radd studies his people's history, locating the origin of their moral decline in their first attempts at space flight. He recounts, "An entire universe was beckoning to us. . . . We had the will . . . to probe the vastness of the distant unknown! Our greatest heroes were the fearless space-spanning astronauts . . . to whom . . . no world was too forbidding. But then, one day . . . it ended! We had probed the cosmos. . . . We had . . . seen too much! And then . . . we no longer cared! . . . For us, the age of space travel had died. . . . Nothing remains . . . save stark and bleak decay!"[18] Rather than compelling humans toward further technological, moral, and political advancement, space travel enervates Zenn-La's people by granting them a feeling of godhood without moral investment in the well-being of the cosmos. The Surfer's narration of this historical travesty coincides with his musings about a technologically obsessed humankind: he voices doubt about whether or not science will fulfill man's potential or stem it and whether peaceable human relations are possible or doomed to collapse in endless cycles of violence. Presciently foreshadowing the first U.S. trip to the moon the following year, the comic boldly questions the utopian logic of the 1960s space race, appropriating the language of astronauts and physicists as "fearless pioneers," to reveal the nation's exuberant hope for space flight as pipe dreams. According to the Surfer, the most terrifying consequence of this overdetermined hope in technological progress is not violence or death but apathy, a carelessness about the world that would spell the doom of social progress and ethics alike.

As a counterbalance to the hollow spiritual content of false gods and the failed promise of technological progress, the messianic melodrama identified love as a secular emotional force linking religious morality with universal humanism to heal all conflicts, whether individual, collective, or cosmic. In the messianic melodrama, love is seen to transcend the barriers between human and alien identities (revealing the supposedly inherent "humanity" of alien beings), while also functioning as a viscerally felt intensity transmitted between bodies that can fill the vast emptiness of outer space with emotional plenitude. This turn to "love" to ameliorate the failures of political life reiterated the genre's attachment to the logic of the female complaint. Elaborating on the link between the female complaint and a fetishization of romantic love, Berlant states, "Love is the gift that keeps on giving when people can rely on re-experiencing their intimates' fundamental sympathy with the project of repetition and recognition. . . . This explains the fetishistic optimism of romantic love about 'tomorrow,' as in 'tomorrow is another day' when there will be opportunities to try again. Love is the gift that keeps on taking for the same reason; the search for mirroring (desire) demands constant improvisation (anxiety) and taking of accounts (disappointment)."[19] This statement describes exactly the logic of the messianic melodrama, whose cyclical narrative of complaint followed by hope for another day, when humanity's moral failings might be recuperated, is consistently mediated by the messianic hero's romantic love for a distant paramour, a love that marks him as a paragon of human goodness and compassion despite his alien origins.

In issue #6 the Silver Surfer could once again be seen voicing his frustration and rage at being trapped on Earth. This time, however, he attributes his frustration to his lost ties to the woman he loves rather than his limited freedom to roam the stars: "How much longer must I be an alien prisoner upon the savage planet earth? How much longer before the loneliness destroys me?? . . . I am hated—and feared—by the very humans my heart longs to aid! My heart! Did I say my heart? How can that be—since I have no heart! For I have left it—countless galaxies away—with the one whom I love—on the planet Zenn-La! It is there my world begins and ends—it is there that I left—Shalla Bal!"[20] The Surfer invokes the metaphorical image of his heart as the object that compels his compassion for humanity but is vitalized by his love for Shalla Bal. Shortly after this monologue, readers see Shalla Bal willing her thoughts to the Surfer across the reaches of space: "Truly beloved—wherever you may be—there is no place too distant—for my heart to reach you!" Jolted by their psychic rapport, the Surfer thinks aloud, "I seem to hear her voice! I seem to sense her thoughts! . . . They give me the strength—they give me the will—to endure!" Here love is visualized as a literal substance that can traverse the cosmos at any distance as well as infuse one with benevolent intent.

The bonds of romantic love are presented as being so powerful that the suffering experienced when love is threatened or unattainable emaciates messianic heroes. Over the course of *The Silver Surfer*, the hero's muscular frame increasingly loses its definition. By issue #6, as he glides across the night sky bemoaning the loss of Shalla Bal, his body appears limp and enervated, no longer silver but a ghostly white.[21] Male readers in particular complained about his visual metamorphosis, interpreting the change in the hero's former muscularity as a sign of the comic's shifting genre status from science fiction to melodrama. One fan decried, "I can't stand it! Take a good look at the Silver Surfer depicted in his sixth issue. He looks almost like a ninety-seven-pound weakling. Surfy has come from a super-human muscle-bound superhero to a puny nothing. What has happened? Please bring his muscles back!!!!"[22] Another directly lambasted the creators' attachment to hyperbolic displays of emotionality: "When you first introduced the Silver Surfer he was completely unique, due to the fact that he had next to no emotional response to any situation and acted purely on intellect.... Now he is an emotional, moody, lovesick... melodrama."[23] But while some found this transformation appalling, others understood it as an appropriate material expression of the Surfer's psychic anguish, indicating his will to live (presumably for Shalla Bal) despite an array of physical and emotional depredations, as well as his noble suffering on mankind's behalf.

As Berlant argues, this conception of the "will to endure" an array of political and social hardships by virtue of one's hyperbolic love for another "collaborates with a sentimental account of the social world as an affective space where people ought to be legitimated because they have feelings and because there is intelligence in what they feel that knows something about the world that, if it were listened to, could make things better."[24] Readers confirmed this fact when they lauded Stan Lee and artist John Buscema for creating a character with such an authentic emotional response to human suffering. They described the Surfer as embodying a "noble anguish" over human failure, a superhero who "evokes emotion" as no other could, and "the most compassionate 'god' in the Marvel pantheon."[25] Perhaps most telling was the statement of this reader: "Here we have a superhero who wins his battles, not with his fists, but with a tear."[26] In the classic formula of the female complaint, the hyperbolic emotionality of figures like the Silver Surfer worked through an intimate reading public that valued "positive" human feelings like love, compassion, generosity, and dignified suffering. It is through these intensely embodied feeling states, in fact, that the messianic melodrama consistently effaces the vicissitudes of lived social inequality, subsuming them within a sentimental vision of universal intimacy.

Only once did *The Silver Surfer* present a human ally to its title hero. In issue #5 readers were introduced to Al Harper, a brilliant but humble African American scientist working on developing a technology that might help the Surfer escape his earthbound prison. After his initial meeting with the Surfer, Harper thinks to himself, "He's treated like an outcast wherever he goes.... Just because of the way he looks! Just because he's different! Maybe it takes a guy like me to really understand!"[27] At the end of the story Harper sacrifices his life to diffuse a bomb placed on Earth by a god-like being named the Stranger that would exterminate mankind. Unlike the Surfer, the Stranger is unconvinced of mankind's potential for good, believing that the cosmos would be safer if the violent species were wiped out. Despite his own experiences with bigotry and racism, Harper sacrifices himself for the people who've shunned him. Rather than an unfair martyrdom, his death is presented as a noble gesture akin to the Surfer's compassion. One fan claimed that the story's affective intensity brought him to tears: "To see one man who met with persecution and misunderstanding all his life give himself for mankind was truly noble. . . . I actually wept after reading the last panel of the story. Perhaps . . . because I could identify with Al since I too am a black American, or maybe because I take a sentimental look at things."[28]

Though Al Harper represents one of the rare instances when the messianic melodrama directly addressed historical experiences of racial inequality, the messianic melodrama could cultivate compassion for such experiences only through the attachments of romantic love.[29] In the opening sequence of the following issue, the Surfer's memory of Shalla Bal precedes a melancholic visit to Al Harper's abandoned home and laboratory, where he worked tirelessly to free his alien friend from his shackles. It is only after imagining Shalla Bal's love traversing the galaxies to reach him that the Surfer is compelled to pay his last respects to the one human who had ever shown him kindness. By framing Harper's relationship to the Surfer in affective terms—through the rerouting of the Surfer's love for Shalla Bal toward a human friend—rather than shared political investments in values like antiracism and nonviolence, the series shut down possibilities for further exploring affiliations between racial minorities and similarly minoritized heroes, leaving the messianic hero to wander the spaceways alone with only his righteous virtue to guide him.

Despite its initial popularity, the messianic melodrama was a short-lived generic formation. The subgenre's highly formulaic narrative structure restricted attempts to develop its central heroes beyond their moral lament against humankind. Similarly its depiction of a seemingly endless array of human cruelties contradicted its investment in combating political cynicism, while its inability to distinguish among different forms of human aggression—such as that between military violence and activist protest—dulled its ability to make politically salient claims about contemporary geopolitics. In one of the more judicious critiques of *The Silver Surfer* a fan wrote, "Surely, Stan, the human race must have learned something about tolerance in the past 20 centuries! In *The Silver Surfer* . . . you portray humanity as being grossly selfish, cowardly, unbelievably cruel and ignorant. . . . I'm hoping this is not your true opinion of 'we, the people.'"[30]

It was the Silver Surfer's refusal to remain within the confines of the melodramatic mode that spelled the demise of the messianic melodrama almost before it even came into its own as a fully formed subgenre. In his final adventure, in issue #18, the Surfer encounters the Inhumans when he spies their sanctuary, the Great Refuge, during one of his tours of Earth. Black Bolt's royal family initially mistake the Surfer for one of Maximus's assassins, attacking him without warning. Though the Inhumans quickly realize their mistake and try to make amends by welcoming the Surfer into their home, their initial hostility proves the last straw for the space-faring hero, whose repeated abuse by nearly every population on Earth finally breaks his spirit. The last page of the series depicts a tight close-up of the Surfer's enraged face as he screams to the world:

> Too long have I displayed restraint! But now—my very soul is aflame with burning rage! In a world of madness—I tried to practice reason—but all I won was hatred and everlasting strife! So I'll have done with reason—and with love—or mercy! . . . Since a fiendish fate has trapped me here with a hostile race in a nightmare world! . . . I'll . . . blot out my space-born ethic—no longer will I resist their earthly madness! No longer mine a lonely voice, pleading peace in a world of strife! From this time forth, the Silver Surfer will battle them on their own savage terms![31]

Where the series began as an extended complaint against human intolerance, it ends as screed against both liberal politics and sentimental compassion as viable sites of moral redress. Unable to offer solutions to the emotional experience of liberal exhaustion, the messianic melodrama concludes with the one feeling it assiduously repressed: unbridled rage. While this vitriolic abandonment of liberal tolerance appears to jettison any possibility for social change, its radical negativity short-circuits the melodramatic imaginary, destroying the clear line between "good" and "evil" and questioning the capacity of emotion or sentiment alone to make up for the failures of American political life.

The Surfer's last statement was so powerful that it derailed the series. Below this final portrait, a banner advertised "The Savagely Sensational NEW Silver Surfer!," who would presumably appear in the next issue. This new Surfer never made an appearance, as the series was canceled following this issue. According to Lee, the creative direction they had taken the character was so different from what he was originally intended to represent that the series' producers couldn't decide how to narrate a character who had renounced the very ideals they thought they were upholding.[32] Torn between a variety of competing responses to the collapse of left political coalitions in the late 1960s, among them the search for alternative models of human interconnectedness, moral regeneration through spiritual awakening, the "loosening up" ideology of the counterculture, cynicism and alienation, and unadulterated rage, the messianic melodrama served as testing ground for exploring the role of the superhero in a world where the unifying categories of humanism—universal rights, free will, and rational thought—were in terminal crisis. The messianic hero explored all these avenues of redress, taking on a variety of guises—biblical martyr, ecological spokesperson, and god-like judge of humanity—discarding each in turn as all proved unequal to the task of reinventing the humanist tradition. The Surfer's final dramatic break from the generic conventions of the melodramatic form offered an opportunity to move beyond a visually redundant complaint about the state of contemporary politics toward productive attempts to imagine what the unwritten pages after the hero's final proclamation might look like.

In the mid-1970s no comic book would expand the generic limits of the space opera more boldly or successfully than the X-Men, a series that narrated the universe-spanning exploits of a band of outcast mutant superheroes. With the X-Men the messianic melodrama gave way to the galactic space war, a modality of the space opera that narrated grand conflicts between alien civilizations that brought Earth into their crosshairs. The galactic space war popularized stories involving hundreds of characters, conflicts spanning multiple galaxies, and interpersonal relations that tied everyday lives to cosmic events. The transformation of the space opera from the moral lament of messianic melodramas to the messy entanglements of galactic space wars marked a creative and ideological shift in superhero storytelling from a politics of liberal exhaustion to a politics of world making. By celebrating the existence of nonhuman species that included the mutant and the alien, while highlighting the internal heterogeneity of the human race, the galactic space war depicted cross-species affiliations based on shared social interests rather than an assumed moral commitment to the category of the human.

From Humanity to Mutanity

First published in 1963 as part of the Marvel Revolution in superhero storytelling, *The X-Men* introduced readers to five suburban teenagers gifted with extraordinary abilities stemming from an evolution in their genetic makeup. In the fictional Marvel Universe, such beings came to be known as mutants, constituting a distinct population alongside those made superhuman by radioactive materials, scientific experimentation, or extensive physical training. Under the guidance of world-class telepath Professor Charles Xavier, the X-Men honed their abilities while exploring the complex and often contentious relations between humanity and an emergent mutantkind. By popularizing the genetic mutant as a social and species minority, the series laid the foundation for reimagining the superhero as a figure that, far from drawing readers to a vision of ideal citizenship through patriotic duty or righteous suffering, dramatized the politics of inequality, exclusion, and difference.

Popular use of the term *mutation* long predated *The X-Men*, circulating widely throughout the 1950s in conjunction with concerns over incidences of radiation-related death due to atomic testing. In 1962, *The X-Men*'s first year of publication, Rachel Carson's best-selling book *Silent Spring* rerouted national discourse on the negative effects of radiation to the widespread use of insecticides, whose chemical qualities, Carson claimed, could wreak havoc on the human genome.[33] Resignifying the meanings attached to *mutation*, *The X-Men* fused real-world fears about the disabling effects of radiation exposure with the impossible notion that such effects could accelerate the evolution of the human species, granting people remarkable "mutant powers." Simultaneously the series revalued physical disability and visible difference from ordinary humanity as the ground upon which new forms of social and political community could be articulated. The elasticity of mutation as a metaphor for a variety of embodied and cultural differences made it a potent popular fantasy for vitalizing Marvel Comics' cosmopolitan ethos at the level of both comic book content and public reception. The ongoing stories of the X-Men's conflicted relationship to humanity encouraged readers to identify with the band of mutant outcasts and even desire the team's pariah status as a defining feature of their own subjectivity.

As generative as the concept of mutation was for a popular appraisal of cultural difference, *The X-Men*'s all-white suburban cast seemed out of place in the popular culture milieu of the late 1960s, especially when juxtaposed with the increasingly racially and culturally diverse casts of other Marvel Comics series, like *The Fantastic Four* and *The Avengers* (1963). Despite its initial success, the series foundered in the late 1960s and was canceled. In the case of the original *X-Men*, the failure to explicitly articulate mutation to race, gender, and sexuality evacuated the political purchase of the category by leaving it an empty placeholder for a variety of real-world differences.[34]

In 1975, five years after its cancellation, *The X-Men* was reborn under the creative direction of Marvel editor Len Wien and newcomers Chris Claremont and Dave Cockrum. Reinventing the team as an international cadre of mutants with diverse and often traumatic personal histories, Claremont and Cockrum helped make *The X-Men* the single most successful comic book in industry history. The revamped team included Ororo Monroe (Storm), an African weather goddess able to manipulate atmospheric forces like lightning, hurricanes, and hail; Peter Rasputin (Colossus), a Russian farmer capable of turning his body into impenetrable steel, granting him superhuman strength, stamina, and invulnerability; Kurt Wagner (Nightcrawler), a German elf and circus acrobat able to teleport to any location within visible range; Logan (Wolverine), a rapid healer with "adamantium"-laced bones and retractable claws capable of cutting through nearly any material; and Sean Cassidy (Banshee), able to produce supersonic sound waves powerful enough to slice steel.[35] By expanding the racial, geographic, and gender makeup of the mutant species to include characters and identities previously ignored by the series, the new *X-Men* articulated mutation to the radical critiques of identity promulgated by the cultures of women's and gay liberation.[36]

Throughout the 1970s these social movements developed critiques of heteropatriarchy that celebrated gender nonconformity, alternative community building outside heterosexual coupling, and the politicization of private life as a way of building alliances between people of disparate identity groups. Within this political logic the developing category of "gay identity," which initially described same-sex desire, became conceptually linked to a variety of identities that similarly thwarted the normative expectations of traditional heterosexual life paths. Writing about the Gay Liberation Front, the first radical gay activist organization in the early 1970s, Richard Meyer explains, "The GLF understood the term gay as part of a broader reinvention of traditional categories of sex and gender and, by extension, of society itself. 'Gay,' wrote Allen Young in his manifesto . . . 'in its most far-reaching sense, means not homosexual, but sexually free. . . . It is sexual freedom premised upon the notion of pleasure through equality.'"[37] In this way an expansive understanding of gay identity as a category that bound people across racial, gender, and class differences through their shared experience of alienation from heteropatriarchal norms emerged as a socially viable popular fantasy that was as culturally and politically capacious as the concept of "mutation."[38]

Echoing Xavier's recruitment of the original X-Men as students at his school, the legendary first issue of the revamped title opens with a series of vignette's depicting Xavier traveling the world searching for new mutants to join his team. These snapshots display the diverse ethnoracial background of each new recruit while vividly foregrounding the struggles of mutants to survive in a world where they are "hated and feared" by a human majority. In the opening scene Xavier saves Kurt Wagner's life when he telepathically pacifies a mob of German villagers prepared to lynch the defiant mutant for his elfish features and blue skin. Equally poignant is Peter Rasputin's struggle to leave the Russian village where he and his family have lived since his youth; raised under communism, he questions whether to use his powers or hide them, fearing they grant him unfair advantage in a world populated by the working poor. As these and other scenes attest, the new X-Men visually linked the popular fantasy of mutation to concrete differences grounded in histories of race hatred, cold war political oppression, and Western imperialism.[39]

From the outset the newly revamped X-Men staged a conceptual standoff between the team's old guard and their new, transnational incarnations, revealing the ways the original team would need to adapt to a new world order if they expected to evolve, and survive, as heroes and mutant ambassadors. This was dramatized in the iconic cover image of Giant-Size X-Men #1, which depicts the new team in full color bursting through a blue-hued portrait of the original team, whose faces appear contorted in horror as they are superseded by this interracial mutant generation (plate 14). The disparity in formal color between the two sets of mutants underscores the obvious racial differences that distinguish the two teams, which is highlighted by the presence of black, brown, and even blue-skinned figures in the central image, set against the homogeneous all-white cast behind them. At the same time, the new X-Men's literal "tearing through" the borders of the frame suggested that the shift in team membership could effect an equivalent transformation of the comic book's visual politics, now tasked with depicting an expanding set of characters and their myriad social identities.

Between 1975 and 1978 Claremont and Cockrum constructed the developing relationships between the new X-Men and their predecessors around epic space adventures that forced them to realign their traditional local affiliations with alien civilizations whose internal conflicts allegorized the social and political strife that dogged human and mutant relations on Earth. Neither uniformly affiliated with any nation nor properly human in their biological makeup, the X-Men forged alliances across difference that exceeded even *The Fantastic Four*'s inhuman anthropology. *The X-Men* developed the popular fantasy of the mutant superhero not only to resist a variety of repressive social norms—including racial segregation, sexism, and xenophobia—but also to facilitate new kinds of choices about political affiliation and personal identification. Within the comic book's narrative the encounter between geographically and ethnically diverse mutants who had formerly struggled to survive independently of a mutant community transformed the political investments each of these figure previously held, reorienting their everyday choices around an ethical commitment to protect one another from various threats posed by antimutant activists, government agents, and other mutants bent on their destruction. They proposed an alternative to the seemingly all-inclusive sign of "universal humanity" in the form of a cross-species kinship network more properly described as a "queer mutanity." This coalition took shape through three key innovations in superhero storytelling that would define the *X-Men*'s popular appeal for the next four decades.

First, the series developed a distinctly feminist approach to forging alliances across difference. As a corollary to its critique of normative identity, *The X-Men* shifted the traditional locus of affective and political identification in mainstream superhero comics from white male heroes to powerful and racially diverse female superheroes whose emotional strength anchored mutant kinships and whose superpowers granted them unprecedented ability to reshape the material world. Where formerly the messianic hero's suffering male body anchored the emotional identification of reading publics around the shared experience of liberal exhaustion, now the vital body of the female superhero audaciously announcing her visual presence on the comic book page reconfigured audience identification around a proactive assertion of bodily agency and collective world making. The X in the team's name refers to the fictional X gene that gives each member his or her mutant powers, yet it also identifies mutants as both literal and figurative "ex-men," neither considered proper members of humanity nor embodying the ideals of superheroic masculinity.

The depiction of empowered female superheroes indexed the political values of feminism while visualizing those ideals through the aesthetics of feminist and gay cultural formations, including the politics of sexual liberation and disco culture. Specifically the comic book presented the superheroine's exercise of her mutant abilities as a psychedelic flowering of self-awareness that enabled a refashioning of the terms that organized her identity as woman, mutant, X-Man, or other. This was depicted in extravagant explosions of color and quasi-mystical graphics that linked female acts of superhuman energy projection, telepathy, and telekinesis to sumptuous displays of feminist empowerment. The female superheroes of *The X-Men* linked the pleasures and dangers of deploying one's mutant powers to the work of forging new bonds between unlikely allies that transformed both psychic and physical states of being, as well as the visual organization of the comic book page.[40] These newly elaborated female characters—most powerfully embodied by the African weather goddess Storm and the telekinetic powerhouse Jean Grey—performed multiple, overlapping, and often contradictory identities, even as they sought to articulate a coherent sense of self.

These characters' varied practices of self-making reflected a second key feature of *The X-Men* series: its commitment to visually dramatizing the intersectional nature of identity. In the X-Men's countless adventures, the series repeatedly highlighted the difficult labors of each team member to negotiate multiple, conflicting identifications with national, biological, familial, ethnic, and geographic loyalties. Simultaneously the creators' innovative deployment of the comic book form—through the display of racially diverse bodies in expansive tableaux exceeding any single panel, and the use of comic strip seriality to dramatize shifts in time and space corresponding to changes in personal identity—confirmed the medium's exceptional capacity to map these multiple affiliations visually. Third, *The X-Men*'s adventures collectively produced an evolving cognitive map of individual histories as they came into contact with broader collectives that included mutants, humans, and aliens of many stripes. These latter encounters were part of the X-Men's epic space travels, which resignified the meanings attached to outer space not simply as a symbolic void of alienation and anomie but as an imaginative playground where encounters with cosmic forces and alien life forms offered forms of recognition previously denied to mutant outcasts like the X-Men and their manifold allies.

"Enter the Phoenix!" *The X-Men's* Feminist Cosmology

No female figures dominated the visual and affective narrative of the new *X-Men* more than the African weather goddess Ororo Monroe, claiming the moniker "Storm," and the team's first superheroine, Jean Grey, who would become the all-powerful cosmic being "Phoenix." In these two characters readers witnessed the absorption of popular feminist politics into the pages of mainstream superhero comics. By the mid-1970s images of sexually liberated and psychologically empowered women had begun saturating both mainstream and independent cultural production, as evidenced in popular narratives of sexual awakening like Erica Jong's *Fear of Flying* (1973) and Rita Mae Brown's *Rubyfruit Jungle* (1973), the creative work of feminist science fiction authors and alternative comics artists, and popular cinema in genres from science fiction to blaxploitation. *The X-Men's* belated entry into this cultural archive allowed the comic book to straddle the ideals of a dominant white liberal feminism, celebrating consciousness raising and sexual self-determination, as well as the values of an emergent multiracial women of color feminism that highlighted the need to produce alliances across difference and question the articulation of gender hierarchy to race and class. Applauding this project, the teenage reader Marilyn Brogdon wrote in *X-Men* #103, "I've been an X-fan since 1967. All this time, I thought it highly unlikely that all 'good' mutants were Caucasian who just happened to live on the east coast of the United States. The emergence of an international and interracial team is a great step forward. As a young black woman, I am particularly interested in Chris' development of Ororo. I wonder how Chris will handle her relationship with a group of white males."[41] Articulating her personal investment in the X-Men, and Storm in particular, through her identity as an African American woman, Brogdon joined countless readers who found in the revamped series a narrative testing ground for new social relations across race, class, and gender. To be an X-fan was to inhabit a new subject position that produced a "democratic equivalence" between the political worldview of individual readers whose affinity to the comic book indicated a shared investment in the progressive ideals of racial tolerance, sexual equality, and radical inclusion.[42]

Ororo is a character with few, if any, genuine antecedents in American superhero comic books: a superpowered black woman, orphaned at age four, who grew up a vagabond surviving on the art of thievery in Cairo until deciding to traverse the desolate landscape of the Sahara Desert to Kenya. She is discovered by Xavier in a small Kenyan township, where villagers worship her as a rain goddess. Although committed to those she has considered her people and basking in the glow of godhood, Ororo is convinced by Xavier to acknowledge her mutant identity and develop her skills under the rigorous training of the Xavier Institute.[43] When the original X-Men take temporary leave of the team with the arrival of a new generation of mutants, Storm replaces Jean Grey as the female heart of the group, proving herself as formidable as her teammates by displaying exceptional strength of will and adept use of her powers. Most important, she represents a new affective relation between the teammates that derails the heterosexual order that had prevailed in the original team.

Untrained in the sexual and gendered norms of the United States, Storm questions the strictures of normative femininity—initially refusing to wear clothes around the mansion grounds because she deems them needlessly restrictive and training with her male teammates at their level—and consistently rebuffs the romantic overtures of her colleagues, recoding their relationship in familial terms by naming Colossus, Wolverine, and Nightcrawler her brothers.[44] Simultaneously Storm's embodiment of the black female "disco diva" that dominated gay and African American visual culture—namely through her cascading mane of white hair, her hyperbolic performance of an "African goddess" persona, and her skin-tight costume, which sported thigh-high boots, a leotard with cut-outs, a flowing cape, and a tiara—positions her as a figure capable of taking pleasure in the performance of a variety of racial and gender identities. Exploring the agency afforded by her newfound kinship network, Storm at times takes on the role of team matriarch and female confidant to her sister mutants while alternately asserting leadership of the team, a warrior protecting her fellow X-Men. Storm's feminist sensibility, then, did not emerge as a wholesale abandonment of all gendered relations but from her demand to be a free agent who chooses her own affiliations rather than allowing them to be dictated by social expectations.

This fact is most evident in two narrative tropes that came to define Storm's character. The first is her ability to balance collective intimacies with her need for personal autonomy, a skill figuratively reflected in her mastery over atmospheric forces, which demands a similar understanding of the natural world and her place within it. Although Storm grows increasingly close to her teammates, she maintains an enclave of her own in Xavier's mansion, a lush greenhouse that serves as a space of contemplation and connection to nature. In between the X-Men's many adventures, the comic book presented emotionally charged scenes of Storm returning to the greenhouse to give sustenance to her beloved plants, speaking to them as though they are sentient creatures. At other times she strips naked and bathes in the moisture of a miniature rain shower in her room, liberating her mind and body from the constraints of costumes (both superheroic and social) that wed her to specific identities and expectations. These isolated "weather events" sustain the lush garden she oversees, encouraging life and growth for both herself and the organic life around her.[45]

In Storm's character the comic book identifies the central condition of producing social worlds as that of cultivating an interior domain of self-reflection: Storm is at once a willful agent and a living ecosystem producing and sustaining relations through the use of her abilities. In these moments the series attaches the activity of "worlding"—the production of social bonds and the maintenance of a complex natural order—to the female body. In one sense, then, *The X-Men* essentialized the category of "woman" as a kind of divine force (akin to "Mother Earth") maintaining networks of relations seemingly inaccessible to men; at the same time, these moments of strategic essentialism worked precisely because they universalized particular identities only to ultimately relocate them in the daily lives of individual characters.

This phenomenon is dramatized in Storm's key weakness: a debilitating claustrophobia. Her paralyzing fear of enclosed spaces initially appears as another manifestation of her Mother Earth persona, a desire for freedom and mobility echoed by the romantic language of whole earth environmentalism. But contrary to this assumption, readers learn that her claustrophobia is linked to her history as the orphan of parents killed in the military strikes on Cairo during the 1956 Suez crisis. In issue #102, when the X-Men battle the villain Juggernaut beneath Banshee's Irish castle, Storm is physically incapacitated by her claustrophobia.[46] Her psychic anguish occasions a vivid flashback sequence that relates how Ororo's parents, an American photojournalist and a Kenyan princess, moved from Harlem to Cairo in 1951, only to be killed five years later when a French fighter plane destroys their apartment building.

Following the bombardment, Ororo awakens to her mother's limp hand jutting from beneath a pile of debris, unable to provide the comfort her frightened child so desperately seeks. The flashback concludes with a dramatic splash panel depicting the child escaping from the rubble, living among thieves in Cairo, and finally, at age twelve, walking the length of the Sahara to Kenya. This series of images is immediately followed by the memory of Xavier's call to join the X-Men, galvanizing Storm's mental connection with the professor and recalling her multiple loyalties to her African heritage and her mutant kinship. Storm's personal history, unfolding from the geopolitics of postcolonial military conflicts, intersects with the struggle to define a mutant solidarity as the ground for a new collective history shorn of the violence and despair that have occasioned her own.

When the battle destroys one side of the castle, Storm regains her senses, joyfully taking flight while exclaiming, "I—can see the sky! Free! Gods of the Earth and air be praised! I am free!" (figure 4.1). This spirit of freedom as a condition of mutant kinship presciently captured the dual identities of Storm as otherworldly weather goddess and historical immigrant. The very "Gods" she praises, natural deities that wed her to an ethereal vision of Mother Earth, are also allegories for her biological mother, to whom she first calls out when struck by claustrophobia in the tombs of Cassidy Keep. A historical ghost, Ororo's mother ties her to the world of forced migrations, dual African and American identities, and global violence that make up the lineaments of her identity.

Storm's embodiment of the shifting demands of gendered and racialized identity is echoed in the evolution of the X-Men's first lady, Jean Grey. Where Storm's sisterly affection for her fellow teammates reorganizes the patriarchal structure of the nuclear family form, Jean's transformation into the mythical powerhouse Phoenix illustrates her liberation from the constraints of traditional American womanhood. Formerly known as Marvel Girl, Jean was introduced in the X-Men's 1963 inaugural issue as the team's first female recruit, a shy telepath and burgeoning telekinetic. Jean enthralled her teammates with her beauty and intelligence, but the strength of her abilities initially paled in comparison to her teammates' powers. In the new series' first year of publication, Jean outgrows her shrinking violet persona, moves out of the Xavier School, and develops an intimate bond with Storm. These changes paved the way for the fundamental transformations the series had in store for Jean over the next two years, while presaging the forms of alliances that Ororo and she would develop between black and white women alongside the posthuman categories of mutant and alien.

FIGURE 4.1. Storm unleashed. Chris Claremont (writer) and Dave Cockrum (penciller), "Who Will Stop the Juggernaut?," *The X-Men* #103, December 1976, reprinted in *Uncanny X-Men Omnibus Vol. 1* (New York: Marvel Comics, 2006), 223.

Between 1975 and 1978 the X-Men undertook two outer space adventures that served as narrative vehicles for the evolution of Jean's character. In their first exploit the X-Men become trapped on a space station run by a malevolent scientist who has rebuilt the mutant-hunting Sentinels—giant robots programmed to exterminate mutants—that plagued the X-Men in their youth. To save her teammates from certain death, Jean sacrifices her life by piloting their damaged space shuttle back to Earth, using her telekinetic abilities to shield the hull from a deadly radiation storm. Her corporeal body is destroyed by radiation exposure, only to be reknit by the power of a mythical cosmic entity known as the Phoenix Force.[47] The moments leading up to her death literally split Jean between her corporeal and psychic selves, the former screaming out to her beloved Scott Summers (Cyclops), while a psychic projection of her terror-stricken face speechlessly surrounds the ship in a fiery halo reminiscent of the globular motion of a lava lamp, her consciousness flowing through space as her body plummets to Earth along with her crew. When the rocket ship crash lands in the ocean off Cape Canaveral, Florida, the X-Men are shocked to see their friend torpedo up from the water, garbed in an unfamiliar costume (later identified as emblematic of the Phoenix), vitalized with new life. Jean's commanding first words capture the thrust of her transformation: "Hear me X-Men! No longer am I the woman you knew! I am fire! And life incarnate! Now and forever—I am Phoenix!" The full import of Jean's statement would become clear only later, but in the immediate context it reinterprets "the last moments of a young woman's life" not as literal death but as a transformation from naïve youth to empowered womanhood, wherein the mental expansion of her psyche into the vastness of the cosmos occasions the absorption of unprecedented liberatory energies into the body.

Jean's hallucinatory transformation into the Phoenix visually marshals the "getting loose" discourse of the hippie counterculture as a corollary to the concept of feminist consciousness raising. Sam Binkley explains the counterculture's philosophy: "The world this new vocabulary unfolds is one in which states of conformity and self-regimentation are undermined. . . . Related through metaphors of eruption, epiphany, and release . . . to 'be yourself,' to 'let it all hang out' . . . was to release a primordial vitality, to become an artist of oneself and of one's identity."[48] Much as the feminist rhetoric of self-determination worked to unleash women's dormant political energies by refashioning them into agents of their own social destinies, so too the Phoenix brought "a primordial vitality" into the world, granting Jean a repertoire of abilities to transform the fabric of reality and the contours of her own identity.[49] Simultaneously the visual spectacle of Jean's transformation accompanied by a verbal declaration of her newfound identity performed gay liberation's injunction to "come out" of the proverbial closet and declare one's homosexuality, where "'coming out' was framed . . . not simply as a private act of self-disclosure but as a public demand for visibility."[50] In "coming out" as Phoenix, Jean arguably became the most visible member of the X-Men.

Materializing the feminist mantra "I am woman, hear me roar," Phoenix commonly appears rising in cruciform shape, arms alight with energy and mouth agape in a primal scream that symbolizes an extraordinary show of self-determination as well as an exhilarating potential for a loss of self-control.[51] The famous cover of *X-Men* #101, which depicts the Phoenix's birth, presents in stark visual terms both the emancipatory dimensions of the Phoenix Force and the threat it poses to existing affiliations between Jean and her fellow X-Men (plate 15). Poised dramatically at the center of the cover, Jean launches from the depths of the Atlantic garbed in the green and gold costume of the Phoenix as bolts of energy radiate from her upturned hands, her fiery mane of red hair in full bloom. Below her imposing figure, Storm struggles to lift an arm from the water, her features contorted in terror, while Cyclops faces the reader, gasping for air. If the Phoenix may be read as a popular fantasy embodying the concept of feminist consciousness raising—a physical transformation representing Jean's "coming into consciousness" as a feminist—Storm and Cyclops iconically stand in for the figures most alienated by this performance of liberated white femininity, namely black women and white men, here literally drowned out by the forces of Jean's self-actualization. Accompanying them, though left of center, is Nightcrawler, his blue features and elfish hand barely staying afloat in the roiling waters; as the single visibly "mutant" figure in the scene, he joins Storm and Cyclops as part of a constellation of identities effaced by the empowering but solipsistic personal emancipation the Phoenix Force enables.

In the figures of Storm and Phoenix, *The X-Men* dramatized two distinct but overlapping feminist projects of the mid-1970s that could be materialized and critiqued through the popular fantasy of mutation: the desire for female autonomy and self-actualization and the development of alternative intimacies and solidarities outside of heteropatriarchy. The series located the former project in an important but narcissistic white liberal feminist worldview and the latter in the alliances forged by radical women of color through their articulation of feminist goals to diverse categories of identity. Storm's willful remembering of her mutant kinship in a moment of fear and isolation and Jean's absorption of the Phoenix force as she faces obliteration by a radiation storm reflected the capacity of popular fantasy to offer tools for reimagining personal identity when the terms that organize one's sense of self no longer make for a "livable life."[52] The feminist visual iconography of Storm and Phoenix would find its greatest expression in *The X-Men*'s epic 1977 space opera, "The Phoenix Saga." Here the liberatory vision of female powers and agency embodied by these two fantasy figures became the material for responding to galactic crises that threatened to destroy the fabric of reality and, with it, the alternative kinships developed within the intimate sphere of the X-Men's mutant solidarity.

"Where No X-Man Has Gone Before!"

Arguably the most canonical story line in *The X-Men*'s publishing history, "The Phoenix Saga" tells the story of the alien princess Lilandra Nermani's desperate effort to gain allies in a cosmic struggle against the machinations of her tyrannical brother, D'Ken, emperor of a vast alien civilization known as the Shi'ar Empire. The empire was torn apart by civil war when Lilandra turned against her kin, refusing to support his plan to obtain the power of the deadliest force in the universe, the M'Kraan Crystal, to achieve absolute rule over the cosmos. Although Lilandra and her supporters fight valiantly, her resistance crumbles. As she explains, "I was jinking through the binary system, trying to shake off my pursuit, when . . . in my mind, I saw a face. . . . It was as if I'd found a missing piece of my soul. . . . In that instant I was bound to Charles Xavier . . . and he to me."[53] In her time of need Lilandra discovers a psychic rapport across the galaxies that leads her to Earth and Xavier's X-Men, calling forth a monstrous mutant kinship against the tainted bonds of blood and empire.

Responding to Lilandra's plea, Phoenix employs her newfound cosmic powers to teleport the X-Men thousands of light years from Earth to "the World," an uninhabited planet where the M'Kraan Crystal, a massive gem containing the energies of a caged miniature universe, is besieged by D'Ken and his forces. The X-Men learn that D'Ken plans to shatter the crystal and unleash the power of the universe within, supported in his maniacal plans by the Shi'ar Guard, a formidable cadre of superhumans sworn to protect their emperor. The three issues that compose the narrative core of "The Phoenix Saga" chronicle the X-Men's epic battle with the Shi'ar Guard, their newfound alliance with the Starjammers—interstellar space pirates and sworn enemies of the Shi'ar, led by the swashbuckling Corsair—and their entry into the crystal itself, where Phoenix faces the task of reweaving the tapestry of the cosmos.[54] This final project is visually depicted as a metaphorical bonding of the X-Men's multiple identities—across race, gender, nation, and generation—through the literal bonding of Storm and Phoenix, figures whose differences could be reconciled by visual reference to the cross-racial and sexual culture of disco, where difference was dissolved in the psychedelic pleasures of the dance floor.

To achieve this reconciliation, the X-Men must first contend with the cultural divisions that structure their encounter with the Shi'ar Guard, dramatically captured in the saga's opening double-page spread in *The X-Men* #107 (plate 16). Presciently titled "Where No X-Man Has Gone Before!," the image presents an awesome tableau of superhuman figures flanking the edifice of the M'Kraan Crystal, a giant pink jewel atop a mechanical pedestal. No less than twenty-five figures fill the scene, the X-Men entering the fray from the left with the Shi'ar Guard standing opposite. Across the field of action, a Shi'ar warrior exclaims, "Comrades! Who are these people?! They materialized out of the stargate . . . but are they friends? Or Foes?" Bursting from the center of the spread is the singular declaration of another guardsman: "Aliens!"[55]

Marshaling the epic visual vistas of the space opera, this inaugural image depicts an intergalactic conflict that brings within its orbit unexpected encounters between manifold figures who far exceed the label "human." The scene's central declaration, "Aliens!," functions as a floating signifier attaching itself to everyone in the panorama; to the imperial guard, the X-Men are quite literally extraterrestrials and vice versa, while both these groups are aliens to the resting place of the M'Kraan Crystal. This last fact is reiterated in the scene's title, "Where No X-Man Has Gone Before!," which echoes the famed slogan of the popular television series *Star Trek* ("Where no *man* has gone before!") while transforming the putatively "human" referent of the term *man* to indicate something radically different from humanity. At the same time, it derails the imperial thrust of the original use of the phrase, "where no *one* has gone before," first printed in a 1958 White House press booklet on American space travel, which identified the Moon as a site for Americans to claim as a victory in the cold war space race. Here, traversing the galaxies to arrive at the World is not an imperialist project but a liberatory undertaking to protect the M'Kraan Crystal from D'Ken's colonial aspirations. The confusion between the categories of alien, mutant, and human is rendered in both semiotic and visual terms, for the ostentatious garb of the imperial guard appears identical to the X-Men's' costumes, both groups resembling the polyester menagerie of a 1970s disco dance floor surrounding a massive mirror ball in the form of a cosmic gem.

Expanding its visual horizon to absorb a seemingly limitless cast of characters whose encounters embody the struggles of an entire social universe, the first part of "The Phoenix Saga" laid the groundwork for the X-Men's entry into the M'Kraan Crystal itself, where histories of conflict would dissolve in a stunning network of solidarities born of a shared will to save the world from destruction. As the structure housing the forces that maintain the order of the universe, the crystal is a quintessential example of popular fantasy, an imagined object that metaphorically equalizes the disparities between friend and enemy, human and alien, dictator and subject, by depicting the cosmos as a network of relations rather than a series of antagonisms. Reaching into the minds of those who would intrude upon its sanctum, the crystal forces each to experience his or her worst nightmare: Nightcrawler relives his fear of being lynched by a bigoted mob, now composed of his friends, the X-Men, while Corsair remembers the murder of his wife at the hands of D'Ken's henchmen years before. With each image, entire psychic histories flash before our eyes, linking the affective lives of each character to the universal network of relations held together by the crystal's center of gravity. Awakening from her own hallucination—the memory of her death and rebirth as Phoenix—Jean sees Cyclops lash out uncontrollably with his optic blasts, inadvertently rending the surface of the crystal's core. As it fractures, she calls out, "What do I do now?! I don't know what's in there, and even if I did, how am I supposed to stop it! I—I'm all alone."[56]

Combating her fear, Jean finds strength in her identity as a member of the X-Men: "The first thing—is not to panic. I am an X-Man. I've been in tough spots before and I've always come through with flying colors." Speaking these words aloud, Jean projects the Phoenix Force from her body, a cosmic flame in the shape of the mythical bird. Beholding the torn latticework binding the universe at its core, she intones, "I'm Jean—yet I'm Phoenix. And I feel as if, for the first time . . . I'm truly alive. This lattice, it's alive. And it's dying." The consequences of the crystal's destruction unfold in her mind's eye: the universe torn asunder, her loved ones swept into the void. In this moment of expanded consciousness, Jean weds her self-actualization to the necessity for affiliation and connection beyond the self; she understands that the process of negotiating multiple identities—to be Jean and Phoenix and an X-Man simultaneously—requires her to declare emancipation from the limits of her former life while affirming the manifold relations that define her as a living part of the world, a vital lattice of social bonds.

So vast is the latticework's reach that even Phoenix's power is not enough to heal it. "It's absorbing me!" Jean rages in frustration. "It's pulling me so far away from the human plane of reality—that it's as if I no longer exist!" In her moment of greatest need, her desperate plea is answered by her chosen sister, Ororo Monroe. "But you *do* exist!" Storm exclaims, reaching for her friend's hand across the chasm separating them. "You need an anchor in this cosmic maelstrom, Jean. I will be that anchor." Held back by her conscience, Jean replies, "No! Storm—Ororo . . . the anchor you offer is your life-force!" Storm responds to Jean's caveat, "It is my life to give, my friend." As she utters these words, a panel depicts Storm's hand reaching through the energy field to clasp Jean's in a gesture that affirms her material existence (figure 4.2).

Storm's embrace galvanizes Jean to expand the network, stretching out her free hand to Corsair, who first refuses her call but relents when she recognizes him as Cyclops's father. Acknowledged as the X-Men's kin, Corsair joins Storm in psychically anchoring Jean and giving life to the Phoenix. The double embrace of Storm and Corsair unifies the previously rent identities depicted in the famous cover image to *X-Men* #101,

FIGURE 4.2. Storm offers Phoenix a psychic anchor. Chris Claremont (writer) and John Byrne (penciller), "Armageddon Now!," *The X-Men* #108, December 1977, reprinted in *Uncanny X-Men Omnibus Vol. 1* (New York: Marvel Comics, 2006), 325.

joining categories of male and female, black and white, while bridging the gap between the liberal and cultural feminist worldviews embodied by Storm and Jean, respectively. In light of the internal divisions over questions of race and class privilege that plagued women's liberation in the mid-1970s, to see a black woman join hands with a white woman to save the universe was no minor representational achievement; that popular fantasy would engage this vision in mass media concurrent with radical political attempts to articulate cross-racial alliances and mutual recognition between women indicated fantasy's imbrication in the political life of the feminist counterculture.[57] By figuratively completing the grasp her mother could not reciprocate years before, Storm's gesture of solidarity engenders a cross-racial sisterhood that ameliorates the historical atrocities marking the individual lives of those bound within it by producing new intimacies based on agency rather than the vicissitudes of identity and political history.

Flying into the heart of the latticework, Jean and Phoenix become one, and above the fray of Shi'ar civil war, of mutant and human conflict, all of Jean's identities merge into one cosmic form enveloping the crystal to heal the wounds inflicted upon it by a universe of strife. Finally the Phoenix becomes all, "the patterns of her life, of the X-Men's lives, becoming one with the lattice pattern":

> She falters—panic seizing her as she realizes that for all her awesome
> power, she still can't do it alone. And then, suddenly she isn't alone.
> The spirits of the X-Men are with her, giving of themselves as Storm
> and Corsair gave. In that instant—she feels her power, the powers of
> her friends sing within her; as she reenergizes the energy lattice.... A
> new pattern forms—shaped like the mystic tree of life—with Xavier
> its lofty crown and Colossus its base. Each X-Man has a place, each
> a purpose greater than him or herself and the heart of that tree,
> the catalyst that binds these wayward souls together is Phoenix.
> Tiphareth... the vision of the Harmony of Things.[58]

Experiencing a state of literal ecstasy repairing the latticework, Jean's identity is thrown into disarray, no longer able to distinguish herself from the Phoenix, the Phoenix from the cosmos. Much like her initial transformation into Phoenix, Jean's encounter with the M'Kraan Crystal is visualized through the sensory discourse of gay and feminist public cultures, specifically the language of bodily transformation through a variety of states of ecstatic pleasure that included the intoxicating highs of the disco dance floor and the orgasmic intensities of sexual liberation. Robert McRuer explains, "For ... most historians of disco ... the dance floor was a place where one's individual identity could disintegrate and be absorbed into the larger mass of writhing bodies. Through ... openness to others and ... a range of bodily pleasures, the self could be remade."[59] This description parallels Jean's experience of reknitting the fabric of the cosmos: as her body is subsumed within the vast power of the Phoenix, Jean is recast as a being made up of the many lives, histories, and experiences that constitute a social world.

Though the visual appropriation of gay and feminist public cultures was a recurrent motif throughout *The X-Men* series, it was not the only cultural resource from which the comic book gleaned its most powerful figural metaphors. As Jean's transformative experience in the heart of the M'Kraan Crystal attests, the comic book's invocation of "Tiphareth," a Kabbalan term denoting the universal order of all things (literally, "the tree of life"), uses spiritual myth for the purpose of articulating alternative social bonds. Similarly, in the figure of the M'Kraan Crystal, "The Phoenix Saga" fashioned a fictional cosmic force of legitimation for the X-Men's mutant kinship in the absence of worldly political ones: recall that the Crystal recognizes Nightcrawler's greatest fear as the disintegration of his bond with the X-Men into xenophobia and hatred, while it simultaneously offers Jean the vision to ensure that such a fate doesn't befall the mutant cadre. Where the heroes of messianic melodramas spanned the spaceways only to face alienation and violence, the X-Men flew headfirst into the far reaches of space and found, to their surprise, a confirmation of the complex knitted-togetherness of the universe and its manifold inhabitants.

Whether depicted in the mutated bodies of superhuman outcasts, the visual politics of gay and feminist public cultures, or the iconic figures of ancient myth, the narration of mutually transformative encounters between unlikely allies in "The Phoenix Saga" was also the central concern of a variety of stories across *The X-Men* series. *The X-Men*'s cultural purchase thus lay in its ability to visualize alternative solidarities at a moment when traditional political affiliations, notions of normative family life, and heteronormative sexual relations were being radically reorganized in American culture. Rather than rail against such changes and the loss of formerly "stable" binding categories of political and social identity, *The X-Men* sought to engage the contradictions, labors, and potential pleasures of fantasizing new modes of relationality.

This fact was repeatedly impressed upon readers not only by *The X-Men*'s narrative content but by the dialogues between fans and creators. In one early issue of the series, a fan castigated writer Chris Claremont for his depiction of Lorna Dane, the mutant superhero Polaris, as overly codependent and doting on her fiancé, Alex Summers, the former X-Man Havok. He remarked, "The script was well written but . . . hasn't [Chris] ever heard of a women's movement? Someone should tell Lorna that she shouldn't have to depend on a man to feel 'complete' and 'fulfilled'—this is 1975 after all." The writer concludes by lauding the introduction of the character Storm, claiming to be "all in favor of [creators] continuing to put this powerful lady in a more dominant position."⁶⁰ Perhaps the only thing more striking than this bold demand that *The X-Men* continue to live up to its feminist ideals was Stan Lee's unexpected response:

> Hold your horses . . . Dan! Cheerful Chris Claremont has indeed heard of the women's movement, and believes in many of their goals. But where in their manifesto does it say that a woman cannot feel "complete" or "fulfilled" by being with a man she loves—or a man feeling the same way about the woman he loves? If you refer back to the same page . . . you'll notice that Chris mentioned "doctoral candidates" Alex and Lorna. Plural, not singular. Two people working together . . . each giving as much as is received. And when you think about it, isn't that the ultimate goal of all these People Liberation movements: to give every person—regardless of race, creed, or sex—the right to be whatever he, she or it wants to be, and not play a role imposed on them by the society around them?⁶¹

Lee's spirited response revealed the letter writer's putatively liberal standpoint as potentially conservative in its dogmatic framing of feminism as reducible to a woman's individual freedom from men. Against this view Lee links ideals of feminist agency to cosmopolitan investments in relations of equality and reciprocity to suggest that the counterculture's vision of social liberation involves the ability of all people to choose their own affiliations regardless of the identities imposed on them by society. Lee's use of the pronouns "he, she and it" also references the posthumanist vision of *The X-Men*, which depicts countless figures for whom the labels "he" and "she" are too narrow to accommodate the potential variety of subject positions that exist in the universe. In so doing *The X-Men* figured popular fantasy as the site for revitalizing a cosmopolitan world-making project in the age of identity politics.

In issue #119, one year after saving the universe from annihilation, the X-Men convene in Japan at the home of their former teammate Sunfire to celebrate the Christmas holiday. Struck by the intimacy of the scene, Storm thinks to herself, "So much has changed between we six since we became X-Men. . . . We began as loners. And have grown into a family." Filled with emotion, she turns to Nightcrawler and says, "Kurt? I just wanted to tell you . . . that I love you very much." In the following panel, Storm confronts Colossus, brooding apart from the group; he admits, "I feel as close to you, to the X-Men, as to my own family. And that's the problem. I have a family. I think I am the only X-Man with roots, and tonight, I miss them."⁶² This moment of shared intimacy impressed upon readers both the powerful connections the X-Men had developed and the ongoing struggles they faced to honor the manifold bonds that made up their individual lives. Just as Phoenix offered a political myth for describing cosmopolitan networks of kinship and affiliation, so too was the desire to reconcile the competing demands of varied loyalties another kind of myth-making, a fantasy of unity amid stunning heterogeneity. As a new decade of threats to the survival of mutant-kind appeared on the horizon, this was one reality the X-Men dared not dream away.

5 / Heroes "That Give a Damn!": Urban Folktales and the Triumph of the Working-Class Hero

Green Lantern exhibits drama and dialogue comparable with the likes of "Easy Rider" and "Midnight Cowboy." Issue #76 summed up the despair and unreality of our times as no piece of literature I've read this year.... The characters balance perfectly. Green Arrow, totally aware of the sickness of today's America, hip, alive, angry, human. Green Lantern, hesitant, uncertain, looking back to the old ordered and simple universe, slowly coming to the realization that that type of world is dead.
—PETER MARZANO, letter published in *Green Lantern/Green Arrow #81*
(December 1970)

In 1979, only a few years after she had joined the X-men and made the Xavier Institute her home, Ororo Monroe would go in search of her roots. Despite her mother's Kenyan heritage, Storm did not pursue her lineage to Africa but traveled only a few miles from Xavier's Westchester mansion to Harlem, the place of her early childhood. Seeing the decaying stoops, trash-filled streets, and abandoned homeless in what used to be a vibrant black neighborhood, Storm thinks to herself, "In my father's tales, this was a magical place—wicked yet joyous, poor, rough-edged but alive. He was so happy to leave it, yet also so sad. But that was long ago. The magic seems almost gone now. If it was ever truly here." Visiting the apartment where she was a toddler, Ororo is shocked to see it now inhabited by teenage heroin addicts. Her musings about her parents are cut short by a group of junkies who attack her with knives for entering uninvited. Though she initially overpowers them with her combat training, she is saved from an unseen attacker by Luke Cage, New York's premier black superhero and by then a popular fixture in the Marvel Pantheon. "They're so young," she pleads. "Is there nothing we can do?" Cage replies, "They live in a society more concerned about cagin' 13 year-olds for life than tryin' to give 'em a decent chance."[1] The scene of urban degradation that Storm stumbles upon reflected the failed democratic hope of universal equality and economic opportunity that Lyndon Johnson's Great Society programs had promised neighborhoods like Harlem in the mid-1960s and early 1970s. Civil rights, the war on poverty, and urban renewal no longer appeared as milestones on the path to a more inclusive democracy; instead they seemed long forgotten myths, idealistic social projects that spoke of a time "long ago" whose "magic seems almost gone now." Compared to the affective bonds Ororo and her teammates developed as they spanned the spaceways of the Shi'ar Empire months before, the real-world political conditions of American society seemed to offer no ground upon which to enact social change through the seemingly defunct category of national citizenship.

Storm's visit to Harlem marked the conclusion of Marvel and DC Comics' decade-long exploration of the sociopolitical milieu of the American cityscape. Across the span of the 1970s, DC Comics would compete with the rising popularity of Marvel's space operas by infusing political "relevance" into the plot lines of their longest running superhero titles. This move was also motivated by Marvel's willingness to depict contemporary social concerns that pushed the limits of the Comics Code Authority in the late 1960s. In 1969 Marvel broke the Comics Code guidelines to publish a *Spider-Man* story addressing drug addiction among American youth. Ironically Marvel demurred on the Code Authority's recommendation to remove references to drug use because the U.S. Department of Health, Education, and Welfare had requested that the company use their influence on American teenagers to support a national antidrug campaign.[2] As had been the case in the mid-1950s, government pressure on comic book publishing companies, now to help America's youth, wedded the comics industry to state power while also offering opportunities for unprecedented creative innovation.

Following Marvel's bold decision to thwart the Comics Code Authority, both major comic book publishers provided some of their freshest talents—most notably Dennis (Denny) O'Neil and Neal Adams at DC and Steve Englehart at Marvel—the opportunity to revamp a variety of classic heroes as contemporary social critics who used their powers to uncover political corruption, redress social inequality, and demand democratic justice for all. This investment in directly addressing the political issues of the day and the revamping of the American superhero as an agent of social justice was short-lived, most prominently displayed in DC's *Green Lantern/Green Arrow* series from 1970 to 1974 and in Marvel's *Captain America and the Falcon* between 1974 and 1975.[3] Though the period in which superhero comics explicitly identified and critiqued the sociopolitical concerns of the post–Vietnam War era seemed transitory, the generic formations that emerged from these explorations would far outlast any specific political issues the comics themselves addressed.

In the 1970s the urban folktale became the primary generic vehicle for creators to reassert the superhero as a uniquely American icon in a period when the notion of a distinct national character appeared conceptually bankrupt in light of the country's waning economic, political, and military power. Yet the formerly taken-for-granted relationship between the superhero and national culture had to be reconceived in relation to an emergent discourse of identity-based politics and an ethnic revival that celebrated America's ethnoracial diversity. The proliferation of meanings surrounding the category of national identity was acknowledged by Captain America himself in 1974, when he declared to his heroic colleagues, "America is not the single entity you're talking about. . . . In the land of the free, each of us is able to do what he wants to do—think what he wants to think. That's as it should be—but it makes for a great many different versions of what America is."[4] In order to maintain the superhero's capacity to speak to these "many different versions of what America is," creators distanced the figure from its former ties to the state and popular science—institutions now associated with racism, political corruption, and global violence—and stressed the superhero's quest to embody a form of authentic national citizenship based on individual will and agency distinct from government intervention.

In one sense the space opera and the urban folktale responded to the same sociopolitical concerns, including the collapse of New Left and liberal political coalitions, the Vietnam War, corrupt political leadership, and the failure of social services to redress the material inequalities continuing to plague the nation. Yet each genre proposed alternative creative strategies and ideological positions for responding to the failures of American political life. While the space opera took up the superhero as a character whose creative evolution made it effective for developing alliances beyond the assumed limits of liberal humanism, the urban folktale looked to the superhero's roots in American culture as a populist icon upholding the nation's democratic traditions. Consequently, where the space opera's critique of human violence, bigotry, and greed relied on allegorical fantasy to project lived atrocities onto fictionalized interplanetary struggles, the urban folktale used documentary realism to situate superheroes in the everyday circumstances of the most socially and economically oppressed members of American society. This unprecedented focus on America's economic underclass in the pages of mainstream comics made sense in the context of an increasingly corporatized and hierarchical comic book industry.

By the mid-1970s both Marvel and DC Comics had been bought out by media corporations, Cadence Industries and Warner Communications, respectively, that made revenue by licensing popular comic book characters for toys and merchandise alongside the sale of television and film rights. The least profitable portion of this booming licensing empire was the sale of comic books, whose circulation figures had been dropping for two decades despite their growing cultural capital. (Sales figures of comics rarely reflected real-world circulation, which far exceeded official statistics due to the medium's hand-to-hand portability.) In this period former full-time creators were forced to become freelance laborers for the major comic book companies, who owned the rights to creators' work and could adjust their pay based on sales revenue rather than time spent producing a finished comic. This restructuring of comic book labor was indicative of the absorption of neoliberal business practices into the comic book industry in the early to mid-1970s, including the outsourcing and individuation of creative labor, the implementation of austerity measures to reduce corporate costs (including refusal to pay creators stable salaries or benefits), the diversification of company products to increase revenue streams, and the pooling of company resources to upper management to wring increasing profits from underpaid creative labor.

Though comic book writing and drawing had never been especially lucrative careers, the 1960s boom allowed some creators unprecedented job security working on successful titles for years at a time. In the new corporate structure of Marvel and DC Comics, some of the longest-running industry talent became expendable because of flagging comic book sales, while industry unknowns and newcomers found themselves catapulted to stardom on the basis of one best-selling comic. The potential for long-term economic success in the industry began to appear all but impossible in light of the unstable distribution of steady employment and the looming reality that comics might go extinct as a viable commodity, replaced by licensing and media adaptations of comic book characters.

This history of corporate restructuring and the subsequent acrimony that developed between creative talent and company management is chronicled in a number of historical and journalistic exposés of the comic book industry since the 1970s.[5] Yet few studies have explored the aesthetic and narrative dimensions of these structural transformations, particularly how the content of superhero comics became a creative battleground upon which the shifting economic realities of the industry were negotiated at the level of genre, character, and narrative form.[6] These negotiations were most visible in the aesthetic and narrative content of the urban folktale, a genre that emerged at the nexus of corporate demands for "politically relevant" comics, creators' interest in revitalizing their self-image as socially conscientious cultural produc-ers, and audience demand that comics live up to the egalitarian progres-sive values they had articulated in the prior decade. In the 1960s writers and artists had, with substantial secretarial assistance, run the primary operation of comic book production while having to account directly to their readership for their creative decisions. With the corporate buy-outs of Marvel and DC, creators now had to approach their vocation as a highly complex negotiation between a diversified readership and a newly appointed managerial staff of editors, CEOs, and licensing and market-ing experts.

Attempting to reconcile competing corporate and public interests, creative producers embraced the urban folktale as a genre that could address contemporary social inequality (namely persistent racism and classism in American society) as a metaphor for their own labor exploi-tation, thereby pleasing corporate higher-ups who wished to capitalize on hot-button social issues while also articulating progressive values to a putatively liberal or progressively minded readership. Specifically creators framed the superhero as a champion of American democracy through his promotion of racial equality, while recasting the superhe-roes' commitment to progressive race politics as equivalent to the strug-gle to uncover and redress economic inequality across race lines. Doing so allowed the urban folktale to function as a genre that compensated for the *economic* undervaluation of creative labor in the comic book industry by celebrating the *cultural* value of the superhero as a popular embodiment of American liberal democracy.

The urban folktale accomplished this by zeroing in on the Ameri-can city as the location where the contradictions of liberal democracy, especially around issues of race and class, were most visible. The urban landscape highlighted contemporaneous racial conflict, poverty, over-population, and environmental decline in a concentrated geographic space historically identified with upward economic and social mobility and democratic progress; simultaneously the history of the American superhero as a cultural icon rested on his image as a guardian of an urban municipality that represented American technological progress and individual liberty. (Superman had, after all, been a champion of the working class in the late 1930s, valiantly defending laborers of many stripes against corrupt bosses in his city of Metropolis.)[7] Following the lead of *The Fantastic Four*, in the 1970s superheroes increasingly came to represent real rather than fictional cities and faced a diverse population of urban dwellers who often resented superheroes, who they assumed were lackeys of the police, morally corrupt, or simply naïve about the realities of city life. By shedding light on the social crises that afflicted the American city, the urban folktale combined liberal progressive representational politics (making visible and critiquing racism, urban decline, corporate greed, and pollution) with a traditional commitment to American democratic ideals.

In this chapter I analyze DC's *Green Lantern/Green Arrow* miniseries and Marvel's *Captain America and the Falcon* in the mid-1970s to show how the urban folktale positioned itself as a narrative about informed citizenship that demanded superheroes acknowledge the material and lived conditions of the people they claimed to fight for as a requirement of their heroic activity. A new generation of comic book creators deployed a documentary visual style and an ethnographic focus on the everyday lives of ordinary people to recuperate experiences and stories previously barred from representation in mass-market superhero comics, including those of racial minorities, the urban poor, and drug addicts. Rather than using feminist or gay imaginaries to constitute new forms of solidarity that might ameliorate the problems of urban America, these stories turned toward cross-racial male bonding between white and African American superheroes whose partnerships came to represent the liberalization of Golden Age heroes like Green Lantern and Captain America, now agents of racial progressivism. In so doing creators sought to identify their work as a democratic contribution to twentieth-century American popular culture in much the same way that their forebears had championed the liberal struggle against fascism after World War II. Now, however, their struggle was ironically against the economic structures and widening social and political inequalities that postwar prosperity had enabled.

"No Evil Shall Escape My Sight!"
Awakening the Hero's Political Consciousness

In the early 1970s Denny O'Neil and Neal Adams's *Green Lantern/ Green Arrow* miniseries epitomized the rise of political relevance in mainstream comics. Green Lantern was one of the oldest and most beloved superheroes of the Golden Age of comics; by 1969, however, the space-faring hero had fallen out of favor with readers, who complained about the Lantern's lackluster adventures and the failure of writers to make the character relevant to contemporary audiences. To save the series from cancellation, DC Comics hired two rising stars—writer

Denny O'Neil and artist Neal Adams—to creatively overhaul the comic book and revitalize interest in the Green Lantern mythos among young adult and college-age audiences. To do so O'Neil and Adams eschewed stories about the Lantern's epic space adventures, grounding the super-hero in the heart of his native Star City (a stand-in for Philadelphia), where his former Justice League compatriot, Green Arrow, would join him on a tour of the social degradation of urban America. Though the partnership between the two heroes lasted only thirteen issues, the mini-series swiftly became one of the most lauded works of comics artistry ever published, combining an increasingly popular "realist" visual style with an ethnographic interest in depicting the encounter between super-heroic fantasy figures and the everyday realities of urban America.[8]

Two years after DC's dramatic reconceptualization of one of their most classic heroes, Marvel hired up-and-coming writer Steve Englehart to similarly revamp their *Captain America* series. In the politically conscious style pioneered by O'Neil and Adams, Englehart reinvented the latter day World War II veteran and icon of American democracy as a disillusioned citizen questioning his allegiance to a corrupt U.S. government. Unlike the former's documentary approach, the newly retitled *Captain America and the Falcon* juxtaposed the hyperbolically cartoonish style of Jack Kirby in the 1960s with 1970s political realities. In both series the superhero's proximity to contemporary urban realities—namely the social and eco-nomic inequality experienced by people of color, the negative effects of consumerism on political freedom, and the forms of public violence that discouraged collective social action—forced the title characters to reevalu-ate the meaning of heroism at a moment when the category of citizenship had increasingly lost its political purchase.

Just as superheroes had become disillusioned with the supposed transparency of American democracy and its promise of collective freedom and equality, so too comic book creators had lost faith in the promise of artistic freedom and community building that characterized the industry in the 1940s and 1950s. For these writers and artists, char-acters like Green Lantern, Green Arrow, and Captain America were not only figural representations of American democratic ideals that could be used to develop a critical stance toward contemporary U.S. society; they were also cultural tools for redeeming the undervaluation of their creative labor by framing their politicization of such figures as a positive contribution to American cultural history.

This allegorization of the superhero's struggle to regain ethical meaning in his vocation as a foil for the plight of exploited comic book labor was presented in the ~~urban folktale through three narrative moves. First, the~~ urban folktale began by presenting its lead superhero as a failed citizen or political dupe due to his inattentiveness to the needs of everyday Americans and naïveté regarding the stark inequalities of contemporary American social life. Second, the heroes of these stories responded to the charge of failed citizenship by becoming lay cultural ethnographers, returning to the urban environments they had long ignored to gain knowledge about the daily political, economic, and social workings of the cities they claimed to protect. Third, the formerly failed citizen superhero would become a folk hero to the inhabitants of his urban locale whose commitment to the specific needs of local communities made him uniquely equipped to represent America's transformed social landscape. In each of the urban folktale's narrative transitions, the city was the catalyst for the hero's transformation, foregrounding the social atrocities he had failed to acknowledge, offering a vast social field for the visual exploration of urban life, and accommodating the marginalized "folk communities" the hero would ultimately come to recognize as his own.

The urban folktale's double move of deconstruction and moral regeneration is performed in the opening sequence of O'Neil and Adams's first issue of *Green Lantern/Green Arrow*, which introduced readers to the politically conscious perspective of the revamped series. The issue opens with a splash panel depicting Green Lantern majestically flying through the bustling downtown streets of Star City, his body gliding between buildings with a purpose and conviction befitting the classic image of the superhero as distinguished guardian of an urban municipality. Along the left side of the page, however, the narration reads, "For years he has been a proud man! He has worn the power ring of the Guardians, and used it well, and never doubted the righteousness of his cause. . . . In the next dozen seconds, an event will occur which will signal the end of his grandeur, and the beginning of a long torment. . . . His name is Green Lantern and often he has vowed that 'No Evil Shall Escape My Sight!' He has been fooling himself" (plate 17).[9] Immediately following this image, Lantern swoops down through the streets to visit his friend Green Arrow in what appears to be a "ghetto" neighborhood. Nearing ground level, Lantern witnesses an older, portly white gentleman being harassed by a young street thug. Using his power ring to scare the hoodlum away, Lantern quickly turns his attention to the man he just saved to ensure his safety. As he does so an unseen voice hails him from beyond the frame, "Hey—Super-hero!," to which Lantern affirmatively replies, "There's no need to thank me, people! I was just doing my duty." At this statement an empty bean can slams into the side of his forehead, followed by a barrage of trash being hurled by the building's tenants (figure 5.1). Before Green Lantern can respond, Green Arrow intervenes. He explains that the people of this neighborhood are poor minorities living in a dilapidated tenement owned by a corrupt landlord who intends to evict them, the same man Green Lantern helped minutes before. In the span of two panels, what appeared to be an ordinary performance of heroic action is reframed as the presumptuous interference of a bourgeois white superhero uninformed about the lives of the people who call this neighborhood their home. When Lantern yells, "Green Arrow! You're defending . . . these anarchists?! Can't you see they're breaking the law?," his friend responds, "Yeah, I can see . . . lots of things! Like that you've no business here—I was almost tempted to throw a can at you myself. . . . Come on . . . I'll give you a guided tour . . . a look at how the other half lives—if you can call it living."

What follows is a brief but powerful visual tour of the slum conditions in which the building's tenants eek out a wretched existence. Along the way Lantern and Arrow debate the legality of the tenants' actions, including their harassment of the corrupt landlord and inciting a public riot. Arrow refuses to follow Lantern's rigid legal logic, justifying the tenants' actions by appealing to a moral code that acknowledges their retaliation as a necessary response to the terrible conditions under which they live. As they arrive at the building's roof, their heated debate is interrupted by the voice of an elderly African American man who says to Lantern, "I been readin' about you . . . how you work for the blue skins . . . and how on a planet someplace you helped out the orange skins . . . and you done considerable for the purple skins! Only there's skins you never bothered with! . . . The black skins! I want to know . . . how come?! Answer me that, Mr. Green Lantern!" A dejected Lantern shamefully whispers, "I . . . can't." In the following panel a narrative frame reads, "In the time it takes to draw a single breath . . . the span of a heartbeat—a man looks into his own soul, and his life changes."[10]

This introductory scene offers a template of the urban folktale's deconstruction of the traditional ideological thrust of the superhero as protector of law and order. O'Neil and Adams structure the sequence to appear like any commonly recognizable scene of crime fighting from the Golden Age of comics; in this instance, however, Adams's artwork depicts the cityscape and the neighborhood that Green Lantern visits with a level of detail that allows readers to identify the slum conditions from the very outset. Comic strip visuality essentially becomes ethnographic in

FIGURE 5.1. Experiencing urban life from the bottom up. Denny O'Neil (writer) and Neal Adams (penciller), "No Evil Shall Escape My Sight," *Green Lantern/Green Arrow* #76, April 1970, reprinted in *Green Lantern/ Green Arrow Collection Vol. 1* (New York: DC Comics, 2004), 13.

content, attempting to realistically render the conditions under which "the other half lives," which are obscured by certain forms of superheroic fantasy. Consequently readers can see that it is Green Lantern, rather than the creators of the comic book, who is fooling himself by neglecting to acknowledge the baleful social conditions of his own city. This irony is redoubled through the deliberate titling of the issue, "No Evil Shall Escape My Sight!," a citation of Green Lantern's famous mantra, now presented as a hollow performance coming from a hero who is blind to everyday social evils. This failure is then corrected by the comic book itself through Green Arrow's subsequent tour of the miserable conditions of tenement living. Green Lantern's political naïveté is also visually compensated for through a perspectival shift away from the title hero toward the previously "invisible people" that characters like Green Lantern are thought to protect but who more often than not go unacknowledged as actual citizens worthy of interest.

This is illustrated by the pairing of Lantern's first brief interaction with the white landlord and his subsequent encounter with the African American tenement dweller. In the first scene, when Lantern protectively asks if the man has been hurt, the man replies, "Just fine, Lantern—thanks to you! But another second, that kid mighta hurt me. . . . You're my kind of guy, Lantern! More guys like you, this old world'd be a better place!" Lantern's initial identification with the landlord is visually undercut by the elderly African American man in the tenement building, whose indictment of Lantern's ignorance of race and class inequality brings to the surface what was disavowed in the landlord's celebratory praise: that Lantern is indeed exactly the "kind of guy" white fat cats like, a gullible sap easily controlled by those who reside at the top of the economic ladder.

The scene unhinges the visual politics of World War II–era superhero comics, which associated justice with white figures of authority (and criminality with ethnic minorities, the disabled, and the mentally disturbed), by developing an emergent identification between the superhero and marginalized figures, including racial minorities, the homeless, and the working class. In Marvel Comics' *Captain America and the Falcon*, this form of cross-racial and cross-class identification was narrated through the superhero's own transformation into a minority citizen. In the acclaimed 1974 story "Secret Empire," Captain America is accused of being a traitor to the nation. Cap consequently loses his legal standing as a citizen and is forced to inhabit the minority role of the illegal immigrant until he uncovers the plot against him. In an early scene he is horrified to see a televised public service announcement in a store-front window declaring him a public menace. As a crowd begins to form around the shop window, the announcer declares:

> Good day my fellow Americans. . . . For years, Captain Amer-ica has been a one-man vigilante committee, attacking anyone he deemed a criminal. Some were clearly such—but others were private citizens—men the recognized legal agencies had never molested! . . . Who is Captain America? He wraps himself in our nation's proud flag, yet no one in our government is responsible for . . . his actions. Perhaps the reason for this lies in the chemi-cal—which, many rumors allege, created his unnatural abilities in a secret laboratory! Yet he continues to roam the streets, striking at will at those who displease him! He claims he does it all for Amer-ica! *You're* America?[11]

Trusting in people's ability to discern false from true advertising, Cap recalls an earlier conversation with his former lover Peggy Carter: "None of that is true! They deliberately used negative phrases—distor-tions! . . . This was what Peggy warned me about: the advertisements try-ing to turn the public against me! But something that absurd is bound to blow itself out when it comes up against my record, eh?" In the next scene Cap finds himself futilely defending his years of hero work to a growing crowd who look upon the once vaunted hero with suspicion and fear. As this scene unfolds, another television advertisement blares in the background, "Success . . . love . . . you know these depend on what others think of you . . . and our new, improved washday miracle delight promises cleaner—brighter . . . "[12]

In *Green Lantern/Green Arrow* the hero is indicted for his failure to acknowledge the disjoint between the nation's political promise and its lived social realities. Here Cap's misstep is his failure to recognize the corrupting influence of mass media and consumerism on American political ideals. His implicit trust in rational deliberation and democratic justice leaves him baffled by the reality that such egalitarian concepts could be articulated to deeply antidemocratic projects, including public slander and propaganda. Shortly after this scene we learn that a political lobby called "the Committee to Regain America's Principles" (CRAP, as it were) has paid for the public service announcement denouncing Cap's heroic exploits. The committee's critique of Captain America works to redefine his exceptional status as a righteous superpowered vigilante as a mark of his alienation from the American people. The advertisement singles him out by hyperbolically individuating him as a "one-man vigi-lante committee" with an "individual concept of law and order" who stands in contrast to the ad's intended audience, a collectively conceived community of "fellow Americans" potentially threatened by Cap's sin-gular status as a man who merely mimes American iconography but fails to embody its values. Ironically the advertisement's ideology encourages viewers to make an *individual* judgment about Captain America based on their subjective view of what kind of America they wish to live in (indicated by the rhetorical question "*You're* America?"). The fact that the ad intends to elicit uniformly negative judgments, however, reveals its ideological manipulation of both individual and collective life in order to obscure Cap's own commitment to truly democratic ways of life. Simultaneously the speech uses the language of anti-immigrant pro-paganda to delegitimize Cap's status as a U.S. citizen by marking him as "unnatural," not a naturalized citizen and potentially nonhuman.

At the story's conclusion, readers learn that the committee is an arm of the government, the very institution that created Captain America. In a sense Cap's liberal democratic perspective on American politics is exactly what blinds him to the possibility of a government that would disavow its own creations as well as its own purported political values. The crooning sound of the "Washday Miracle Delight" advertisement following CRAP's public service announcement—which sells a utopian vision of love and success through commodity culture—lets the reader in on the secret that Cap will soon find out: that the promise of indi-vidual satisfaction through consumption and upward mobility has made Americans insensible to political truth and critique of government cor-ruption. As a result he is forced to become a fugitive in his own country, running from the law, hitchhiking across America to uncover the com-mittee's fascist plot, and relying only on his African American sidekick, the Falcon, for backup. He inhabits the experience of the American underclass, simultaneously living as an illegal immigrant, down-and-out homeless wanderer, and ethnoracial minority.

This newfound identification between the superhero and margin-alized or second-class citizens is one of the ways superhero comics in the 1970s absorbed and redirected the burgeoning language of identity politics in the post–civil rights period. For superheroes like the X-Men, the experience of being a mutant offered them a ready-made cultural identity through which to articulate a variety of alliances between mar-ginalized groups. For national icons like Captain America and Green Lantern, however, being a superhero only confirmed their privileged social position as white heterosexual men. To overturn the traditional image of the iconic superhero as an emblem of white privilege, creators had to alienate him from the institutions of power that once conferred the privilege of ideal citizenship—including government and family—and grant him an ulterior identity through which he could become affiliated with minority cultures.

This racially progressive identity was modeled by Green Arrow in the famous epilogue to the first issue of Green Lantern/Green Arrow, a supplement to the issue's central story that explicitly references contemporary civil rights politics in its critique of the complacent white superhero. In this brief interlude Green Arrow hurls a stunning critique at his partner for his short-sighted adherence to outmoded laws that serve corporate interests: "You call yourself a hero! Chum . . . you don't even qualify as a man! You're no more than a puppet. . . . Forget about chasing around the galaxy! . . . and remember America. . . . It's a good country . . . beautiful . . . fertile . . . and terribly sick! . . . On the streets of Memphis a good black man died . . . and in Los Angeles, a good white man fell. . . . Something is wrong! Something is killing us all. . . . Some hideous moral cancer is rotting our very souls!"[13] These final words feature Green Arrow's face twisted in sorrow with the etched faces of Martin Luther King Jr. and Robert Kennedy displayed behind him (figure 5.2). By marshaling the notion of an abstract American democratic ideal and wedding it to the bodies of those similarly considered paragons of ethical citizenship, the comic book piously contends that superheroes should be conceived of as humble civil servants striving to live up to the example of such figures as King and Kennedy. Consequently, by helping transform the content of traditional fantasy comics through a turn to political relevance—which involved articulating the messianic hero's previous moral lament to specific contemporary social problems—the creators placed themselves in a position to be thought of as conscientious citizens in the eyes of a broader American public.

If the response of readers was any indication, this project was largely successful. Within the first three issues of the Green Lantern/Green Arrow miniseries, a regular letter writer to the series, Juan Cole, would claim, "The current issues of Green Lantern are more political essays than anything else—and are much related to the works of the muckrakers at the turn of the century; but it's not exactly embarrassing to have such distinguished predecessors as Upton Sinclair and Lincoln Steffens—or even more modern figures such as Norman Mailer. So I wish Julie, Denny, and Neal good luck with their search for America. I only

FIGURE 5.2. "It's a good country . . . but terribly sick!" Denny O'Neil (writer) and Neal Adams (penciller), "No Evil Shall Escape My Sight," *Green Lantern/Green Arrow* #76, April 1970, reprinted in *Green Lantern/Green Arrow Collection Vol. 1* (New York: DC Comics, 2004), 30.

hope the rest of the U.S. has the good sense to follow you."[14] Statements like these bolstered the creators' attempts to link the heroes of urban folktales with the liberal democratic spirit of World War II superhero comics by identifying characters like Green Lantern and Green Arrow, as well as the writers and artists who depicted them, with an even earlier twentieth-century American progressive tradition. For instance, by having Green Arrow use the phrase "how the other half lives" when he indicts Green Lantern's naïveté about slum conditions, Denny O'Neil cannily referenced a founding text of American muckraking, Jacob Riis's *How the Other Half Lives: Studies among the Tenements of New York* (1890), revealing creators' understanding of their relationship to a lineage of socially conscious journalism. One method by which creators politically aligned themselves with their audiences was to provide their title heroes with crime-fighting partners who stood in for a liberal democratic worldview and helped classic superheroes negotiate a new, more progressive relationship with "the folk."

Both *Green Lantern/Green Arrow*'s and *Captain America*'s various plot lines revolved around the central conflict between a classic superhero and his strong-willed crime-fighting partner who served as an ideological foil for the lead character. As its title suggests, from the outset, *Green Lantern/Green Arrow* presented a dialectical struggle between two heroes representing opposing visions of justice, one based on law and order, the other on ethical judgment. In his original incarnation, Green Lantern's allegiance to the peacekeeping Guardians of Oa was understood as an honorable characteristic that reflected his devotion to aiding humanity through the use of his cosmic power ring, which embodied the values of self-determination and will power by granting its wearer the ability to materialize any shape or form he can imagine. In *Green Lantern/Green Arrow* this same allegiance is reread by Green Arrow as a sign of Lantern's blindness to the corrupt workings of power and his obsequious fealty to false authority. In the series' first issue, when Lantern defends his actions protecting the crooked landlord as his heroic duty to uphold the law, Arrow retorts, "Seems I've heard that line before . . . at the Nazi war trials!" By hyperbolically equating Lantern's ignorance of modern social ills with the complicity of Nazi war criminals, Arrow invokes the spirit of midcentury antifascism as a force with continued relevance to contemporary social justice, while also implying that 1970s culture has produced a murderous complacency within the nation that allows human atrocity to take place in the name of law and order.

A former corporate mogul turned bohemian Robin Hood, Green Arrow stands in for everything that Lantern is not: Oliver Queen possesses no superpowers—using only his archery and combat skills to fight crime—and is truly a "man of the people," living in the degraded tenements of Star City's ghetto and protecting its inhabitants from corrupt landlords, drug dealers, and supposedly well-intentioned superheroes like Green Lantern. By introducing crime-fighting partners whose heroic origins and moral commitments stemmed from the everyday happenings of local city life, urban folktales used contemporary superheroes like Green Arrow and Captain America's crime-fighting partner, the Falcon, to ground iconic World War II figures like Green Lantern and Cap in 1970s American culture.

When Arrow first admonishes Lantern for failing to see the plight of the neighborhood's residents, he appears perched atop a pedestal above the building's doorframe, then jumps down to meet Green Lantern at the bottom of the stoop (figure 5.1). As he does so, for the first time we see the actual tenants of the building standing behind Arrow and witness firsthand the decay of the building's façade. By physically leaping off his pedestal to lead Green Lantern through a tour of the dilapidated tenement—moving from the bottom of the building upward—Green Arrow reverses the meanings attached to traditional hierarchies of superheroic power, which read the superhero's upward flight as a sign of his physical and moral superiority. Now it is the value of seeing the world from the position of those at the bottom of the economic totem pole that elevates the superhero. This orientation visually facilitates Lantern's shift in political and personal identification by redirecting his line of sight away from outer space to the city beneath him.

The various methods by which the urban folktale deconstructed the superhero's claim to ideal citizenship—through a reversal of his assumed ideal relationship to "the people," the depiction of his political naïveté, and the construction of narrative foils in politically savvy urban crime-fighting partners—paved the way for the figure's moral regeneration by encouraging him to respond to critiques of his character through a will to self-improvement and political education that could similarly be imparted to the reader through the comic book form itself. As a consequence the superhero comic itself was reformulated as an ethnographic educational tool that, in visualizing its heroes' attempts to discover the "real America" beneath the twin evils of racism and classism, offered a material index of the social realities of its time.

The Superhero as Cultural Ethnographer

The first five issues of O'Neil and Adams's *Green Arrow/Green Lantern* miniseries framed this journey of self-discovery as a road trip across America that leads the crime-fighting duo to a community of exploited mine workers in an Appalachian town, a racist cult modeled on the Manson family, and a Native American reservation threatened by white industrialists. The second half of the series offers a variety of stories focused on hot-button social issues, including drug addiction, pollution, child abuse, and overconsumption. In nearly every issue O'Neil and Adams narrate heroic adventure stories using a documentary style that transforms instances of traditional superheroic action into opportunities to visually detail the everyday living conditions of marginalized or underrepresented communities.

This ethnographic impulse was most dramatically displayed in the two-part antidrug tale, "Snowbirds Don't Fly" and "They Say It'll Kill Me . . . but They Won't Say When." Framed as an exposé on teenage drug addiction, the story functions both as a public service announcement—the cover image to part 1 features a banner reading, "The Shocking Truth about Drugs!"—and a visual ethnography of the American drug trade.[15] The narrative addresses the issue of drug addiction at both personal and structural levels, linking the revelation that Green Arrow's teenage sidekick, Speedy, is a heroin addict, to a larger quest to stop the drug traffickers who supply Speedy and the city's youth. The cover to part 2 features a tableau of the faces of grief-stricken teenagers, many of them racial minorities, overlaid by an image of a giant needle (plate 18). Green Arrow stands in the foreground with his head down in silent mourning as he carries a presumably dead Speedy in his arms; Green Lantern appears to the left, wringing his hands at the sky, his mouth agape in a silent scream of grief and rage. Across the bottom of the page, a banner reads, "More Deadly Than the Atom Bomb."[16] In its layered and politically charged imagery the cover links the plight of an individual addict (Speedy) to the nation's (minority) youth at large, who appear as apparitions potentially suffering *for* or *with* Speedy depending on their individual circumstances. As with so many tropes of the urban folktale, the image's reference to the atomic bomb ties the comic book to the medium's historical relationship to World War II national culture, while stressing the need to take contemporary American social crises as seriously as foreign threats to national security.

The story begins with a local incident in which Green Arrow is mugged by a group of teenagers looking to make quick cash to score drugs. After one of the young men wounds Oliver with one of his own arrows, arrows only Speedy could have access to, he begins to suspect that drug pushers might have abducted his young charge. Green Lantern joins Arrow in trying to find Speedy by tracking down the drug addicts who initially cornered Oliver. Their detective work leads them from a single street crime to a full-blown drug trafficking ring run by a wealthy pharmaceutical company owner named Salomon Hooper. Hooper, they discover, is a high society mogul whose ties to major politicians, judges, and local police have shielded him from prosecution as a drug trafficker. When Arrow and Lantern discover Speedy at one of Hooper's drug dens, they assume he is similarly following the trail of the criminals they intend to bust; as it turns out, however, Speedy is one of Hooper's clients, and finally admits his drug addiction to his shocked mentors. The story narrates Speedy's struggle with drug addiction and uses Arrow and Lantern's detective work to identify the various agents who facilitate the drug trade, visually mapping the circulation of drugs from offshore labs to city airstrips and docks, to individual pushers, and finally into the hands of customers. Throughout, the story line highlights the racial and class dimensions of drug trafficking; it reveals that the drug trade is often run by wealthy white businessmen who control both the means of production (the scientists and labs where drugs are produced) and the circulation of illegal substances, which are commonly sold to working-class minorities enslaved to their addictions. Simultaneously readers are shown the various reasons that disaffected youth have turned on to drugs. Among Speedy's cohort of teenage users are two racial minorities, Asian and African American, who claim that drugs have offered them a way to deal with the burden of racism. When Speedy asks his Asian American companion why his father keeps a collection of ancient weaponry in his basement, the teenager replies, "All day long, he answers to 'chink'... 'slant.' At night he comes home and grooves on the armament—pretends he's Genghis Kahn or somebody... pretends he's killing his bosses... instead of kissing their feet.... Me, I've found another escape." Chiming in, their African American companion exclaims, "'Chink's' nothin' compared to the names I'm called.... Nigger is for openers.... But it ain't the names they call you, it's what's behind their eyes, baby. This is my reason for shootin'.... It makes life more bearable."[17] At the story's conclusion, Speedy offers yet another explanation for the scourge of teen drug addiction, indicting an "uncaring and unthinking society" that turns its back on the American youth after betraying their trust by supporting an illegal war in Vietnam and celebrating corporate greed above democratic freedom. Both the story's visual commitment to mapping the heterogeneous institutions that make up the drug trade, as well as its repeated suggestion that social realities affect individual life trajectories, encourages readers to develop what C. Wright Mills has called a "sociological imagination," the cognitive capacity to scale upward and downward from individual troubles (such as joblessness and drug addiction) to the larger social and economic realities (including racism and unequal distribution of wealth and privilege) that lead to destructive life trajectories.

Even as the comic book uses character likes Speedy to lobby a broader critique of the structural realities that make the drug trade possible—including class inequality, racism, and generational conflict—it also personalizes the experience of drug addiction by framing it as a coming-of-age story for both Speedy and his role models, Green Lantern and Green Arrow. Though Speedy is initially pictured as the weak-willed addict, by the conclusion his overcoming of his addiction and his willingness to take responsibility for his choices reflect his entry into true "manhood." Alternately Green Arrow's stubborn refusal to see Speedy's perspective or take responsibility for abandoning his young charge displays an overinvestment in liberal individualism above collective well-being and empathy for the suffering of others. In this way the urban folktale's ethnographic lens developed empathy not with the suffering hero, as had been the purpose of the messianic melodrama, but with "the people" or the folk communities that gave their heroic work its meaning. The final move of these texts was to reframe the superhero not as a national icon but as a folk hero, now equipped with critical knowledge of the gap between the nation's political ideals and its lived realities through his intimate relationship to ordinary people.

To do so urban folktales borrowed from the language of the ethnic revival, a wider contemporaneous cultural movement that celebrated ethnic American heritage as a purportedly progressive response to the traditional narrative of assimilation. This project appeared strikingly similar to the political program of identity politics; it differed, however, in its desire to transform identity politics from a radical or oppositional mode of affiliation that spoke to the distinct needs of minority groups to a general category that could be inhabited by any American who could lay claim to immigrant ancestry, regardless if they were understood as putatively "white" citizens with the privileges that designation entailed. The ethnic revival elicited a newfound investment among many Americans in their historical roots, encouraging them to revisit their cultural origins and develop affiliations to their ethnic past. Similarly the urban folktale was repeatedly framed as a story about returning to one's roots as an American hero, but now with an acknowledgment of the heterogeneous cultural experiences that define a distinctly American identity.[18]

"What Can One Man Do?" Visualizing the Urban Folk Hero

Both *Green Lantern/Green Arrow* and *Captain America and the Falcon* developed distinct aesthetic techniques for depicting the ascendancy of their title characters from cultural ethnographers to folk heroes. In the *Green Lantern/Green Arrow* miniseries, the superheroes' ability to develop an empathetic relationship to ordinary people indicated that they had been transformed from icons of naïve Americanism to socially conscious members of the folk. To visualize this transformation, O'Neil and Adams combined the use of documentary realism with a visual technique that I call the "psychic overlay." In this mode a full-page splash panel depicts a scene of urban degradation overlaid by the outline of one of the title hero's silhouettes. The silhouette functions as a stylized projection of his moral character—usually displaying his face mournfully brooding over society's social and political woes—while the emplacement of scenes of urban decline within the outline visually links sociopolitical crises to the hero's psyche by figuratively introjecting social ills into his "headspace." This technique works as a visual shorthand for the mental transformation of the hero, who experiences a crisis of identity when faced with social ills his superpowers have no way of combating.

One of the most striking psychic overlays in the *Green Lantern/Green Arrow* series appears in issue #87, titled "What Can One Man Do?" In this story Green Arrow debates whether he can best serve his community as a superhero or an elected official. The opening splash panel captures the dual nature of this weighty decision as one that will have both personal consequences and wide-reaching social ramifications for the residents of his underprivileged neighborhood. Two full-body silhouettes of our hero appear at the center of the page standing back to back, one of him as Green Arrow, the other as Oliver Queen (plate 19). Both versions of his identity look down with expressions of melancholy stoicism. This split imagery is redoubled in a series of light sketches that appear on either side of the silhouettes. Across the top left side of the page we see Green Arrow fighting crime in his heroic garb, while to the right are images of Oliver in a business suit as a hard-nosed CEO, his vocation before losing his fortune. In the space where the two silhouettes meet, we see a documentary-like image of a young African American boy leaving his tenement apartment, which is surrounded by overflowing garbage cans. Oliver's psychic struggle to identify with the social realities that surround him literally and figuratively split him in two, even as both of his identities are overshadowed by the single glaring reality of urban decay. In the story that follows, Green Arrow witnesses the boy pictured in this first image get shot in an urban race riot the hero fails to diffuse. The scene takes place shortly after Oliver receives a call from the mayor's office encouraging him to run for public office, a role all of his superheroic colleagues dismiss as untenable for a superheroic adventurer.[19] The issue ends with a dramatic image of Arrow's tear-stricken face as he hears that the young boy has died in surgery. Following this display, a short epilogue depicts Arrow visiting his longtime girlfriend, Dinah Lance (the superhero Black Canary), to let her know that he has decided to run for public office despite his colleagues' misgivings. From the perspective of the story's conclusion, the psychic overlay that opens the narrative cements Green Arrow's identification with the plight of African Americans by visually wedding his internal conflict of identity to his investment in the well-being of inner-city minorities. It is this very internal crisis of conscience, one that Arrow has never previously displayed in his self-righteous screeds to Green Lantern, that speaks to his newfound political maturity and his true commitment to "the people" rather than to himself or any ideological dogma. Ironically this maturity is signaled by his decision to pursue public office as a democratically elected representative of "the folk," a vocation that is seen to unify the dual identities of superhero and CEO into the legally sanctioned but morally righteous path of civic leadership.

Where *Green Lantern/Green Arrow* combines elements of documentary realism with melodramatic scenes of stylized empathy through psychic overlays, in *Captain America* the hero's evolution from political naïveté to informed citizenship is visualized through a series of encounters between the hero and the symbols of his nationalist past. As he faces the iconic emblems of his heroic career—his battle against the Nazi menace, the Lincoln Memorial, and his own red, white, and blue costume—Cap can only think how the sacred meanings that previously attached to these symbolic events and objects have been twisted by political corruption. Following the events of "Secret Empire," the story line in which Captain America's reputation is tarnished by a vast political conspiracy to overthrow the U.S. government, the series dedicates an entire issue to Cap's torturous decision to abandon his identity as America's official superhero. As the issue unfolds, his friends and colleagues offer him powerful reasons to maintain his heroic identity, each in turn eliciting a visual memory of Cap's exploits throughout the years that produce a series of mnemonic links between Cap and the long history of American democracy: Iron Man reminds Cap of his service to the country against the Nazi menace in World War II; the Falcon reminds his partner of the influence superheroes wield as role models for American youth, recounting his own inspirational first encounter with Cap, which made him decide to become a superhero; and Peggy Carter implores him to consider the symbolic weight of his heroic exploits, through which he represents the founding ideals of the nation.[20]

FIGURE 5.3. The "many different versions of what America is." Steve Englehart (writer) and John Buscema (penciller), "Captain America Must Die!," *Captain American and the Falcon* #176, August 1974, reprinted in *Captain America and the Falcon: Secret Empire* (New York: Marvel Comics, 2005), 157.

Pushing back against these idealistic pleas, Cap tells Peggy, "America is not the single entity you're talking about. It's changed since I took my name. There was a time, yes, when the country faced a clearly hideous aggressor and her people stood united against it! But now, nothing's that simple. Americans have many goals—some of them contrary to others. . . . That's as it should be—but it makes for a great many different versions of what America is." This final statement is delivered in a rectangular panel that depicts the outline of the United States foregrounded by a series of stereotyped images of racial minorities wearing culturally identifiable headpieces (a sombrero, a Middle Eastern kaffiyeh, an afro, and a sedge hat), while Cap's disembodied head looms in the middle with a furrowed brow (figure 5.3). Like these minorities, Cap wears a distinct headpiece, the cowl of his famous costume, with a capital A etched on the front.[21] Though the faces of these minorities appear as bald stereotypes, Cap also appears as a hyperbolic expression of Americanism, more like a clown in a costume than a true hero amid the array of people who now represent the "many different versions of what America is."

This critical retrospective of Captain America's career followed by his declaration of America's changed character serves to show that his ascendancy to the status of folk hero can take place only if he can find a way to experience America through the perspective of the diverse peoples who now claim the nation as their own rather than through his personal history as an idealized American fetish whose identity is shaped by government propaganda. Cap essentially needs to become an immigrant, much like the second-generation Jewish Americans who celebrated their allegiance to their chosen country by creating characters like Captain America to support the cultural war against fascism during World War II. He becomes a wanderer of sorts, seeking out America the way that Green Lantern and Green Arrow had through their cross-country adventures, only this time through a personal reinvention of his costumed identity.

After much deliberation Cap develops a new superheroic identity as "Nomad: Man without a Country." Before arriving at the name, Steve works his way through a variety of possibilities, including "gypsy, vagrant, migrant, hobo, and bum," deciding that these monikers are not "classy enough" before coming up with his final title. Steve linguistically moves through a series of ignominious epithets traditionally given to immigrants, social outcasts, and refugees so that he might finally redeem the status of the stateless subject as a nomad in control of his own destiny rather than a social pariah necessarily driven to seek political recognition from national institutions.[22] At the conclusion of this story line, Steve returns to his former heroic identity as Captain America, convinced that his time as Nomad has given him the foresight to embody the democratic ideals of the nation without being blind to the evils that beset it. Reuniting with the Falcon, he declares:

> The country didn't let me down—I let her down, by not being all that I could be! If I'd paid more attention to the way American reality differed from the American Dream . . . If I hadn't gone around thinking the things I believe in were thirty years out of date—then I might have uncovered [the Secret Empire], and stopped [them], before it was too late! . . . There has to be somebody who'll fight for the dream, against any foe . . . somebody who'll do the job I started. . . . The man who Nomad is won't die. . . . Everything he's learned will live on—only now, once again, it'll be as . . . Captain America![23]

Steve associates the ability to discern between the "American Dream" and the nation's sociopolitical realities with the experience of being a nomad, a wanderer who ultimately chooses his affiliations with nations, people, and political institutions on the basis of informed choice rather than taken-for-granted duty. Simultaneously, even as Cap's wandering alter ego is celebrated for facilitating his political growth and maturity, Nomad is fetishized as the purest expression of "genuine" Americanism rather than a radical political stance *against* the nation. In this way the concept of Nomad is exploited much as ethnic identity was in this period, for the purpose of reaffirming a shared national identity despite the heterogeneity of the country's ethnoracial origins and political viewpoints.

In the early 1970s *Green Lantern/Green Arrow* deployed the logic of white liberalism and the critique of racial privilege to reframe the bourgeois superhero as a "man of the people"; by mid-decade *Captain America and the Falcon* deployed the logic of the ethnic revival, depicting Cap willfully abandoning his natural ties to the nation that he might perform the experience of a newly arrived immigrant forced to construct their relationship to the United States from the ground up. Even as they used different political and visual rhetorics to do so, both series ultimately framed the evolution from icon to folk hero as a story of remasculanization; while the nation itself was often feminized in urban folktales, repeatedly referred to as a vulnerable yet noble woman, folk heroes were conceived of as the country's powerful and virile male guardians.

In *Green Lantern/Green Arrow* the hero's reclaiming of his masculine self-image involved a willingness to abandon his powers and fight social injustice as a man rather than a superhero. In a circuitous logic, it was only by proving himself capable of fighting his own battles without the aid of superpowers that the title character could actually *live up to* the legendary status of the superhero. In Green Lantern and Green Arrow's first cross-country adventure, they battle a fascist mine owner, Slapper Soames, who has violently subjected an Appalachian community to slave labor. During a fight with Soames's armed thugs, Lantern realizes that his ring won't protect him from mortal injury as it has previously. Facing the barrel of a gun without the ring's power to shield him, he declares, "I was chosen for my job because I'm supposed to be brave—courage is easy when you can't die! The ring is constantly playing mother hen! So . . . am I really courageous—? To heck with the ring." In the next frame he springs forward to land a blow to his opponent's cheek, thinking to himself, "Ah! To be able to prove myself again . . . to face danger alone . . . and to best it by my own strength! Ever since I joined the Lantern Corps . . . something's been missing from my life! Something called self-reliance! That last hood's jaw was like granite—! Hurt my knuckles . . . and it's the nicest pain I've ever felt!"[24] In this instance it is the hero's return to human status rather than his exercise of superhuman ability, alongside a commitment to a rugged American individualism, that places him on equal footing with the people he seeks to protect. Unlike "The Phoenix Saga," in which Jean Grey elicits the help of her teammates to heal the M'Kraan Crystal, Green Lantern's struggle is internalized and reconciled through an independent expression of masculine will power, exemplified by his show of brute physical force and disavowal of feminine authority in his dismissive description of the ring as a "mother hen" holding him back from true "self-reliance."

Male readers of *Green Lantern/Green Arrow* understood this as a key ideological point of the series and applauded O'Neil and Adams for reaffirming the title heroes' masculinity. One letter responded to this particular scene by stating, "Never before has GL been so real, so palpable. . . . The clincher of this is was when GL's ring lost the power to protect him from mortal danger. I often wondered why they went to all the trouble of finding a man born without fear when the ring would protect the wearer from fearful calamity. Now GL can stand on his own two feet and be a real man."[25] Rather than depicting the powerful bonds of cross-racial and cross-species alliance forged between female superheroes like Storm and Phoenix, urban folktales celebrated the interracial male bonding between African American and white male heroes. Green Arrow's invocation of Martin Luther King Jr. and Robert Kennedy as putative allies in the struggle for civil rights reaffirmed this fact by linking race and class difference to figures of liberal masculinity who reconciled these conflicting identities through their iconic status as male folk heroes.

The affirmation of white and African American masculinity mutually reinforced by the partnership of iconic white superheroes with powerful urban black heroes (the latter helping their white counterparts face the social and economic inequalities they had previously overlooked) was impressed upon readers in *Captain America and the Falcon*, which depicted the contentious but brotherly relationship between America's national hero and an urban crime fighter. In this series masculinity is measured by the superhero's commitment to interracial male bonding based on an assumed social equality between partners. The opening scene of the story line "Secret Empire" introduces readers to his African American partner, the Falcon (Sam Wilson), walking the streets of Harlem just before a group of thugs are about to attack him. The narration reads, "How is it when you're the Falcon? Well, there's the warming thrill of being partner to a national hero like Captain America—although the thrill is mixed with the nagging frustration that you live within the shadow of Cap's far greater strength."[26] This nagging frustration comes back to haunt Falcon in the following scene, when his struggle to best the thugs who ambush him is ended by Cap himself, which leaves Falcon fuming at his inferior physical capabilities next to his famous partner. Performing the role of the white liberal, Cap responds to Falcon's frustrations, "Sam . . . if you really feel that badly about it, I'll do anything I can to help—even though I really feel you're fine the way you are." Despite Cap's reassurances, a determined Falcon seeks out the Black Panther to fashion him a pair of wings that grant him new powers so that he might become Cap's heroic equal.

Unlike *Green Lantern/Green Arrow*, which identifies masculinity with feats of physical strength independent of superpowers, in *Captain America* successful "manliness" is identified with willful control over one's personal identity and the tenacious pursuit of self-improvement to achieve equality with one's peers. Sam's desire to improve his heroic capabilities and, later, Cap's decision to be independent of the U.S. government are presented as symbolic acts of masculine self-determination that initially divide the partners but ultimately bring them closer together through their mutual recognition of each other's personal development. Even as it strove to equalize white and black superheroes, however, the comic book consistently positioned black masculinity as reliant on whiteness for its meaning. The Falcon's wish to be seen as Cap's heroic equal is presented as stemming from his personal insecurities as a black man in a racist society, while Cap's struggle to escape the institutional structures of government power is framed as the universal struggle to be a free man in any context regardless of race.

The most telling example of this unequal relationship appears in the opening scene to the story line "Nomad," which depicts a nightmare the Falcon has shortly after Steve Rogers gives up the title of Captain America. In a fitful sleep Falcon relives the famous World War II scenario in which Cap and his sidekick Bucky fight their final battle with the Nazis. In the original 1940s narrative, Bucky dies in an airplane explosion during their escape, while Cap falls into the English Channel, to be discovered years later preserved in ice. In his dream Falcon imagines himself in Bucky's place, only this time both he and Cap die together in a furious explosion. Waking up in a cold sweat from this final haunting image, Sam exclaims, "[Cap] had his faith in America shattered, and I've had the same thing happen to my faith in him! He was my idol—my touchstone with the way things were supposed to be—and now he's just dropped out!"[27] The Falcon's nightmare vision of Cap's death in the war is presented as an allegory for the death of cross-racial alliances between black and white men in the postwar period, since Captain America's symbolic death in the present (equated with the countercultural injunction to "drop out" of society) has rent the former partnership between himself and the Falcon. In a stunning display of white liberal hubris, this scene suggests that Falcon's self-image hinges on his ability to live up to the democratic ideals Cap represents, while implying that the racially progressive partnership the two share cannot exist without Captain America's presence in American culture.

The urban superhero's narrative trajectory from failed citizen, to cultural ethnographer, to folk hero mirrored the desired career path for creative producers who developed these stories as a way to move their industrial position from emasculated worker to esteemed auteur. Presciently tapping into the key national discourses on citizenship during this period—namely the emergence of post–civil rights identity politics, the ethnic revival, and the related discourse of diversity and multiculturalism—comic book creators saw an opportunity to link their particular interests as a community of economically and culturally marginalized creative laborers to the forms of marginalized citizenship on the basis of ethnoracial difference that these emergent discourses articulated and embraced.

The linking of the economic plight of creative workers to the marginalized political status of racial minorities was vividly captured in *Luke Cage: Hero for Hire* (1971), the first mass-market comic to feature an African American superhero as its lead character. In his origin story Luke Cage is introduced as Carl Lukas, a young black man who struggles to escape a life of crime in Harlem, only to be framed for possession of narcotics by his former business partner. In prison Lukas is selected to undergo an experimental procedure that hardens his skin to the density of steel and exponentially increases his strength. During the procedure a racist guard bent on Lukas's demise attempts to derail the experiment. Instead Lukas ingeniously uses his newfound strength to escape the prison and make his way back to New York City. There he invents a new name, Luke Cage, an homage to his incarceration, moves into a dilapidated apartment next to an old movie theater, and sells his newfound skills to those in need of his superheroic services.[28] Unlike his heroic colleagues in the Marvel Universe, Cage approached being a superhero as labor worthy of monetary recompense, something that discomforted Captain America, who would claim in the mid-1970s, "I've never even met Luke Cage—and I'm not really sure I want to. This whole 'Hero for Hire' bit rubs me the wrong way! I mean, being an adventurer is a special kind of life—at least it is for me! I'd never do it simply for money!"[29] If characters like Captain America represented the seemingly idealistic white liberal view of hero work, Cage undercut such self-serving claims by pointing out that those superheroes who gave away their services were not ethically superior to him, merely more economically well-off and backed by institutional power unavailable to a black man with a criminal record.

At every stage of his development as a superhero, Cage considers the financial burden of hero work, making decisions based on what he can afford. In the first two issues readers watch as Cage has business cards made with his name and telephone number, carefully selects an affordable superhero outfit from a costume shop, and finds a reasonably priced office to rent. Like the artistic talents who helped bring him into being, Cage is a freelance laborer, a "hero for hire." Though marginalized at the level of race and class, he is depicted as the paragon of black masculinity. His embodiment of ideal manhood (especially in the visual depiction of his hypermuscular black body) compensates for these forms of marginalization, much as the remasculanization of heroes like Green Lantern and Captain America made them ideal folk heroes.

"Hero for Hire" presciently foreshadowed Marvel's and DC's adoption of the "Work Made for Hire" clause in the Supreme Court's revised copyright law decision in January 1978. Under the revised law, employers own the rights to any work they contract from a creative producer unless explicitly stated otherwise in their contract.[30] Soon after this ruling was issued, both Marvel and DC circulated new contracts stipulating that no artist or writer could work for either company if they did not sign away rights to ownership over the materials they produced. Where the practice of Work Made for Hire stripped creators of their power to control their own labor, Luke Cage creatively embodied a hypermasculine, independent, and self-employed hero who willfully chose his clients. In one sense, then, Cage could be read as a racialized fantasy of what white working-class creative laborers might have wished they were. As if to ensure that readers understood the full import of Cage's masculine persona, he was depicted as living in a run-down apartment next to a movie theater that exclusively played classic American westerns. Few issues of the series went by without the voices of John Wayne, Clint Eastwood, and Gary Cooper wafting through the walls as Cage waylays another of the countless thugs who try to ambush him at his workplace.

Perhaps most important of all is the visual correlation of Cage's superhero work with the creative labor of former denigrated workers in the mass entertainment industries. In one of Cage's early adventures, the search for a ghostly apparition that haunts his apartment leads him into the bowels of the Gem Theatre, the movie house next door, where he discovers a network of tunnels housing a long-abandoned penny arcade and circus. Through his detective work he learns that the apparition is merely a costumed man, a former circus worker who was the son of Adrian Loring, "the last of the Ziegfeld types," who "owned most of the theaters on 42nd before the movies took over."[31] At the story's conclusion Loring's son tries to exact revenge on a corporate mogul who murdered his father for his money. Though Loring's son and former partner die in a terrible fall from a high-rise building, Cage becomes the living memory of Loring's former work, the new local attraction on 42nd Street that even the movies can't compete with. In this way the creators of *Luke Cage* acknowledged the raw deal dealt to the ghosts of mass entertainment past, even as they worked to assert their own often denigrated profession as a triumphant survivor of this bygone era of American popular culture. According to the logic of this story, what separated the labor of comic book producers from the defunct theater owners and out-of-work carnies of the past was that it had evolved with the times as a bastion of racial progress.

In racially conscious comic series like *Luke Cage* creators attempted to distinguish themselves from their corporate higher-ups and improve their public image in the eyes of contemporary readers. And readers enthusiastically responded to the introduction of the first independent African American superhero in mainstream comic books, highlighting the series' attention to the intersection of race and class as its distinguishing feature. In turn, creators' replies to these sentiments reflected the eagerness with which they hoped to project themselves as paragons of racial progressivism. In one early letter to the series, a fan named Matthew Graham wrote:

> It has become fashionable to prove oneself open-minded by portraying all members of a minority with a semblance of reality, which results, somehow, in a stereotype. It may have been the awfully stilted dialogue or the characteristic "hard dude" appearance. The concept of a man who puts his power on the open market is one of the few exciting things about this whole series. I've always wondered why someone fought crime for free. . . . I certainly hope you realize you have a winner on your hands as long as you treat it with the same loving care you've built an empire upon.[32]

Graham chastises the industry for its hyperbolic attempts to turn racial progressivism into a fad but also identifies the distinctness of *Luke Cage* with its approach to class. At the same time, in his reference to the Marvel "empire," he reveals a canny understanding of the fact that Marvel (and the comics industry more broadly) has built its own corporate success on the portrayal of economically downtrodden characters, especially racial minorities.

As if to ward against their comics' potential association with economic opportunism, creators responded by stressing their contributions to politically progressive comic book content: "Matt, just for a moment, consider the various black characters in our mags. Luke Cage, the Falcon, T'Challa [the Black Panther], Robbie Robertson [and] his son Randy, Jim Wilson in *The Hulk*—each one is a unique, individual personality. If, to your mind, Luke Cage happens to dovetail with a newly-emerging racial stereotype, it's purely coincidence. Because in all the time we've been portraying black people in our magazines—long before it became sickeningly 'fashionable' by the way—we've never had a character like him!"[33] This bizarrely defensive response to a largely flattering letter indicates the level of anxiety creators experienced over convincing readers of their political sincerity. Their insistence on the diversity of their African American characters displays a desire to be seen as nuanced cultural ethnographers—depicting everyday lived experience in all its diversity—rather than well-intentioned white liberals unwittingly promulgating racial stereotypes through a naïve form of progressive politics.

This is made even clearer in a response to a young reader, Judy Rivas, who encouraged Marvel to distinguish between different racial minorities with more accuracy in future publications:

> I have a suggestion which applies to all comics in general: it concerns a small problem with inking. Comics have made it a habit of drawing everyone who is not white alike. When drawing blacks, you always make them ashen. Also when drawing orientals, the inkers insist on making them yellow or orange. Then there is a group newly arrived to comics, Latins, especially Puerto Ricans, are always made to look exactly like each other. You know, we come in hundred[s] of different shades, sizes, and shapes. While I'm on the subject of Puerto Ricans, do you think you could possibly introduce a new character to the script? Perhaps a cute Puerto Rican girl like . . . (well, I'm really very modest).[34]

To which the editors responded:

> Sure, we know people are different, Judy—as the Cage saga unfolds before you, you'll be seeing all sorts of them. Cage isn't restricting

his clientele to any one type, and, just in living and working in New York, he'll be meeting all races, ages, and social strata. . . . One correction, though—the inker is not the same as the colorist in most cases, and to avoid such misconceptions in the future, we've started adding the colorist's name to each Marvel credit roster—though maybe we should call it the blame roster after the mistakes you mentioned![35]

Despite her criticisms of the comic book industry's lack of nuance in depicting racial minorities, the letter writer Judy Rivas still conceives of comics as a legitimate space for enacting ideals of racial diversity. The ability of a Puerto Rican teenager to identify with the characters of contemporary superhero comics and feel empowered to write directly to the creators regarding both her misgivings about racial representation in comics and her hopes for greater diversity in their creative content, speaks volumes about the politically expansive character of superhero comics in this period. As with Matthew Graham's letter, however, the editors respond by reaffirming their supposed knowledge of true diversity while stressing their commitment to nuanced racial representations through their documentary-like attention to the American cityscape. More important, the response uses Rivas's critique of racial representation against her by pointing out her own failure to distinguish between different kinds of laborers in the comic book industry. The ability of creators to interpret their own mistakes in racial representations as comparable to Rivas's own lack of nuance in the distinctions of comic book labor implied that they understood questions of race and creative labor as two sides of the same coin, much as they were figured in the character of Luke Cage.

Even more revelatory than these published correspondences is the unpublished letter of Jana Hollingsworth to Chris Claremont, writer of *The X-Men*, in response to the depiction of Ororo Monroe returning to Harlem in 1979. Questioning the racial politics of this creative decision, Hollingsworth boldly stated:

> I've disliked Ororo's Harlem background ever since it was introduced. . . . Nearly every city in the country has a black slum; if Ororo had to have an American father, why did he have to be from Harlem? But there's more to it than that. I've always felt that giving Ororo an American father diluted the unique international nature of the X-Men. If she's supposed to be African, damn it, she should be African! I was encouraged by her thought that, though Harlem

is in her heritage, she can chose [*sic*] to reject it. The Falcon, Luke Cage, even the Black Panther contentiously maintain their links with "the street," which is a fine thing. But on Ororo it will look like a political cliché: "good" blacks maintain their connections with the street. Ororo is very much different from every other character at Marvel, black and white. She may well decide that, heritage or no, she personally won't accept Harlem as a part of her life.[36]

In this shockingly astute letter, Hollingsworth joins other fans in critiquing simplistic formulations and deployments of race in 1970s superhero comics. Yet her criticisms reach a new level of nuance by demanding a more intersectional understanding of race as an internally heterogeneous and contingent category of identity that is always produced in relation to other modes of identification, including national heritage, gender, class, and geographical location. Hollingsworth takes Claremont and Byrne to task for feeding the stereotype of African American urban culture as reducible to the figure of Harlem, yet she also questions the equation of blackness with African American identity more broadly, as opposed to a heterogeneous racial category embodied by different communities globally. Like Rivas, Hollingsworth doesn't simply identify creators' representational missteps but demands that comics *live up to the precedent they have already set* of true intersectionality in the form of the X-Men's internationalism, which undermines simplistic reductions of the various teammates' global ethnoracial lineages to *American* racial identities. The demand that ethnoracial identity be a choice, taken up or refused on the basis of one's willed affiliations, is the core of cosmopolitanism. Hollingsworth voices ambivalence toward the urban folktale's movement *away* from such cosmopolitan values toward a monolithic understanding of race as an essential identity in the ethnographic impulse.

What mainstream readers would likely not have known in this period was the contentious nature of these same kinds of fine distinctions of identity among industry professionals in relation to their own creative labor. With the institution of the Work Made for Hire clause in the late 1970s, the value of distinct kinds of creative laborers—including writers, pencillers, inkers, colorists, and letterers—became a question of serious concern. Previously all creators on a comic book were understood as part of a seamless team working simultaneously on a single product regardless of their specific task. Under Work Made for Hire these laborers were contracted independently of one another, giving companies greater leeway to hire and fire individual laborers on a project at their discretion.

This encouraged creators to look out for their own interests, which led to vitriolic battles over who could be said to have contributed the most significant portions of a given comic book.

In 1978 creators met to discuss the formation of a comics guild that would represent the interests of artistic laborers in the field. Almost from the start the meeting devolved into a yelling match between different creative talent over who legitimately counted as a primary contributor to any given issue of a comic book. Though the meeting was organized with the intention of developing a legally functional definition of collective labor, participants used the venue to air personal frustrations with their lack of prestige despite their creative successes, reducing the act of artistic production to individual struggles with company management. This struggle was repeatedly framed by a description of the relationship between company management and creators as one of infantilization. Capturing this sentiment, *X-Men* writer Chris Claremont claimed, "Everything that has been done to us in the past years has been from the attitude, 'Here, my boy, have a lollypop.' It's been a parent dealing with an unruly child. We're not children! . . . We're creators!"[37] Ironically the writers and artists who most often deployed the discourse of infantilization to decry the paternalistic structure of Marvel and DC—including Claremont, Adams, and Steve Englehart—were generally the most successful creative producers in the industry and those granted the most creative license by their respective companies.[38]

This dual rhetoric of infantilization and emasculation worked to aggrandize predominantly white, male creative labor—positioning them as courageous combatants against the institutional aggression of an unjust authority figure, much like the superheroes of the urban folktale—while sidestepping the material inequalities that had defined the field of comic book production since its inception. Not only did this discussion ignore the question of racial homogeneity in comic book labor (which was almost uniformly white), but by equating the major comic book companies with castrating father figures, the rhetoric of infantilization relied on a patriarchal logic that assumed all creative producers were men who similarly saw their relationship to their employers in these terms, essentially ignoring the professional interests of women in the field. Prior to the meeting, Mary Jo Duffy, a recent editorial hire at DC Comics and one of the few women working in the industry, presciently offered the following critique of the guild based on her perception of the male creators who were organizing it (including Neal Adams, the artist of the *Green Lantern/Green Arrow* miniseries): "I don't see how, when you work in a syndicated medium . . . you can have individual creator's rights. When it's a group effort, I don't see how each individual can claim it's his or her work . . . .There are a lot of good things that could come out of a Guild, but I don't think a group of people whose only interest is getting a better piece of the actions for themselves . . . can accomplish those good things."[39] Duffy recognized that the purported investment in protecting creative labor was often a cover for economic self-aggran-dizement among already establishment male talent. Even as the primary writers and artists of both companies struggled to convince readers of their political acumen in relation to questions of race, class, and gender hierarchy, their participation in the comics guild debate revealed a stun-ning lack of self-reflection about the internal inequalities of their own profession.

While the urban folktale began as a seemingly progressive attempt to develop a double-pronged critique of American sociopolitical life and the increasingly conservative conditions of comics production in the 1970s, by decade's end it overtook the space opera as the vanguard genre of a fully corporatized comic book industry. Even as it worked to reaffirm the cultural capital of comic book producers and make visible the social conditions that devalued U.S. citizenship and creative labor alike, the urban folktale's insistence on grounding such affirmation in the indi-vidual psychic struggles of iconic male superheroes rather than in the collective world-making projects of the space opera ultimately served to contain the potential expansiveness of its critique. Consequently, where the urban folktale emerged out of the conditions of and *against* the cor-porate restructuring of the comic book industry, it ultimately devolved into a celebration of a neoliberal politics of personal responsibility grounded in bootstrap individualism. This contradictory conclusion to the urban folktale's initially transformative project reflected conflicting desires among industry professionals to push back against the corporate structures of comic book publishing while benefiting financially from the industry's expansion into the realms of product licensing.

As the 1970s came to a close, creative producers recognized, even if implicitly, that their capitulation to the industrial demands of the major publishing companies reflected their collective failure to develop a united front against their own economic exploitation. At the same time, those whose work sold well reaped the benefits of the direct market—the emer-gent mode of selling comics through devoted comic book retailers rather than newsstands and bookstores—by becoming celebrated auteurs among hardcore reading audiences. The greater the fan base became for any particular writer or artist, the more creative license he (or, less often, she) received from the companies, so that the artistic freedom comic book producers had long sought through failed professional organizations could finally be found by successfully living up to the company's standard of high sales figures.

In many ways the seemingly local and narrow world of superhero comics in this period presciently mapped the broader transformations and crises of the American left throughout the decade. Just as the left increasingly turned to identity politics as a way of recuperating its failing reputation at the close of the decade, so too did the urban folktale largely succeed over the conceptual project of the space opera by celebrating the individual achievement of hardened male superheroes against a corrupt "system," an ongoing allegory for creative producers' own self-image as battle-weary laborers who had valiantly fought against the corporate machine and lost. By the mid-1980s *The X-Men*'s alternative kinship was ghettoized into an *X-Men* franchise, a highly successful but limited slice of superhero comic publishing now dominated by stories of vigilante justice rather than collective political action. Absorbing both a growing professional fan community's vitriolic critique of superheroes as fascist iconography and the industry's hyperinvestment in sales, comics creators of the early 1980s often reflected disdain for the very characters they propelled into the American imagination, producing dystopian tales of the superhero's failed project to protect humanity from its internecine conflicts and his own loss of faith in humanity's social and political redemption. In one sense the creative producers of the 1970s had sold their soul to the proverbial devil, and in turn, their most famous creations would increasingly find themselves struggling with their own literal demons, the terrifying representatives of a new era of economic greed and national excess following the privations of the stagflationary 1970s.

6 / Consumed by Hellfire: Demonic Possession and the Limits of the Superhuman in the 1980s

The goal of the Hellfire Club's Inner Circle is power—[we] wish to rule the world. Mutants are a means to an end. . . . There are too many super-beings—mutants and otherwise—people have begun to realize their value. The person, group, corporation—country—that possesses them . . . has an incalculable advantage over those that don't. We used to be hated, now we are desired. . . . They still fear us . . . but now they wish to use us. . . . You must decide whether you wish to be ruler—or slave.
— EMMA FROST, the White Queen of the Hellfire Club,
The New Mutants #16 (June 1984)

I didn't want this, my dear ones—and yet, it was something I had to do. By striking you down, I cut myself free of the last ties binding me to the person I was, the life I led. You and I are quits now, X-Men. Our paths will cross no more. My destiny lies in the stars!
— DARK PHOENIX, *The Uncanny X-Men* #135 (July 1980)

Speaking to the nation in the midst of a devastating energy crisis in July 1979, President Jimmy Carter boldly asserted, "In a nation that was proud of hard work, strong families, close-knit communities, and our faith in God, too many of us now tend to worship self-indulgence and consumption. Human identity is no longer defined by what one does, but by what one owns. But we've discovered that owning things and consuming things does not satisfy our longing for meaning. We've learned that piling up material goods cannot fill the emptiness of lives which have no confidence or purpose."[1] In what is now widely considered the most important speech of his presidency, Carter reframed the nation's struggle for energy independence not as a crisis of political leadership or government policy but as stemming from a breakdown in national morale. Self-interest, overconsumption, and profligate investment in immediate pleasure at the expense of future security had shorn Americans' investment in a common good that had been the bedrock of the nation's historical progress. One year later, in the pages of America's most popular superhero comic book, *The Uncanny X-Men*, Jean Grey would transform into the Dark Phoenix, a monstrous version of her former benevolent self, now possessed by the Phoenix Force's ravenous hunger for energy.

To sate her boundless appetite, Dark Phoenix would devour the energy of an entire star, obliterating five billion inhabitants of a distant planet. Where once the Phoenix Force had symbolized the generative network of relations that bound together the universe and the X-Men's mutant kinship, now, "to feed her [infernal hunger]," Dark Phoenix threatened to "consume all that exists."[2]

How did it come to pass that in two short years the radical vision of egalitarian alliances across difference so dramatically depicted in "The Phoenix Saga" would come to this? What made it possible for the symbiotic relationship between Jean and the Phoenix Force to be recast as a form of possession prompting Jean's megalomaniacal drive to devour the cosmos? Most important, how did a national discourse about overconsumption and political self-interest come to inform this transformation in superheroic fantasy? From the late 1970s onward, the superhero's susceptibility to possession by outside forces—demonic, alien, or otherwise—as well as her increasing willingness to respond to repressed desires for unlimited power became the central anxiety around which superhero comics produced their most epic stories. In this period the interior psychic world of the superhero was laid bare, its characters revealed as self-loathing, guilt-ridden, and ambivalent about their capacity, or more accurately *incapacity* to control their powers. Simultaneously an increasingly cynical fictional public grew to view superheroes as paragons of psychological dysfunction who embodied the worst forms of narcissism, sadism, and egomania.

This image of the superhero as a self-interested free agent untethered from ethical commitments to family, nation, or species echoed a broader national discourse about the fraying of generational ties and familial responsibility in the late 1970s and early 1980s dubbed "the culture of narcissism." In August 1976 journalist Tom Wolfe famously labeled the 1970s "the 'Me' Decade," lobbing a sarcastic critique of the baby boom generation as a self-absorbed, pleasure-seeking mass of consumers whose self-definition rested on a childish disavowal of their ties to previous generations.[3] In many ways this image of self-actualization through an active break with one's history described Jean Grey's initial manifestation of the Phoenix Force in the mid-1970s as a liberatory power granting her freedom from an oppressive and sexist past. Eliding such radical possibilities for self-reinvention, Wolfe blamed the dangerous "presentism" of the baby boomers on postwar affluence, which afforded a new generation of upwardly mobile Americans the promise of seemingly boundless material wealth to improve their self-image and social status.[4] Transforming this critique into a full-fledged social theory, in 1979 the historian Christopher Lasch published his best-selling book, *The Culture of Narcissism*. Lasch identified the expansion of the narcissistic type in American culture—a superficial and self-aggrandizing personality incapable of empathy and obsessed with recognition from others—as a symptom of a broader breakdown in generational ties that was grounded in the historical collapse of the nuclear family. According to Lasch, the family's invasion by professional caregivers, government regulation, and mass media had alienated its members from one another, creating emotionally distant mothers and absent fathers who produced insecure and recognition-seeking children incapable of developing an authentic sense of self.[5]

While all of these thinkers linked the psychological category of narcissism to a critique of overconsumption (often defined by an obsession with material possessions), they consistently criticized individual consumers for their self-interested choices rather than a larger system of acquisitive capitalism that endorsed the accumulation of wealth as the primary vision of the good life. As Natasha Zaretsky has shown, in the various writings and speeches of cultural critics, politicians, and journalists in this period, the critical energies that might have been devoted to indicting capitalist ideals instead zeroed in on the left-wing social and countercultural movements of the 1970s, particularly feminism. These critics accused feminism of convincing women to abandon family and child rearing and of recasting the relationship between men and women as a battleground that negated possibilities for fulfilling heterosexual reproductive futurity.[6] In its various manifestations the culture of narcissism thesis linked a self-interested and psychologically dysfunctional nation to an overinvestment in the superficial pleasures of material life, which had been spurred on by radical identity movements whose philosophies of personal liberation damaged the capacity of Americans to feel genuine emotion and attachment to others.

Throughout the 1980s demonic possession stories initially appeared to perform the popular narrative of the culture of narcissism but ultimately linked the psychic corruption of their central superheroic characters to the machinations of global capitalism. These texts repeatedly placed the individual psychic conflicts of possessed superheroes within larger institutional structures—including corporate capital and the state's increasing investment in private industry above the interests of citizens' rights and freedoms—to show how apparent narcissistic tendencies were spawned not by radical identity movements but by capitalism's obsessive attachment of economic value to all social relationships.

As the example of Dark Phoenix made patently clear, demonic possession stories followed the larger discourse around narcissism in linking possession to gender and sexual deviancy. These stories presented the superhero's monstrous transformation as distorting her traditional gender identity and bringing forth a voracious sexual appetite expressed in sadistic pleasure in the violent use of her powers. In its zealous quest to critique neoliberal systems of economic value, the demonic possession story *devalued* the kinds of gender and sexual transformations that superhero comics like *The X-Men* had celebrated in the mid-1970s. By linking demonic possession to visual expressions of nonnormative or "perverse" performances of gender and sexuality, these stories paradoxically relied on a misguided erotophobic (or antisex) logic that indirectly echoed another emerging discourse of this period: the feminist sex wars. At the same time that writers like Wolfe and Lasch were indicting radical feminism and sexual liberation for degrading American cultural morale, radical feminists themselves were embroiled in a series of internal conflicts regarding the politics and pleasures of alternative sexual practices, pornography, and the depiction of women's sexuality in popular media. By the mid- to late 1970s a cohort of radical feminist theorists and activists had reversed the earlier feminist emphasis on sexual freedom and polymorphous pleasures as avenues for women's liberation by developing a powerful critique of sexuality as *the* primary site of women's oppression. Citing the prevalence of pornographic imagery and violence toward women in media, increasing rates of rape and battery, and the continued legal and economic subjection of women within marriage, these feminists argued that sexuality was fundamentally structured by the logic of patriarchy and could be made amenable to women's freedom only if it were stringently regulated rather than reinvented or inhabited in new ways, as earlier feminists and gay liberationists had argued. To combat structures of patriarchal sexual domination, these "antipornography feminists" pursued legislative measures to curtail the production and circulation of pornography, while mounting a vitriolic intellectual campaign against sadomasochistic sexual cultures that explored relationships of submission, domination, and pleasure in pain. They interpreted these forms of sexuality as reproducing the structural domination of men over women, regardless of the consent of the actors involved.[7] Against this formation sex-positive queer writers and activists struggled to reaffirm the critical importance of feminism as a resource for supporting, sustaining, and valuing the possibilities inherent in alternative sexual cultures, as well as rallying against activism that sponsored censorship as a tool for opposing patriarchy.[8]

The feminist sex wars revealed a deep ambivalence among feminists about the cultural outcomes and values promulgated by feminist sexual freedom in the early 1970s; it also produced unlikely coalitions between conservative critics of the "culture of narcissism" and supposedly radical feminists who claimed to fight on behalf of women's liberation. With its equally ambivalent relationship to sexuality, the demonic possession story exhibited a struggle over some of the central questions of the feminist sex wars, namely whether or not any expression of personal agency, sexual self-expression, or pleasure could be disentangled from structures of acquisitive capitalism and patriarchal domination. This seemingly intractable question manifested in the dichotomy between narrative plots that explicitly indicted possessed heroes for their greed and sadism and visual depictions of possession that spectacularized this state of being as a site of visual pleasure and fascination that potentially liberated the superhero from narratives of social value. At every level demonic possession was a story of extreme ambivalence in the face of the shifting historical realities of American capital and the waning ability of left-wing imaginaries to respond to its ferocious forward movement.

This chapter tracks the development of demonic possession as the primary trope of superhero storytelling in the 1980s. The ascendancy of demonic possession stories signaled a dramatic shift in the political values of superhero comics, namely the move away from radical left world-making projects toward an internal critique of the superhero articulated through the language of political catastrophe and despair. Where in the 1970s the superhuman body was opened up to a variety of ecstatic states of being that enabled a reinvention of the self in the service of heightened forms of consciousness, now these euphoric performances of psychic liberation were replaced by terrifying experiences of bodily discorporation, loss of self-control, and the obliteration of one's identity by nonhuman agents of evil. Possessed by malevolent forces, superheroes questioned their capacity for benevolence and compassion, the sincerity of their own heroic intentions, and ultimately their humanity. These stories also embodied the shifting emotional landscape of creative producers within the comic book industry from initial rage to despair, whose decade-long struggle against their economic undervaluation by the major comic book companies had failed to produce collective bargaining rights for their creative output. The rapid assimilation of up-and-coming artists and writers to the economic interests of Marvel and DC Comics—often through strategic concessions that granted creative producers limited royalties for particular projects and advertised the careers of celebrity auteurs—looked like nothing so much as a form of demonic possession by corporate power.

Despite the diversity of figurations through which the trope was presented and the equally diverse meanings that attached to it, demonic possession consistently accomplished a single primary goal: to question both the viability of human agency and the underlying notion of a universal "moral good" that informed human action. Where superhero comics had nearly always affirmed the capacity of humans and superhumans alike to make moral judgments based on rational thought—assuming that most would seek to better the world by guarding against threats to its survival or producing alliances across difference—demonic possession framed individuals as having little to no control over their own destinies and desires. It undercut the very political foundation on which the superhero was built, in particular the pursuit of justice in the service of producing a more egalitarian world. Yet far from curtailing the superhero's capacity to offer radically imaginative alternatives to present political circumstances, this transformation freed him from a predetermined trajectory binding him to liberal ideals of moral justice or neoliberal conceptions of economic value, making him available for a variety of unpredictable engagements with other forms of political freedom.

To analyze this phenomenon I develop an extended case study of two of the most sensational demonic possession stories of the early 1980s: the evolution of Jean Grey into the malevolent Dark Phoenix in "The Dark Phoenix Saga" (1979–80) and the epic battle of wills between Spider-Man and the alien symbiote Venom in "The Birth of Venom" (1984–91). On the one hand, these stories framed demonic possession as a metaphor for the rapacious expansion of late capitalism, where the possession of the superhero's ethical core by a desire to consume life offered a visual corollary to the perceived destruction of individual Americans' psychic life by corporate greed. On the other hand, these texts linked the superhero's loss of self-possession with a loss of control over one's sexual and gender identity, depicting those blighted by demonic forces as sexually narcissistic and lascivious, taking on the characteristics of opposing genders, and lacking control over their desires. Mapping this double move, I argue that rather than merely a backlash narrative against the political thrust of radical sexual and gender politics these narratives lamented the co-optation of feminist and gay liberation social values by consumer capitalism, while embodying a deep ambivalence over the pleasures and dangers of those values in a world where they had become so explicitly commodified. By depicting demonic possession as a crisis of both psychic and social proportions, comic books used the superhuman body to visualize the link between nonnormative or queer desires and larger structures of economic and political power in 1980s America.

Supermen in Dark Times

Each time, it becomes easier to touch Jean's mind—as our psychic rapport grows ever closer—and why not? I'm merely giving her a taste of some of her innermost— forbidden—needs and desires. Within her angel's soul—as in all our souls—lurks a devil, a yang counterpart to the surface yin. All I'm doing is freeing that negative part of her "self" from its moral cage.—MASTERMIND, *The Uncanny X-Men* #127 (January 1980)

Peter and I used to be very close—but he's changed so much in the past few years. I don't feel I know him anymore. We've become strangers, and I don't think he even cares. . . . The Peter Parker I used to know wouldn't have dropped out of college. He wouldn't have thrown his future away. He had a sense of responsibility.
—AUNT MAY, *The Amazing Spider-Man* #254 (July 1984)

More than any other heroes of the Marvel Universe, Jean Grey and Peter Parker—Phoenix and Spider-Man—would come to represent paradigmatic examples of demonic possession in the 1980s. At first glance few characters would appear more dissimilar. Where Jean was born a mutant, Peter was an ordinary bookworm gifted with extraordinary abilities by a radioactive spider bite. Where Peter was an agile acrobat who fought with his fists, Jean was a skilled telepath who fought with her mind. And where Jean found a home in the mutant kinship of the X-Men, a heroic ambassador to the human race, Peter remained the consummate loner, a freelance photographer with only his beloved Aunt May as family. Despite their differences, Jean and Peter shared a common experience: in the course of their heroic careers, both became possessed by otherworldly and alien forces beyond their control that allowed them to achieve their greatest potential as heroes while unleashing the darkest aspects of their psyches. In narrating the demonic transformations of these two characters, comic book creators addressed a key contradiction that plagued superheroic fantasy in an age of mass consumerism: as a figure that embodied notions of bodily freedom and agency, the superhero now dwelled in a medium fully possessed by market forces. Consequently the mainstream comics of this period offered readers a vision of their own potential possession by the values of global capital by identifying the besieged soul of the superhero as an allegory for the vulnerability of the individual citizen to the unceasing psychic assaults of consumer society. In their respective narratives Phoenix and Spider-Man embodied a general notion of "moral good" and also personified the key political projects that defined superhero comics in the postwar period. On the one hand, Peter Parker was the ideal liberal citizen, an ordinary boy unwittingly gifted with powers beyond his wildest imagination who rejected the use of his abilities for personal gain in order to protect the lives of fellow New Yorkers. The series' famed tag line, "With great power, comes great responsibility," defined Spider-Man's outlook on the world: to deploy one's powers in the service of collective good above personal interest. On the other hand, through her transformation into the cosmic entity known as Phoenix, Jean Grey came to represent a vision of radical political community where one's powers were not merely a resource for the common good but a mark of difference that bound mutant, alien, and human outcasts through the shared experience of exclusion from the dominant institutions of everyday social life. Like Peter, Jean wedded her powers to the interests of a broader collective, in her case a monstrous mutant kinship whose chosen bonds could articulate new ways of relating and affiliating in the world. Though both represented different approaches to the notion of collective well-being, they shared a common assumption: that underlying all social progress was an agentic subject capable of choosing his or her fate and willfully allying with particular political projects for the betterment of mankind. For these two figures to lose sight of their personal identities necessarily questioned the efficacy of the political visions their actions previously espoused.

In "The Dark Phoenix Saga" and "The Birth of Venom," comic book creators narrated the descent of Phoenix and Spider-Man into madness and their subsequent loss of control over their physical powers and personal identities. Yet in both stories the psychic unraveling of these characters—which appeared as individual experiences of mental crisis—unfolded as part of a broader cultural logic that implicated institutional forces such as global capitalism in corrupting the ability to reason and make moral choices, as well as nullifying the wider democratic values that framed such reasoning. In one sense these stories framed Jean Grey and Peter Parker as the profligate consumers denigrated by Carter in his "Crisis of Confidence" speech, wayward citizens whose maniacal desire to possess unlimited power over others would lead to chaos and fragmentation. As narratives that mapped the psychic life of particular characters onto the collective consciousness of the nation during a period of massive capital expansion, "The Dark Phoenix Saga" and "The Birth of

Venom" can be read as cognitive maps of the shifting political values of the superhero comic book and the state of U.S. citizenship in the 1980s. A brief look at the central plot lines of these stories will help ground a broader analysis of the structural logic that came to organize the trope of demonic possession.

Released in twelve issues between 1979 and 1980, "The Dark Phoenix Saga" narrated Jean Grey's loss of control over the Phoenix Force and her subsequent transformation into the Dark Phoenix, the malevolent aspect of the cosmic entity whose power she had once used to save the universe from destruction. Jean's transformation is catalyzed by the machinations of the villainous mutant Mastermind, a skillful illusionist who conjures an elaborate fantasy that he and Jean are eighteenth-century English aristocrats betrothed on the eve of their travels to the British colonies. Projecting this illusion into Jean's psyche, Mastermind influences her to question her identity and her sanity, consequently weakening her control over the psychic barriers that have held the power of the Phoenix at bay. We soon learn that Mastermind is a member of the Hellfire Club, a secret cabal of mutant billionaires with ambitions to rule the world by economic means. Mastermind has been tasked with convincing Jean that she is a member of the Club so that they might use her extraordinary power to destroy all opposition to their plans. The Club almost succeeds, even getting Jean to declare herself their Black Queen and turn against her teammates. When she is finally released from her delusion by her fiancé, Scott Summers (Cyclops), Jean's rage at her manipulation causes her to lose psychic control over the Phoenix Force until she is consumed by its power. In an explosive echo of her original rebirth as Phoenix, Jean becomes Dark Phoenix, rending her emotional ties with the X-Men and ravaging the cosmos in search of sources of energy to feed her hunger for power. In the saga's final chapter, the Shi'ar Empire returns to Earth to sentence Jean for her crimes against the galaxy; championing the rights of their teammate and sister, the X-Men challenge the Shi'ar Guard to a duel on the dark side of the Moon for Jean's life. Watching her teammates fall one by one, Jean decides to sacrifice her own life by telekinetically training an ancient laser gun at herself, choosing to rob Phoenix of its human host rather than see the universe, and her mutant family, obliterated by its power.

Where "The Dark Phoenix" saga unfolded over the course of a single year, Spider-Man's struggle with his alter ego, Venom, was told in two parts across the span of nearly seven years of publication, the first narrated in 1984–85 and the second in 1989–91.[9] During an epic space conflict on a distant world, Spider-Man discovers an alien substance in the form of a rubbery black ball that bonds to his skin, replacing his tattered superhero costume. Mistaking the material for an advanced synthetic fiber, Spider-Man becomes enamored of its many wondrous capabilities. Acting as a metamorphic liquid surface, the obsidian-hued material envelops Peter's body, responding to his every thought by taking on the shape and form of any clothing he imagines while enhancing the physical strength and agility of his superhuman abilities. Peter develops a deep psychological connection to the suit on the basis of its ability to boost his self-image during a period marked by failed romances, financial troubles, and professional uncertainty. Despite its advantages, the suit is revealed to be an alien symbiote attaching itself to a host body until they become inseparable. In an epic struggle to detach the suit, Peter exposes himself and the symbiote to the deafening gong of a church bell that nearly kills them both, sonic waves being the alien's only known weakness. Though Peter is briefly free of the suit, it returns three years later in the guise of a former professional rival, the journalist Eddie Brock. Swearing vengeance against Spider-Man for ruining his career, Brock accidentally stumbles upon the symbiote suit when he visits the church where Peter last fought with his alien alter ego. Sensing in Brock its own desire for vengeance against the man who had spurned its companionship, the symbiote bonds to its new host, the two becoming the villain known as Venom. After repeatedly terrorizing Peter and his loved ones, Venom stages a final showdown with his sworn enemy, during which Spider-Man cajoles the symbiote suit away from Brock's body by offering himself once more as its host. As the symbiote releases itself from Brock to reunite with its former host, Brock and the alien are incapacitated by the attempted separation, finally granting Peter freedom from both.

As the central conflicts of these plots suggest, "The Dark Phoenix Saga" and "The Birth of Venom" displayed a deep ambivalence about the ultimate culprit of demonic possession and its material consequences. These stories simultaneously indicted Jean and Peter for their lack of psychological fortitude against the machinations of the Phoenix Force and the symbiote, while implicating larger social and institutional forces in their moral corruption. At the same time, both narrated demonic possession as a distinctly gendered and sexual experience that exposes the body to "feminine" forms of vulnerability to outside forces, while also granting extravagant power associated with masculine forms of domination and control. This dual ambivalence formed the core logic of the demonic possession story, which offered readers a spectacular story of psychological unraveling whose material consequences—including physical violence inflicted upon one's former allies and the destruction of personal relationships, if not entire worlds—propelled the narrative outward toward a wider network of sociopolitical relations both affected by and shaping the perceived motives of the characters at their center.[10]

The Psychic Story

In the months following the dramatic events of "The Phoenix Saga," Jean's newfound self-confidence in her abilities quickly evolves into a potentially dangerous form of self-indulgence, making her a threat to herself and her fellow teammates. While watching Jean exercise her cosmic powers—ones she increasingly deployed in manipulating the world to suit her needs—her teammates remarked on the disparity between the Jean Grey they knew and loved and the detached god-like creature she was becoming. In a telling scene early in "The Dark Phoenix Saga," Jean mentally pacifies the indignant parents of a potential new recruit to the Xavier Institute, the teenage genius Katherine (Kitty) Pryde, who threaten police action against Xavier after Kitty is drawn into one of the X-Men's adventures. Witnessing Jean effortlessly erase and reorganize the Prydes' memories, Ororo and Scott share a worried conversation:

ORORO: Scott, did Jean do what I think she did?
SCOTT: She used her telepathic abilities against an innocent person's mind, something that used to be an anathema to her.
ORORO: We both sense a . . . wrongness about her. There is a dark side to the Phoenix that could consume her! It's almost as if something—or someone—was manipulating her, helping that wrongness to grow! If that is the case, we must find out who or what is doing this . . . before it is too late![11]

In the logic of the demonic possession story, what Scott and Ororo find difficult to describe about Jean's transformation—a "wrongness about her"—is the manifestation of a narcissistic personality in previously altruistic heroes. In both "The Dark Phoenix Saga" and "The Birth of Venom" narcissism encompasses a variety of characteristics antithetical to the classic superhero, including an extraordinary hubris about one's superhuman abilities, overindulgence in personal (and sexual) desires, and exhibitionistic pleasure in exercising one's powers to manipulate the physical world. As Ororo's worried statement made clear, the emergence of such traits was nearly always interpreted as a sign of a psychological loss of self to malevolent outside forces. The inability to individuate one's ego from the outside world, the hallmark of narcissism, became the sine qua non of the Dark Phoenix persona that overtook Jean's mind and body.

Following her initial transformation into the Dark Phoenix, Jean takes to outer space in search of sustenance, effortlessly absorbing the energy of a distant star without a thought for the life forms that might exist in its orbit. The narrative relates, "Months ago . . . when her power saved the universe, Jean Grey had a vision of herself as Tiphareth . . . heart and soul of the mystic tree of life. She was a dream, representing the order and harmony of all things. She was all that was *great* in us. But now, the dream is twisted. She knows this—knows what she was, what she has become—and she does not care. . . . All creation is her domain—to do with as she pleases." Describing the spectacular reversal of Jean's former benevolent spirit into an all-consuming force of destruction, the narrative begins by equating her original manifestation of Phoenix with the universal "goodness" of the human race, even interpolating the reader into this vision by invoking a collective "us" to describe the cosmopolitan ideals Phoenix once represented. What is most distressing about Jean's subsequent loss of humanity is that she consciously recognizes her moral corruption yet revels in the power she now possesses. In turn, through the rhetorical logic that links Phoenix to the human race, a universal "us," Jean's transformation offers an indictment of what the human race "has become," not merely narcissistic but cognizant of the destructiveness of our desires yet willfully ravaging the Earth's resources.

On a smaller scale, Peter similarly becomes absorbed with the new-found power afforded him by the symbiote suit, taking excessive pleasure in his ability to manipulate the suit's form and function at will. After an argument with Aunt May about his future professional goals, Peter attempts to erase all thought of his personal problems by donning his new costume and taking to the streets to fight crime. As he leaps into the New York skyline, he thinks, "Ahh! Now, that's better! Nothing like a little web-slinging to chase the blues away! Besides, I always seem to think clearer up here! Maybe I'm a little weird or something, but I really get off on this!" Peter compensates for his feelings of inadequacy over his unraveling academic career and failed romantic relationships by enjoying the control he maintains over the suit and the bodily freedom it grants him. The longer Peter wears the suit, the more self-confident he becomes in both his acrobatic skill and his self-image, convinced the suit projects an impression of him as a mature superhero rather than the young upstart others in the Marvel Universe consider him to be.

When Peter finds a spare costume from his early heroic career, he considers molding the black and white symbiote suit into the bright red and blue of his original uniform but quickly scraps the idea: "When I designed my very first Spider-Man outfit I was looking to strike it big in show business! I wanted something flashy! . . . Over the years, it came to . . . symbolize . . . so much more to me . . . but even so, it couldn't do stunts like this! . . . It's time to put the past behind me! I've grown older, and, hopefully wiser in the last years. . . . Maybe my new look will help reflect those changes."[12] This moment of self-reflection cannily reveals the psychic conflict the new suit engenders in him. Even as he disclaims a former immature desire for show-biz fame, he still revels in the fact that the new costume can do stunts the previous one never could. Convinced he has invested the suit with new meaning, Peter fails to see that it is the suit's power that has reshaped his self-image by fueling his ego; what appears to him to be a progressive movement toward psychological maturity is actually a more intensified return to his fantasies of celebrity with better resources.

Echoing the broader national discourse about narcissism and self-interest promulgated by cultural theorists like Lasch and reaffirmed in Carter's "Crisis of Confidence" speech, these texts linked narcissistic tendencies to a loss of one's ethical investment in others. As Phoenix's ecstatic pleasure in boundless consumption and Spider-Man's "getting off on" his own superhuman dexterity make clear, however, narcissism was simultaneously framed as facilitating deviant sexual pleasures that derail the assumed trajectory of heterosexual desire by rerouting it toward the self. This deviation in the "appropriate" direction of sexual desire was understood as coterminous with the breakdown of traditional gender identity. In "The Dark Phoenix Saga," Jean's malevolent transformation is linked to her acquiring masculine qualities—including an aggressive sexuality and a violent temper—while Peter's intimate proximity to the parasitic symbiote suit feminizes him by metaphorically "opening up" his body to alien forces. This performance of improper gender roles is paired with visual expressions of excessive sexuality: in Jean's case, her hyperbolic "lust for power" depicted by the twisting of her facial features into a diabolical mask of lascivious pleasure while inflicting pain on others; in Peter's, the transformation of his body into an object of passionate sexual desire by the women in his life, as well as the symbiote itself, which clings to him like a lover.

This dual anxiety over the breakdown in traditional gender roles and excessive sexuality was highlighted in an early scene in "The Dark

Phoenix Saga" in which Jean and Scott Summers visit a seedy underground disco in search of an unidentified mutant Xavier hopes to recruit to the X-Men. When Scott asks Jean to mentally scan the crowd with her telepathic abilities, she thinks to herself, "That's easier said than done. . . . I can't screen out everyone's thoughts. Some of the images I'm receiving are so . . . vile. But, I can handle that. Part of me almost finds those thoughts . . . attractive."[13] No longer perceived as a site of liberatory political energies as it had been throughout the 1970s, disco culture is now equated with deviant forms of desire, presumably of the sexual variety. Jean's admission of her personal attraction to these seemingly amorphous "thoughts"—characterized as "vile," leaving the reader to imagine all manner of lascivious horrors (or pleasures) filling the psychic space of the disco—indicates a flaw in her character that leaves her susceptible to moral corruption. Her seeming openness to deviancy also positions her as a potential gender outlaw, a woman willing to seek out a variety of desires rather than simply be a sexual object for men. In the aftermath of the sexual revolution, this transformation in Jean's character initially appears as a logical extension of her freedom from traditional womanhood, which the Phoenix facilitated in the second half of the 1970s, yet the ultimate telos of her increasing openness to deviant desire is her evolution into the Dark Phoenix, a figure for whom the former "ecstasy" of healing a damaged cosmos is now recast as a narcissistic and destructive pleasure in her own power.

In the narrative of "The Dark Phoenix Saga," Jean's progressive inability to distinguish between personal pleasure and the pain of others becomes the index of her narcissistic personality. In a number of scenes her use of her abilities to inflict pain on her loved ones is described simultaneously in emotional and sexual terms. When Jean first confronts the X-Men as Dark Phoenix, Cyclops exclaims, "Jean's enjoying this! Using her power is turning her on—acting like the ultimate physical/emotional stimulant!" Echoing Cyclops, Storm thinks, "She was like this when she saved the universe. But then her power was tempered by joy, and *love*. There is no joy—no love—in Dark Phoenix. I sense pain, great sadness—and an awful all-consuming *lust*." When Jean seeks to obtain more power from the cosmos, the narrative reads, "She reaches for the sky—summoning the lightning—laughing as the awesome bolts of energy caress her body like a lover."[14] Just as her telepathic scan of the disco reveals a potential proclivity toward deviant desire, her cosmic abilities become figured as a material manifestation of her excessive sexuality fueled by a narcissistic desire to transform everything in her path into a source of personal pleasure. In this sense the Dark Phoenix was presented as a cosmic fetishist.

The conversion of the Phoenix from a benevolent force of sexual liberation into a violent sexual predator is visually depicted by three transformations in Jean's gender identity across the narrative (plate 20). Early in "The Dark Phoenix Saga," Jean repeatedly finds herself trapped in Mastermind's illusion as an eighteenth-century British lady preparing to marry the dashing gentlemen Jason Wyngarde (Mastermind's fantasy projection of himself). After Jean succumbs to Mastermind's manipulations, she appears as the leather-clad Black Queen of the Hellfire Club. Finally, once she is freed from her brainwashing, she loses control of her abilities and transforms into the power-hungry Dark Phoenix. As Wyngarde's betrothed, Jean paradoxically goes against the gender norms of her historical moment (the early 1980s) through her performance of an obsequious hyperfemininity, dressed in frilly pre-Victorian hoop skirts and lace blouses while fawning over Wyngarde. As the Black Queen of the Hellfire Club, she appears as a dominatrix, donning a black lace corset, thigh-high boots, and a short cape (with a whip and leather wrist cuffs). Though reminiscent of Storm's sexually alluring costume, the Black Queen's attire reflects the twisted sexual accoutrements of a deviant aristocratic sexuality that take pleasure in practices of sexual domination and submission rather than the playful erotics of Storm's disco diva persona. When Jean shifts from Black Queen to Dark Phoenix, the green of her former costume becomes a crimson red and her physical features appear frighteningly predatory, her face alight with a maniacal smile that displays her pleasure in the destructive force of her power.

Each of these personas represented distinct but related performances of deviant gender and sexual roles: feminine submissiveness, masculine domination, and monstrous Schadenfreude. These various roles and Jean's movements through them modeled the political logic of antipornography feminism, which argued that both women's sexual submissiveness and any fantasies of domination they might have (embodied in the figure of the sadomasochistic dominatrix) were socially inculcated positions that were expressions of patriarchy's perversion of natural, presumably universal desire into desire for unequal distributions of power in all sexual encounters. What could be a more potent allegory of this logic than the depiction of Jean's psyche infiltrated by a villainous male "mastermind" who represents a patriarchal institution of economic power intent on transforming a woman into an exploitable object (by making her wear a dominatrix suit no less)? Such a staging of this scenario initially appears to argue that the various gendered and sexual subject positions Jean inhabits are not of her own choosing but rather the consequence of extreme patriarchal manipulation: by being treated like a fetish object, she *becomes* an even greater fetishist of herself and others. No surprise, perhaps, that in the late 1970s the Hellfire Club was the name for an underground bondage, discipline, sadism, and masochism (or BDSM) club in the meat-packing district of Manhattan boasting an elite, invitation-only membership. In the context of "The Dark Phoenix Saga," the real-world Hellfire Club functions to represent or invoke the "deviant" sexual cultures that emerged from the era of sexual liberation.

However, despite the seemingly transparent narrative of mental manipulation that presented Jean as an unwitting dupe to the Hellfire Club, there remained a powerful undercurrent of uncertainty as to whether she was being coerced into losing hold of her own desires or secretly wished to inhabit these various gender and sexual roles. As the earlier epigraph from Mastermind suggests, even as it appeared to structurally position Jean in a relation of submission to male power, the story also implied that this encounter was potentially unleashing her "innermost—forbidden—needs and desires." Ultimately, then, the narrative complicates the antipornography position by presenting human desire and its purported manipulations as so deeply intertwined that any attempt to identify an authentic desiring subject beneath the coercive regimes of capitalism and patriarchy would be impossible.

This ambivalence is redoubled in the visual pleasure potentially elicited from readers in seeing Jean inhabit these various roles, which begs the question of whether we are taking pleasure in hypersexualized depictions of women's bodies or genuinely fantasize about witnessing female characters inhabit classically masculine forms of power. In the famed cover image of *Uncanny X-Men* #135, Dark Phoenix is depicted taking pleasure in the destruction of her former mutant kinship, dramatically towering over the battered bodies of her teammates as she crushes the X-Men logo between her hands (plate 21). As a full-figured female giant, Jean once again exhibits a deviant form of female masculinity, the strength of her grasp and her powerful stance clearly at odds with her former feminine demeanor, while the sensuousness of her body and her look of maniacal pleasure give the image a lascivious flare absent in the first empowering but desexualized portrait of the Phoenix Force in *X-Men* #101. The image depicts havoc being wreaked upon the members of the X-Men but also conceptually wreaks havoc on any easy form of feminist visual critique. Where does visual pleasure lie here? Is it in Jean's hypersexualized body, in the dramatic rending of mutant solidarity, in the spectacle of female domination, in the novelty of Jean's spectacular visual presence, or in all of these? What we see here is an opening out of possibility in visual pleasure and the willingness to render female power as negative, antisocial, and riven by ambivalence rather than redemptive or valuable for its presumed moral superiority.

This remarkable reversal of the visual politics of the original "Phoenix Saga," which presented Jean's powers as an expression of feminist liberation through unfettered self-actualization, would be echoed in the most referenced sequence in "The Dark Phoenix Saga," in which Jean consumes the power of a distant star, obliterating the five billion inhabitants of another solar system (plate 22). Like her destruction of the bonds of mutant kinship, this operatic ten-page sequence uses the visual rhetoric of sexual conquest. In four consecutive panels we witness Jean plummet to the heart of a distant star, her body subsequently alight with energy at the center of the glowing orb, and finally the star's implosion "as it is suddenly, completely, consumed by Dark Phoenix." Next we see the blue-skinned denizens of an alien planet gaze with terror at the sky as their world is engulfed in flame. The narration reads, "And in the center of the super-nova she created, Dark Phoenix thrills to the absolute power that is hers. She is in ecstasy. Yet she knows that this is only the beginning—that what she feels now is nothing compared to what she experienced within the great M'Kraan Crystal. She craves that ultimate sensation."[15] This scene renarrates the conclusion of "The Phoenix Saga"—in which Jean travels to the center of the M'Kraan Crystal to mend the rift in its latticework—as a moment of immanent destruction in which Phoenix willfully terminates the life of a vital celestial body. The sequence reverses the meanings attached to Phoenix's original labor and figures her as a violent masculine force whose upending of traditional gender roles similarly overturns the generative relations of heterosexual reproduction. As she jets through the galaxy, Dark Phoenix's comet-like body resembles human sperm penetrating the surface of an ovum-shaped star. Rather than fertilize this figure of reproductive futurity, Jean obliterates it to reproduce herself in an act of narcissistic self-aggrandizement. Chris Claremont himself, the writer of the story, claims of this scene, "It was the quest for the cosmic orgasm. . . . Her feeding on the star, was an act . . . of self-love, of masturbation probably."[16]

In "The Birth of Venom," Peter similarly experiences a loss of control over his gender identity that manifests as both feminization (his metaphorical penetration by the suit's power over his mind and body) and hypersexualization (the suit's involvement in a series of failed romances that send Peter's private life into a tailspin). The scene where readers are first introduced to the alien foreshadows Peter's emasculation at the hands of the symbiote by offering a gendered explanation for its initial visual appearance. When the alien substance first bonds to Peter's skin, appearing as a sleek black bodysuit with a dramatic white spider emblem on its chest, he thinks, "I wonder why it didn't come out like my old one? . . . Maybe I was subconsciously influenced by that new Spider-Woman's suit! Hope she doesn't mind!"[17] Peter's nonchalant reference to Spider-Woman's costume offers a potential "original symptom" for the gendered meanings that later come to attach to the symbiote suit: a representation of his unconscious attraction to femininity through his female superheroic counterpart, Spider-Woman. Similarly the depiction of the suit as a metamorphic liquid visually attached feminine characteristics to Peter's body. Soon after he first dons the costume he realizes that he can open up a seam in its surface that reveals a convenient storage pouch. On the first of two occasions where readers witness this phenomenon, the seam appears as a flower-shaped hole in Spider-Man's torso, reminiscent of a vaginal orifice.[18] Similarly the scenes in which the suit visits Peter during his sleep are framed in the form of the Adam and Eve fable, with Peter the innocent, docile Eve unwittingly influenced by the charms of the devil in the from of the liquid suit, which is described as "slinking" or "slithering" its way like a snake onto Peter's body. Just as Jean dons the attire of a dominatrix on her way to ultimate power as the Dark Phoenix, Peter's relationship to the suit and the power it confers is figured in sadomasochistic terms: the suit's sleek black exterior echoes the black leather of slave and master (S/M) gear while its forceful physical domination of Peter superficially appears to embody the relations of S/M practice by making Peter its slave.

The Economic Story

In both "The Dark Phoenix Saga" and "The Birth of Venom," the critique of narcissism and its dislocation of normative gender and sexuality was always ambivalent and provisional. This indecision over the ultimate root of individual narcissism and its gendered ramifications spoke to a broader confusion among both comic book creators and the American public about the origin of national malaise. Had the nation's loss of morale and ethical direction been facilitated by institutional forces like global capitalism or the morally lax worldviews of the sexual revolution and women's and gay liberation? Without this underlying ambivalence, the demonic possession story's apparent critique of gender and sexual nonnormativity could be misread as merely a story of backlash against feminism, seeking to recontain the energies of the women's movement and sexual liberation by associating them with the decline of the national character or else a reflection of the sex negativity of antipornography feminism. The symbolic presence of backlash ideology in these stories, however, was outweighed by a larger anxiety about the power of capitalism to co-opt and corrupt feminism and other identity movements of the 1970s, transforming what had once been a struggle for individual liberation from social and sexual constraints into a narrow-minded pursuit of self-interest.

Attempting to understand the ambivalent relationship between the politics of liberation and contemporary capitalism, the demonic possession story mapped the primary psychological crisis depicted in the narrative onto a second, underlying story of class conflict. This secondary story would initially appear as a series of minor references to the economic circumstances of the lead characters: in one instance, readers see Peter Parker fretting over his low checking account as he prepares to take photos of his heroic exploits to sell to the *Daily Bugle*; in another, the narrator of "The Dark Phoenix Saga" describes the sleek jetliner owned by the Hellfire Club, while a panel shows its plush eighteenth-century interior.[19] Though these moments initially appear to be unassuming instances of comic book "realism," the recurrent visual references to economic life soon begin to interrupt the flow of the primary story line, increasingly appearing as gratuitous symptoms of narrative anxiety over the class struggles of its characters.

Far from innocent, the symptoms of class conflict that dot the narrative landscape of these texts offered readers tools to reinterpret the primary narrative of psychological crisis as having economic rather than personal or psychological origins. In "The Dark Phoenix Saga," the narrative reveals a canny understanding of the economic realities of modern urban life: when the X-Men arrive at the downtown Manhattan disco club in *Uncanny X-Men* #130, the opening page depicts their arrival in Xavier's Rolls-Royce while the narrative reads, "It's hardly the sort of neighborhood where you'd expect to see a Rolls-Royce at midnight. . . . Delano Street, in lower Manhattan—in its heyday this was one of the busiest manufacturing centers in New York. The businesses are closed now, crumbling. Only junkies and derelicts live here full time." In a later scene the Dark Phoenix transmutes an entire tree into solid gold, to which Nightcrawler drolly responds, "Mein Gott—that solid gold oak tree should solve New York's fiscal crisis for sure." And when Night-crawler demands to know why the Hellfire Club has captured the X-Men alive, the Club's leader, Sebastian Shaw, explains, "There's no profit in simply killing you. . . . If my associates and I can isolate the genetic quirk that created us . . . and then 'custom build'—through genetic engineer-ing—mutants at will, the possibilities are . . . limitless." Alongside these broader references to the discourses of postindustrialism and free mar-ket capitalism, the story displays a heightened attention to the individual class backgrounds of the various members of the X-Men, histories of unequal economic standing rarely mentioned in the early years of the series. When the X-Men prepare to infiltrate a lavish party at the Hellfire Club's headquarters, a tuxedo-clad Colossus reflects, "I have never worn clothes as fine as this. They feel marvelous . . . yet, it does not feel . . . right to wear a suit that cost more than my father earns in an entire year."[20]

Echoing this rumination on the economic meanings attached to the high-class suit, in nearly every instance in "The Birth of Venom" where the reader is alerted to the symbiote suit's psychological hold on Peter, the moment is paired with a reference to its material qualities, particu-larly the financial benefits of its ability to enhance Spider-Man's outward appearance. In one scene Peter is ecstatic when he realizes that the suit "reacts instantly to my thoughts—and it can mimic the appearance of any set of clothes I can imagine! It's a complete wardrobe in itself. I may never have to buy clothes again!"[21] The costume is an extension of Peter's psyche—responding to his every whim and desire—and his material interests. Struggling to keep his finances in order, Peter certainly ben-efits from the promise of "never having to buy clothes again." His ability to exploit the visual novelty of the suit itself, which photographs bril-liantly for newspaper stories, proves to be the only thing keeping him from destitution.

By encouraging readers to assess demonic possession as a psychologi-cal experience born of broader economic conditions, these stories offered a hypothesis about the state of contemporary citizenship not unlike that posed by Jimmy Carter: that the desire for material wealth and upward mobility, once understood as the bedrock of American progress, might itself represent the potential evil that lurked within all human beings and posed the greatest threat to robust national citizenship. On its sur-face "The Dark Phoenix Saga" appears to possess all the trappings of a psychological thriller, taking as its focus the mental unraveling of a beloved heroine as she struggles to reconcile the competing halves of her split identity. Yet even as Jean and her teammates work to understand the complex psychological motives of the Phoenix Force and its insatiable hunger, they find themselves trapped within a grand web of competing institutional forces that seek to lay claim to the Phoenix's incredible power. In the Hellfire Club the series maps the economic and political relationships that structured contemporary global capitalism. The Club embodies capitalism's elite ruling class, rich, manipulative industrialists whose mutant abilities span the gamut of psychic control, domination, and seduction, figuratively mimicking capitalism's ability to co-opt and repurpose the energies of political projects that seek to combat it. Among the Club's highest ranking mutant members are Sebastian Shaw, capable of absorbing all forms of kinetic energy, including any blow dealt by a foe, which fuels an extraordinary physical strength and invulnerability; Emma Frost, the White Queen, a telepath who manipulates the thoughts and desires of others to do her bidding; and Mastermind, a world-class illusionist able to implant desires and motives in his hapless victims. All of these abilities map onto the ideological apparatus of capitalism, including its capacity to absorb and repurpose challenges to the profit motive and its production and shaping of consumer desire through psychic manipulation. As their internal role-playing suggests, the Hellfire Club's world is like a game of chess modeled on the economic relations of eighteenth-century Great Britain rather than a genuine practice of competitive business interests. When a new inductee questions their eccentric garb, Shaw explains, "Our costumes signify our abandonment of the modern age—with its cloying ethics and bourgeois mercantile principles, where society is bent on protecting people from themselves at any cost—for a far simpler one where a man was limited solely by the scope of his imagination, his ambition, his daring, and bound only by his own personal sense of honor. Society—the common herd—means nothing, the individual all."[22] Shaw's outline of the Hellfire Club's underlying social values articulates the central logic of an emergent neoliberal ideology in the early 1980s as a system in which "the political sphere, along with every other dimension of contemporary existence, is submitted to an economic rationality ... [and] equally important is the production of all human institutional action as rational entrepreneurial action, conducted according to a calculus of utility, benefit, or satisfaction against a micro-economic grid of scarcity, supply and demand, and moral value-neutrality."[23] To the members of the Hellfire Club, the potential immorality of manipulating Jean Grey, not to mention the apparent intragroup disloyalty of exploiting fellow mutants for financial gain, are meaningless concerns within an economic calculus that views the Phoenix Force as a priceless asset in their plans for world domination. To them, controlling the Phoenix simply makes good business sense.

Throughout "The Dark Phoenix Saga" the narrative of Jean's psychological unraveling is undergirded by this secondary story about the institutional powers that seek to extract financial gain from her loss of control over the Phoenix Force. Mastermind's illusion initially appears to work purely at the level of Jean's psychological insecurities, convincing her that her love for Scott pales in comparison to her passion for the dashing Wyngarde. Yet the architecture of the illusion is ultimately built on the desire for upward mobility. In this elaborate fantasy Jean is a bourgeois lady preparing to marry a wealthy aristocrat. Over time the illusion takes on the shape of a story, narrating Jean and Wyngarde's travels to the colonies, followed by their marriage and her anointment as the Black Queen of the Hellfire Club. Once again the story functions on the level of personal desire and economic mobility; Jean's sexual passion for Wyngarde, which leads to their marriage, also leads to her ascendancy in the ranks of the Hellfire Club, the consummation of their marital vows coterminous with her inauguration as the Black Queen. The visual appearance of the illusion in the text signals an alternate way of reading Jean's transformation into the malevolent Dark Phoenix: rather than an expression of Jean's inability to control her evil impulses, it is the Hellfire Club's manipulation of her personal investments away from the X-Men toward the aristocratic trappings of the Club's inner circle that facilitates the birth of Dark Phoenix. Even as the eighteenth-century illusion presents Jean with a false image of the world, the comic book presents it to readers as a metaphor for the *real relations of production* that define contemporary economic life in the United States: the rich ruling over the poor, capitalism enslaving the masses, class inequality occluding all other forms of political solidarity. In fact the crowning achievement of the Hellfire Club's influence on Jean's psychic life is to convince her that she "owns" the X-Men, who, in the logic of Mastermind's illusion, appear to her as three members of George Washington's Continental Army and a turncoat slave.

In one of the most shocking scenes of the "The Dark Phoenix Saga," Jean appears before the X-Men as the Black Queen of the Hellfire Club, her teammates Colossus, Storm, Nightcrawler, and Cyclops all manacled after being defeated by the Club's inner circle. Two consecutive overlapping panels offer the reader a view into the dual perspectives of each party in the scene: first, we see the X-Men staring incredulously at their transformed friend and teammate, baffled by her brainwashing at the hands of the Hellfire Club. The following panel presents the same image from Jean's eyes, the room they stand in now appearing as the interior of a plantation home with the three men dressed as eighteenth-century colonial rebels and Ororo a runaway slave wearing large hoop earrings and a colorful headscarf. In the next set of panels, Jean reprimands Ororo, "I expected better of you. In all the years you have been my slave, I have never mistreated you. I trusted you, only to see that trust betrayed." "Slave?!" Ororo thinks to herself. "Goddess, there's such . . . evil in Jean's voice." Jean taunts Ororo, first insulting her with the English translation of her name ("beauty"), then dangling a set of keys in front of her face: "Is this what you want Beauty? The keys that will free you and your companions?" In the subsequent image, however, those same keys appear as Storm's tiara and lock picks, visually cuing the reader to the disjuncture between Jean's manipulated worldview and reality. When Storm attempts to reason with her friend, Jean lashes her across the face with a whip, exclaiming, "Silence! You dare speak so to me. Slave?! I am not your friend—but your mistress! I own you! And—as my right—mine will be the hand that ends your worthless existence" (figure 6.1).[24]

In this extraordinary sequence the comic book visually maps the dissimulations of the Hellfire Club while unmasking the story's underlying economic logic. The purpose of Mastermind's illusion is to align Jean with the economic and social interests of a time when the kinds of affiliations and solidarities engendered by the X-Men's mutant kinship did not exist but where class and social standing, violently enforced through racial hierarchy, were the differences that mattered. The erotic position of the dominatrix as figurative master of a sexual slave is here recast in terms of the racist underpinnings of historical slavery to reveal economic hierarchy as the founding logic that organizes sexual deviancy. It is particularly telling that this shift in Jean's loyalties is initially depicted by her turning against her chosen sister, Ororo, for in so doing Jean appears to simultaneously adopt the economic worldview of the Hellfire Club (she deems Ororo literally "worthless" or lacking in economic value) and obliterate her commitment to the feminist politics that had formerly bound her and Ororo together. In this light the depiction of Jean as a psychologically unstable powerhouse was less a critique of feminist liberation itself than of the co-optation of the category "woman" and feminist sisterhood by patriarchal economic forces, even as it relied on an erotophobic disavowal of S/M sexual cultures to make its charge.

FIGURE 6.1. The Black Queen treats Storm as her slave. Chris Claremont (writer) and John Byrne (penciller), "Wolverine: Alone!," *The Uncanny X-Men* #133, May 1980, reprinted in *Marvel Legends: The Dark Phoenix Saga* (New York: Marvel, 2003), 83.

This practice of visually uncovering the dissimulation of vested economic interests is similarly deployed to uncover the underlying political motives of the Shi'ar Empire in its mission to bring Dark Phoenix to justice for her crimes against the galaxy. If the Hellfire Club stands in for the machinations of global capital, the Shi'ar Empire functions as its political double, representing the corruption of governmental power by the interests of economic imperialism. When Lilandra summons her grand council, she dramatizes the threat Dark Phoenix poses to the galaxy in the following way: "When I first met Phoenix, she was a terran female named Jean Grey, a beneficent entity. . . . Now, it seems, the child is beneficent no longer. I fear as well that she means to pick up where my brother left off. Ministers of the empire—if the universe is to survive . . . Phoenix must be destroyed."[25] Lilandra disavows the Shi'ar Empire's own imperialist claim to the galaxy by equating Jean with a political tyrant, her brother D'Ken, while basing the value of Jean's life on her level of "beneficence" or lack thereof to the Shi'ar Empire.

Ultimately Jean chooses to sacrifice herself through cosmic suicide rather than see her friends and the universe suffer for her loss of control over the Phoenix Force. Her rationale for this final drastic action rests upon her guilt over what the Dark Phoenix has compelled her to do to the millions of innocents who died for her infernal hunger. Jean internalizes Phoenix's actions as her own, interpreting her consumptive desires as an effect of a flaw in her moral character, consequently absolving the institutional forces that corrupted her mind and body. This final desperate action solidifies Jean as the paragon of the neoliberal subject, forced to take personal responsibility for the institutional consequences of market rationality. As Wendy Brown elaborates, neoliberalism "configures morality entirely as a matter of rational deliberation about costs, benefits, and consequences [so that] the rationally calculating individual bears full responsibility for the consequences of his or her action no matter how severe the constraints on this action."[26] Unleashed as the Dark Phoenix, Jean Grey's unrestrained pursuit of energy to feed her "infernal hunger" as well as her extraordinary ability to transform the fabric of reality to "service her ambitions" embody the self-interested market logic of neoliberal ideology; her self-sacrifice brings this logic full circle, locating the impetus and responsibility for such self-interest in the individual subject regardless of the manipulations of the capitalist institutions (the Hellfire Club and the Shi'ar Guard) that encourage market rationality as the driving force of social relations.

"The Dark Phoenix Saga" trains readers to identify the class narrative underlying Jean's psychic conflict through a reduplicative visuality that offers competing images of the world as it appears through the eyes of the X-Men (a world defined by mutant solidarity and affiliation) and alternately through the perspective of the Hellfire Club (a worldview defined by a dehumanizing economic calculus). In "The Birth of Venom" this same effect is produced through another kind of visual duplication, namely the doubling of Peter's body in the form of his nemesis, Venom, a new incarnation of the original symbiote suit, now bonded to Peter's former journalistic rival Eddie Brock. In the first years of Peter's conflict with the symbiote, his financial troubles recurrently appeared as a point of interest in the story line that intersected with the symbiote's derailment of his ability to manage his personal affairs. Despite this, the underlying narrative of class struggle in this first part of Spider-Man's demonic possession (published in 1984–85) remained focused on his ongoing efforts to rid himself of his psychological and physical dependency on the suit. In 1988 the symbiote made its long-awaited return. In this narrative sequel to the original alien saga, the battle between competing psychological impulses that defined Peter's initial engagement with the symbiote is recast as a battle between competing class interests in the figures of an upwardly mobile Spider-Man and the downwardly mobile alien parasite.

The return of the symbiote suit was primarily a sales gimmick to celebrate the twenty-fifth anniversary of the *Amazing Spider-Man* series. At the same time, it offered an opportunity to reflect on the core values that had shaped Peter Parker's character by narrating the reencounter between himself and his alter ego. As prologue to the story, the creators offered a glimpse of the menace that would soon terrorize Peter and his wife-to-be, Mary Jane Watson, in a three-page spread that reintroduced the symbiote suit in the form of a mysterious Spider-Man stalker (plate 23). The first page tellingly opens with an image of a dilapidated tenement in the South Bronx. Inside a figure shrouded in darkness stares at a wall covered in newspaper clippings, all stories related to Spider-Man and his heroic exploits. The figure thinks to himself, "The darkness that blankets this city is nothing, nothing! Not compared to the shroud that Spider-Man pulled over me! He stole my life[,] shattered it . . . then cast it aside like yesterday's news! So it is only fitting that I do the same to him!" Following these words a rapid-fire sequence of vertical panels shows the figure's burly white hands as he pounds his fist into his palm. With each impact, the hands grow blacker, a sticky substance encircling the skin, until at last it is fully covered.

At the top of the next page, we cut to a new location, Manhattan's up-and-coming Chelsea neighborhood, where Mary Jane walks into her and Peter's posh new apartment building carrying shopping bags. The image is a visual echo of the tenement that opened the previous page, only now in an area of New York City reserved for its most upwardly mobile denizens, presumably those who can afford to go shopping as a cure for emotional stress.[27] Entering her darkened apartment, Mary Jane is horrified to see Peter's former black-and-white suit materializing from the darkness. Drawing closer, the figure's massive white eyes are joined by a jagged clown-like grin reflecting its diabolical pleasure in Mary Jane's terror as it intones, "Hi, honey . . . I'm home!" With these final words, the figure is presented in full form, a towering black bogey-man with rippling muscles and claw-like fingertips reaching out to Mary Jane from the darkness. Though the figure leaves Mary Jane unharmed, he informs her that he knows Spider-Man's secret identity, offering her advance warning of his intentions to destroy her fiancé and their loved ones.

In this sequence the symbiote suit is reintroduced to readers as the hyperbolic stereotype of a vermin-like home invader, creeping up from the lower classes to haunt the lives of the rich. Clearly identified with the "darkness" associated with the working-class slums of the South Bronx, and racialized through the stereotype of the hypermasculine black man sexually terrorizing innocent white women, Venom recasts the symbiote suit as an expression of working-class resentment toward the wealthy, a point reiterated by his new moniker (the term for a deadly poison and symbolizing acrimony or resentment) and by his sarcastic appropriation of the bourgeois sitcom cliché, "Hi, honey . . . I'm home!"[28] Moreover, at the height of the AIDS epidemic, when thousands of gay men were being evicted, or else removed post mortem, from affordable housing in lower Manhattan, the specter of the sexually excessive muscle-monster haunt-ing the home of new heterosexual renters gentrifying neighborhoods of former artists and bohemians was unmistakable.[29] From this perspec-tive, the towering muscular black figure of Venom (including the power-ful black fist he pounds against his palm) harkens back to the gay leather, S/M, and fisting cultures of the 1970s and 1980s—cultures decimated by AIDS—and the muscular, leather-clad "clones" who strolled the streets of the Lower East Side seeking a variety of gay sexual encounters. In this visually overdetermined sequence, Venom comes to materially embody a long history of class conflicts in the shifting demographic makeup of lower Manhattan refracted through ethnic, racial, and sexual divisions in the twentieth century.

A few days later, while Peter and Mary Jane are moving their belong-ings into their new apartment, Peter glimpses Venom web-slinging near their building. Donning his costume, Peter follows Venom to the South Bronx, where the two have a violent confrontation in an abandoned building. In the course of their battle Venom reveals himself to be Eddie Brock, a former journalist at the *Daily Globe*, where Peter freelances as a photographer. In response to Spider-Man's incredulity at his identity, Brock gives a detailed account of the circumstances that led to his trans-formation into Venom. He begins by decrying his loss of social status after Spider-Man publicly revealed that his news stories were based on lies. Brock explains, "My column in *The Daily Globe* was read by millions! I was a solid reporter, a respected member of the fourth estate!" After revelations of his false reporting, however, "the *Globe* was a laughing stock. I was fired. My peers questioned my ethics, shunned me. I was forced to write venomous celebrity exposes . . . for scandal rags, just to eke out a living. . . . The garbage I was forced to write began to rot my soul." Moving to the South Bronx, Brock took up body building in the hopes of reducing his stress, but his training regimen only fueled his revenge fantasies against Spider-Man. Unable to bear his misfortune, Brock considered suicide. As a devout Catholic, however, he felt incredible guilt for his sinful thoughts, wandering "from church to shadowed church, praying for forgiveness." Then one night, while praying at Our Lady of Saints Church, Brock claimed, "a shadow moved. Caressed me. I was joined. But this was a shadow filled with light. It clarified my anguish, focused my purpose its hatred for you matched my own. It knew who you were and it had power, oh such powers!"[30]

Through his backstory Brock relates a narrative of downward mobility that leads him back to the symbiote suit, whose own rise to power through its attachment to Spider-Man, followed by an ignominious demise at the hands of its former host, helped forge its hatred for the man who had spurned its affections. Brock thus represents a specifically *classed* figuration of the symbiote suit, the two bound by shared affective "venom" toward the people and institutions that contributed to their fall from grace. As Brock's narrative suggests, it is the experience of performing the work of "lower-class" journalists that "rots" his soul, making him susceptible to the hatred, self-loathing, and resentment that drew the symbiote to him. The visual geography of the story literalizes the metaphorical rotting of Brock's soul as nearly every battle between Spider-Man and Venom takes place in a site of economic decay and destitution: the tenements of the South Bronx and a downtown Manhattan meat-packing plant where Venom topples a canister of rotting blood and offal on Spider-Man during their brawl. All of these narrative and visual frames depict Venom as a symbolic reflection of working-class resentment in the 1980s, an emergent identity as a victim of class conflict that reorganized left-liberal political energies around what Brown has called "wounded attachments."

For Brown, the investment in grounding a political identity on one's victimization by oppressive social forces—a concept culled from the identity politics of the 1960s and 1970s and co-opted by the conservative right to describe the frustration of the white working classes with the upward mobility of women and people of color—is a devastating sign of a loss of political vision on both the right and the left. Rather than offering the possibility of political freedom based on the value of collective action, the politics of identity rehashes an attachment to one's own social oppression. Venom is a hyperbolic metaphor for this phenomenon, literally seeking out a physical attachment to the symbiote suit on the basis of shared emotional and economic wounds inflicted by Spider-Man and the journalistic community that "shunned" him following the revelation of his false reporting.[31] Just as Jean Grey's psychological realignment with upper-class identity as a member of the Hellfire Club was distinctly gendered, so in corollary fashion Eddie Brock's realignment with lower-class status is associated with the unraveling of white working-class masculinity.

Where Spider-Man's original encounter with the suit appeared to emasculate him, Brock's turn to bodybuilding and the suit's subsequent inflation of his physical form mark him as hypermasculinized by his relationship to the alien symbiote. Brock's performance of a hyperbolic, even grotesque masculinity is coded as a pathologically excessive response to his own feelings of inadequacy as a working-class washout, once a member of "the fourth estate," now transformed into a physical stereotype of the working-class tough. Throughout the story he is presented as a hulking muscle man towering over Peter's lithe frame, the skin-tight fit of the symbiote suit accentuating his excessive physique. Glimpses of Brock's South Bronx hideout reveal that he has no furniture except training equipment. By framing Brock as the embodiment of the kind of pathologically insecure host most amenable to the suit's manipulation, this arc of the broader story of Peter's demonic possession worked to recuperate Spider-Man's former openness to the symbiote by positioning him as having nobly disavowed the narcissistic tendencies of his past and no longer burdened with insecurities about either his professional or personal performance. In fact the narrative gratuitously offers scenes of Peter and Mary Jane's seemingly boundless sexual appetites for one another to highlight Peter's recuperation of virile masculinity.

Even this relationship, however, is now cast in economic terms: when Peter and Mary Jane first move into their luxurious Chelsea apartment, she is the primary breadwinner, paying for their extravagant lifestyle with her modeling. As the narrative unfolds, Mary Jane's career takes a nosedive, and she and Peter are forced to move to Queens to live with Aunt May. Rather than presenting this experience of downward mobility as a blow to Peter's masculinity, the story depicts the spiraling of Mary Jane's career as a psychological boon to Peter as he can now resolve to become the family's breadwinner, taking up his photography again and returning to his graduate studies. Peter is then presented as the ideal of proper (and balanced rather than excessive) masculinity, so much so that downward mobility actually offers him a chance to become an even more idealized version of his former self, locating him firmly in the middle class (between the extremes of upper- and lower-class identity).[32]

The disparity between Peter's and Eddie's performances of middle- and working-class identity—the former a paragon of normative masculinity, the latter an icon of pathological insecurity—is underscored in Spider-Man and Venom's final showdown. At the story's conclusion, Brock visits Aunt May's home to issue an ultimatum to Peter: meet for a final duel to the death or expose his family to Venom's wrath. Venom hopes to claim victory over his rival at the location that symbolizes his own former professional standing and the upper-class lifestyle he had worked so hard to achieve, the Long Island estate of the *Daily Globe*'s publisher, his former employer during his years as a successful journalist. Brock's preparation for this long-awaited face-off is his own physical fitness regimen. Taking a different tack, Peter seeks the advice of a professional psychiatrist, hoping to understand the motivations driving both the symbiote suit and Brock to their shared revenge against him. After detailing to the psychiatrist his personal history with the symbiote and the recent emergence of Venom, the doctor suggests, "The symbiote show[s] signs of a classic love-hate relationship.... When someone is spurned by a love object, they sometimes channel their feelings in a strongly opposite direction but the emotion at the core of it all is still love!" Armed with this information, Spider-Man arrives for battle at the appointed time hoping, that this insight will help him defeat his archnemesis.[33]

Unable to defeat Venom with physical force, Peter is almost at his breaking point when he has an epiphany: if the suit still loves him beneath its exterior rage, as the doctor suggested, why not simply give himself over to it, encouraging its feelings of attachment and care to negate Brock's hatred? In a bizarre gesture that looks like a sexual solicitation, Peter removes his costume down to his underwear, offering himself to the suit, body and soul. Though Venom initially laughs off Peter's gesture as a bluff, the suit betrays him, revealing its unresolved emotional attachment to its original host. As the symbiote detaches from Brock and begins to flow over Peter's body, Peter nervously worries that his ploy will fail, leaving him permanently bonded to the alien. As the symbiote nears full attachment, however, it suddenly wrenches back in a horrifying snap that slams both men to the ground.

Regaining consciousness, Peter witnesses the suit sloughing off his body. "The alien couldn't sever its bond with Eddie completely," Peter thinks, "but the pain of trying must've been too much—knocked them both out!" As he walks away from the Long Island estate, Peter's final thoughts are of the good news he has for Mary Jane: that the nightmare of Venom is over. His triumph over the suit's emotional hold reverses his former subservience to the suit's wiles by forcing it to recognize him as its object of desire. In so doing he projects his own emotional excesses (represented by his former attachment to the symbiote) back onto an abject working-class body through recourse to the language of psychopathology; in the doctor's logic, Venom's working-class resentment can be rewritten as a secret love or desire for the upwardly mobile identity that Peter embodies. Peter's own perfectly sculpted, lean body—presented on the page as sexy underwear model—is a visual index of what kind of male body ideally magnetizes this kind of desire, which is set against the overly muscled, hairy, "ugly" (and presumably "black" and "gay") body of the lower-class Brock. Like Jean's willful act of self-sacrifice, which highlighted her moral fiber while obscuring the broader institutional forces that facilitated her descent into madness, Peter's act of submission to the suit's emotional attachment allows him to reflect his newfound psychological fortitude against its advances while negating the complex social consequences of Brock's struggle with his class identity.[34]

* * *

In the early 1980s "The Dark Phoenix Saga" and "The Birth of Venom" imagined what the American superhero might look like in the absence of its former claim to agency and self-determination. This was a radical move in a storytelling mode that had rested on a fantasy of enhanced bodily mobility, strength, and power since its inception five decades earlier. Struggling to reconcile the former nobility of heroes like Jean Grey and Peter Parker with their narcissistic insanity, these stories sought to locate the perpetrators of demonic possession either in the soul of the victim or in the institutional structures that facilitated their villainous transformation. To definitively identify the source of these demonic transformations, however, was in a sense to decide who was to blame in the evolution of American culture into a consumer society: the weak-willed and self-interested citizen consumer or the pernicious influence of free market capital.

Even as the creators used the figure of the superhero to work through these broader cultural anxieties and questioned the market rationality that demanded they extract economic and cultural value from superheroic characters, they held out hope that the broad ethical ideals embodied by the superhero—its assumed commitment to social justice and peacekeeping—would provide the basis for its moral redemption. In fact the conclusion of "The Dark Phoenix Saga" was so intent on recovering a notion of universal good that it offered a long-winded philosophical rationale for Jean's suicide articulated in the language of universal humanism. Following Jean's self-annihilation, the story cuts to the perspective of the Watcher, an alien Oracle who observes all the events of the Marvel Universe. When his assistant, a sentient robot named the Recorder, inquires why Jean Grey was "hounded unto death" by the Phoenix Force despite her benevolent actions to save the universe, the Watcher explains:

> All beings carry within them a capacity for good and evil. . . . Our *reason* makes us aware of these forces and likewise gives us the responsibility of choosing between them. . . . This child achieved a level of power that placed her as far above humanity—on the evolutionary scale—as they are above the amoeba. She had only to *think* and that thought would become instant reality. But the Phoenix is also a force of primal passion, and homo sapiens is still as much a creature of passion as of intellect. Such passion is by its very nature seductive and violent. Jean could not help but respond to it, be changed by it, and in time *overwhelmed* . . . yet when faced with a choice between keeping her god-like power—knowing she would then wreak death and destruction across the stars—and dying herself, she chose the *latter.* That is what makes humanity virtually unique in the cosmos . . . this extraordinary capacity for self-sacrifice. . . . Jean Grey could have lived to become a god. But it was more important to her that she die . . . a human.[35]

In the Watcher's speech "The Dark Phoenix Saga" negated an entire postwar history of comic book critiques of liberal humanism and its narrow conception of political freedom as merely equivalent to the idea of individual agency. As the Watcher suggests, the Phoenix is a cosmic force that obliterates the rigid humanistic distinctions between reason and passion, good and evil, the individual and collective life. This was precisely what made Phoenix a liberatory force akin to the left worldmaking projects of the 1960s and 1970s, a creative metaphor for new conceptions of political freedom based on shared identity and collective action rather than individual sovereignty. By making Jean's sacrifice a token of moral fortitude and humanistic triumph, the story effaces her distinct commitments to mutant and feminist identity, seeking a solution to the problems posed by demonic possession in a flight from the radicalism that had once defined the meaning of individual freedom in the superhero comic book.

Like the messianic melodrama before it, the demonic possession story reached a creative impasse when it came to deciding what to make of the identity crises it portrayed: either the superhuman hosts had to sacrifice themselves to save the world from the demons that possessed them (Jean Grey in "The Dark Phoenix Saga") or else the demons themselves had to be excised and destroyed (Spider-Man in "The Birth of Venom"). Such conclusions rehashed the age-old call for moral fortitude against a general notion of evil that echoed both left liberal responses to a decline in national morale (embodied by Jimmy Carter's demand for self-sacrifice and moral integrity in the face of the energy crisis) and right-wing conservative calls for a renewed American traditionalism (represented by Ronald Reagan's celebration of marriage and the nuclear family ideal as the twin pillars of Americanism). What these stories seemed unable or unwilling to imagine was what the superhero could be if it was never "cured" of its possession but rather dwelled in the experience of being ever at odds with its own demonic impulses. In other words, what would the superhero look like if it were no longer animated by an overriding impulse to "do good"?

This question haunted the creative limits of demonic possession in the early decade, and it would become the central concern of superhero comics across the second half of the 1980s. One response was to recast the superhero as an alienated vigilante whose desire to help others was revealed to be an expression of an egomaniacal pursuit of power. This image of the superhero as a self-interested and potentially psychologically deranged icon of narcissism became the hallmark of the decade's most famous independent comics, most notably Alan Moore's *The Watchmen* (1986–87) and Frank Miller's *Batman: The Dark Knight Returns* (1986). These miniseries unabashedly deconstructed the assumed moral character of the American superhero by telling stories of superhuman vigilantes at odds with the very nation they had once dutifully served; unsurprisingly they did so by reasserting superheroic masculinity, and its perversion into a fascistic drive to dominate or control the unthinking masses, as an indicator of the nation's political decline. Another avenue, however, was to embrace the contingency of the superhero and to use the comic book medium to visualize what superhuman community might look like *without* the shared imperative to improve the world or protect it from villainous threats. In this vision the superhero's loss of purpose did not necessarily result in a full-scale abandonment of egalitarian political ideals or cynical skepticism about the possibility for social transformation but rather prioritized the mutual acknowledgment among superhuman companions who must renegotiate their solidarities on the basis of something other than an assumed commitment to saving the world.

In light of the mutant superhero's long-standing role as a catalyst of comic book innovation, it might come as little surprise that the most bold explorations of this new terrain in superhero storytelling would take place in the acclaimed *X-Men* franchise, whose expanding cast of characters and increasingly complex fictional world of mutants would ultimately place the original mutant kinship of the X-Men in crisis. In the mid-1980s Chris Claremont would develop an original series, *The New Mutants*, as a contemporary spin-off of the *X-Men*, narrating the story of six new recruits to the Xavier Institute forced to forge unexpected alliances in the absence of a shared commitment to mutant or superheroic identity. Children of the late cold war and a world experiencing the growing pains of globalization, the New Mutants found themselves caught within a web of geopolitical conflicts that made any claim to free will a farce. Realizing that their attachment to minority identity only served to make them targets of economic and political exploitation in this new world order, the teammates strove to reinvent the very nature of mutant and superhuman community by articulating alternative grounds for solidarity beyond the limits of identity politics. What superheroes might become, or how they might act in the world, absent their former role as morally righteous peacekeepers and crime fighters, remained to be seen. The choice itself, however, opened a world of possibilities that even the Watcher could not predict.

7 / Lost in the Badlands: Radical Imagination and the Enchantments of Mutant Solidarity in *The New Mutants*

In 1984 Marvel Comics released *The New Mutants*, an offshoot of the *X-Men* series that introduced readers to a new generation of mutant teenagers struggling to make sense of their unwieldy abilities.[1] Like its predecessor, the series narrated Xavier's recruitment and training of an international group of mutant heroes. Though at first glance the series appeared a mere rehashing of the original X-Men mythos, its narrative would radically reassess of the concept of the "mutant superhero." The X-Men of the 1970s were a diverse cadre of mutants whose mutual experience of alienation from the human race bound them together in an ethical mission to forge peaceful relations between humans and mutantkind. In this vision "mutant" functioned as a coherent but elastic identity that defined a distinct population of superpowered beings, including those who allied themselves with the biological deviants indicated by that name. Unlike the X-Men, the New Mutants were brought together not for the purposes of an egalitarian peacekeeping mission but to learn the proper use of their powers, which they experienced as monstrous physical burdens threatening their own safety and that of their loved ones. The exuberance and pleasure of exercising mutant powers as an extension of a liberated identity that inhered in *The X-Men*'s vision of mutant solidarity was now presented as a traumatic experience of shame, self-hatred, and guilt at the expression of latent superhuman abilities that alienated the members of this cohort from all their intimate relationships. The New Mutants existed in a world where the promises of an expansive liberationist rhetoric seemed long gone, broken by the collapse of left world-making projects into distinct identity movements, a right-wing backlash against civil rights, feminism, and gay liberation, and the commodification of cultural identity. In a world of narrowing political possibilities, *The New Mutants* asked what might bind mutant outcasts together when the terms that defined their exclusion from proper humanity no longer functioned as a shared ground of identification. The series' attempt to imagine new terms for the production of solidarity in a neoliberal world order echoed the various world-making projects of superhero comics in the postwar period, including the Justice League's ethical citizenship, the Fantastic Four's comic book cosmopolitics, and the X-Men's queer mutanity. What distinguished *The New Mutants* from these previous iterations of the superhero was that it abandoned the underlying assumption that the purpose of alternative community building was to improve the world or bring justice to those wronged by social and political oppression.

The notion that the superhero's purpose was always necessarily to ameliorate social injustice meant that the figure was merely a creative means to an alternate social end: to improve race relations, to combat cold war conservatism, to liberate women, to enact social justice. While these ends were often creatively depicted through the visual rhetoric of left-wing politics in the 1960s and 1970s, positioning the superhero as an embodiment of new forms of political community and solidarity, by the early 1980s the superhero no longer had a creative life of its own but instead was repeatedly deployed as a vehicle for imparting public service announcements or melodramatic stories of social uplift. This was reflected in the scores of comic book specials that pitted Marvel's and DC's most famous superheroes against human injustices, including South African apartheid, world hunger, racism, and religious intolerance.[2] Despite the ethical worthiness of these causes, using the superhero to bring attention to these crises reduced the figure to an instrument of social justice—and linked its cultural utility to its economic value—rather than a site of popular fantasy where the kinds of solidarities required to transform the conditions that enabled these atrocities could be brought into being.

Against this trend *The New Mutants* jettisoned the question "What is a superhero good for?," instead asking, "What can a superhuman *be*?" In so doing it reanimated the postwar superhero's commitment to world making, that is, to developing the worldly conditions under which new political affiliations and public dialogue could be enacted in the absence of "natural" or universal binding categories, without any assumed trajectory or purpose that the superhero must fulfill. According to *The New*

Mutants, in a world of superhumans every exercise of extraordinary powers offered not a means to a specific end—to save the world, to do good, to promote citizenship—but an unpredictable act whose consequences could never be known in advance. This creative transformation captured the real-world trajectory of radical left-wing politics in the United States, which had shifted from a liberationist project of individual consciousness raising as the ground for collective freedom in the 1960s and 1970s to an identity-based politics of minority group interests in the 1980s and, finally, to a postmodern anti-identitarian politics of difference.[3] This final shift, realized in social movements like ACT UP (the AIDS Coalition to Unleash Power) and third-wave feminism, affirmed difference itself as the wellspring for a radical politics based on affinity and shared political values rather than the assumed sameness between political actors on the basis of ethnoracial identity or a putatively shared "humanity." Like the social movements of the 1980s that destabilized instrumentalist understandings of politics, *The New Mutants* recast the figure of the superhero as a contingent political actor detached from an assumed role as a purveyor of liberal ideals. In so doing the series became a creative space for depicting, exploring, and judging various articulations of superhuman power to alternative political solidarities. This was perhaps the most innovative creative challenge to the neoliberal calculus of market rationality that comics had ever conceived, and it would revitalize the promise of a comic book cosmopolitics within the very structure of a fully corporatized comic industry.

Rather than lament this loss of a putatively stable mutant identity, *The New Mutants* engaged the work of refashioning mutation (and the superhero more broadly) as a contingent category whose meanings and purpose could not be taken for granted but required continual redefinition through public debate. Who counted as a mutant, what mutant identity might mean for different actors, and what role mutantkind played in relation to an antagonist humanity were now questions open to reinterpretation. In this way *The New Mutants* engaged in a practice of radical imagination that involved projecting taken-for-granted identities like "mutant" and "superhero" into new contexts where they could be taken up in unpredictable ways, allowing one to see how these categories might function for a variety of subjects across an array of differences.[4] The development of a faculty of radical imagination around the category of mutation took a variety of forms, including sustained dialogue between the characters about their conflicted feelings toward their mutant biology, the dramatization of telepathic mutant powers that allowed members of the team to project themselves into other people's point of view, and the depiction of villains who metaphorically embodied the historical traumas experienced by various members of the team.

Embodying this set of values, 1980s radical movements suggested that the aim of politics should not be the pursuit of a universal human identity, a utopian world free of oppression, or the procurement of rights from a liberal state but rather the practice of developing significant social responses to concrete differences that were at once democratic and critical. Linda Zerilli elaborates this form of politics in her description of the political values of the Milan Women's Bookstore Collective, a radical third-wave feminist group formed in the late 1980s: "The Milan Women's Bookstore Collective does not restrict the question of freedom to liberation from oppression. Rather, it is centrally concerned with freedom understood as the capacity to found new forms of political association. . . . These forms cannot be thought apart from the difference of sex, for 'to be born a woman is an accident that conditions all of life.' . . . A contingent fact that has the force of necessity, the difference of sex is not to be destroyed or transcended, bur rather resymbolized, transformed 'from a social cause of unfreedom into the principle of our freedom.'"[5] The collective's 1987 mission statement was developed as a response to the impasses of second-wave feminist identity politics. It elaborates a feminist theory of political association that acknowledges women's differences while "resymbolizing" forms of feminist solidarity that are not based on a universal conception of "woman" or an essentialist view of shared female traits or dispositions. Similarly the political activism of the radical AIDS activist movement ACT UP (1987) fought against homophobia and inaction in the face of the AIDS crisis and also actively transformed the meanings attached to gay and lesbian identity in the 1980s. ACT UP's politics were articulated through the rubric of a new queer (as opposed to gay and lesbian) politics, where "queer" came to symbolize "fury and pride about gay difference and about confrontational activism, antipathy toward heteronormative society, and aspirations to live in a transformed world."[6] Movements and organizations like the Milan Women's Bookstore Collective and ACT UP upended traditional liberal politics, which aspire to create a conflict-free public sphere whose utopian horizon ends in universal political equality and a postracial, postgender, *postdifference* society. Instead these movements saw the goal of politics as facilitating spaces of productive political conflict, acknowledging both oppressive and generative aspects of difference, while developing sophisticated theoretical and practical responses to those differences.

Similarly engaged in the struggle over the shape and form of a postidentity politics, the members of the New Mutants seemed stuck between two difficult choices: they could abandon all investment in mutant solidarity by declaring the category of "mutant" unfit for political use due to its tainted associations with capitalism and state power, or they could cling to mutation as the sole shared experience that bound them together, affiliating on the basis of a wounded attachment to a victimized identity as genetic deviants. Innovating beyond this impasse, the New Mutants "resymbolized" mutation as a figure of plurality, inhabited by a vast array of subjects who may or may not be biologically mutant but potentially identified with mutation as a category of political freedom. In this context "plurality is not a demographic or existential fact, but a political relation to . . . differences; it requires that I do something in relation to such differences, that I count them in some politically significant way."[7] For differences to be politically significant means that they must be articulated to questions of public concern rather than remain markers of private or individual character. This is precisely what radical left movements of the 1980s endeavored to accomplish and what *The New Mutants* theorized.

Mutation as a "Figure of the Newly Thinkable"

In the mid-1980s *The New Mutants* boasted the most diverse cast of any mainstream superhero comic. This cohort included Xi'an (or Shan) Coy Manh (Karma), a nineteen-year-old Vietnamese refugee able to telepathically possess the bodies of multiple hosts; Danielle Moonstar (Mirage), a young Cheyenne warrior able to project the greatest fears of others as living illusions; Roberto da Costa (Sunspot), the debonair son of a Brazilian corporate mogul whose body transforms into a powerful wellspring of solar energy, granting him superhuman strength and stamina; Sam Guthrie (Cannonball), the son of an Appalachian coal miner able to transform into an invulnerable ball of kinetic energy; and Rahne Sinclair (Wolfsbane), a shape shifter capable of transforming into a superpowered wolf, exiled by her Irish Catholic foster parents, who claim she is possessed by the devil.

These heroes hailed from all parts of the globe and differed in age, experience, religious upbringing, and social commitment. *The New Mutants* troubled the notion that mutant identity could serve as a universal category binding all social outcasts by linking the fictional category of mutation to an expanded array of real-world differences that exceeded the categories of ethnoracial and gender identity central to *The X-Men* a decade before. This project included a revitalized class critique that identified how people understood mutant identity in vastly different ways depending on their economic background. Consequently the series foregrounded the material conditions that were redefining what it meant to be a mutant in the neoliberal order.

At the height of the cold war, mutants were biological freaks and potential weapons of mass destruction capable of obliterating the human race. Their individual differences of race, class, and gender mattered less than the fact that they belonged to a distinct biological species that purportedly threatened the future of mankind. The advent of globalization, however, helped recast mutants as "commodities of great value . . . like oil or gold—or slaves." Hailing from locales as diverse as war-torn Vietnam, the Native American reservation system, rural Appalachia, and communist Russia, the New Mutants were familiar with globalization, U.S. imperialism, and mass consumerism; at the same time, they understood that their own mutant identities were shaped by these historical phenomena in ways that made them targets of economic exploitation even as they remained putative members of a social underclass defined by their racial and mutant differences.

By addressing the teammates' varied experiences of economic class and unequal social standing, the comic book located each character within the broader geo-political context of the post-Vietnam era. When Shan Coy Manh first arrives at the Xavier Institute, she worries that attending the school will require her to juggle a full-time job and her studies, leaving no time to tend to her younger siblings. Xavier offers a solution: "Come to work for me. I need someone to help me run the school. . . . You're bright, well educated, articulate, multi-lingual—a perfect choice. Your salary and benefits will be more than adequate. And you'll be able to work and study at the same time." Shan's predicament is a direct consequence of the global dislocations of cold war military conflict. An orphaned Vietnam War refugee, she is unexpectedly thrust into the role of full-time guardian to her twin siblings while struggling to make a life for herself in the country whose military and political policies forced her to flee her native home. Ironically her Vietnamese-language skills, which in other contexts might negatively identify her as an illegal immigrant, are an asset to the Xavier Institute, whose educational mission is global in scope. For Shan the promise of mutant solidarity cannot erase a simple truth: providing for herself and her family requires financial resources that can be garnered only by exploiting her skills in cross-cultural communication. In order to survive she must flexibly accommodate the economic crises that U.S. imperialism have precipitated.[8]

The inequalities of economic and social class in the era of globalization were most sharply rendered in the characterization of Sam Guthrie and Roberto da Costa, the two male members of the New Mutants who become fast friends despite their vastly different class backgrounds. The son of a coal miner in rural Kentucky, Sam is poised to be the first member of his family to attend college. When his father dies of "the black lung" after years of backbreaking mine work, Sam forfeits his college scholarship, taking his father's place to provide for his family. On his first day of work the mine suffers a cave-in. Sam's overwhelming fear unexpectedly triggers his latent mutant powers, which allow him to save a fellow mine worker's life and escape certain death by launching his body through the rubble like a cannonball. Witnessing this extraordinary feat through surveillance cameras, the owner of the mine, Donald Pierce (a member of the Hellfire Club), decides to exploit Sam's mutant ability by hiring him as a security guard for a genetic engineering facility he has recently opened. Sam's economic struggles embody the contradictions of late capitalism; despite his low economic standing, his mutation becomes an unexpected asset that, ironically, places him in a position to accept a job from the very man whose coal mine led to his father's death.

In contrast to Sam's working-class childhood, Roberto da Costa was raised in the lap of luxury as the only son of a billionaire corporate mogul, Emmanuel da Costa, in Rio de Janeiro. In an early issue of *The New Mutants* readers are given detailed background on Emmanuel's rise to power. The son of a servant woman who worked for one of the richest families in Brazil, Emmanuel drove the family's heir to ruin, building an economic fortune for himself by running a "world-wide industrial empire." Sickened by his father's obsession with wealth and power, Roberto disavows his inheritance and joins the New Mutants, a solidarity based on mutual trust rather than economic gain.[9] Meanwhile Roberto's father is recruited to the Hellfire Club's inner circle. In their eyes his wealth outweighs the fact that he is not a mutant like the other members.

In these two portraits the series depicts the multiple articulations that mutation can have in a world where class and wealth play a central role in defining social status. Unlike so many mutants who experience their genetic difference as a mark of difference that makes them species outcasts, Sam is primarily marginalized by his working-class background.

In fact his mutation helps him escape the lethal labor of coal mining, though his new job involves protecting a facility intended to develop methods for economically exploiting mutant genetics like his own. At every level, then, Sam is caught in the cross-hairs of neoliberal capitalism, forced to play his mutation against his working-class identity to make a living wage. Similarly, when we are first introduced to Roberto, he is playing in a soccer match against an all-white high school team whose members verbally assault him with racist epithets; regardless of his economic standing, Roberto and his family are still seen as outsiders to upper-class society because of their racial background. When Roberto manifests his powers on the soccer field for the first time, his mutation is understood as an expression of his racial identity; his transformation into a solar-powered strongman even turns his body pitch black (like a figurative "sunspot").[10] Paradoxically Roberto's greatest experience of marginalization is linked to his decision to disclaim his inheritance, which leads his father to disown him. As was the case with Sam, Roberto's experience of difference is primarily tied to the vicissitudes of his economic and racial identities rather than his mutation, reminding readers that mutation intersects with multiple axes of identity. By willfully abandoning his father's expectations, Roberto placed himself in a position to develop bonds of friendship with the New Mutants, and Sam in particular. Without such a choice, Sam's economic class would have left him forever alienated from someone like Roberto, who could very well have been his future employer as an heir to the Hellfire Club's many industrial operations.

As Sam's and Roberto's stories show, the class conflicts that wove their way through the narrative of *The New Mutants* were doubly framed as generational struggles over opposing social values and political worldviews. Where the original *X-Men* stressed the conflicts between humans and mutants as the central concern around which the team's mutant kinship was organized, the narrative of *The New Mutants* is fueled by the contentious relationship between developing youth and their generational antecedents. Throughout the series readers learn about the complicated family histories of each of the characters and the struggles they face to escape the expectations set for them by their parents. Not only do the characters express ambivalence toward their parents' values and life choices, as is evident in Roberto's refusal to follow in the footsteps of his father; they also come into conflict with Professor Xavier and his dream of peaceful relations between humans and mutants. The New Mutants are originally brought to the Xavier Institute after the

X-Men are abducted by a savage alien species known as the Brood.[11] Seeking to protect another generation of mutants from the same fate, Xavier recruits a new cohort of students to train. This time, however, his dream of shaping a team of mutant superheroes into cross-species ambassadors appears to have vanished along with his mutant family as the New Mutants express doubts about the efficacy and desirability of equality with humankind. They develop in the shadow of the team that had embodied Xavier's dream but that no longer held the imagination of a new generation of mutants.

In one poignant moment, Danielle Moonstar stumbles upon the young X-Man Kitty Pryde's bedroom. Carefully inspecting a wall of photos depicting the X-Men in a variety of familial scenes, she thinks to herself, "What strange-looking people . . . the Professor never talks about the X-Men. Something terrible happened to them. Are we supposed to take their place? Will their fate . . . be ours? Who cares? I probably won't be around to share it . . . even if I wanted to. My powers are destroying my life—and any chance for friendship or happiness here . . . just like they did back home" (figure 7.1).[12] Far from a desirable vision of mutant kinship, the X-Men now represent a literal and symbolic dead past that hangs over the heads of the living. Not only does the team's untimely demise appear as a monstrous fate that might befall all those who choose to affiliate with the dream they represented, but they no are longer even visually recognizable to a new generation of mutants, to whom they seem "strange-looking people" garbed in gaudy, outdated costumes.

Unable to square her own identity with the terms once used by her mutant forebears, Dani finds herself dislocated from the historical narratives and models of self-understanding that long prevailed in *The X-Men* series and the superhero comic book more broadly, ones that grounded solidarity on the basis of an assumed moral imperative to engage in hero work for the betterment of humankind. Shortly after visiting Kitty's room, however, Dani discovers Storm's lush greenhouse, the plants suffering from lack of care during her long absence. She thinks, "I've never seen so many plants. They're so beautiful! Doesn't anybody look after them? They're dying for lack of water. People are so cruel. Plants are living things—they deserve as much consideration as human beings."[13] Dani introduces herself to the plants, speaking to them as sentient creatures, unaware that Storm shared the same philosophy about the ties between humans and the natural world. Through her encounter with Storm's greenhouse, Dani forges an unconscious link with the history of the Xavier Institute and a broader mutant solidarity, one that, in being

FIGURE 7.1. Dani explores the X-Men's past. Chris Claremont (writer) and Bob McLeod (penciller), "Initiation!," *The New Mutants* #1, March 1982, reprinted in *New Mutants Classic Vol. 1* (New York: Marvel Comics, 2006), 58.

freely pursued, is divorced from the coercive demands of Xavier's dream. According to the narrative, the New Mutants' ability to forge an alternative future for themselves requires them to face the history of their forebears without losing sight of their own values.

To do so *The New Mutants* invested deep historical significance in the mutant abilities of its lead characters. Unlike their superheroic forebears, whose powers were commonly characterized by enhanced physical ability, the New Mutants possess powers of psychic projection, mental manipulation, and bodily morphing that materialize the dislocations of time and space occasioned by forms of neoliberal capital. Shan's ability to shunt her mind across space, Dani's ability to project spirit forms of people's greatest fears, and Rahne's ability to morph between human and animal form place each of these characters' sense of self in flux as they project their subjectivity onto external objects or else transition between varied physical forms. In one sense the "out-of-body" experiences occasioned by the use of such powers reflect the alienation from self and history that defines postindustrial society, a culture of mass consumption that relies on people's ability to flexibly accommodate the rapid movement of market trends by transforming themselves from historically rooted subjects with ethical and political loyalties into free-floating commodities unburdened by affective ties and available for consumption in any venue (much as Shan is required to do to secure employment at the school). In the context of the New Mutants' developing kinship, however, these powers become a vehicle for articulating social bonds beyond the level of language, offering unpredictable forms of intuitive communication (through telepathic rapport, psychic projection, and affective responses to one another's transformations) that function outside the logic of economic exchange, exceeding the ability of capitalist forces to easily co-opt and commodify because of their constant state of flux. *The New Mutants* suggested that even if mutant identity itself had become a commodity to be bought and sold in a free market, the manifold expressions of mutant powers themselves, and the way each mutant chose to enact those powers in relation to others, had the potential to change the direction of history.

To stress unpredictability and contingency as the defining characteristics of mutant ability, *The New Mutants* turned to the realm of magic, defining mutant powers not merely as a material effect of unique biology but also as an enchanted form of acting upon the world. Magic is an inaugural act that brings something into being that previously did not exist or remained invisible to the eye. Consequently magic forges seemingly impossible relationships between objects separated by time, space, and kind. In this way it functions like the practice of politics, which "consists in building a relationship between things that have none" for the purpose of "articulating matters of common concern."[14] Just as the affinities forged by political action can never be fully predicted in advance—one's political claims having the potential to be taken up by any number of actors across the social field—magic similarly introduces novel terms for articulating previously inchoate or unseen social relationships while revealing the imaginative constructedness of political acts. In *The New Mutants* magic came to represent the realm of the imagination where new ways of articulating one's sense of self and alternative visions of what the future could be like are developed and materialized.

For example, early in the series Dani joins the New Mutants to free Xavier from the clutches of Donald Pierce, the malevolent corporate mogul who employed Sam Guthrie. When Rahne transforms into a wolf to break into Pierce's guarded compound, Dani discovers that her rapport with animals extends to Rahne when she is in wolf form, allowing the two to communicate through their mind-link.[15] The experience forges a psychic and emotional bond between the two teenage mutants that shapes their developing friendship. This rapport appears as a form of magic, a mental link across time and space that exceeds scientific explanation. After all, if Rahne remains psychologically a human even in wolf form, then her metamorphic powers unravel the distinction between human and animal consciousness in order to allow Dani's entry into her psyche. Despite being culturally and socially worlds apart, Dani and Rahne are unexpectedly connected by a psychic bond that materializes without either character directly willing it, by simply *acting* in the world with their mutant abilities.

Scenes of enchanted encounter like this capture the work of radical imagination by modeling Hannah Arendt's contention, "Imagination is a means to see things in their proper perspective . . . to be generous enough to bridge abysses of remoteness until we can see and understand everything that is too far away from us as though it were our own affair." This capacity to "[be and think] in my own identity where actually I am not," enables genuine plurality as well as the ability to bridge differences through an enlarged perspective on similar phenomena.[16] The faculty of radical imagination was central to the left-wing political movements of the 1980s that struggled against the limited perspective of identity politics, "which assumes that individuals who share the same" racial, gender, or sexual identity also necessarily share a "common experience, outlook, and set of values and interests."[17] *The New Mutants* used popular fantasy to visually depict what it might look like to actually inhabit another person's perspective, using the unpredictable developing mutant powers of its characters as an avenue for performing and developing the faculty of radical imagination.

Though magic signaled the open-ended nature of human action and choice, such unpredictability required some ethical ground upon which to forge solidarities despite the unwieldiness of one's identity. In *The New Mutants* that ground was a bond of trust between the teammates based on a promise to protect their companions and facilitate one another's personal growth in an atmosphere of mutual support. Theorizing the concept of entrustment in relation to radical feminist political practice in the late 1980s, the Milan Women's Bookstore Collective claimed, "In its most crystallized form, the person to whom one entrusts oneself is the woman (or women) who supports one's desire for freedom, who says, 'Go on.'" Zerilli elaborates: "This phrase, in its utter simplicity and multiple, quotidian articulations, symbolizes . . . an exit from the impasse of feminism's freedom of the will. To say or to hear 'Go ahead,' and to act publicly in accordance with that phrase, is to take leave of feminism's injury identity . . . without denying one's membership in a group called women."[18] In this understanding of political association, the legitimacy vested in another person who authorizes one's desire to "go ahead" is garnered from women themselves, not from an outside source of authority like the state, social norms, or a universal figure of "woman" as an injured identity. In similar fashion the New Mutants model a form of mutant entrustment that is a "contingent yet necessary" response to the lack of symbolic figures of freedom for young mutants, whose only recourse in making sense of their place in the world is to latch on to an injured identity as genetic outcast. This demanded a willingness to recognize and affirm one another's ability to act in the world despite myriad oppositions to one's freedom, while accepting the judgments of one's fellow teammates as genuine interlocutors.

This is exemplified in a scene where Sam and Rahne debate the nature of mutation. When Rahne declares her mistrust of a new teammate, Illyana Rasputin, because of Illyana's knowledge of witchcraft, Sam flippantly remarks, "Big deal, you're a werewolf." Rahne shamefully responds, "D'you not think I know what I am! She and I're two of a kind—witch and were-thing—spawn of Satan!" Horrified that his friend would hold such self-hating beliefs, Sam offers her another interpretation of the Holy Bible, directly critiquing her minister's suggestion that

Rahne is born of the devil: "[Your minister's] a human being, Rahne, like you an' me! It isn't for us to understand the Lord's actions or design. That isn't possible. . . . He'll judge you in his own time, his own way—till then, you do the best you can with what you got. Mutant is a label, like 'colored' used to be. It doesn't matter. What's important is that you live your life. Give yourself a chance, Rahne—an' then, give Illyana the same."[19] Sam performs entrustment by authorizing Rahne's desire to act as herself, to "go ahead," as it were, as both human *and* werewolf, despite the beliefs that have convinced her otherwise. He engages in an act of radical imagination by recasting the very religious criteria through which Rahne has judged herself in a different light, offering her a new way of understanding herself not as a monstrous deviation from God's intended plan for the world but as an embodiment of his wish for a world of diverse, free-thinking subjects judged on the basis of their choices rather than what they are or appear to be (a racial minority or species outcast). He implores Rahne to recognize and embrace her capacity to act in concert with others and to grant the same recognition to her companions, regardless of her identity as mutant, woman, or Catholic. In the logic of the series, the practice of entrustment is framed as a form of magic that alters the relations between groups of people in the midst of a chaotic and unpredictable world.[20]

Where *The X-Men* of the 1970s forged bonds through their shared experience of mutant identity, the contemporary contingency of that same identity now made such bonding an intellectual labor that, far from inevitable, had to be actively cultivated among unlike companions. To cement the critical role entrustment played in the lives of these characters, *The New Mutants* would offer a contemporary retelling of the most noteworthy story of entrustment to appear in the original *X-Men* series: the bond between Storm and Phoenix. Specifically the series performed the liberatory solidarity of Storm and Phoenix in its two primary female characters, Dani Moonstar (Mirage) and Illyana Rasputin (Magik). Unlike Storm and Phoenix, however, who ultimately repair their traumatic histories through a mystical reunification at the heart of the M'Kraan Crystal, Mirage and Magik become interlocutors with one another, constantly questioning each other's self-understanding to create a space where "opinions" and worldviews can be "judged and perhaps unsettled to the point of crisis."[21] According to *The New Mutants*, it is precisely such crises that demand the production of social bonds that help negotiate the unpredictable and chaotic transformations of self when one acts in concert with diverse others.

"Do You Believe in Magik?"

The creative innovations *The New Mutants* brought to the *X-Men* franchise manifested in a variety of forms, including the redefinition of mutant identity from a utopian universal to a contingent political category; the refocusing of plot from mutant villains who threatened peaceful relations between humans and mutants to historical demons that threatened the very viability of mutant solidarity; and the transformation of the underlying political mission of the original *X-Men* in the 1960s and 1970s from mutant ambassadors to the human race to practitioners of a politics of radical imagination. Yet, like its fictional forebear, *The New Mutants* grounded these innovations in the unfolding stories of the characters themselves, most notably in the female members of the team, Dani Moonstar and Illyana Rasputin, who came to embody the shifting political meanings of mutation in a new decade.

Where Storm and Phoenix personified alternative visions of feminist liberation in the previous decade, Dani and Illyana now stood in for varied experiences of generational trauma. They respectively manifested the struggle to make peace with one's indigenous heritage and the process of mourning the premature loss of childhood innocence. For Storm and Phoenix the competing discourses of feminist liberation circulating throughout the 1970s provided a rich language to describe the willful exercise of mutant powers as a metaphor for feminist consciousness raising and freedom from the repressive hold of normative gender and sexuality; in the 1980s the dramatic internal fracturing of the American women's movement and the vitriolic public backlash against feminism rendered this previous creative framing naïve, if not ideologically suspect. Unable to rely on the discourse of second wave feminism to make sense of their burgeoning mutant powers or forge a path for reinventing their identities beyond the limits of their tormented childhoods, Dani and Illyana turned instead to their own wounded histories in search of an explanation for how and why their lives had led them to their present circumstances as conflicted members of a new mutant generation. The exercise of their powers was less an extension of their will or agency and more an unpredictable attempt to act upon the world whose results were impossible to determine in advance.

Like her fictional counterpart, Storm, Dani Moonstar was one of a kind: the first female Native American superhero in a mainstream comic book. Raised as a proud Cheyenne warrior and the granddaughter of a respected clan chief, Black Eagle, in the town of Sundance, Colorado,

Dani's life is upended by the emergence of her mutant powers. Soon after her abilities manifest, she unwittingly projects a spirit form of her father's greatest fear, a monstrous Demon Bear. Weeks later her parents mysteriously disappear on a hunting trip. Devastated by the loss, Dani assumes that her spirit forms presaged, and perhaps caused, their deaths. Outcast by her people for her mutant abilities and with only her grandfather to look after her, Dani flees "to the mountains, to live as a hermit." When her grandfather first seeks out Xavier's help in teaching her the skills to control her mutant talents, Dani lashes out in anger, "A white!?! You would send me to an Anglo?!? No! I won't do it! I won't go! . . . He's an enemy! All white men are our enemies!" In her anger she projects a spirit form of her grandfather's death at the hands of the Hellfire Club's henchmen. Horrified by her own malicious actions, Dani hugs her grandfather close and weeps, "I'm so sorry. I didn't mean to—I was so angry I summoned the dream shapes without thinking. Just as I did at home and in town before I fled to the mountains. I . . . I couldn't help myself, I don't know how I do this—or how to stop." Embracing his granddaughter, Black Eagle responds, "Which is *why* you need Xavier." That night the same men who appeared in Dani's spirit vision murder Black Eagle. In her grief she realizes that Black Eagle foresaw his own death and sought Xavier's help to protect his granddaughter's future from the villainous forces that would seek to kill her.[22]

As her initial reaction to Black Eagle's request displays, Dani's Cheyenne heritage is the source of her fierce determination and warrior skill. Yet the wounded history of her people, which she carries as a personal burden, prevents her from creating a new path for herself outside the narrow antagonisms between her people and the "whites" who long sought their extermination. Not only does Dani feel dislocated from her heritage by her mutant ability, but the solution to her troubles—to train with Xavier and his New Mutants—seems to her a form of selling out to white culture. Though she initially seeks to avenge her grandfather's murder alone, she ultimately joins forces with the New Mutants to battle Donald Pierce, the man responsible for Black Eagle's death and a rogue member of the Hellfire Club intent on exploiting and dispatching this new generation of young mutants. In the midst of a heated struggle with Pierce, Rahne is badly hurt. Forced to choose between pursuing Pierce and tending to a fellow mutant and newfound friend, Dani rushes to Rahne's side. In choosing to save the life of her teammate rather than murder the man responsible for her grandfather's death, Dani honors Black Eagle's commitment to life while uneasily offering her loyalty to a different tribe, the New Mutants. Torn between multiple allegiances to her family, her tribe, and her mutant identity, Dani seeks to maintain loyalty to her native heritage however she can. When she first dons the official garb of the X-Men, she replaces the traditional red belt and yellow boots with a turquoise amulet and her leather moccasins. When Xavier asks Dani to explain her refusal to follow school rules, she proudly responds, "I am Cheyenne. Nothing—no one—will ever make me forget or abandon my heritage. I'm also an individual, professor. You say we must wear these clothes—I will do as you ask, but in my own manner."[23]

Where Danielle Moonstar struggles to maintain her historical ties with an endangered native heritage, Illyana Rasputin wishes for nothing more than to be rid of her tainted history. The younger sister of X-Man Peter Rasputin (Colossus), Illyana was barely a child when her sibling left their family's Russian farmstead to join the ranks of the Xavier Institute. Two years later she was abducted by the sorcerer Belasco, a master of black magic and the demon lord of Limbo, an otherworldly domain akin to the biblical Hell, who wishes to lay claim to Illyana's soul. Though mere minutes go by for the X-Men, seven years pass in Limbo, during which time Belasco and his demon henchmen S'ym corrupt Illyana's soul to use her as a living conduit between Limbo and Earth. In the last years of her entrapment, Illyana secretly learns the demonic enchantments that fill a vast library of magical knowledge in Belasco's castle. Using this power, she materializes a piece of her darkened spirit, transforming it into an enchanted weapon, a Soulsword that embodies the combined power of her magical knowledge. In a final showdown with her mentor and captor, Illyana wields her Soulsword against Belasco, forcing him to flee Limbo, leaving her to take on the mantle of the Demon Queen of the realm. Finally free of the enchantments barring her escape from Limbo, Illyana returns to her own time, now a young woman wielding dark magic of extraordinary power. Alongside her mastery of the dark arts, during her last years in Limbo she manifests her mutant power, the ability to teleport herself and others across time and space through the use of "stepping discs," circular portals that open rifts in the fabric of reality. Upon her return she joins the New Mutants in the hopes of reknitting her ties to the world of the living and learning more about her magical and mutant powers. Even as she seeks to rebuild her life, she carries the knowledge that within her soul lies the heart of a demon.[24]

Illyana emerged in the 1980s as the one of the most complex figures of demonic possession in any mainstream superhero comic book. On the one hand, she embodied the stereotype of the innocent blue-eyed, blond-haired young girl obsessively worried over in the decade's popular discourse on child abduction and abuse. As readers learn more about Illyana's life in Limbo, it becomes clear that physical torture, even suggested sexual abuse at the hands of the demon S'ym, defined her lost years.[25] On the other hand, Illyana's susceptibility to Belasco's enchantments and her own ambivalence about her relationship to the demon lord (at times considering him a loving father figure) put her perceived purity in question: Could Illyana have halted Belasco's transformation of her spirit, or was her soul predestined for corruption? In the months following her escape from Limbo, Illyana worries over her demonic nature, questioning her own motives toward those she loves most; it was only a matter of time, she would think to herself, until the demon gods trapped in Limbo would use her to enter our world and extinguish all life on Earth. Like Dani torn between her multiple loyalties to her native heritage, familial bonds, and mutant kinship, Illyana similarly struggles to develop bonds with her new teammates following years spent in a hellish dimension where all friendships and solidarities were destroyed beneath the weight of crushing evil.

Unlike the powers of their feminist forebears, Storm and Phoenix, Dani's and Illyana's mutant abilities do not grant them liberation from the constraints of normative gender and sexuality but reveal the wounded attachments that have formed their identities. Dani's spirit forms visualize the greatest fears of those she comes into contact with. By deploying her abilities, she projects the traumatic psychic lives of others, often seeing in their fears a reflection of her own anxieties and insecurities about her mutant identity and her failure to live up to the expectations of her Cheyenne heritage. When Shan, Rahne, and Xavier first visit Dani's Colorado home, Dani attacks Shan with her psychic power. Suddenly the rocky landscape of the Colorado Mountains transforms into a Vietnamese forest where an all-out blitz attack by American troops is unfolding. By reaching into Shan's thoughts, Dani materializes her terrifying memories of the Vietnam War, trapped by an onslaught of gunfire and explosive artillery exchanged between opposing American and North Vietnamese troops. The unexpected juxtaposition of the forests of Vietnam and Colorado's arid mountain landscape reveals a historical resonance between the experience of U.S. imperialism in Southeast Asia and Native American genocide at the hands of white settlers. In the next panel the illusion of violence occasioned by Dani's powers becomes all too real when a firebomb thrown by the Hellfire Club's thugs explodes before them. The imagined war zone of Vietnam then comes into contact with an actual war zone in the Colorado Mountains, the antagonists no longer American troops against native peoples and Vietnamese guerrilla fighters, but a new generation of mutants and the forces of global capitalism in the form of the Hellfire Club. [26] Dani's spirit forms thus offered a picture of the various histories of violence that shape hers and Shan's perspective in their struggles to respond to new threats arrayed against their mutant rather than their racial or indigenous identities.

In this and countless other scenes *The New Mutants* used Dani's powers to visually depict the concept of radical imagination. By externalizing interior psychological states as living images available for all to see, Dani reveals how one takes into account another person's perspective on the same phenomenon or experience. In one moving scene Dani accidentally projects the greatest fears of Amara Aquilla, a new recruit to the team capable of transforming into living magma and controlling the heat of the Earth's core. Before them appears a vivid image depicting Amara using her powers to incinerate Dani. Dani responds to this vision by thinking, "She's scared of killing me . . . of her power getting out of control! She doesn't want to hurt me . . . she's as spooked as I was when I first discovered what I could do."[27] Rather than fleeing for her life or turning against Amara after witnessing a vision of her own death, Dani interprets the affective thrust of her spirit-form as a site of shared experience between the two strangers. Through a variety of similar experiences, her repertoire of skills expands dramatically over the course of the series. With practice she is able to materialize a range of affective states, including people's most beloved memories as well as their greatest desires. Consequently her guilt over the devastating emotional effects of her abilities is tempered by her capacity to elicit great joy and pleasure from those around her, but also by the knowledge that her power grants her empathetic insight into other people's psychological struggles.

Where Dani's powers visually display the psychic lives of others, Illyana's mutant and magical abilities reveal her own demonic nature and the childhood torture that facilitated its birth. With the use of her stepping discs, she can transport herself and others across time and space. Yet to do so requires her to travel through Limbo. Every use of her abilities unwittingly grants her friends a view of the hellish realm where she lived most of her childhood as an apprentice to the demon lord Belasco. In one of her first adventures with the New Mutants, Illyana is forced to teleport the team to aid her in defeating the demon S'ym, who follows her from Limbo to exact revenge for her disloyalty to Belasco. As Demon Queen of Limbo, Illyana's stepping discs are wedded to the dark realm, requiring her to pass through Limbo with each teleport. As the stepping disc engulfs the teammates, they briefly witness a fiery wasteland of stalagmites surrounding a young girl who reaches out to them for help. Roberto yells, "That's Illyana!," to which Sam responds, "It can't be, Bobby—she's too young!" Before they can react the teammates are teleported back to Xavier's mansion, where they join Illyana in battle against her demon stalker.[28] Taking this journey through Limbo numerous times in later adventures, they learn that the little girl they first saw was indeed Illyana, a toddler when she first arrived in Belasco's realm. Crossing through time as well as space, the stepping discs offer devastating images of Illyana's past, forcing her companions to reconsider their earlier judgments against her in light of what she suffered as a child. Just as Dani's powers encourage her and others to literally and symbolically see from another person's perspective, so too Illyana's powers demand that her friends come to understand the world through her eyes, a former prisoner of Limbo whose only hope of escape was to master the dark sorcery that would corrupt her soul.

At the same time that her powers reveal glimpses of her own childhood suffering, Illyana's stepping discs also move *forward* through time, granting her the ability to see different versions of the future. Through a series of unexpected travels into alternative futures, she gains a repository of dangerous knowledge about the potential outcome of the teammates' newfound alliance. When the New Mutants battle their villainous counterparts, the Hellions (a team of mutant teenagers organized by the Hellfire Club), all the teammates save Dani and Illyana are captured by the White Queen. Using Illyana's stepping discs to evade detection, they escape into Limbo before returning to free their friends. When they attempt to return to the present, however, Illyana mistakenly transports them one year past their original encounter with the Hellions. There they witness a horrifying scene: all of their former teammates now dressed in Hellions attire, "acting like the best of friends."[29] Had their friends deserted the Xavier Institute to join the Hellions? Why had Xavier not returned to save his former students? Was this an image of things to come or one possible reality of many? From that moment onward, all of these questions would weigh on Dani and Illyana as they fought on behalf of a team they feared could betray them at any moment. What Illyana revealed about herself as well as her teammates potentially placed into crisis the New Mutants' entrustment. Yet it forced them all to face the contingency of their choices by acknowledging that each had the same capacity for evil as Illyana.

If Illyana's stepping discs offer a window into the demonic realm that had shaped her childhood, her magical abilities similarly function as another kind of portal for the very demons that inhabit Limbo. Her sorcery relies on the ability to marshal the primal forces of Limbo to manipulate reality and combat demonic agents when they appear in our world. The depiction of Illyana as a literal conduit for Limbo's demonic forces found its greatest expression in the emergence of her two alter egos, Magik and Darkchylde (plate 24). Shortly after joining the New Mutants, Illyana notices an alarming phenomenon: each time she deploys her sorcery to battle various foes, a shimmering armor begins to cover various parts of her body.[30] At first the armor appears wherever a foe lands a blow to her body, protecting her from physical harm. Soon it covers large swaths of her arms and torso, automatically appearing each time she calls upon the power of her Soulsword. She learns that the enchanted "Eldritch Armor" is an extension of her mystical weapon, literally materializing her identity as the hybrid mutant/sorceress Magik. Yet the armor presages a third transformation from Magik to Darkchylde, a monstrous cloven-hoofed demon whose scaly red skin, curved horns, and bright yellow eyes increasingly replace Illyana's armor whenever she deploys her magic for violent or destructive ends. Illyana's sorcery is at its most powerful when she manifests the Darkchylde, yet it is in this same guise that her humanity is most compromised, losing control of her actions and her ability to discern between good and evil, friend and foe.

In the figures of Illyana, Magik, and Darkchylde, *The New Mutants* dramatized Illyana's split subjectivity as an embodied experience of transformation across various physical forms. Where previous demonic possession narratives merely rehashed a story of the cosmic battle between good and evil that manifested in a character's transformation from benevolent hero to villainous alter ego, Illyana's struggle with the demonic forces that made up her being results in the birth of Magik, a liminal figure (or third term) that exists between the binaries of good and evil, innocence and corruption. For Illyana to choose innocence and purity meant losing the extraordinary powers she had gained, and potentially her identity, which was now irrevocably shaped by her years spent in Limbo. At the same time, for her to fully give in to the black magic at her disposal would inevitably lead to her transformation into the devilish Darkchylde, losing any semblance of her humanity. Either choice involved dire consequences Illyana was unwilling to accede to. In turn, the persona Magik came to embody Illyana's willingness to accept that every choice she made would always be riven by ambivalence.

Across the span of series Dani's and Illyana's mutant powers were defined by their sheer unpredictability. Though both figures are tortured by the idea that their personal histories have already predestined them to doom—Dani in the form of the Demon Bear she believes will ultimately cause her death, and Illyana through her inevitable enslavement to the gods of Limbo—their mutant powers consistently put in question the very notion of destiny or fate, instead revealing seemingly immutable categories such as time, space, history, and identity as highly contingent and open to infinite permutations. Despite her increasing skill in psychically reaching out to other people's minds, Dani can never determine in advance what secret fears, joys, or desires she might uncover. To engage her power always involves a leap of faith that she can withstand the emotional effect of her revelations. Similarly Illyana's mutant powers can be activated only with the possibility of unintended effects in time and space. As we have seen, though Illyana's stepping discs are a tool for transportation and combat, they are also unwieldy, requiring extraordinary amounts of mental and physical energy from her to control the temporal and spatial dimensions of every teleport. Each time Illyana uses a stepping disc, she risks transporting herself and her comrades to any number of dangerous scenarios in Limbo or else to lose her place in time.

Though both Dani and Illyana initially see the unwieldiness of their powers as reflecting their lack of control over their mutant abilities, they soon realize that this very unpredictability can function as the ground upon which the teammates can build their developing kinship. This kinship would be based on the contingency of all actions, political or otherwise, rather than the false promise of a predetermined identity or destiny. If the various members of the New Mutants came to the team burdened with the heavy weight of personal histories that appeared to foreclose the possibility of a different life path for each, it would be the unpredictability of their choices and the willingness to authorize one another's decisions that would hold out the possibility of a collective future defined by mutual trust rather than the assumption of a shared investment in a mutant identity. Readers would catch a glimpse of this collective future in the figures of Dani and Illyana, for by visualizing the histories that shaped the childhoods of each New Mutant they made the past itself a point of common public debate to be contested, reinterpreted, and grappled with from a variety of perspectives. This project would be most eloquently captured in "The Demon Bear Saga," a story of the epic struggle between the New Mutants and the eponymous avatar of Dani's native past. In this tale of generational conflict, all the political values of the New Mutants—the practice of radical imagination, the will to entrustment, and the embrace of human contingency—are put to the test as the teammates are forced to develop a collective response to a previously imagined threat that now appears frighteningly real.

Lost in the Badlands

"The Demon Bear Saga" (1984) dramatized the violent psychological and political effects of generational conflict by depicting it as a battle between youth and their forebears that plays out on the landscape of American history.[31] The eponymous villain is a demonic embodiment of Dani's Native American heritage. When Dani's mutant powers were still developing, she unwittingly reached into her father's mind, visualizing a terrifying nightmare in which a giant bear murders a majestic Palomino and a fierce Golden Eagle. Because her father was of the Eagle clan and her mother the Horse clan, Dani could not help but think that she had projected her parents' deaths, transforming what had once been an immaterial terror into immanent reality. Forever plagued by guilt, the fiercely brave Dani fears only one thing: facing the Demon Bear that tore her family apart.

Unlike "The Phoenix Saga" of the 1970s, which depicts the unification of competing identities under the sign of a "queer mutanity," "The Demon Bear Saga" narrates the struggle of mutant youth to sever histories of trauma that prevent them from pursuing new kinships and alliances outside the limits of their familial or biological lineage. Where in "The Phoenix Saga" the X-Men traveled the length of the galaxy bound to one another by an expansive sense of mutant kinship, the New Mutants initially faced the murderous Demon Bear as wary comrades unsure of themselves and the strength of their precarious alliance. The central thematic of "The Demon Bear Saga" lay not in an image of the harmony of all things but in each teammate's development of a faculty of radical imagination, the ability to see from each other's viewpoints as they faced a shared threat from competing perspectives.

The narrative itself is visually organized around the teammates' transition from individual and atomized worldviews born of personal experience to acceptance of the plurality of experiences that shape their diverse kinship. This shift moves the story's initial focus from Dani's attempt to defeat the monstrous bear of her dreams to her teammates' battle with the bear for the life of their friend. A second movement across time and space simultaneously signals this transition from Dani's singular strug-gle to the collective efforts of the team: Dani's initial battle with the bear takes place in the present on the grounds of the Xavier Institute, while the team's epic struggle against its demonic enchantments unfolds in an otherworldly realm, the Badlands, a demonic version of the American West prior to the arrival of white settlers. This final showdown requires the New Mutants to combine the full physical force of their powers to combat the supernatural strength of the beast, an act that hinges on their ability to develop a mutual trust and shared interest in each other's well-being despite their differences. To do so meant that all the team members had to first imagine Dani's struggle as their own, to understand their collective life as shaped by *her* past as much as by their own individual histories.

As if to foreshadow its conclusion, "The Demon Bear Saga" begins with the critical question of trust, or lack thereof, between the neophyte band of New Mutants. In the weeks prior to the bear's arrival, Dani prepares to face the Demon Bear that murdered her parents but chooses to keep her knowledge of the impending attack a secret from her teammates. Illyana suspects that something is awry when she presides over a series of Danger Room sequences in which Dani programs the Xavier mansion's advanced combat simulation system to run a test requiring her to fight a grizzly bear on frozen terrain. When Illyana questions Dani about the purpose of her workouts, Dani merely claims that she wants to stay fit for her duties as team leader. That night, as a snowstorm pummels the mansion, Dani thinks to herself, "Illyana didn't believe a word I said . . . and didn't bother hiding her anger, either. She trusted me with her secrets. . . . It hurts that I won't do the same. She'd help if I asked. They all would. They don't under-stand—this is something I have to do alone." Following these words, a brief sequence depicts Dani recalling her parents and her sense of responsibility for their deaths. As she adorns her face with war paint and braves the blis-tering cold to confront the Demon Bear of her dreams, Dani proclaims, "It's my fault my folks died, my spirit-sending that made them ride into the mountains to face the bear. They did it to protect me. . . . I won't see anyone else suffer in my place. I am Cheyenne! My father—my ancestors—were the proudest warriors of the plains. I will be true to my heritage no matter what! Tonight, I'll prove myself worthy!"[32] These opening scenes display Dani's split loyalties to her native heritage and her mutant family. Despite the many friendships she has developed at the Xavier Institute, she still perceives her decision to join the New Mutants as a cowardly turning away from her duties to the Cheyenne. By framing her impending battle with the Demon Bear as a personal struggle to regain her honor rather than a bid for freedom from the demons of her past in the name of a collective solidarity with the New Mutants, Dani remains bound to a history of wounded attachments, unable to develop the bonds of trust with her newfound teammates that are a necessary component of common political life.

Summoning the bear to battle, Dani finally comes face to face with the nightmare beast. In a terrifying full-page splash panel the Demon Bear appears before her, its body a giant black void dwarfing its prey (plate 25). Reaching into the Demon Bear's psyche, Dani projects a spirit form of what the monster fears most. She is shocked to see an image of herself materializing between them. "Me?!?" she declares incredulously. The projected figure appears unarmed, its back to the reader, a version of Dani garbed in her New Mutants uniform yet still in her traditional native braids and moccasin boots. In violent terror the Bear lashes out at the image, giving Dani the chance to shoot an arrow into its throat. Though outweighed many times over, Dani escapes the bear's clutches to shoot two more arrows before it falls. As she turns away from the hulking carcass, she exclaims, "I don't believe it—I won! The demon beast that murdered my parents! At last, their spirits are at rest. And my nightmare is . . . over!" With these last words, the Demon Bear's eyes flicker with rage, while Dani triumphantly walks away, unaware the monster still lives. The following page opens with Rahne bolting up from a fitful sleep yelling Dani's name. Through her psychic rapport with Dani, Rahne instinctively realizes that her friend is in terrible danger. When the New Mutants follow her into the raging snowstorm, they encounter Dani's beaten body lying in blood-covered snow.

In her desperate wish to avenge her parents and be free of the Demon Bear's hold over her life, Dani misreads the meaning of her initial revelation that she is the bear's greatest fear. It is not her that the bear fears most, but her dual identity as both a member of the New Mutants and a Cheyenne.[33] In her time spent with the New Mutants, Dani gained the confidence to see that these two aspects of her personal history could sustain one another rather than exist in contradiction. Yet her own reluctance to jettison the idea of a singular or pure loyalty to the Cheyenne people and her self-imposed guilt over the perceived betrayal of her people's history offered the bear an avenue through which to terrorize Dani in her dreams. In this context her exclamation "Me?!?" suggests her own disbelief at seeing herself embody both aspects of her identity simultaneously.

The transition from the Demon Bear to Rahne shifts the affective weight of the narrative from Dani's individual struggle to the collective actions of the New Mutants. Where Dani fails to call upon the power of her collective solidarity with the New Mutants to aid her in her battle with the Demon Bear, the visual structure of the comic book itself forges a link between her suffering and the interwoven lives of her new companions. At the local hospital Dani is wheeled into emergency surgery. As the team frets in anguish over their inability to help their friend, Sam reminds them that Dani will need their collective protection when the Demon Bear returns for its prey: "Stands to reason, ever since we've known her, Dani's had a special fear of a spirit bear she said murdered her parents. None of us really gave the story much credit—after all, who b'lieves in magic? 'cept, Illyana's a real witch, we've fought demons an' sorceresses. . . . T'night, [Dani] walked out into a storm, alone, armed with bow an' arrows an' wearin' war paint! An' got mauled. We were wrong t'doubt her. We should'a listened. . . . If ah'm right, the New Mutants are the only hope she's got."[34] Sam's statement acknowledges that the missing link between the teammates has been a shared sense of trust. Though Dani's refusal to seek the help of her friends betrayed her lack of trust in them, their unwillingness to acknowledge her fears and anxieties about her haunted past—understood as their refusal to "believe in magic"—similarly made the development of mutual trust impossible. The very nature of the threat they face, a demonic avatar with malevolent magical abilities, now requires the New Mutants to place their trust in the one teammate they have all feared since the day she joined their ranks: the Demon Queen of Limbo, Illyana Rasputin.

When Rahne exclaims, "Oh, Sam—how can we fight such a fearsome creature?! It's magic!" Illyana boldly responds, "So am I. And when you want to be, Rahne, you can be pretty fearsome yourself. We'll give the beast a run for his money." As the Demon Queen of Limbo, Illyana is imbricated in the same dark magic that fuels the Demon Bear's malevolent character, a point impressed upon readers earlier when Dani claims, "There's a part of [Illyana] that's as evil as the bear."[35] As a child of both light and darkness, Illyana is able to discern the true meaning of the New Mutants' encounter with the Demon Bear: a trial that will force the teammates to come to terms with the contingent nature of their own humanity by recognizing that the only force with the potential to bind them together despite the unpredictability of their identities is trust. Or, in Illyana's language, "magik." As soon as Illyana casts a protective spell around Dani's operating room, the bear reappears, using dark magic to teleport itself and the New Mutants across time and space.

A panoramic double-page spread depicts the New Mutants arrayed before the massive figure of the Demon Bear against the horizon of a midwestern plain (plate 26). To the right, the Demon Bear's towering body takes up nearly half the page length, a jagged black void along the horizon line. Above the bear's outstretched hands float his two demonic hosts and a red orb reflecting the events taking place in the operating room, the floating sphere a physical manifestation of Illyana's protection surrounding Dani's surgery ward. In the upper left-hand corner of the spread appears a white grid framed by stylized southwestern borders and marred by black smears. A label above reads, "Darkness Descends: A View from 2,000 Feet," accompanied by a note elaborating, "Black areas represent . . . land consumed by the Demon-Bear's shadow." The narrative explains that this is "the Bear's own domain . . . a virgin America untouched by the white invaders from across the sea. A pure, unspoiled land—rich with power. The bear is part of the natural scheme of things here—yet at the same time apart from it. An abomination. A symbol of strength and order twisted into a loathsome travesty of its true self, its very presence corrupting the Earth like a plague." Baffled by the scene before them, the New Mutants turn to Illyana to explain this turn of events. While Roberto and Sam implore Illyana to use her magic to free the bear's prisoners and save Dani, Rahne thinks to herself, "Tha's na' right! How dare we trust Illyana when she's as much a demon as yon bear?"[36]

In this single panorama the manifold stakes of "The Demon Bear Saga" are made visible. Though the New Mutants are intent on protecting their friend and teammate from the clutches of the Demon Bear, doing so requires them to face the wounded history it embodies, namely the scars of white imperialism and Native American genocide. As the narrator suggests, the bear stands in not only for the violence of these events but also for the memorialization of the native past as a series of historical traumas to be relived into the indefinite future. This depiction of the Demon Bear once again figures the monster as a literal cut or rift in time and space, a jagged black void that rends the fabric of history, remaking an idealized, "unspoiled" past into an irreparable wound. In its reference to the midwestern plains, the title "Badlands" not only locates the scene in an iconic American landscape but also transforms the Native American past into a "bad land" in much the same way that the endless litany of false treaties and broken political promises made to native peoples created a bad land out of the very landscape they once considered home.[37]

By identifying the Demon Bear as "part of the natural scheme" of the Badlands yet also an "abomination . . . apart from it," the narrative invoked the central trauma at the core of indigenous identity as a category that simultaneously describes an original state of natural belonging to a place as well as the violent dispossession of that attachment by genocide and forced migration.[38] Where in the 1970s the categories of race and ethnicity allowed *The X-Men* to dramatize questions of inclusion and exclusion within the framework of a queer mutanity, indigeneity was a category that allowed *The New Mutants* to question the very nature of original belonging to any group, land, history or political vision. In a world where mutation had become a valuable commodity worth massacring populations of vulnerable genetic outcasts to exploit, "mutant" had become a modern form of dispossessed identity. Each of the team members had fled their place of origin under threat of war, abuse, enslavement, and death, seeking safe haven at the Xavier Institute, where they were forced to reimagine belonging and solidarity in the absence of their former ties to family and nation. The Demon Bear embodied these horrors in the form of the foundational indigenous trauma, the genocide of Native American peoples. This is impressed upon readers when the Demon Bear violently tears the surface of Illyana's protective sphere attempting to reach Dani while she lies in surgery; ripping through time and space, the bear creates a window between the Badlands and Dani's surgical ward, visually linking the wounds of a native past to Dani's literal wounds in the present. Seeing this past resonate with their own limited histories, the teammates must make a critical choice: to be swallowed up by the loss of a foundational belonging or to inaugurate a new indigenous identity in their own solidarity.

After a series of unsuccessful attacks on the bear, the teammates regroup. A massive panorama depicts the horizon occluded by blue-black clouds, a few glimmers of light barely shining through. Scanning the foreboding horizon, Illyana thinks, "What do we do next?! The shadowlands are growing—and with them, the bear's power. We have to act now, and we dare not make a mistake—but our ignorance cripples us." Struck by an epiphany, Illyana reminds the team that Dani holds the key to their victory for she is what the bear fears most. Rahne balks at the possibility of entering Dani's mind to recover the knowledge they need to destroy the bear, fearing that the mind link might kill her while in such a weakened state. "Without that information, the bear will kill her anyway—and us as well!" Illyana implores the team. "And that's just the beginning! Don't you see?! Any of you?! Once the bear conquers this earth, he'll come after our own! We're the only thing standing in its way. We don't have a choice, Rahne. It's Dani's life versus everyone else's in the world."

On the brink of permanent darkness, Illyana breaks the team's deadlock by making a critical judgment: risk Dani's life with the hope of defeating the bear and changing the course of history or remain paralyzed before its power and abandon all claims to their future. Illyana reminds her teammates that in the absence of certainty about the future, their mutant powers still grant them the ability to procure the knowledge they need to act with purpose, as long as they are willing to trust in each other's skills. Through a practice of radical imagination—depicted in the psychic rapport between Dani and Rahne—the teammates seek to understand the meaning of the Demon Bear from Dani's perspective. Only then is each New Mutant able to conceive of Dani's struggles with the demons of her past as akin or indigenous to their own.

Among Chris Claremont's papers archived at Columbia University's Rare Books and Manuscript Division is a sheaf of historical and anthropological information about Cheyenne culture collated by a fan named Larry Marder during the first years of *The New Mutants'* publication. Marder annotates a page that outlines the central philosophical values and worldview of the Cheyenne. The text explains that in the Cheyenne cosmology, the universe "is fundamentally a mechanical system with a limited energy quotient which progressively diminishes as it is expended." This energy is rechargeable through "mimetic acts of sympathetic ritual." Consequently the Cheyenne postulate that "acts are more effective than words." In his annotations Marder circled this last postulate in blue ink, with an arrow pointed at it, and in bold outlined letters wrote, "Marvel Gospel!" The description of the Cheyenne belief in "mimetic acts of sympathetic ritual" as a source for expanding the world's energy is a corollary to the concept of radical imagination: the ability to act on behalf of others in sympathetic rapport. By identifying acts as having the highest value of the Marvel Universe, Marder sees an analogous mimetic sympathy between Marvel's fictional world-making and the Cheyenne cosmology. Whether Claremont received his inspiration from these sources or elsewhere, it is undeniable that this worldview underwrites the narrative of "The Demon Bear Saga." In her demand that the New Mutants recognize their capacity to learn from Dani what they must do to reenergize the darkening universe, Magik reminds her teammates that their mutant powers offer them the ability to engage in acts of sympathetic rapport that can potentially transform the world.

As Rahne prepares to mind-link with Dani, the team begins working in tandem to combat the bear's dark magic. Just as the tides turn in their favor, Rahne reemerges from her rapport with Dani and exclaims, "Tha's the key! Yuir sword!! Dani's was the knowledge, ours th' power! The mutants—actin' as a team! It must be cut to its heart and soul!" Encouraged to "go ahead," Illyana acts decisively. Facing the bear head-on, her final encounter with the monster recalls Jean Grey's moment of epiphany at the heart of the M'Kraan Crystal:

> At last, their eyes meet—hers and the bear's—and she hesitates. The bear dwarfs her to the point of insignificance, its demonic nature kin to the evil within her own soul. It is as ancient as the planet—a malfeasance that has ever been, shall ever be . . . while Illyana, for all her dread power, is still very much a child. What hope has she to even match her foe, much less overcome it? Then, with a cry torn from the core of her being—Soulsword radiating so much energy it turns night into day—she splits the monster's skull![39]

With these words, we see a terrifying image of the bear's monstrous face shattered in half. As it discorporates, a vivid splash panel reveals two figures emerging from beneath the bear's former cloak of darkness: William and Peggy Lonestar, Dani's parents. In this extraordinary sequence the New Mutants come to understand the necessity of working as a team for their mutual survival. For Rahne to authorize Illyana to go ahead despite her previous misgivings about Illyana's demonic nature suggests a radical transformation in the relations among all the New Mutants, made possible through each character's willingness to inhabit the worldviews of the others. In her final encounter with the beast, Illyana sees in its visage an image of herself, acknowledging her kinship to the very malevolent forces embodied by the bear. While the beast represents a history frozen in memory by unforgiven historical atrocities, echoed by Illyana's lost childhood spent in Limbo, Illyana's future is yet to be decided, an open landscape of possibility underwritten by the bonds of trust she shares with her teammates. With that trust now in place, the future waits only for her to act. And she does.

In the logic of "The Demon Bear Saga," it was no surprise that the villain of the story would be revealed as a symbolic embodiment of Dani's personal history in the form of her parents. When asked to explain their link to the Demon Bear, William Lonestar says, "We weren't killed, but enslaved—transformed into the demon bear you fought, a foul corruption of our sacred symbol of courage and integrity. We were meant to do the same to you."[40] In William and Peggy Lonestar the story offered an allegory for wounded generational attachments that had barred the

New Mutants from forging their own identities and acting in concert. In turn, though Illyana's actions appeared to free the Lonestars from their enslavement, the killing of the Demon Bear was an act of freedom for herself and her generation. The point was not to dismiss or negate the historical past of native cultures, nor deny the genocidal atrocities they had endured as victims of European imperialism, but to suggest that any given generation of an indigenous culture should have the chance to forge a distinct relationship to their past, informed but not predetermined by the worldviews of their elders.

Like the radical social movements that projected the limited categories of identity politics into new contexts in the 1980s, so too the New Mutants' entrustment "posited a figure of the newly thinkable" in the image of a mutant solidarity grounded in mutually shared values rather than an injured identity as social outcasts.[41] In the coming years this practice of collective freedom would become the sine qua non of *The New Mutants*, displayed in countless stories in which the teammates band together to battle the historical demons of their friends and colleagues. This freedom was not based on a struggle for inclusion within a larger human majority that hated and feared them but rather on each teammate's willingness to authorize the actions of his or her companions, to "give each other a chance," as Sam once put it. This seemingly simple practice of entrustment helped reinvent the superhero in the late twentieth century from a champion for social justice to a fantasy of political freedom.

* * *

Since the moment she escaped the clutches of the demon lord Belasco, Illyana Rasputin feared the day when the gods of Limbo would finally seek their dominion on Earth. In her heart she knew that when that time came, she would be their gateway. What she could not foresee was whether she would have the power to stop them, or if she would want to. Though much time and many adventures would pass in her years with the New Mutants, as the 1980s came to a close Limbo would wait no longer. In 1989 Marvel Comics published *X-Men: Inferno*, a monumental twenty-part miniseries depicting the X-Men's epic battle with the demonic hordes of Limbo and Illyana's final showdown against the dark forces that had corrupted her soul as a child.

Inferno tells the story of the demon sorcerer N'astirh's plan to cast a spell that will open a portal between Limbo and Earth, allowing Limbo to pollute the world with its evil. To accomplish his plan N'astirh requires Illyana's stepping discs, which provide a direct link between the two worlds. Choosing Manhattan as the site for his takeover of Earth, N'astirh casts an enchantment that transforms the city into an epicenter of demonic energies. The spell is timed to coincide with the New Mutants' arrival in Limbo following a previous adventure in which Illyana taxes her mutant abilities to their limit. Lacking sufficient power to teleport her friends out of Limbo, she is forced to make a bargain with N'astirh. In exchange for the last vestiges of her soul, N'astirh will allow her friends to go home unharmed. To save her friends Illyana accepts his deal and is transformed into the dread Darkchylde. At the moment that she deploys her mutant power to open a stepping disc back to New York City, however, Illyana realizes that this was N'astirh's plan all along: to use her darkened soul to bring the demon hordes of Limbo to Earth. Unable to close the gateway, Illyana makes the ultimate sacrifice, propelling her Soulsword, the weapon that represents her demonic spirit, into Limbo and using its power to seal the portal between the two worlds. In so doing she effectively obliterates the entire history of her time in Limbo. In a Christ-like moment of death and resurrection, her teenage body dissolves to reveal the seven-year-old Illyana before she became Magik. Though Earth would be saved from Limbo's reign, the Illyana that had become the New Mutants' companion and friend was gone forever, now only a memory to those who had known her.[42]

At first glance *Inferno* appears to offer yet another example of the classic demonic possession story depicted in narratives like "The Dark Phoenix Saga" and "The Birth of Venom," a struggle between good and evil that ends in the purification of the soul through an act of self-sacrifice. Yet if these former stories were underwritten by an economic narrative describing the institutional forces of capitalism acting upon the psyche, *Inferno* offered a new reading of demonic possession as the experience of being overtaken by scientific and technological forces infiltrating the body. When Illyana and her teammates first arrive in Limbo prior to her deal with N'astirh, they realize that the entire realm has been infected with the trans-mode virus, a techno-organic disease brought to Limbo by one of the New Mutants' recent villains, the Magus. Consequently, when Illyana opens a portal between the two worlds, the demon reign that falls upon Manhattan is presented as the massive infection of the city by a techno-organic virus for which there is no cure. Perhaps even more telling, at the same time that the New Mutants are battling N'astirh, the X-Men are locked in struggle with the Goblin Queen, a clone of Jean Grey created by the mutant geneticist Mr. Sinister. Readers soon learn that N'astirh's entire plot to bring Limbo to Earth has been bankrolled by Sinister, who seeks to gain access to the X-Men and their unique genetic information in the hopes of producing an army of mutant clones to wipe out the human race.

In a stunning rearticulation of the trope of demonic possession, *Inferno* reinterpreted spiritual possession as biological contagion, the literal vulnerability of the body to a virus and the figurative vulnerability of the body politic to corrupt scientific practices. If this wasn't impressed upon readers firmly enough in *Inferno*, two years later, Illyana Rasputin would be the first mutant to contract the Legacy Virus, a fictional mutant disease akin to the AIDS virus that unravels the genetic sequence of its host, degenerating her body and her powers until death.[43] Thus Illyana becomes the first victim of a virus that would ravage the mutant community throughout the 1990s, and her death would memorialize a new era of the superhero as an icon of biological citizenship, a figure of genetic deviancy that now embodied the dehumanized object of genocide, eugenics, and scientific exploitation. By choosing purity over contingency—to rid her soul of the evil influence of Limbo and return to a state of innocence—Illyana thought she had cured herself of Limbo's corruption.

The Legacy Virus reaffirmed what readers had known all along: that Illyana could never be pure and that the desire for purity itself embraced a false hope to rid the world of contingency. No surprise that that same desire for a world of absolutes was concurrently reflected in the rise of genetic testing and the international debate about the Human Genome Project. As the 1990s began, scientific hopes for the production of a genetic database to sequence the full spectrum of human DNA were coupled with dreams of predicting and potentially manipulating every human characteristic, from physical features to personal proclivities. Where once the genetic or species outcast was a fantasy figure that helped readers articulate new forms of citizenship outside the idealized social norms of liberal politics, now the idea of genetic deviancy was a full-fledged reality made explicit by the drive to map an "ideal" or "normal" human genetic sequence against which to measure a variety of anomalies that could be exploited (if deemed valuable) or expunged (if deemed harmful) from the species.

In a world where advanced genomics had become a scientific reality, mutants were no longer merely a metaphor for outsider status; now they symbolized the proliferation of an emergent category in modern political life: the deviant biological citizen who did not conform to a scientifically measured ideal. The emergence of the deviant biological citizen threatened the entire project of radical left politics to articulate new alliances on the basis of shared values by reasserting rigid biological categories of identity as the basis for political solidarity. Just as the American superhero was abandoning identity politics, genomics helped resuscitate the age-old myth that human identity—everything from race, gender, sexuality, and ability—could be explained by indisputable biological evidence. One could now "prove" ethnic and racial heritage through genetic tests, for instance, while immunology claimed to solidify the biological basis of homosexuality by falsely associating HIV with gay men's bodies. It was in this context that *The X-Men* would inaugurate an emergent era of biological citizenship by introducing a new threat to the survival of mutantkind in the late 1980s: the malevolent geneticist.

Through a decade-long engagement with magic, the superhero comic book had come full circle back to the scientific concerns that had propelled its content in the early postwar period. As we have seen, the turn to magical and occult phenomena in the 1980s was not a turning away from science but an attempt to articulate empirical realities as unpredictable, contingent, and open-ended rather than easily quantified and explainable in the language of institutional science. This language of contingency was similarly the language that radical political movements were deploying in this period to combat the deeply conservative rhetoric of the religious right, whose claims about the moral bankruptcy of American culture were absorbed by science and government institutions in a rigid political logic that distinguished citizens on the basis of their perceived moral worth rather than their rights as human beings. This was displayed in the decade's heart-wrenching political battles over the AIDS epidemic, an international crisis largely ignored by the conservative right based on moral judgments against the perceived sexual deviancy and social worthlessness of the populations most affected by its spread, namely gay men, IV drug users, and minority women. On the radical left, emergent movements like ACT UP began to engage in the same kind of political practices embraced by the members of the New Mutants, developing alliances on the basis of shared political investments rather than identity, questioning all the major categories that seemed to divide people's reactions to the epidemic (including gay/straight, deviant/normal, at risk/safe), and stressing the contingent nature of scientific knowledge production around the disease.[44]

As its name suggests, the Legacy Virus was not simply a disease but a powerful material expression of the mutant race's ugly inheritance: a legacy of xenophobia and violence that would once more rear its monstrous head in the figure of the human genome, now no longer a site of radical potential as the atom had been in the aftermath of World War II but a tool of biological determinism. In the 1990s the demonic avatars through which the superhero's shifting political values were rearticulated in the previous decade would be replaced by threats that issued forth from the language of genetic rather than spiritual purity. As Americans watched genocides unfold in Rwanda and Kosovo, as the threat of biological warfare expanded in a resurgence of military science, and as national citizenship became defined by bids for inclusion through assimilation rather than the production of alternative political communities, the American comic book would once more take up the charge of addressing these complex realities through the unpredictable body of the superhero.

Yet in the four decades since its initial revival in the postwar comic book boom, the American superhero had become a dramatically different kind of icon, progressively losing its attachments to nationalism, universal humanism, the politics of identity, and even the vicissitudes of national history itself; now threatened by genocide and species extinction the American superhero would combat the politics of biological determinism by offering ever proliferating visions of alternative genetic futures for the mutants, cyborgs, aliens, and superhumans among its ever-evolving ranks. Whether dystopian, utopian, or altogether foreign to the imagination, these potential timelines—presenting everything from the extinction of mutantkind to the transformation of vigilante superheroes into government agents and a world where every member of the human race had superpowers—worked to present humanity's future as an open horizon of possibilities, even one where the very concept of a universal humanity had passed into history.

Epilogue: Marvelous Corpse

Under what practical conditions is the right to kill, to allow to live, or to expose to death exercised? Who is the subject of this right? What does the implementation of such a right tell us about the person who is thus put to death and about the relation of enmity that sets that person against his or her murderer? . . . Imagining politics as a form of war, we must ask: what place is given to life, death, and the human body (in particular the wounded or slain body)? How are they inscribed in the order of power?
—ACHILLE MBEMBE, "Necropolitics" (2003)

Sharon Carter: *"The rule of law is what this country is founded on."*
Captain America: *"No . . . it was founded on breaking the law. Because the law was wrong. . . . The Registration Act is another step toward government control. . . . And, while I love my country, I don't trust many politicians. Not when they're having their strings pulled by corporate donors. And not when they're willing to trade freedom for security. 'Those who expect to reap the blessings of freedom must undergo the fatigue of supporting it.'"*
Sharon Carter: *"Okay, how about this one—'To argue with a person who has renounced the use of reason is like giving medicine to the dead.'"*
—*CAPTAIN AMERICA* #22 (January 2007)

In April 2007 Captain America died. Where little more than a decade earlier Superman died a martyr to the human race, now the nation's ultimate patriot would die a traitor to his country, assassinated on the steps of a New York City courthouse. Captain America's patriotic legacy would be eclipsed by his support of the Superhuman Liberation Front against the regulatory powers of the U.S. government.[1] In the months leading up to his demise, a civil war between Marvel Comics' greatest heroes would place Captain America on the wrong side of the law with fatal results, fighting against a superhuman Registration Act requiring all masked superheroes to list their identities with the government, becoming a new arm of the security state. In the early 1990s the death of Superman unfolded a story about the changing contours of national citizenship by projecting an expanded vision of who might legitimately count as part of the national "circle of we," including racial and class minorities, youth, immigrants, and even yet-to-be-realized cyborgs. In the midst of a war on terror, the death of Captain America offered a scathing critique of the radical narrowing of citizenship to the mere exercise of state power in the years following 9/11. That Captain America, the paragon of citizenship, would die as a result of exercising his democratic right to dissent was an irony few could miss.

Yet where DC's controversial publicity stunt in killing its banner superhero had garnered widespread hostility for its glaring opportunism, Cap's death was treated as a serious cultural critique of the war on terror and the dramatic undercutting of American civil liberties in the twenty-first century. Financially secure, Marvel Comics did not need to kill Captain America to boost comic book sales; rather the decision appeared to be an attempt to use the heightened cultural capital of the company as an opportunity to develop a genuine dialogue about the deleterious effects of American nationalism. The visual advertising for the story was telling in this respect. In its second printing the cover to *Captain America* #25 featured Cap bleeding out on the steps of the courthouse, his body riddled with bullets while his colleague and lover Sharon Carter cradles his head (plate 27). They are surrounded by the dropped protest signs of the crowds who had only minutes before been demanding either his death or his release. The picture is framed by a white border with the words "Captain America: The Death of the Dream," printed at the top against a folded American flag in an upside-down triangle. On the back cover a white page features this triangle insignia with the words "Where were you when Captain America died?"

The cover links Captain America's death to national public culture in at least two ways. First, it invokes the image of empty or hollow protest in the face of a violent security state. The front image displays Cap surrounded by the kind of dissent he believed American political culture should foster—indexed by the protest signs that appear at the edges of the frame—yet his dead body speaks to the evacuation of political meaning from these gestures of protest, less arguments for social change than battles over ownership of Cap's symbolic history. At the same time, by placing Cap's dying body on the steps of a New York City courthouse, the creators underscored the irony that the very institutions meant to protect citizens and foster justice under the law had become sites of political violence and oppression. Second, the front cover symbolically links Captain America's death to that of another national icon, John F. Kennedy, and the back cover invokes the question most commonly associated with the president's assassination: "Where were you when JFK died?" The repeated visual reference to the folded American flag, a traditional icon at the funerals of public officials and military personnel, associates Captain America with the highest levels of national service.

If JFK's passing signaled the death of one kind of American dream—a vision of liberal progress defined by racial equality, economic prosperity, and political consensus projected by Kennedy's New Frontier campaign in the early 1960s—Captain America's demise signaled the death of a related dream, that of a democratic public life where dissent could galvanize social transformation. The meaning of Captain America's death, however, was not limited merely to the unjust murder of a freedom fighter; the broader narrative surrounding his assassination unfolded an elaborate story about government corruption at the highest levels of power that threatens to undermine the political freedom of every American citizen. In the events leading up to Marvel's civil war, Captain America traces a vast conspiracy orchestrated by his archnemesis, the Red Skull, to bring about the ruin of the United States. This conspiracy is linked to Kronas, a transnational corporation, and its global affiliates, all culled from former cold war alliances among a network of terrorist organizations, bribed politicians, and corrupt scientists. In this way the creative producers positioned Cap's body as one node within a locus of points that collectively reveal a secret national history tying global capital, cold war political intrigue, and government corruption to the geopolitical realities of the post-9/11 period.

In the deaths of Superman and Captain America we can identify a figure that has propelled the American superhero into the new millennium, a marvelous corpse that unravels the national fantasies that attach to its previously vital skin, pointing us toward unsettled national identities, irreconcilable histories of state and corporate violence, and the visual politics that struggle to articulate them. Since the early 1990s the highly publicized deaths of iconic heroes like Superman and Captain America have garnered passionate responses from both non-comics-reading audiences and fans who have mourned the passing of these characters as symbolic of the loss of American political idealism. More important, the deaths of these iconic figures gained their cultural meaning alongside a broader trend in superhero comics to depict superhumans as perpetually threatened by mass extinction, genocide, and hostile conflict with humankind. In the 1990s and 2000s the cosmopolitan world-making projects celebrated by superhero comics after World War II have been increasingly depicted as running up against the limits of postnational tolerance. I want to suggest that the contemporary obsession with images of the superheroic body subjected to physical torture or death is intimately related to public perceptions of citizenship as a bankrupt category of political life and the failure of postwar human rights discourse to prevent mass suffering and global violence.

Simultaneously the narrative profusion of "crisis" events in postmillennial superhero comics symbolizes the full absorption of the comic book industry into the workings of neoliberal capital. Rather than being exceptional narrative occurrences that punctuate broader stories of fictional world making, earth-shattering crisis events—including the deaths of iconic heroes, the destruction of alien planets and star systems, the erasure of fictional timelines, and the extinction of entire populations of humans and superhumans—are now the primary storytelling mode of superhero comics. These narratives are relentlessly exploited for their ability to sell comics because of their visual spectacle and violent unmaking of fictional worlds. They embody in fantasy form the actual temporal rhythms of the neoliberal security state, which unfolds historically as a series of seemingly never-ending political crises, economic shocks, acts of local and state violence, and mass death in the name of corporate profit and upward mobility for the privileged few at the expense of the world.[2]

Historically Marvel and DC Comics have offered a host of reasons for "killing" their characters: to encourage new readership, to reinvent a character by dramatizing a transformative resurrection, to increase sales figures, to highlight supporting characters, or to decisively end a series. The most telling of these, however, is the desire to imagine what kind of world might emerge when an iconic figure no longer occupies it. Superheroes die when they no longer make sense in a particular world. Their return signals either an attempt to reinstate the authority of the heroic liberal fantasy—to claim, for instance, that the world "needs" Superman—or a demand that the body of the superhero perform a new kind of discursive work. In texts like Robert Morales's *Truth: Red, White, and Black* or Mark Millar's *Superman: Red Son*, writers have imagined alternative histories for iconic characters, including an originary black Captain America and a Soviet Superman. These stories rely on the conceptual (if not actual) death of characters to clear a space for narrating alternative stories of heroic development that highlight the erasure of complex racial and national politics in the production of American superheroes.[3] Morales's *Truth* follows the lives and deaths of four African American soldiers exploited by the U.S. government as guinea pigs for the superserum that would ultimately transform Steve Rogers into the officially recognized Captain America. The narrative explicitly links the image of the white nationalist superhero to histories of medical violence, exploitation, and murder of black bodies in the name of national security. In this way the marvelous corpse can reveal the superhero to us anew, staging a scene of misrecognition whereby we may see in the image of the superhero not ourselves, uncritically sutured to the ideals of national culture, but rather the uneven material realities that unfold from such a fantasy. The deaths themselves open up spaces, both discursively and literally on the comic book page, where national culture can be redefined and inhabited by new figures. Consequently the visual dramas that ensue from the deaths of figures like Superman and Captain America are battles over who will ultimately hold power over these new spaces of possibility.

Despite its many variants, the marvelous corpse has found its most generative expressions in two related figurations: the physically enervated corpse and the superhero's diseased body. The former has been popularized in the deaths of Superman and Captain America, which depict the violently murdered body of the superhero as a visual metaphor for the political enervation of democratic citizenship, while the latter has become most visible in the *X-Men* series whose introduction of "The Legacy Virus" in the early 1990s, a comic book corollary to the AIDS epidemic, links the mutant superhero to the suffering of racial minorities, the working poor, and sexual and gender outlaws murderously neglected by government and medical institutions. In both cases the marvelous corpse has offered a visual meditation on what it would mean for the superhero to develop an antisocial relationship to the state and the national community, to embrace the value of death as a way to galvanize public action against constricting political possibilities.

The marvelous corpse overturns one of the single longest-running assumptions of liberal political thought: the idea that life is indicative of political freedom and agency, while death signals the ultimate limit of political recognition. In the marvelous corpse, superhero comics have vitalized a figure of political impotence through the recognition that the vulnerability of the body can be a site for developing an ethical responsibility for one's fellow companions on Earth.[4] Within the logic that animated the Golden Age superhero of the World War II period, the very idea of the dead or dying superhero would have been impossible, or at least illegible; after all, the constitutive fantasy of the superhero in its original form was its physical *invulnerability* and its symbolic immortality. For superheroes to face death was to suggest that they were not superhuman to begin with. The marvelous corpse, then, is a figure whose conditions of possibility were forged with the reinvention of the superhero in postwar America as an icon of vulnerability existing at the limits of the human. In this framework the superhero's death implies that the figure has become like any other citizen, capable of harm and needing the collective protection of others. Through their deaths, these figures place the onus of responsibility for thinking alternative modes of political community in the hands of reading audiences rather than in the fictional worlds of superhero comics.

The death of Captain America offers a paradigmatic example of the marvelous corpse as a figure that demands action in the face of political despair. Murdered in the midst of uncovering a vast conspiracy that ties the U.S. government to corporate espionage and fascist political organizations, Captain America leaves behind a political mystery that is taken up by his heroic friends and colleagues. At the same time, his corpse becomes a visual index of the failures of public culture, demanding readers to acknowledge the real-world networks of power that deny the possibility of public dissent and constrict the alternative practices of citizenship. In the death of Captain America the narrative returns to his corpse only twice following his assassination: in the hospital he is taken to immediately following the shooting, where a vacant eye stares out at the reader from a bloody gurney, and then on an autopsy table where Sharon and Tony Stark (Iron Man) stare in disbelief at the remains.[5] In this disturbing second image, Cap's body is displayed before the reader as a husk of its former vital self, having degenerated beyond recognition in a matter of days. Echoing iconic images of holocaust victims from World War II, the scene jolts the reader's memory of the very people Captain America had been tasked with liberating in the 1940s. Stark suspects that the superserum injected into Cap by the U.S. government in 1941 has reversed its effects following his death. In Captain America's emaciated cadaver, we see the national subject reduced to a body significant only as a corpse carrying the trace of a former life vitalized by the state. Not a monolithic symbol, Cap's body bears the burden of time as it deteriorates before our very eyes across the span of the comic strip. Here the narrative grants Cap a corporeal history previously denied him by the state, which sought to preserve his body as a youthful simulacrum of its own symbolic immortality.

In "The Death of Superman," we learn that Superman's body remains vital even after his passing, as though his symbolic and corporeal status could easily stand in for one another. Here there is no reconsolidation or vitalizing resurrection to be had; there is only the fact that death unfolds as a corporeal reality of the symbolic politics of national security. If the fear of death is what allows the security state to maintain power over its subjects, continually reminding them of threats to their physical security as a way of legitimizing the dismantling of civil liberties, the marvelous corpse offers to bear the burden of death so that others may be free of the fear that prevents them from claiming their political liberty. The marvelous corpse reverses the logic of political security by encouraging one to fear the loss of liberty more than the threat of death.

And yet. If the mainstream comic book industry has been willing to explore the deathly underside of contemporary citizenship, it is in part because it has survived, even thrived, beyond its *own* figurative death. In 1994, after years of ceaseless character licensing, successful corporate marketing campaigns, and the diffusion of direct-market publishing, Marvel surprisingly filed for bankruptcy. Despite their relative success in reviving the comic book industry in the 1980s, both DC and Marvel had invested themselves in the speculation markets that had sprung up to take advantage of increasing comic book values, especially those of vintage and rare issues of classic Golden and Silver Age comics. Both attempted to create expanded value in their contemporary comics by overproducing collectible special editions, so-called variant and holographic covers, memorabilia, and limited-run licensed products. Ultimately they invested in high-cost products that a newer generation of young noncollectors could not afford to buy. The speculation bubble they helped produce inevitably popped, leaving both companies in a massive economic slump. Yet, in the most exceptional of neoliberal comebacks, both companies, rather than fold, managed to flexibly accommodate the shifting market trends of the mid-1990s. Kept afloat by their larger corporate ownerships (Marvel Entertainment Group and Warner Bros., respectively) during their economic tribulations, the comic book production arms of Marvel and DC shifted the focus of their operations toward the film and television industries, global branding, and character licensing campaigns. These areas of production have dominated the industry ever since. In 1994 Marvel was bankrupt; in 2009 Walt Disney bought the company and its stable of characters for over $4 billion. This was arguably one of the greatest feats of flexible corporate management of the late twentieth century, a death and resurrection to rival that of any superhero.

In the realm of comics the real-world economic upheavals of the market that Marvel and DC have managed to weather find their fictive corollaries in the countless crisis events that superhuman characters must survive, manage, overcome, or be obliterated by since the mid-1990s. These cataclysms shock the fictional worlds of both companies, yet they have also proven to be best-selling narrative events that encourage

Marvel and DC to make each apocalyptic crisis outdo the last. Since the late 1980s DC Comics has rebooted (or erased and restructured) its fictional universe at least four times in narrative crossover events, including "Crisis on Infinite Earths" (1985), "Zero-Hour: Crisis in Time" (1994; in which the formerly benevolent Green Lantern becomes a god-like psychopath, Parallax, who destroys time itself), "Infinite Crisis," (2005–6), and "Final Crisis" (2008). Similarly Marvel Comics' *X-Men* franchise, which was once driven by rich character development and visually exuberant adventures stories, is now narratively organized around a series of escalating mutant extinction events. As the titles of just some of these stories since the late 1980s suggest—"Fall of the Mutants" (1988), "X-tinction Agenda" (1990), "Age of Apocalypse" (1995–96), "E Is for Extinction" (2001), and "Endangered Species" (2007)—mutants no longer have much time to engage in cross-cultural encounter and global humanitarianism since they spend most of their days trying to survive genocide. Despite its production of mass superheroic deaths, the narrative and visual rhetoric of crisis might be seen as the political antithesis of the marvelous corpse. The narrative rapidity of crisis narratives, and their visual imperative to depict acts of world-rending violence, leaves minimal creative space to address complex political categories like citizenship, the nation, race, human rights, and democracy. If the marvelous corpse makes citizenship and its uneven distribution visible by locating the dead superhero's body as the site of an undemocratic injustice that must be redressed, crisis reduces the complex field of superheroic action to flexible survivors or unlucky victims. In a recent issue of the newly revitalized *New Mutants*, the X-Men team leader Cyclops tells Dani Moonstar, "Managing change is our specialty."[6] Against the former depiction of the mutant as a figure of radical flux, negotiating multiple identities and affiliations in a complex social world, the mutant has now become a stolid icon of neoliberal flexibility, adapting with clenched jaw and an instinct for survival to the heightened crises of late capitalism. Such crises now repeatedly include the genocide of socially undesirable or economically unviable mutant populations. Of course, representing the genocidal destruction of mutants has made billions for Marvel.

Unsurprisingly, many contemporary superhero comics appear enamored of both the perils and the mystique of neoliberal capitalism, oscillating between a distrust of corporate power (most forcefully expressed in corporate conspiracy narratives like "The Death of Captain America") and a gleeful depiction of conspicuous consumption. For example, in the recently revamped Marvel Comics title *All New X-Factor*, yet another of the many series in the *X-Men* franchise, readers are presented with a fully corporate superhero team that bears the logo of their company, Serval Industries (read "serve all"), on each issue's cover. The first collected volume of the series is titled "Not Brand X," an attempt to rebelliously distinguish the *All-New X-Factor* from the classic *X-Men* franchise.[7] Yet in this supposedly ironic move, the comic book openly admits that the *X-Men is* a full-fledged Marvel Comics brand, while *X-Factor*'s "rebellion" against that imprint merely involves taking on the name of a fictional corporate brand. This further obscures the fact that both comics are the product of a real corporation, Marvel Entertainment Group, whose logo appears on *all X-Men* titles. If this weren't enough, the recent storylines of the *X-Men* franchise reveal an almost pathological obsession with money: even as they are figured as an "endangered species" fighting for their survival, the X-Men are also repeatedly presented as "kadjillionaires" whose funds come from a variety of corporate ventures that allow them, among other things, to relocate to San Francisco, buy thousands of acres of property in the Marin Headlands, and build a state-of-the-art mutant sanctuary called Utopia, equipped with the world's most advanced technology, weapons, flight gear, and medical facilities.[8] In light of creative decisions that refuse to acknowledge the realities of global recession, the national wealth gap, and rampant poverty among minority populations, one wonders how the X-Men can continue to be identified with outcasts, misfits, and queers if they are part of the economic 1 percent.

The answer to this question lies in the comic book industry's contemporary identity politics, which involves obscuring corporate profits through the spectacular representational diversity of Marvel's and DC's character rosters. In the same period that Marvel and DC have recovered from financial loss, made exceptional gains in film, television, and licensing, and upped the stakes of their most popular superhero stories with countless crisis events, both companies have found their previous investment in left-wing political imaginaries dovetailing with contemporary rights-based discourses and the politics of representation, most notably in the form of gay rights advocacy. Unsurprisingly they have unabashedly capitalized on this fortuitous alliance. Both companies have invested huge amounts of creative talent and marketing in depicting gay superheroes and a wider array of racial minorities and women, framing each one of their decisions to expand the range of superhero representation as an expression of their progressive values and their supposedly benevolent attention to the needs of a diverse readership. The mass deaths of iconic characters in numerous crisis events is now offset by the introduction of an expanding list of iconic racial, sexual, and gender minorities: a disabled Batgirl, a Muslim Ms. Marvel, a gay Batwoman and Green Lantern (from a parallel Earth), a teenage gay couple in Marvel's *Young Avengers*, a transgender alien teenager in Marvel's *Runaways*, a black Captain America, and a female version of Thor, not to mention the late coming out of formerly straight characters like Shan Coy Manh (Karma) of the New Mutants, among countless others. If this trend weren't clear enough, in 2008 writer Matt Fraction relocated the X-Men from their Westchester headquarters to San Francisco, the unofficial "gay mecca," finally making explicit the analogy between mutants and gays and lesbians that had been implicit in the series for decades.[9] Of course, even though the X-Men were now framed as an "endangered species," the analogy did not extend so far as to compare their dwindling numbers to the loss of countless gay and minority lives over the past three decades from AIDS (an analogy the franchise had been willing to make in the early 1990s with the introduction of the Legacy Virus); rather, in the contemporary neoliberal moment, in which gays and lesbians appear to be achieving their full civil liberties with their assimilation into the capitalist economy and the wedding complex, mutants and queers could be compared only if both appeared as economically thriving denizens of the Golden Gate city, or the land of Oz.

Certainly these representations are not all equivalent, nor do they collectively prove a single, unified philosophy of neoliberal multiculturalism shared by creators and corporate management. Yet they do illuminate a trend toward diversification *without* creative world-making practices that has undoubtedly dulled, if not wholly undermined, the radical political edge of comic books in the contemporary moment. This is, in part, due to the fact that modern American culture no longer has a visible, clearly defined set of radical political movements that can provide an alternative to both liberal and conservative U.S. politics and consequently offer comics a language of radical difference to address the unique realities and social demands of a world dominated by the logic of globalization. Of course, as this book as sought to show, the popular fantasy spaces of comic books successfully invented new kinds of political imaginaries throughout the late twentieth century when faced with the impasses of left-wing movements. Not only do those movements no longer hold sway on the popular imagination, but comics are no longer motivated to revitalize them. In the absence of attachments to world-making movements such as black power, the Third World left, women's and gay liberation, and AIDS activism, creators now promise audiences the pleasure of seeing their own diverse identities—as gays and lesbians, Muslims, Buddhists, Catholics, and African and Asian Americans—represented in their favorite superhero comics, but no sense that the heterogeneity of those identities could and *should* change the world.

The depiction of the first gay superhero wedding in comics' history in the pages of the *X-Men* is a case in point. In spring 2012 Marvel made the shocking announcement that it would feature its first gay superhero, Northstar (who had come out in 1992 but subsequently remained a minor character until the mid-2000s), getting married to his African American boyfriend, Kyle. Like the deaths of Superman and Captain America, the event made headline news, upping the ante on Marvel's racial and sexual progressivism by featuring an interracial gay marriage. Yet the story's purported political progressivism hinged on downplaying these "real" differences in order to highlight a greater fictional interpersonal conflict between the two lovers over their differences as an ordinary human (Kyle) and superhuman mutant (Northstar). The story of their wedding (which depicted the lovers overcoming this fictional difference) was less interesting than the visual advertising for the event, particularly the cover image to the variant edition of *Astonishing X-Men* #51, the wedding issue.[10] The cover is a double-page wrap-around spread that appears as a wall of family photos (plate 28). On the back cover we see eight framed photos of famous superhero weddings from the history of Marvel Comics: Storm and Black Panther, Scarlet Witch and Vision, Jean Grey and Scott Summers, among others. They are a motley crew of mutants, aliens, cyborgs, and minorities of all stripes appearing in various romantic unions. On the bottom are two more images: to the left a portrait of Marvel's first couple, Reed Richards and Sue Storm, on their wedding day, and to the right, the two grooms, Jean-Paul and Kyle, embracing each other in their matrimonial tuxedos. Above these images of the first and latest Marvel weddings appears an oversize white frame with a stenciled outline, presumably available for the reader to insert a picture of his or her own wedding beneath the famous X-Men logo.

Where Marvel's cosmopolitan ethos of the 1960s and 1970s offered conceptual tools for readers to scale upward from individual experiences to broader networks of collective life, this image promotes a dramatic scaling downward from the heterogeneous political imaginaries of superhero comics to the personal, sentimental narratives of romantic coupling. Specifically the cover transforms the complex history of Marvel's various characters into a progressive narrative of interracial and cross-cultural marriages that embody the assimilation of difference in the values of heterosexual life narratives. The blank space allows Marvel Comics itself to be a perpetual bearer of the gift of assimilation, allowing any and all readers to insert themselves into this string of iconic weddings in perpetuity. This is underscored by the fact that the cover is a direct visual echo of the famed 2006 *Time* "Man of the Year" cover, which featured a square of reflective paper that could effectively make every reader part of *Time*'s vision of the information age, defined by anonymous identities contributing user content to the World Wide Web. In borrowing this visual iconography, the *Astonishing X-Men* cover similarly flattens (or at least sentimentally homogenizes) the heterogeneity of individual readers' life experiences into the traditional image of heterosexual reproduction and generation, another photo to add to the family wedding album.

In late June 2014, nearly two years after the special wedding issue was published, I saw a copy of this variant cover issue displayed at a comic book store in San Francisco's Castro district, arguably the nation's most recognized gay neighborhood. It was displayed front and center, at eyeline from the front door, in the week leading up to Gay Pride, the most visible public gay event in the country. Weeks later, in case anyone had missed the point, the display now had a sign attached to it: "Tape your wedding photo on the wedding album inspired cover!" I was mesmerized by the confluence of a highly corporatized gay national event (the San Francisco Gay Pride Parade, which city residents have protested for its corporate sponsorship and profiteering) with the gay representational politics of the nation's best-selling superhero comic book. Who could blame gay comics readers for feeling pride and exhilaration when a beloved series that had implicitly celebrated their experience of oppression for four decades finally came out of the proverbial closet and acknowledged their existence? Yet who could ignore the fact that after decades of queer world-making, Marvel Comics had chosen to capitalize on one of the most conservative political issues of contemporary gay and lesbian cultural life, the demand for assimilation into the institution of marriage? By 2014 queerness, like mutation, had become so profitable as to make a single comic book issue continue to sell two years after its initial publication, and to the very demographic—the LGBT community—that had provided the series with its greatest conceptual force as a distinctly queer world-making project since the 1970s.

The fact that recent creative decisions in superhero comics often lack the cosmopolitan spirit of postwar comic book production does not mean that such possibilities no longer exist. As the figure of the marvelous corpse suggests, those possibilities are now most commonly found at the margins of contemporary superhero fantasy worlds, appearing in bodies, spaces, and narratives of political negativity that resist the demand to flexibly accommodate the attrition of political life in the name of capitalist profit. These marginalized narratives and figures wield the conceptual power of the *What if?* that creators so masterfully deployed in their reinvention of the superhero as a social and species outcast in the postwar period: What if the superhero was no longer human? What if the superhero was no longer only a national citizen? What if superheroes belonged to no single person, nation, or planet, but to the world? These were the questions that animated the postwar superhero comic book and galvanized a three decades long exploration of the nature and possibility of alternative citizenship, belonging, and affiliation that would define the long Silver Age of comics history.

Contemporary *What if?* narratives are stories that take place in alternate universes separate from the official fictive timelines of traditional superhero narratives. These stories provide a space where the cosmopolitan political visions of postwar comics make their limited return, sometimes putting enough pressure on the traditional continuity of superhero comics to break through and become legitimate happenings in their own right. They range from the brilliantly conceived and executed—such as Robert Morales's "historical" recovery of the black Captain America corpse in *Truth: Red, White and Black*, and Mark Millar's conception of Superman as a Soviet everyman in *Superman: Red Son*—to the scattershot, the clumsy, and the bizarre. Regardless of their aesthetic purchase, all *What if?* stories have the potential to experiment with creative possibilities that remain beyond the political scope of contemporary comic book imaginaries, much as the mainstream comics that preceded them had done across the second half of the twentieth century. The value of *What if?* stories, then, lies in their imaginative premise, namely the possibility of asking the superhero, and its most compelling fantasies, to *do* and to *be* something else.

In May 2011 DC Comics announced that in an upcoming storyline, Superman would officially renounce his U.S. citizenship. Though it was not officially touted as a *What if?* story, this short nine-page feature presented near the end of the milestone *Action Comics #900* (the series that introduced Superman in its inaugural 1939 issue) quickly gained legendary status as a kind of speculative fiction meditating on the future possibilities for remaking the Man of Steel. The story depicts Superman's decision to repudiate his national ties after being criticized by the Iranian government for supporting nonviolent student protest in the country.[11] The Iranian government lambastes Superman on the assumption that his actions are based on orders from the U.S. government. In a heated confrontation with the U.S. president's national security advisor, Superman declares, "I intend to speak before the United Nations tomorrow and inform them that I am renouncing my U.S. citizenship. I'm tired of having my actions construed as instruments of U.S. policy. 'Truth, justice, and the American way'—it's not enough anymore." While some news media, bloggers, and cultural critics marveled over this seemingly radical creative decision to dislodge Superman's national loyalties, others criticized the hype around a seemingly minor (and generally immaterial) storyline to the larger Superman mythos. What few, if any, commentators acknowledged was the fact that Superman's public renunciation of U.S. citizenship simply confirmed his long-standing identity as a citizen of the world, which he had claimed for more than half a century. As I have sought to show in the preceding chapters, this cosmopolitan spirit of global engagement was the defining feature of the postwar superhero comic book, galvanizing its most powerful fantasies and most beloved characters. Such an ethos necessarily relied on the superhero's material and symbolic vulnerability. For Superman to formally renounce his national ties means that he could potentially inhabit one of the most vulnerable political subjectivities of our time: the stateless subject or refugee. Invoking the marvelous corpse as a symbolic "dead" citizen, this seemingly minor story poses a question of philosophical magnitude: What if the American superhero no longer had a country? The allegiances and solidarities superheroes can forge once they declare themselves stateless subjects and universal citizens remains to be seen. But if the past forty years of superhero storytelling offers any indication, those unwritten encounters might remake the world as we know it.

Notes

Introduction

1. Dan Jurgens (writer) and Brett Breeding (penciller), "Doomsday!," *Superman* #75, November 1992, DC Comics.

2. Frank Rich, "Term Limit for the Man of Steel: Yes It's Time for Him to Go," *New York Times*, November 22, 1992; Chuck Rozanski, "'Death of Superman' Promotion of 1992," *Comics Buyer's Guide*, July 2004, Tales from the Database, July 2004, http://www.milehighcomics.com/tales/cbg127.html.

3. Six months after Superman's death, DC released a collectible magazine titled *Newstime* that mimicked national periodicals like *Newsweek* and *Time*. The magazine offered a retrospective account of Superman's final battle with Doomsday alongside articles about the state of the world "without a Superman." This counterfactual artifact further articulated Superman's death to public culture both in its packaging as a putatively nationally circulated periodical and in its fictional embodiment of a shared site of mourning for the people of Metropolis. See Terri Cunningham et al., *Newstime: The Life and Death of the Man of Steel* (New York: DC Comics, May 1993).

4. See Dan Jurgens et al., *The Death and Return of Superman Omnibus* (New York: DC Comics, 2007), reprinting "Reign of the Supermen," January–October 1993.

5. See Wright, *Comic Book Nation*, 1–29.

6. A precise definition of liberalism is one of the most contested intellectual projects of modern humanistic thought. Debates commonly circulate around three questions: (1) the relationship between *economic* liberalism (the individual's' right to participate in a free market) and *political* liberalism (the individual's right to be free from the tyranny of governments or unjust law), (2) the specific limits of liberal inclusion (whether or not forms of exclusion based on cultural identity or social status are endemic to liberalism or merely perversions of liberal ideals), and (3) the articulation of liberalism to specific forms of political governance (especially democracy). Most scholars agree, however, that nearly every expression of liberal thought centralizes the importance of

the individual as a rational subject capable of free will and agency and recognizes "the individual" on the basis of an assumed universality between members of the human species. See Brown, "Neo-liberalism," paragraphs 6–7, 21–24; Hariman and Lucaites, *No Caption Needed*, 14–16; Singh, "Liberalism," 139–45. On liberalism in the context of twentieth-century American politics and culture, see Brinkley, *Liberalism and Its Discontents*; Feldstein, *Motherhood in Black and White*; Grestle, "The Protean Character of American Liberalism."

7. On the articulation of liberalism and democracy see Brown, "Neo-liberalism" paragraphs 21–23; Hariman and Lucaites, *No Caption Needed*, 14–16; Mouffe, *The Return of the Political*, 9–22, 102–16.

8. Wright, *Comic Book Nation*, 24.

9. Joe Simon (writer) and Jack Kirby (penciller), *Captain America Comics* #1, March 1941, Marvel Comics.

10. See Susman and Griffin, "Did Success Spoil the United States?," 27–28.

11. The history of government critique of the comic book industry is well documented. See Hajdu, *The Ten-Cent Plague*; Nyberg, *Seal of Approval*.

12. According to the *Oxford English Dictionary*, the term *flux* finds its Medieval origins in physiological descriptions of the flow or movement of bodily fluid; it gains its modern meaning in the eighteenth century as a state of being that is "ever-changing . . . inconstant, variable." As a figure that sutures *physical* expressions of bodily mutation to a *psychic* state of becoming characterized by variability, the postwar superhero is an exemplary embodiment of flux.

13. On the flexible subject see Martin, *Flexible Bodies*, chap. 7; McRuer, *Crip Theory*, 17; Ong, "Edges of Empire," 770–71.

14. Klein, *Cold War Orientalism*, chap. 3.

15. Mickenberg, *Learning from the Left*; Young, *Soul Power*. On the liberal and radical uses of culture in postwar America see Bodrokozy, *Groove Tube*; Braunstein and Doyle, *Imagine Nation*; Young, *Soul Power*.

16. Lipsitz, *Time Passages*, 16–17.

17. On world making as a political practice, see Zerilli, *Feminism*, 14–25, 177–81.

18. Warner and Berlant, "Sex in Public," 558.

19. Muñoz, *Disidentifications*, 195.

20. Myers, *Worldly Ethics*, 92.

21. Hollinger, *Cosmopolitanism and Solidarity*, xvii; Anderson, "Cosmopolitanism, Universalism, and the Divided Legacies of Modernity," 268–69. The term *cosmopolitanism* originally described the privileged rootlessness of the internationally mobile classes of the seventeenth century, a kind of sophisticated connoisseurship of travel and cross-cultural encounter engaged by white colonialists as an exercise in economic and racial power during the Age of Exploration. For some this is reason enough to discard its use altogether when speaking of anticolonial political frameworks for radical democracy and internationalism. I argue otherwise. Rather than seeking the comforts of a utopian category of affiliation somehow free of the violent history of colonial encounters, a revamped cosmopolitanism demands that we remember the precariousness of our engagements, remaining vigilant against the stance of imperial privilege even as we seek out new egalitarian modes of affiliation. See Appiah, *Cosmopolitanism*; Cheah and Robbins, *Cosmopolitics*.

22. I am extending Chute's argument that, "through its hybrid and spatial form, comics lends itself to expressing stories . . . that present and underscore hybrid subjectivities" (*Graphic Women*, 5).

23. Stan Lee, "Stan's Soapbox," November 1968, reprinted in Cunningham, *Stan's Soapbox*.

24. Ferguson and Hong, *Strange Affinities*, 9.

25. Ibid., 11.

26. This accords with Saler's description of early twentieth-century fantasy-reading communities as "public spheres of the imagination" in which engagement with fantasy texts "compelled members to acknowledge the constructed dimension of identities as well as the liberating capacity to juggle multiple allegiances" (*As If*, 19).

27. See for example *The Fantastic Four Annual* #3, October 1965; *Fantastic Four* #80, November 1968; Giant Size *Avengers* #4, June 1975; *X-Men* #30, March 1994.

28. Foucault, "The Subject and Power," 787–93.

29. Tanoukhi, "The Scale of World Literature," 614, 604–5, 613–14.

30. See Howe, *Marvel Comics*; Jones, *Men of Tomorrow*; Raphael and Spurgeon, *Stan Lee and the Rise and Fall of the American Comic Book*.

31. A genealogy of key texts in the theory of literary fantasy might include Freud, *The Uncanny*; Bettelheim, *The Uses of Enchantment*; Todorov, *The Fantastic*; Jackson, *Fantasy*; Warner, *From the Beast to the Blonde*; Jameson, "Radical Fantasy"; Paik, *From Utopia to Apocalypse*; Saler, *As If*.

32. See Jameson, *Archaeologies of the Future*, xi–22, 211–36.

33. Berlant, *Anatomy of National Fantasy*, 5.

34. Ibid., 21, 24, 199–201.

35. On the affective dimensions of enchantment, see Bennett, *The Enchantment of Modern Life*; Muñoz, *Cruising Utopia*; Saler, *As If*.

36. Bennett, *The Enchantment of Modern Life*, 17.

37. Ibid., 4.

38. Gould, *Moving Politics*, 212.

39. Kelley, *Freedom Dreams*, 11.

40. This form of enchantment differs significantly from the affective experience of most cold war speculative fictions, including science fiction b-films, postapocalyptic novels, and science-fantasy comics. The alien encounters depicted in films like *War of the Worlds* (1953), *Them!* (1954), and *Invasion of the Body Snatchers* (1956) and the postapocalyptic scenarios of popular literature like Richard Matheson's *I Am Legend* (1954) or EC Comics' dystopian *Weird Science-Fantasy* comic strips (1954–55), thrilled audiences with fantastical narratives but encouraged a defensive posture against outside forces deemed threatening to human life.

41. Stan Lee (writer) and Jack Kirby (penciller), "The Fantastic Four!," *The Fantastic Four* #1, November 1951.

42. Sedgwick, *Tendencies*, 8.

43. Sedgwick, *Epistemology of the Closet*, 23.

44. Muñoz, *Cruising Utopia*, 1.

45. In 1971 a *Time* journalist reported on rising rates of heroin use among U.S. soldiers in Vietnam as a "new mutant" affecting servicemen demoralized by the stresses of war; in 1982 doctors and gay activists briefly described the as yet unidentified HIV virus as a "new mutant" infiltrating the bodies of gay men. Whether figured in

aesthetic, political, or biomedical terms, the "new mutant" has functioned as an icon of social deviancy and queerness in the late twentieth century. See "New Withdrawal Costs," *Time*, June 7, 1971, 11–12; Richard Berkowitz, Michael Callen, and Richard Dworkin, "We Know Who We Are," *New York Native*, November 1982.

46. Fiedler, "New Mutants," 509–11, 516–17.

1 / The Family of Superman

1. On February 14, 1989, the Ayatollah Khomeini, then the reigning political and religious leader of Iran, issued a fatwa, or Islamic "sentence of death," against Rushdie for the perceived anti-Muslim bias of his 1988 novel *The Satanic Verses*.

2. Rushdie, "Is Nothing Sacred?," 425.

3. The concept of global citizenship, or to be called a "citizen of the world," has a long history dating back to antiquity, when the Greek historian Plutarch quoted Socrates as claiming, "I am not an Athenian or a Greek, but a citizen of the world" (ca. AD 100). The concept's modern American usage emerges out of the international military conflicts of World War II, which encouraged the development of such documents as the Atlantic Charter, the foundation for modern global human rights policy. In his fourth and final presidential inaugural speech in 1945, Franklin Delano Roosevelt stated that the global conflict of that war had taught Americans how "to be citizens of the world, members of the human community." See Franklin Delano Roosevelt, "Fourth Inaugural Address," delivered on January 20, 1945, http://www.bartleby.com/124/pres52.html (accessed January 15, 2013). On the history of the World Citizenship Movement and a biography of its founder, Garry Davis, see the website for the World Government of World Citizens, http://www.worldservice.org/ells.html (accessed January 15, 2013).

4. Gardner Fox (writer) and Mike Sekowsky (penciller), "The World of No Return!," *Justice League of American* #1, October–November 1960, reprinted in *The Justice League of America Archives Vol. 1* (New York: DC Comics, 1992, 97–98. All page numbers reference archive editions, indicated by volume.

5. Wright, *Comic Book Nation*, chap. 1.

6. The ambiguity in the term *league* speaks to this split, simultaneously referring to a global organization like the League of Nations and to national and local forms of affiliation such as unions, teams of scientists (like the Manhattan Project researchers), and popular sports leagues. In the *Justice League of America*'s first five years, the team is variously depicted as a metaphor for all these forms of affiliation, once even presented as a labor union on strike, in "The Case of the Forbidden Superpowers." See Gardner Fox (writer) and Mike Sekowsky (penciller), *Justice League of America* #28, June 1964. On the competing definitions of postwar political versus economic liberalism, see Brinkley, *Liberalism and Its Discontents*, 79–93; Cohen, *Consumer's Republic*, chap. 3; Singh, "Liberalism," 139–45.

7. Borgwardt, *A New Deal for the World*, 1–14.

8. John Budnick, letter published in "The JLA Mail Room" section, Gardner Fox (writer) and Mike Sekowsky (penciller), "The Fantastic Fingers of Felix Faust!," *Justice League of America* #10, March 1962.

9. The Universal Declaration of Human Rights, http://www.un.org/en/documents/udhr/ (accessed January 15, 2013).

10. Gardner Fox (writer) and Mike Sekowsky (penciller), "Starro the Conqueror!," *The Brave and the Bold* #28, March–April 1960, 14.

11. See Borgwardt, *New Deal for the World*, 4.

12. On cold war fears of communist brainwashing, see Carruthers, *Cold War Captives*, chap. 5.

13. *The Brave and the Bold* #28, 38.

14. Steve Erickson, letter printed in "The JLA Mail Room" section, Gardner Fox and Mike Sekowsky, "Journey into the Micro-World," *Justice League of America* #18, March 1963.

15. Borgwardt, *New Deal for the World*, chap. 9.

16. See Klein, *Cold War Orientalism*, chap. 2; Sandeen, *Picturing an Exhibition*, 95–123; Von Eschen, *Satchmo Blows Up the World*.

17. Sandeen, *Picturing an Exhibition*, 39–51. Also see the best-selling exhibit catalogue *The Family of Man*. Between 1955 and 1962 the exhibit toured in more than thirty-eight countries and was seen by nine million viewers.

18. See Hollinger, "How Wide the Circle of the 'We'?"

19. See the following by Gardner Fox (writer) and Mike Sekowsky (penciller): "Challenge of the Weapons Master!," *The Brave and the Bold* #29, May–June 1960; "Journey into the Micro-World," *Justice League of America* #18, March 1963; "Case of the Stolen Super Powers!," *The Brave and the Bold* #30, July–August 1960.

20. In a 1972 interview, *Justice League of America* writer Gardner Fox stated that he maintained an archive of reference material in his home: "Everything about science, nature, or unusual facts, I can go to my files or the at least 2,000 books that I have, and I can dig it out." Interview transcribed in the 1972 New York Comic Art Convention program.

21. Gary Freidrich, letter published in "The JLA Mail Room" section, reprinted from the Jackson (Missouri) High School newspaper *The Sqaw-ler*, Gardner Fox (writer) and Mike Sekowsky (penciller), "When Gravity Went Wild!," *Justice League of America* #5, June–July 1961.

22. Richard West, Dianna Hruska, and Anne Britt, letters respectively published in "The JLA Mail Room" sections of *Justice League of America* #11 (May 1962), #34 (March 1965), and #9 (February 1962).

23. The first twenty-five issues of the series boast thirteen science feature-pages and seven public service announcements covering issues from high school dropout rates to the World Health Organization.

24. Hollinger, "Science as a Weapon," 448.

25. Ibid., 444.

26. See Wang, "Scientists and the Problem of the Public"; Moore, *Disrupting Science*.

27. Krige, "Atoms for Peace," 180.

28. See Gardner Fox (writer) and Mike Sekowsky (penciller): "The Last Case of the Justice League," *Justice League of America* #12, June 1962, and "The Wheel of Misfortune," *Justice League of America* #6, September–October 1961, 238.

29. See Gardner Fox (writer) and Mike Sekowsky (penciller), "Journey Into the Micro-World," *Justice League of America* #18, March 1963, and "The Slave Ship of Space," *Justice League of America* #3, February–March 1961.

30. See for example, Gardner Fox (writer) and Mike Sekowsky (penciller), "When Gravity Went Wild," *Justice League of America* #5, June–July 1961, and "The 'I' Who Defeated the Justice League," *Justice League of America* #27, May 1964.

31. See Gardner Fox (writer) and Mike Sekowsky (penciller), "The Riddle of the Robot Justice League," *Justice League of America* #13, August 1962, vol. 2: 187–89.

32. See Serlin, *Replaceable You*, 5–9.

33. Gardner Fox (writer) and Mike Sekowsky (penciller), "The Super-Exiles of Earth," *Justice League of America* #19, May 1963, vol. 3: 130. See also Gardner Fox (writer) and Mike Sekowsky (penciller), "The Case of the Forbidden Superpowers!," *Justice League of America* #28, June 1964, in which the United Nations places an injunction against the Justice League of America's use of their powers based on false evidence that their abilities threaten international security.

34. Gardner Fox (writer) and Mike Sekowsky (penciller), "The Case of the Disabled Justice League," *Justice League of America* #36, June 1965, vol. 5: 140. This issue pays homage to an earlier *Justice Society of America* story, "A Place in the World" in *All Star Comics* #27, December 1945.

35. Gardner Fox (writer) and Mike Sekowsky (penciller), "The Case of the Disabled Justice League," *Justice League of America* #36, June 1965, vol. 5: 146.

36. Ibid., 162.

2 / "Flame On!"

1. Stan Lee (writer) and Jack Kirby (penciller), "The Fantastic Four!," *The Fantastic Four* #1, November 1961, Marvel Comics, reprinted in *The Fantastic Four Omnibus Vol. 1* (1961–64; New York: Marvel Comics, 2007). Page numbers refer to the reprint editions, indicated by volume.

2. Reumann, *American Sexual Character*, 5–8.

3. Serlin, "The Other Arms Race," chap. 1 in *Replaceable You*; McRuer, *Crip Theory*, 2, 6–10.

4. See May, *Homeward Bound*, chap. 1.

5. Cuordileone, *Manhood*, 67–87; Reumann, *American Sexual Character*, 194–98.

6. Herman, *Romance of American Psychology*, 109–12; Serlin, *Replaceable You*, 3, 11–15.

7. Serlin, *Replaceable You*, chap. 4; Meyerowitz, *How Sex Changed*, chap. 2.

8. On cold war culture as a regime of normalization, see Igo, *The Averaged American*, chap. 5; May, *Homeward Bound*; Serlin, *Replaceable You*.

9. McRuer, *Crip Theory*, 9.

10. On "transition" as a figure for transgender embodiment, see Prosser, *Second Skins*, 5.

11. Ahmed, "Orientations," 543.

12. Spigel, *Welcome to the Dreamhouse*, 113.

13. On the Fantastic Four as a narrative of American supremacy in the space race see Yockey, "This Island Manhattan."

14. See "Men of the Year: U.S. Scientists," *Time*, January 2, 1961.

15. See Cuordileone, *Manhood*, vii, 38; Reumann, *American Sexual Character*, 68.

16. On inner- and other-directed personalities see David Riesman and Nathan Glazer's *The Lonely Crowd* (1950). "The man in the gray flannel suit" was the eponymous title of Sloan Wilson's best-selling 1955 novel. "The doughface liberal" was an epithet originating in conservative critiques of the abolitionist North in the 1850s but taken up by anticommunists like the political scientist Arthur Schlesinger Jr. in the 1950s to describe the perception of liberals as compromising and malleable in their political commitments.

17. Stan Lee (writer) and Jack Kirby (penciller), "The Red Ghost and His Indescribable Super-Apes!," *The Fantastic Four* #13, April 1963, 337.

18. "Fantastic Four Feature Page: Spot-light on Reed Richards, Mr. Fantastic," in Stan Lee (writer) and Jack Kirby (penciller), "The Micro-World of Doctor Doom!," *The Fantastic Four* #16, July 1963, 419.

19. On the "egghead" as a feminized intellectual type, see Cuordileone, *Manhood*, 48.

20. Ibid., 198–99; "Men of the Year," *Time*, January 2, 1961.

21. Stan Lee (writer) and Jack Kirby (penciller), "Sub-Mariner, and the Merciless Puppet Master," *The Fantastic Four* #14, May 1963, 352.

22. Buhle, *Feminism and Its Discontents*, chap. 1; Zaretsky, "Charisma or Rationalization?"

23. Herman, *Romance of American Psychology*, chap. 4.

24. By the mid-1950s psychoanalytic and pop-Freudian terminology—including inferiority complexes, penis envy, and Freudian slips—became common knowledge to the American public through the mass media. In one *Justice League of America* issue, a teenage fan wrote to the editors to chastise them for incorrectly using the word *subconscious* in one of their stories when the correct psychoanalytic term for the suppressed part of the human psyche was *the unconscious*. See Dave Black, letter published in "JLA Mailroom" section of Gardner Fox (writer) and Mike Sekowsky (penciller), *Justice League of America* #21. On the postwar popularization of psychoanalysis, see Hale, *The Rise and Crisis of Psychoanalysis*, chap. 16.

25. Zaretsky, "Charisma or Rationalization?," 351.

26. See Stan Lee (writer) and Jack Kirby (penciller), "A Skrull Walks among Us!," *The Fantastic Four* #18, September 1963, 449, and "The Mad Thinker and his Awesome Android!," *The Fantastic Four* #15, June 1963, 375.

27. Stan Lee and Jack Kirby, "A House Divided!," *The Fantastic Four* #34, January 1965, vol. 2, 130–32. On the popular appeal of the Beatles' embodiment of nonnormative masculinity and androgyny, see Douglas, *Where the Girls Are*, 116–21.

28. Marvel even advertised their fan magazine *Foom* (Friend of Ol' Marvel) with a seal that read "E Pluribus Marvel," replacing the unifying term of *Unim* in the classic Latin motto with the company name, and the misfits and outcasts it implied. See Bullpen Bulletin Advertisement in *Luke Cage: Hero for Hire* #9, May 1973, Marvel Comics.

29. Editor's response to letter from Frank Silverstri reprinted in "Fantastic 4 Fan Page" section, *The Fantastic Four* #45, December 1965.

30. Prosser, *Second Skins*, 69.

31. Ahmed, "Orientations," 554.

32. Stan Lee (writer) and Jack Kirby (penciller), *The Fantastic Four* #1, November 1961, 13–14.

33. Ahmed, "Orientations," 564.

34. James Sturm highlights this rhetorical link in his faux biography of the Fantastic Four, *Unstable Molecules* (2003). "Letters and Notes" section in Sturm, *Unstable Molecules* (New York: Marvel Comics, 2003).

35. This fact was not lost on contemporary comic book writers like James Sturm, whose 2003 graphic novel *Unstable Molecules* renarrates Johnny's boyhood to frame him as a wannabe beatnik. In a deeply homoerotic encounter with a Kerouac-like figure named Joey King, King tells Johnny that he is a "holy flaming flower," invoking

Kerouac's oft-quoted line, "The only people for me are the . . . ones who . . . burn, burn, burn like fabulous yellow roman candles."

36. For the first appearance of the original Human Torch, see Carl Burgos (writer), *Marvel Comics* #1 (New York: Timely Publications, October 1939).

37. Hayden and Students for a Democratic Society, *The Port Huron Statement*, 48.

38. See for example John Kenneth Galbraith, *The Affluent Society* (1958); Vance Packard, *The Status Seekers* (1959); Herbert Marcuse, *One-Dimensional Man* (1964).

39. Ahmed, "Orientations," 565.

40. Stan Lee (writer) and Jack Kirby (penciller), "Sub-Mariner, and the Merciless Puppet Master," *The Fantastic Four* #14, May 1963, 362–64.

41. Meikle, *American Plastic*, 1–2.

42. Muñoz, *Disidentifications*, 11–12.

43. Stan Lee (writer) and Jack Kirby (penciller), "The Return of the Mole Man!," *The Fantastic Four* #22, January 1964, 608–10.

44. Butler, *Bodies That Matter*, 4.

45. Thanks to Adrienne Davis for this insight.

46. Stan Lee (writer) and Jack Kirby (penciller), "The Infant Terrible!," *The Fantastic Four* #24, March 1964, 660.

47. See cover of *Playboy* #1, December 1953; "Fantastic Four Pinup Page: Sue Storm, The Glamorous Invisible Girl," *The Fantastic Four* #10, January 1963, 266.

48. See Gerhard, *Desiring Revolution*, chap. 3.

49. Stan Lee (writer) and Jack Kirby (penciller), "The Coming of . . . the Sub-Mariner!," *The Fantastic Four* #4, May 1962.

50. See Stan Lee (writer) and Jack Kirby (penciller), "Bedlam at the Baxter Building!," *The Fantastic Four Annual* #3, 1965.

51. Ahmed, "Orientations," 543.

52. See 1974 New York Comic Art Convention program, 36–37, artwork by Jack Kirby; "The Cosmopolitan Man: Burt Reynolds," *Cosmopolitan*, March 15, 1972; "Marvel's Greatest Hero: The Thing," *Foom* #5, Spring 1974, artwork by Jack Kirby.

53. Affirming this idea, in 2012 *Fantastic Four* writer Matt Fraction introduced a new character to the series named "Miss Thing," a female Thing impersonator who wears a superpowered suit mimicking Ben Grimm's powers. See Matt Fraction (writer) and Mike Allred (penciller), "Marvel Now! Point One #1" (New York: Marvel Comics, October, 2012).

54. Stan Lee (writer) and Jack Kirby (penciller), "This Monster Forever!," *The Fantastic Four* #79, November 1968.

3 / Comic Book Cosmopolitics

1. Bruce Hall, letter published in "Fantastic 4 Fan Page" section, *The Fantastic Four* #30, September 1964.

2. Editor's note in "Fantastic 4 Fan Page" section, *The Fantastic Four* #3, March 1962.

3. Warner, *Publics and Counterpublics*, 119.

4. Pustz, *Comic Book Culture*, 52–53.

5. See, for instance, Pustz *Comic Book Culture*; Brown, "Comic Book Fandom."

6. An average of 340,000 copies of *The Fantastic Four* were printed and distributed monthly by the mid- to late 1960s, based on numbers listed in the Publisher's Statement of Ownership printed annually in select *The Fantastic Four* issues.

7. Isabelle Kamishlian and J. Geoffrey Magnus, letter published in "Fantastic 4 Fan Page," *The Fantastic Four* #32, December 1964.

8. Editor's note in "The Fantastic 4 Fan Page," *The Fantastic Four* #10, January 1963.

9. Martin Ross, letter published in "Fantastic 4 Fan Page" section, *The Fantastic Four* #6, September 1962.

10. Editor's reply to Martin Ross, "Fantastic 4 Fan Page" section, *The Fantastic Four* #6, September 1962.

11. Scotty Smith, letter published in "Fantastic 4 Fan Page" section, *The Fantastic Four* #5, July 1962.

12. Artie Starr, letter published in "Fantastic 4 Fan Page" section, *The Fantastic Four* #8, November 1962.

13. Editor's Note, "Fantastic 4 Fan Page" section, *The Fantastic Four* #10, January 1963.

14. Larry Tucker, letter published in "Fantastic 4 Fan Page" section, *The Fantastic Four* #11, February 1963.

15. Martin Ross, letter published in "Fantastic 4 Fan Page" section, *The Fantastic Four* #13, April 1963.

16. Stan Lee (writer) and Jack Kirby (penciller), "A Visit with the Fantastic Four," *The Fantastic Four* #11, February 1963, 279.

17. For a related critique of the assumed "realism" of Marvel Comics narratives in the 1960s, see Hatfield, *Hand of Fire*, 122.

18. Fred Bronson, letter published in "Fantastic 4 Fan Page" section, *The Fantastic Four* #12, March 1963.

19. Martha Beck, letter published in "Fantastic 4 Fan Page" section, *The Fantastic Four* #16, July 1963.

20. *The Fantastic Four* #11.

21. Ibid., 271.

22. Ibid., 272.

23. Ginger Church, letter published in "Fantastic 4 Fan Page" section, *The Fantastic Four* #15, June 1963.

24. Jimmy Edelstein, letter published in "Fantastic 4 Fan Page" section, *The Fantastic Four* #25, April 1964.

25. Editor's reply, letter published in "Fantastic 4 Fan Page" section, *The Fantastic Four* #29, August 1964.

26. Alex Nicholson, letter published in "Fantastic 4 Fan Page" section, *The Fantastic Four* #29, August 1964.

27. Jerry Brigers, letter published in "Fantastic 4 Fan Page" section, *The Fantastic Four* #33, December 1964. Brigers is referring to Parson's College in Fairfield, Iowa.

28. Joseph Hartlaub, letter published in "Fantastic 4 Fan Page" section, *The Fantastic Four* #40, July 1965.

29. Marlene Jablon, letter published in "Fantastic 4 Fan Page" section, *The Fantastic Four* #48, March 1966.

30. Stan Lee (writer) and Jack Kirby (penciller), "The Red Ghost and His Indescribable Super-Apes!," *The Fantastic Four* #13, April 1963, 337.

31. Carola Burroughs, letter published in "Fantastic 4 Fan Page" section, *The Fantastic Four* #46, January 1966.

32. Dan Clark, letter published in "Fantastic 4 Fan Page" section, *The Fantastic Four* #41, August 1965.

33. "'Hello, Culture Lovers!' Stan Lee at James Madison University," interview recorded by Jim Dawson, *Comics Journal* 42 (October 1978): 47.

34. See Stan Lee (writer) and Jack Kirby (penciller), "The Hate-Monger!," *The Fantastic Four* #21, December 1963.

35. Self, "The Black Panther Party and the Long Civil Rights Era," 21.

36. Singh, *Black Is a Country*, 197.

37. Hayden and Students for a Democratic Society, *The Port Huron Statement*, 51–52.

38. Stan Lee (writer) and Jack Kirby (penciller), "Behold a Different Star!," *The Fantastic Four* #37, April 1965, vol. 2: 219.

39. Hayden and Students for a Democratic Society, *The Port Huron Statement*, 52.

40. Stan Lee (writer) and Jack Kirby (penciller), "The Way it Began . . . !," *The Fantastic Four* #53, August 1966, vol. 2: 582.

41. Ibid., 597.

42. Baldwin, "The Negro Assays the Negro Mood," *New York Times*, March 12, 1961, 25.

43. See Stan Lee (writer) and Jack Kirby (penciller), *The Fantastic Four* #45–47: "Among Us Hide . . . the Inhumans," December 1965; "Those Who Would Destroy Us!," January 1966; and "Beware the Hidden Land!," February 1966.

44. The Inhumans' displacement also references the history of the Jewish ghetto and the ongoing attempts by the Jewish people to find a permanent home.

45. *The Fantastic Four* #46, vol. 2: 447.

4 / "Where No X-Man Has Gone Before!"

1. Saul Braun, "Shazam! Here Comes Captain Relevant," *New York Times*, May 2, 1971; "O.K., You Passed the 2-S Test—Now You're Smart Enough for Comic Books," *Esquire*, September 1966; Robin Green, "Face Front and Clap Your Hands! You're on the Winning Team," *Rolling Stone*, September 16, 1971, 28–34; Joanne Edgar, "Wonder Woman Revisited," *Ms.*, January 1972.

2. See "To Span the Spaceways," in *Son of Origins of Marvel Comics* (New York: Marvel Comics, 1975), reprinted in *The Silver Surfer Omnibus*. The Silver Surfer is introduced in *The Fantastic Four* Vol. 1 #48, March 1966. His interaction with Alicia Masters appears in *The Fantastic Four* #48–49, March–April 1966.

3. "To Span the Spaceways," n.p.

4. Tom Brown, letter published in "Who Speaks for the Surfer?" section, *The Silver Surfer* #4 (February 1969).

5. Binkley, *Getting Loose*, 3–4.

6. Berlant, *Female Complaint*, ix.

7. Ibid., 2.

8. Ibid., 6.

9. Stan Lee (writer) and John Buscema (penciller), "The Origin of the Silver Surfer!," *The Silver Surfer* #1, August 1968, reprinted in *Marvel Masterworks: The Silver Surfer* (New York: Marvel Comics, 2010), 6. Page numbers refer to reprint editions, indicated by volume.

10. See Dunaway, "Gas Masks"; Rome, "'Give Earth a Chance.'"

11. This mode of ecological thinking was popularized by Rachel Carson in her 1963 best seller *Silent Spring*. On "whole earth" environmentalism see Cosgrove, "Contested Global Visions."

12. Cosgrove, "Contested Global Visions," 273–78.

13. Stan Lee (writer) and John Buscema (penciller), "The Power and the Prize," *The Silver Surfer* #3, December 1968. They battle twice more: "To Steal the Surfer's Soul," *The Silver Surfer* #9, October 1969; "The Flame and Fury!" and "In the Hands of . . . Mephisto!," *The Silver Surfer* #15–16, April–May 1970.

14. Stan Lee (writer) and John Buscema (penciller), "The Power and the Prize," *The Silver Surfer* #3, December 1968, 106.

15. Stan Lee (writer) and John Buscema (penciller), "When Lands the Saucer!," *The Silver Surfer* #2, October 1968, 54.

16. See, for instance, Roy Thomas (writer) and Gil Kane (penciller), *Captain Marvel* #14–16, June–August 1969, in which the eponymous hero discovers that the reigning god of his people, the alien Kree, is a mechanical puppet.

17. See Roy Thomas and Gil Kane, *Marvel Premier #1: Featuring the Power of . . . Warlock*, April 1972.

18. Stan Lee (writer) and John Buscema (penciller), *The Silver Surfer* #1, August 1968, 10–11.

19. Berlant, *Female Complaint*, 15.

20. Stan Lee (writer) and John Buscema (penciller), "Worlds without End!," *The Silver Surfer* #6, June 1969, 202.

21. Ibid., 203.

22. Steve Pizzi, letter published in "Who Speaks for the Surfer?" section, *The Silver Surfer* #13, February 1970.

23. Daniel Preston, letter published in "Who Speaks for the Surfer?" section, *The Silver Surfer* #6, June 1969.

24. Berlant, *Female Complaint*, 2.

25. These comments can be attributed to letters by Charles Oldham, Bruce Coville, and Dick Glass, respectively, published in "Who Speaks for the Surfer?" section, *The Silver Surfer* #7 (August 1969), #3 (December 1968), and #13 (February 1970).

26. Greg Wrobluaski, letter published in "Who Speaks for the Surfer?" section, *The Silver Surfer* #14, March 1970.

27. Stan Lee (writer) and John Buscema (penciller), "—And Who Shall Mourn for Him?," *The Silver Surfer* #5, April 1969, 180.

28. John Stewart II, letter published in "Who Speaks for the Surfer?" section, *The Silver Surfer* #7, August 1969.

29. Stan Lee (writer) and John Buscema (penciller), "Worlds without End!," *The Silver Surfer* #6, June 1969, 204–5.

30. Wendy Fletcher, letter published in "Who Speaks for the Surfer?," *The Silver Surfer* #5, April 1969.

31. Stan Lee (writer) and Jack Kirby (penciller), "To Smash the Inhumans!," *The Silver Surfer* #18, September 1970, vol. 2: 269.

32. Stan Lee, "The Surfer Doesn't Just Talk, He Says Something," introduction to *Marvel Masterworks: Silver Surfer Vol. 2* (New York: Marvel Comics, 1991).

33. See Moore, *Disrupting Science*, 96–129; Carson, *Silent Spring*, 8–37.

34. For the original run of *The X-Men*, see Stan Lee (writer) and Jack Kirby (penciller), *The X-Men Omnibus, Vol. 1* (1963–67; New York: Marvel Comics, 2009) (collects *X-Men* #1–31).

35. For the introduction of the new X-Men, see Len Wein (writer) and Dave Cockrum (penciller), "Second Genesis," *Giant Size X-Men* #1, February 1975, reprinted in *The Uncanny X-Men Omnibus, Vol. 1* (1974–80; New York: Marvel Comics, 2006). Page numbers refer to reprint edition.

36. For a brief time the team also included the Native American superhero Thunderbird. Thunderbird offered a compelling critique of Xavier's utopian intentions in recruiting a band of global superheroes by invoking the history of elite whites' exploitation of indigenous peoples and their skills. Thunderbird's death three issues into the revamped series suggested the inability of the new *X-Men* to address the distinct category of indigeneity alongside race and gender. *The X-Men* would return to questions of native heritage and indigenous belonging in *The New Mutants* (1981), which I discuss in chapter 7.

37. Meyer, "*Gay Power*," 449.

38. On gay liberation's articulation of gay identity to antiracist and antisexist ideals, see Jay and Young, *Out of the Closets*; and McRuer, "Gay Gatherings."

39. *Giant Size X-Men* #1, 12–14, 19–21.

40. On disco culture's gay and multiracial character see McRuer, "Gay Gatherings," 231–34; Schulman, *The Seventies*, 72–75; Dyer, "In Defense of Disco"; Echols, *Hot Stuff*, chap. 2.

41. Marilyn Brogdon, letter published in "X-Mail" section, *X-Men* #103, February 1977.

42. Mouffe, *Return of the Political*, 18–19.

43. *Giant Size X-Men* #1, 17–19.

44. Chris Claremont (writer) and John Byrne (penciller), "Home Are the Heroes," *X-Men* #109, February 1978.

45. See for example Chris Claremont (writer) and Dave Cockrum (penciller), "Enter: The Phoenix!," *X-Men* #101, October 1976, 91; Chris Claremont (writer) and John Byrne (penciller), "Home Are the Heroes!," *X-Men* #109, February 1978, 332–33.

46. Chris Claremont (writer) and Dave Cockrum (penciller), "Who Will Stop the Juggernaut?," *X-Men* #102, December 1976, 210–11.

47. See Chris Claremont (writer) and Dave Cockrum (penciller), "Greater Love Hath No X-Man," *X-Men* #100, August 1976.

48. Binkley, *Getting Loose*, 3.

49. Michals, "'Consciousness Expansion,'" 48–49.

50. Meyer, "*Gay Power*," 447.

51. Songwriter Helen Reddy popularized this phrase in her 1972 hit single, "I Am Woman," cowritten with Ray Burton.

52. Butler, *Undoing Gender*, 3.

53. Chris Claremont (writer) and Dave Cockrum (penciller), "Where No X-Man Has Gone Before!," *X-Men* #107, October 1977, 313.

54. See Chris Claremont (writer) and Dave Cockrum (penciller), "Phoenix Unleashed," X-Men #105, June 1977; Chris Claremont (writer) and John Byrne (penciller), "Where No X-Man Has Gone Before!," *X-Men* #107, October 1977; Chris Claremont (writer) and John Byrne (penciller) Armageddon Now!," *X-Men* #108, December 1977.

55. *X-Men* #107, 303.

56. *X-Men* #108, 333.

57. The key political text working to articulate a radical feminist worldview to a critique of the interlocking oppressions of race, class, gender, and sexuality in this period is "A Black Feminist Statement" by the Combahee River Collective (1977). The Collective's formation in 1974 and publication of their statement in 1977 historically bookends the relaunch of the *X-Men* series in 1975 and the publication of "The Phoenix Saga," arguably Marvel Comics' feminist statement of the 1970s.

58. *X-Men* #108, 337.

59. McRuer, "Gay Gatherings," 231–23. See also Meyer, "*Gay Power*," 453, for a discussion of gay liberation's appropriation of "quasi-mythic" and spiritual iconography as symbols for the discourse of "coming out."

60. Daniel Rako, letter published in "X-Mail" section, *X-Men* #99, June 1976.

61. Editor's reply to Daniel Rako, "X-Mail" section, *X-Men* #99, June 1976.

62. Chris Claremont (writer) and John Byrne (writer, penciller), "'Twas the Night before Christmas," *X-Men* #119, March 1979, 550.

5 / Heroes "That Give a Damn!"

1. Chris Claremont (writer) and John Byrne (penciller), "Cry for the Children," *X-Men* #122, June 1979.

2. See Wright, *Comic Book Nation*, 239. Stan Lee discusses this decision in "'Hello Culture Lovers!' Stan Lee at James Madison University," *Comics Journal* 42 (October 1978): 47, 49.

3. On the politicization of superhero comics in the 1970s, see Ashby, *With Amusement for All*, 432–34; Wright, *Comic Book Nation*, chap. 8.

4. Steve Englehart (writer) and Mike Friedrich (penciller), "Before the Dawn," *Captain America and the Falcon* #175, July 1974, reprinted in *Captain America and the Falcon: Secret Empire* (New York: Marvel Comics, 2005). Page numbers refer to reprint editions, indicated by volume.

5. See Howe, *Marvel Comics*; Jones, *Men of Tomorrow*; Raphael and Spurgeon, *Stan Lee and the Rise and Fall of the American Comic Book*. The *Comics Journal* (first issue published in 1977) is the longest running comic arts criticism publication in the United States and is a rich resource for documenting shifts in the mainstream comic book industry's business history.

6. In a rare gesture toward such interpretative work, Howe shows how creators' increasing sense of professional devaluation at Marvel led them to depict internal company politics allegorically, by presenting a variety of comic book villains as fictional versions of Marvel publishers and corporate higher-ups (*Marvel Comics*, chap. 9, 217–18).

7. On the superhero as a fantasy of unlimited urban mobility, see Bukatman, *Matters of Gravity*, chap. 8.

8. Denny O'Neil (writer) and Neal Adams (penciller), *Green Lantern/Green Arrow* Vols. 1–2 (1970–72; New York: DC Comics, 2004) (collects *Green Lantern/Green Arrow* #76–89). Page numbers refer to trade paperback edition.

9. Denny O'Neil (writer) and Neal Adams (penciller), "No Evil Shall Escape My Sight," *Green Lantern/Green Arrow* #76, April 1970, 10–13.

10. Ibid., 15.

11. Steve Englehart (writer) and Mike Friedrich (writer), "When a Legend Dies!," *Captain America and the Falcon* #169, February 1974, 11.

12. Ibid., 12.

13. *Green Lantern/Green Arrow* #76, 30.

14. Jaun Cole, letter published in "Green Lantern's Mail Chute," *Green Lantern/ Green Arrow* #83, November 1970.

15. See Denny O'Neil (writer) and Neal Adams (penciller), "Snowbirds Don't Fly," *Green Lantern/Green Arrow* #85, August–September 1971; "They Say It'll Kill Me but They Won't Say When," *Green Lantern/Green Arrow* #86, October–November 1971.

16. *Green Lantern/Green Arrow* #86, 75.

17. *Green Lantern/Green Arrow* #85, 63.

18. On the ethnic revival see Jacobson, *Roots Too*; Zaretsky, *No Direction Home*, chap. 4.

19. Eliot S. Magin (writer) and Neal Adams (penciller), "What Can One Man Do?," *Green Lantern/Green Arrow* #87, December 1971–January 1972, 116, 122–24.

20. Steve Englehart (writer) and John Buscema (penciller), "Captain America Must Die!," *Captain America and the Falcon* #176, August 1974, 157.

21. Ibid.

22. Steve Englehart (writer) and John Buscema (penciller), The Coming of the Nomad!," *Captain America and the Falcon* #180, December 1974, 71.

23. Steve Englehart (writer) and Frank Robbins (penciller), "Nomad: No More!," *Captain America and the Falcon* #183, March 1975, 133–34.

24. Denny O'Neil (writer) and Neal Adams (penciller), "Journey to Desolation!," *Green Lantern/Green Arrow* #77, June 1970, 48.

25. Carl Gafford, letter published in "Green Lantern's Mail Chute" section, *Green Lantern/Green Arrow* #80, November 1970.

26. Steve Englehart (writer) and John Buscema (penciller), "When a Legend Dies!," *Captain America and the Falcon* #169, January 1974, vol. 2: 5–10.

27. Steve Englehart (writer) and John Buscema (penciller), "Lucifer Be Thy Name," *Captain America and the Falcon* #177, September 1974, vol. 2: 7–9.

28. Archie Goodwin (writer) and George Tuska (penciller), "Out of Hell: A Hero!," *Luke Cage: Hero for Hire* #1, June 1972.

29. Steve Englehart (writer) and Frank Robbins (penciller), "Nomad: No More!," *Captain America and the Falcon* #183, March 1975, vol. 2: 133–34.

30. See Gary Groth, "The Comics Guild," *Comics Journal* 42 (October 1978): 15–17. The official title of this clause was "Work for Hire." Comic book creators referred to it incorrectly as "Work Made for Hire," but the name stuck.

31. Archie Goodwin (writer) and George Tuska (penciller), "The Phantom of 42nd Street," *Luke Cage: Hero for Hire* #4, December 1972.

32. Matthew Graham, letter published in "Comments to Cage" section, *Luke Cage: Hero for Hire* #4, December 1972.

33. Editor's reply to Matthew Graham, "Comments to Cage" section, *Luke Cage: Hero for Hire* #4, December 1972.

34. Judy Rivas, letter published in "Comments to Cage" section, *Luke Cage: Hero for Hire* #5, January 1973.

35. Editor's reply to Judy Rivas, "Comments to Cage" section, *Luke Cage: Hero for Hire* #5, January 1973.

36. Jana C. Hollingsworth, unpublished letter, Chris Claremont Papers, Columbia University Rare Book and Manuscript Library.

37. Quoted in Gary Groth, "The Comics Guild: The First Meeting," *Comics Journal* 42 (October 1978): 26.

38. See Howe, *Marvel Comics*, 208–9.

39. Quoted in Gary Groth, "What Do the Pros Think?," *Comics Journal* 42 (October 1978): 18.

6 / Consumed by Hellfire

1. Reprinted in Horowitz, *Jimmy Carter*, 113.

2. See Chris Claremont (writer) and John Byrne (penciller), *X-men Legends Vol. 2: The Dark Phoenix Saga*, reprinting *The Uncanny X-Men* #129–37 (1979–80; New York: Marvel Comics, 2006). Page numbers refer to the collected trade paperback edition.

3. Zaretsky, *No Direction Home*, 193. See also Tom Wolfe, "The 'Me' Decade and the Third Great Awakening," *New York*, August 23, 1976.

4. Zaretsky, *No Direction Home*, 192.

5. Ibid., 209.

6. Ibid., 186–87, 198–99.

7. Rubin, *Deviations*, 290–91.

8. See Gerhard, *Desiring Revolution*, conclusion; Rubin, *Deviations*, chap. 11; Duggan and Hunter, *Sex Wars*, 29–64.

9. For consistency, I use the title "The Birth of Venom" to describe both of Spider-Man's encounters with the alien symbiote. See Jim Shooter (writer), Roger Stern (writer), Louise Simonson (penciller), et al., *Spider-Man: Birth of Venom*, reprinting *Secret Wars* #8, *Amazing Spider-Man* #252–59, 298–300, 315–17, *Spider-Man Annual* #25, *Fantastic Four* #274, and *Web of Spider-Man* #1 (1984–85, 1988–91; New York: Marvel Comics, 2007). Page numbers refer to the collected trade paperback edition.

10. Clover finds a similar logic in occult horror films of this same period, in which a woman's body is made vulnerable to demonic forces as a front for the psychic conflict of an emotionally closed-off male figure (*Men, Women, and Chainsaws*, chap. 2).

11. Chris Claremont (writer) and John Byrne (penciller), "Run for Your Life!," *The Uncanny X-Men* #131, March 1989, 57.

12. Tom DeFalco (writer) and Ron Frenz (penciller), "Introducing . . . Puma!," *Amazing Spider-Man* #256, September 1984, 110.

13. Chris Claremont (writer) and John Byrne (penciller), "Dazzler!," *The Uncanny X-Men* #130, February 1980, 26.

14. Chris Claremont (writer) and John Byrne (penciller), "Dark Phoenix!," *The Uncanny X-Men* #135, July 1980, 112.

15. Ibid., 123–27.

16. Public discourse on narcissism in the late 1970s equated it with antinatalism or the refusal to take on the responsibilities of reproduction. See Zaretsky, *No Direction Home*, 198–99.

17. For the first appearance of the alien symbiote, see Jim Shooter (writer) and Mike Zeck (penciller), *Marvel Super Heroes: Secret Wars* #8 (New York: Marvel Comics, December 1984), 6–7.

18. See for example Tom DeFalco (writer) and Ron Frenz (penciller), "Homecoming!," *Amazing Spider-Man* #252, May 1984, 17, and "Even a Ghost Can Fear the Night!," *Amazing Spider-Man* #255, August 1984, 84.

19. See Tom DeFalco (writer) and Ron Frenz (penciller), "Homecoming!," *Amazing Spider-Man* # 252, May 1984, 23; Chris Claremont and John Byrne, "God Spare the Child," *The Uncanny X-Men* #129, January 1980, 7.

20. See the following by Chris Claremont (writer) and John Byrne (penciller): "Dazzler!," *The Uncanny X-Men* #130, February 1980, 23; "Dark Phoenix!" *The Uncanny X-Men* #135, July 1980, 116, 121; "Wolverine: Alone!," *The Uncanny X-Men* #133, May 1980, 84; "And Hellfire Is Their Name!," *The Uncanny X-Men* #132, April 1980, 65.

21. Tom DeFalco (writer) and Rick Leonardi (penciller), "By Myself Betrayed!," *Amazing Spider-Man* #253, June 1984, 37.

22. Chris Claremont (writer) and Bill Sienkiewicz (penciller), "The Shadow Within," *The New Mutants* #22, December 1984.

23. Brown, "Neo-liberalism," paragraph 9.

24. *The Uncanny X-Men* #133, 82–83.

25. Chris Claremont (writer) and John Byrne (penciller), "Child of Light and Darkness!," *The Uncanny X-Men* #136, August 1980, 132–33.

26. Brown, "Neo-liberalism," paragraph 15.

27. David Michelinie (writer) and Todd McFarlane (penciller), "Chance: Part I," *Amazing Spider-Man* #299, April 1988, 226–28.

28. Brown, *States of Injury*, chap. 3.

29. Schulman, *The Gentrification of the Mind*, chap. 1.

30. David Michelinie (writer) and Todd McFarlane (penciller), "Venom," *Amazing Spider-Man* #300, May 1988, 251–54.

31. Brown, *States of Injury*, chap. 3. Though usually depicted as a murderous psychopath, on at least two occasions Venom shows mercy, even heroic compassion, to working-class people and the homeless. See supplemental story in David Michelinie (writer) and Paris Cullins (penciller), *Amazing Spider-Man* #315, unsurprisingly titled "A Matter of Life and Debt!," May 1989, 293–302.

32. David Michelinie (writer) and Todd McFarlane (penciller), "Dead Meat," *Amazing Spider-Man* #316, June 1989, 310.

33. David Michelinie (writer) and Todd McFarlane (penciller), "The Sand and the Fury!," *Amazing Spider-Man* #317, July 1989, 347–48.

34. Ibid., 346–48.

35. *The Uncanny X-Men* #137, 183.

7 / Lost in the Badlands

1. Chris Claremont (writer) and Bob McLeod (penciller), *Marvel Graphic Novel #4: The New Mutants* (New York: Marvel Comics, 1982), reprinted in *The New Mutants Classic Vol. 1* (New York: Marvel Comics, 2006). Pages numbers refer to trade paperback editions, indicated by volume.

2. See for example, *Heroes for Hope Starring The X-Men #1* (New York: Marvel Comics, 1985); "A Song of Pain and Sorrow!," *Superman and Batman: Heroes against Hunger,* (New York: DC Comics,1986); Marv Wolfman and Denys Cowan, "Black and White," *Teen Titans Spotlight on: Starfire* (New York: DC Comics, 1986).

3. Seidman, "Identity and Politics," 105–11.

4. Zerilli, *Feminism*, 98.

5. Ibid. Zerilli is citing the Milan Women's Bookstore Collective, *Sexual Difference: A Theory of Social-Symbolic Practice* (Bloomington: Indiana University Press, 1990).

6. Gould, *Moving Politics*, 256.

7. Hannah Arendt cited in Zerilli, *Feminism*, 105–6.

8. *Marvel Graphic Novel #4*, 20–22.

9. Chris Claremont (writer) and John Buscema (penciller), "Sunstroke," *The New Mutants* #12, February 1983, vol. 2: 96–100.

10. *Marvel Graphic Novel #4*, 8.

11. The X-Men triumphantly return in Chris Claremont (writer) and Paul Smith (penciller), "The Goldilocks Syndrome! (Or: 'Who's Been Sleeping in my Head?')," *The Uncanny X-Men* #167, March 1982.

12. Chris Claremont (writer) and Bob McLeod (penciller), "Initiation!," *The New Mutants* #1, March 1982, 58.

13. *The New Mutants* #1, 59.

14. Jacques Rancière cited in Zerilli, *Feminism*, 22–23.

15. *Marvel Graphic Novel #4*, 38.

16. Arendt cited in Zerilli, *Feminism*, 148–49.

17. Seidman, "Identity and Politics," 120.

18. Zerilli, *Feminism*, 114, 116.

19. Chris Claremont (writer) and John Buscema (penciller), "Scaredy Cat!," *The New Mutants* #15, May 1984, vol. 2: 182–83.

20. Zerilli, *Feminism*, 114–19.

21. Ibid., 110.

22. *Marvel Graphic Novel #4*, 15–16.

23. Ibid., 46, 49.

24. See *Magik: Storm and Illyana* (1983–84; New York: Marvel Comics, 2008). For Illyana's first appearance as a member of the New Mutants see Chris Claremont (writer), Brent Anderson (penciller) and John Buscema (penciller), "Do You Believe in—Magik?," *The New Mutants* #14, April 1984, vol. 2: 141–63.

25. Sexual abuse by the demon S'ym is implied in "Limbo," *The New Mutants* #71, January 1989.

26. *Marvel Graphic Novel #4*, 23.

27. *The New Mutants* #11, vol. 2: 77.

28. *The New Mutants* #13, vol. 2: 152.

29. Chris Claremont (writer) and John Buscema (penciller), "The New Mutants vs. the Hellions," *The New Mutants* #17, July 1984, vol. 2: 220–22.

30. For the first appearance of Illyana's "Eldritch Armor" see Chris Claremont (writer) and Bill Sienkiewicz (penciller), "Siege," *The New Mutants* #19, September 1984, vol. 3: 42.

31. "Death-Hunt," *The New Mutants* #18, August 1984; "Siege," *The New Mutants* #19, September 1984; "Badlands," *The New Mutants* #20, October 1984: all by Chris Claremont (writer) and Bill Sienkiewicz (penciller).

32. *The New Mutants* #18, vol. 3: 18.

33. Ibid., 20–22.

34. *The New Mutants* #19, vol. 3: 31.

35. Ibid., 34.

36. *The New Mutants* #20, vol. 3: 50–51.

37. Ibid., 54.

38. On the dual nature of indigenous identity, see Byrd, *Transit of Empire*, introduction.

39. *The New Mutants* #20, vol. 3: 67–68.

40. Ibid., 70.

41. Cornelius Castoriados cited in Zerilli, 62–64.

42. See *X-Men: Inferno* (1988–89; New York: Marvel Comics, 2009), reprinting *X-Factor* #33–40, *X-terminators* #1–4, *X-Men* 239–43, *New Mutants* #71–73, and *X-Factor Annual* #4.

43. Illyana's illness and subsequent death are narrated in Scott Lobdell (writer) and John Romita Jr. (penciller), "Legacies," *The Uncanny X-Men* #300–304, May–September 1993.

44. See Gould, *Moving Politics*, introduction.

Epilogue

1. See Ed Brubaker (writer), Steve Epting (penciller), and Mike Perkins (penciller), "The Death of the Dream," *Captain America* #25 (New York: Marvel Comics, April 2007).

2. On neoliberalism as an ideology of crisis management, see Klein, *The Shock Doctrine*; McRuer, *Crip Theory*, 16–17.

3. See Robert Morales (writer) and Karl Baker (penciller), *Truth: Red, White and Black* (New York: Marvel Comics, 2003); Mark Millar (writer), Dave Johnson and Kilian Plunkett (pencillers), *Superman: Red Son* (New York: DC Comics, 2003).

4. On vulnerability as a basis for ethics see Butler, *Undoing Gender*, 22–24; Butler, *Precarious Life*, 28–29.

5. See *Captain America* #25; Ed Brubaker (writer), Steve Epting (penciller), and Mike Perkins (penciller), "The Death of the Dream Part Two," *Captain America* #26, May 2007.

6. Dan Abnett (writer), Andy Lanning (writer), and Leandro Fernandez (penciller), *New Mutants* #27 (New York: Marvel Comics, July 2011).

7. See Peter David (writer) and Carmine Di Giandomenico (penciller), *All-New X-Factor Volume 1: Not Brand X* (New York: Marvel Comics, 2014), collecting issues #1–6.

8. See Matt Fraction (writer), Greg Land (penciller), and Terry Dodson (penciller), *Uncanny X-Men: The Complete Collection by Matt Fraction Volume 1* (New York: Marvel Comics, 2013), collecting *The Uncanny X-Men* #500–511.

9. See Matt Fraction (writer), Ed Brubaker (writer), Gregg Land (penciller), and Terry Dodson (penciller), *Uncanny X-Men* #500 (New York: Marvel Comics, July 2008).

10. Marjorie Liu (writer) and Mike Perkins (penciller), *Astonishing X-Men* #51, variant edition (New York: Marvel Comics, August 2012).

11. See David Goyer (writer) and Miguel Sepulveda (penciller), "The Incident," *Action Comics* #900 (New York: DC Comics, June 2011).

Bibliography

Ahmed, Sara. "Orientations: Toward a Queer Phenomenology." *GLQ* 12.4 (2006): 543–74.

Anderson, Amanda. "Cosmopolitanism, Universalism, and the Divided Legacies of Modernity." In Pheng Cheah and Bruce Robbins, eds., *Cosmopolitics: Thinking and Feeling beyond the Nation.* Minneapolis: University of Minnesota Press, 1991, 265–89.

Appiah, Kwame Anthony. *Cosmopolitanism: Ethics in a World of Strangers.* New York: Norton, 2007.

Ashby, LeRoy. *With Amusement for All: A History of American Popular Culture.* Lexington: University Press of Kentucky, 2006.

Bennett, Jane. *The Enchantment of Modern Life: Attachments, Crossings, and Ethics.* Princeton, NJ: Princeton University Press, 2001.

Berlant, Lauren. *The Anatomy of National Fantasy: Hawthorne, Utopia, and Everyday Life.* Chicago: University of Chicago Press, 1991.

———. "Citizenship." In Bruce Burgett and Glen Hendler, eds., *Keywords for American Cultural Studies.* New York: New York University Press, 2007, 37–42.

———. *The Female Complaint: The Unfinished Business of Sentimentality in America.* Durham, NC: Duke University Press, 2008.

Bettelheim, Bruno. *The Uses of Enchantment: The Meaning and Importance of Fairy Tales.* New York: Vintage, 1975.

Binkley, Sam. *Getting Loose: Lifestyle Consumption in the 1970s.* Durham, NC: Duke University Press, 2007.

Bodrokozy, Aniko. *Groove Tube: Sixties Television and the Youth Rebellion.* Durham, NC: Duke University Press, 2001.

Bongco, Mila. *Reading Comics: Language, Culture, and the Concept of the Superhero in Comic Books*. New York: Taylor and Francis, 2000.

Borgwardt, Elizabeth. *A New Deal for the World: America's Vision for Human Rights*. Cambridge, MA: Harvard University Press, 2005.

Braunstein, Peter, and Michael William Doyle, eds. *Imagine Nation: The American Counterculture of the 1960's and 70's*. New York: Routledge, 2002.

Brinkley, Alan. *Liberalism and Its Discontents*. Cambridge, MA: Harvard University Press, 1998.

Brown, Jeffrey A. "Comic Book Fandom and Cultural Capital." *Journal of Popular Culture* 30.4 (1997): 13–31.

Brown, Wendy. "Neo-liberalism and the End of Liberal Democracy." *Theory & Event* 7.1 (2003). Online.

———. *States of Injury: Power and Freedom in Late Modernity*. Princeton, NJ: Princeton University Press, 1995.

Buhle, Mari Jo. *Feminism and Its Discontents: A Century of Struggles with Psychoanalysis*. Cambridge, MA: Harvard University Press, 2000.

Bukatman, Scott. *Matters of Gravity: Special Effects and Supermen in the 20th Century*. Durham, NC: Duke University Press, 2003.

Butler, Judith. *Bodies That Matter: On the Discursive Limits of "Sex."* New York: Routledge, 1993.

———. *Undoing Gender*. New York: Routledge, 2004.

Byrd, Jodi. *The Transit of Empire: Indigenous Critiques of Colonialism*. Minneapolis: University of Minnesota Press, 2011.

Carruthers, Susan. *Cold War Captives: Imprisonment, Escape, and Brainwashing*. Berkeley: University of California Press, 2009

Carson, Rachel. *Silent Spring*. 1962. New York: Houghton Mifflin, 2002.

Cheah, Pheng, and Bruce Robbins, eds. *Cosmopolitics: Thinking and Feeling beyond the Nation*. Minneapolis: University of Minnesota Press, 1998.

Chute, Hilary. *Graphic Women: Life Narrative and Contemporary Comics*. New York: Columbia University Press, 2010.

Clarke, Alison J. *Tupperware: The Promise of Plastic in 1950s America*. Washington, DC: Smithsonian Institute Press, 2001.

Clover, Carol. *Men, Women, and Chainsaws: Gender in the Modern Horror Film*. Princeton, NJ: Princeton University Press, 1993.

Cohen, Lizbeth. *The Consumer's Republic: The Politics of Mass Consumption in Postwar America*. New York: Vintage, 2003.

Cosgrove, Denis. "Contested Global Visions: One-World, Whole-Earth, and the Apollo Space Photographs." *Annals of the Association of American Geographers* 84.2 (1994): 270–94.

Cunningham, Brian, ed. *Stan's Soapbox: The Collection*. Los Angeles: Hero Initiative, 2008.

Cuordileone, K. A. *Manhood and American Political Culture in the Cold War*. New York: Routledge, 2005.

Douglas, Susan J. *Where the Girls Are: Growing Up Female with the Mass Media.* New York: Random House, 1995.

Duggan, Lisa. *The Twilight of Equality? Neoliberalism, Cultural Politics, and the Attack on Democracy.* New York: Beacon Press, 2003.

Duggan, Lisa, with Nan D. Hunter. *Sex Wars: Sexual Dissent and Political Culture.* New York: Routledge, 2006.

Dunaway, Finis. "Gas Masks, Pogo, and the Ecological Indian: Earth Day and the Visual Politics of American Environmentalism." *American Quarterly* 60.1 (2008): 67–99.

Dyer, Richard. "In Defense of Disco." In Simon Frith and Andrew Goodwin, eds., *On the Record: Rock, Pop, and the Written Word.* New York: Routledge, 1990.

Echols, Alice. *Hot Stuff: Disco and the Remaking of American Culture.* New York: Norton, 2011.

Feldstein, Ruth. *Motherhood in Black and White: Race and Sex in American Liberalism, 1930–1965.* Ithaca, NY: Cornell University Press, 2000.

Ferguson, Roderick, and Grace Hong, eds. *Strange Affinities: The Gender and Sexual Politics of Comparative Racialization.* Durham, NC: Duke University Press, 2011.

Fiedler, Leslie. "The New Mutants." *Partisan Review,* September 1965, 505–25.

Foucault, Michel. "The Subject and Power." *Critical Inquiry* 8.4 (1982): 777–95.

Freud, Sigmund. *The Uncanny.* 1919. New York: Penguin, 2003.

Gerhard, Jane. *Desiring Revolution: Second Wave Feminism and the Rewriting of American Sexual Thought, 1920 to 1982.* New York: Columbia University Press, 2001.

Gould, Deborah. *Moving Politics: Emotion and ACT UP's Fight against AIDS.* Chicago: University of Chicago Press, 2009.

Grestle, Gary. "The Protean Character of American Liberalism." *American Historical Review* 99.4 (1994): 1043–73.

Hajdu, David. *The Ten-Cent Plague: The Great Comic-Book Scare and How It Changed America.* New York: Picador, 2009.

Hale, Nathan G. *The Rise and Crisis of Psychoanalysis in the United States: Freud and the Americans, 1917–1985.* New York: Oxford University Press, 1995.

Hariman, Robert, and John Louis Lucaites. *No Caption Needed: Iconic Photographs, Public Culture, and Liberal Democracy.* Chicago: University of Chicago Press, 2007.

Hatfield, Charles. *Hand of Fire: The Comics Art of Jack Kirby.* Jackson: University of Mississippi Press, 2011.

Hayden, Tom, and Students for a Democratic Society. *The Port Huron Statement: The Visionary Call of the 1960s Revolution.* 1962. New York: Public Affairs, 2005.

Herman, Ellen. *The Romance of American Psychology: Political Culture in the Age of Experts.* Berkeley: University of California Press, 1995.

Hollinger, David. *Cosmopolitanism and Solidarity: Studies in Ethnoracial, Religious, and Professional Affiliation in the United States.* Madison: University of Wisconsin Press, 2006.

———. "How Wide the Circle of the 'We'? American Intellectuals and the Problem of the Ethnos since World War II." *American Historical Review* 98.2 (1993): 317–37.

———. "Postethnic America." *Contention* 2 (1992): 79–96.

———. "Science as a Weapon in *Kulturkämpfe* in the United States during and after World War II." *Isis* 86.3 (1995): 440–54.

Horowitz, Daniel. *Jimmy Carter and the Energy Crisis of the 1970s: The "Crisis of Confidence" Speech of July 15, 1979. A Brief History with Documents.* New York: Bedford St. Martin's, 2005.

Howe, Sean. *Marvel Comics: The Untold Story.* New York: Harper, 2013.

Igo, Sarah. *The Averaged American: Surveys, Citizens, and the Making of a Mass Public.* Cambridge, MA: Harvard University Press, 2008.

Jackson, Rosemary. *Fantasy: The Literature of Subversion.* New York: Routledge, 1981.

Jacobson, Matthew Frye. *Roots Too: White Ethnic Revival in Post–Civil Rights America.* Cambridge, MA: Harvard University Press, 2008.

Jameson, Frederic. *Archaeologies of the Future: The Desire Called Utopia and Other Science Fictions.* New York: Verso, 2007.

———. "Radical Fantasy." *Historical Materialism* 10.4 (2002): 273–80.

Jay, Karla, and Allen Young, eds. *Out of the Closets: Voices of Gay Liberation.* 1972. Twentieth Anniversary edition. New York: New York University Press, 1992.

Jones, Gerald. *Men of Tomorrow: Geeks, Gangsters, and the Birth of the Comic Book.* New York: Basic Books, 2005.

Kelley, Robin D. G. *Freedom Dreams: The Black Radical Imagination.* New York: Beacon Press, 2003.

Klein, Christina. *Cold War Orientalism: Asia in the Middlebrow Imagination, 1945–1961.* Berkeley: University of California Press, 2003.

Klein, Naomi. *The Shock Doctrine: The Rise of Disaster Capitalism.* New York: Picador, 2008.

Krige, John. "Atoms for Peace, Scientific Internationalism, and Scientific Intelligence." *Osiris* 21 (2006): 161–81.

Lipsitz, George. *Time Passages: Collective Memory and American Popular Culture.* Minneapolis: University of Minnesota Press, 2001.

Martin, Emily. *Flexible Bodies: The Role of Immunity in American Culture from the Days of Polio to the Age of AIDS.* New York: Beacon Press, 1995.

May, Elaine Tyler. *Homeward Bound: American Families in the Cold War Era.* 1988. New York: Basic Books, 2008.

Mbembe, Achille. "Necropolitics." Trans. Libby Mientjes. *Public Culture* 15.1 (2003): 11–40.

McRuer, Robert. *Crip Theory: Cultural Signs of Disability and Queerness*. New York: New York University Press, 2006.

McRuer, Robert. "Gay Gatherings: Reimagining the Counterculture." In Peter Braunstein and Michael William Doyle, eds., *Imagine Nation: The American Counterculture of the 1960's and 70's*. New York: Routledge, 2002, 215–40.

Meikle, Jeffrey L. *American Plastic: A Cultural History*. New Brunswick, NJ: Rutgers University Press, 1995.

Meyer, Richard. "*Gay Power* Circa 1970: Visual Strategies for Sexual Revolution." *GLQ* 12.3 (2006): 441–64.

Meyerowitz, Joanne. *How Sex Changed: A History of Transexuality in the United States*. Cambridge, MA: Harvard University Press, 2004.

Michals, Debra. "From 'Consciousness Expansion' to 'Consciousness Raising' Feminism and the Countercultural Politics of the Self. " In Peter Braunstein and Michael William Doyle, eds., *Imagine Nation: The American Counterculture of the 1960's and 70's*. New York: Routledge, 2002, 41–68.

Mickenberg, Julia. *Learning from the Left: Children's Literature, the Cold War, and Radical Politics in the United States*. New York: Oxford University Press, 2006.

Moore, Kelly. *Disrupting Science: Social Movements, American Scientists, and the Politics of the Military, 1945–1975*. Princeton, NJ: Princeton University Press, 2008.

Mouffe, Chantal. *The Return of the Political*. New York: Verso, 2005.

Muñoz, José Esteban. *Cruising Utopia: The Then and There of Queer Futurity*. New York: New York University Press, 2009.

———. *Disidentifications: Queers of Color and the Performance of Politics*. Minneapolis: Minnesota University Press, 1999.

Myers, Ella. *Worldly Ethics: Democratic Politics and Care for the World*. Durham, NC: Duke University Press, 2013.

Nyberg, Amy Kiste. *Seal of Approval: The History of the Comics Code*. Jackson: University Press of Mississippi, 1998.

Ong, Aihwa. "On the Edges of Empires: Flexible Citizenship among Chinese in Diaspora." *positions* 1.3 (1993): 745–78.

Paik, Peter. *From Utopia to Apocalypse: Science Fiction and the Politics of Catastrophe*. Minneapolis: University of Minnesota Press, 2011.

Prosser, Jay. *Second Skins: The Body Narratives of Transsexuality*. New York: Columbia University Press, 1998.

Pustz, Matthew J. *Comic Book Culture: Fanboys and True Believers*. Jackson: University Press of Mississippi, 2000.

Raphael, Jordan, and Tom Spurgeon. *Stan Lee and the Rise and Fall of the American Comic Book*. Chicago: Chicago Review Press, 2004.

Reumann, Miriam G. *American Sexual Character: Sex, Gender, and National Identity in the Kinsey Reports*. Berkeley: University of California Press, 2005.

Rome, Adam. "'Give Earth a Chance': The Environmental Movement and the Sixties." *Journal of American History* 90.2 (2003): 761–814.

Rubin, Gayle. *Deviations: A Gayle Rubin Reader*. Durham, NC: Duke University Press, 2011.

Rushdie, Salman. "Is Nothing Sacred?" In *Imaginary Homelands: Essays and Criticism 1981–1991*. New York: Penguin, 1992.

Saler, Michael. *As If: Modern Enchantment and the Literary Pre-History of Virtual Reality*. New York: Oxford University Press, 2012.

Sandeen, Eric J. *Picturing an Exhibition: The Family of Man and 1950s America*. Albuquerque: University of New Mexico Press, 1995.

Schulman, Bruce. *The Seventies: The Great Shift in American Culture, Society, and Politics*. New York: De Capo Press, 2002.

Schulman, Sarah. *The Gentrification of the Mind: Witness to a Lost Imagination*. Berkeley: University of California Press, 2013.

Sedgwick, Eve Kosofsky. *Epistemology of the Closet*. Berkeley: University of California Press, 1990.

———. *Tendencies*. Durham, NC: Duke University Press, 1993.

Seidman, Steven. "Identity and Politics in a 'Postmodern' Gay Culture: Some Historical and Conceptual Notes." In Michael Warner, ed., *Fear of a Queer Planet: Queer Politics and Social Theory*. Minneapolis: University of Minnesota Press, 1993, 105–42.

Self, Robert O. "The Black Panther Party and the Long Civil Rights Era." In Jama Lazarow and Yohuru R. Williams, eds., *In Search of the Black Panther Party: New Perspectives on a Revolutionary Movement*. Durham, NC: Duke University Press, 2006, 15–58.

Serlin, David. *Replaceable You: Engineering the Body in Postwar America*. Chicago: University of Chicago Press, 2004.

Singh, Nikhil. *Black Is a Country: Race and the Unfinished Struggle for Democracy*. Cambridge, MA: Harvard University Press, 2004.

———. "Liberalism." In Bruce Burgett and Glenn Hendler, eds., *Keywords for American Cultural Studies*. New York: New York University Press, 2007, 139–45.

Spigel, Lynn. *Welcome to the Dreamhouse: Popular Media and Postwar Suburbs*. Durham, NC: Duke University Press, 2001.

Susman, Warren, and Edward Griffin. "Did Success Spoil the United States? Dual Representations in Postwar America." In Lary May, ed., *Recasting America: Culture and Politics in the Age of Cold War*. Chicago: University of Chicago Press, 1989, 19–37.

Tanoukhi, Nirvana. "The Scale of World Literature." *New Literary History* 39.3 (2008): 599–617.

Todorov, Tzvetan. *The Fantastic: A Structural Approach to a Literary Genre*. Ithaca, NY: Cornell University Press, 1975.

Von Eschen, Penny. *Satchmo Blows Up the World: Jazz Ambassadors Play the Cold War*. Cambridge, MA: Harvard University Press, 2006.

Wang, Jessica. "Scientists and the Problem of the Public in Cold War America, 1945–1960." *Osiris* 17.2 (2002): 323–47.

Warner, Marina. *From the Beast to the Blonde: On Fairy Tales and Their Tellers.* New York: Farrar, Straus and Giroux, 1995.

Warner, Michael. *Publics and Counterpublics.* New York: Zone Books, 2005.

Warner, Michael, and Lauren Berlant. "Sex in Public." *Critical Inquiry* 24.2 (1998): 547-66.

Wright, Bradford W. *Comic Book Nation: The Transformation of Youth Culture in America.* Baltimore: Johns Hopkins University Press, 2003.

Yockey, Matthew. "This Island Manhattan: New York City and the Space Race in the Fantastic Four." *Iowa Journal of Cultural Studies* 6 (Spring 2005): 58–79.

Young, Cynthia. *Soul Power: Culture, Radicalism, and the Making of a U.S. Third World Left.* Durham, NC: Duke University Press, 2006.

Zaretsky, Eli. "Charisma or Rationalization? Domesticity and Psychoanalysis in the United States in the 1950s." *Critical Inquiry* 26.2 (2000): 328–54.

Zaretsky, Natasha. *No Direction Home: The American Family and the Fear of National Decline.* Chapel Hill: University of North Carolina Press, 2007.

Zerilli, Linda. *Feminism and the Abyss of Freedom.* Chicago: University of Chicago Press, 2005.

Index

ABOUT THE AUTHOR

Ramzi Fawaz is Assistant Professor of English at the University of Wisconsin, Madison. His manuscript for *The New Mutants* received the 2012 Center for Lesbian and Gay Studies Award for best first book in LGBT studies. His work appears in the journals *American Literature*, *Callaloo*, *Anthropological Quarterly*, and *GLQ*.

CPSIA information can be obtained
at www.ICGtesting.com
Printed in the USA
LVOW06s2045121017
552182LV00004B/20/P